Royal Commission on the Distribution of Income & Wealth

Chairman
Lord Diamond

Report No 8
Fifth report on
the Standing Reference

Presented to Parliament by Command of Her Majesty
October 1979

LONDON

HER MAJESTY'S STATIONERY OFFICE
£7.00 net

Cmnd. 7679

ISBN 0 10 176790 0

ii

The Royal Warrants

ELIZABETH R.

ELIZABETH THE SECOND, by the grace of God, of the United Kingdom of Great Britain and Northern Ireland and of Our other Realms and Territories QUEEN, Head of the Commonwealth, Defender of the Faith, to

Our Right Trusty and Well-beloved Counsellor John, Baron Diamond;

Our Trusty and Well-beloved:

Sir George Neville Butterworth, Knight;

Ernest Henry Phelps Brown, Esquire, Member of Our Most Excellent Order of the British Empire;

Roy Arthur Cox, Esquire;

George Henry Doughty, Esquire;

John Greve, Esquire;

David Edward Lea, Esquire;

Leslie Frederick Murphy, Esquire;

Dorothy Enid Cole Wedderburn,

Greeting!

WHEREAS We have deemed it expedient that a Commission should issue to inquire into, and report on, such matters concerning the distribution of personal incomes, both earned and unearned, and wealth, as may be referred to it by the Government;

NOW KNOW YE that We, reposing great trust and confidence in your knowledge and ability, have authorised and appointed and do by these Presents authorise and appoint to be Our Commissioners you the said John, Baron Diamond (Chairman) to hold office for a term of three years from the First day of August, 1974 and to be eligible for re-appointment on the expiry thereof; and you the said Sir George Neville Butterworth; Ernest Henry Phelps Brown; Roy Arthur Cox; George Henry Doughty; John Greve; David Edward Lea; Leslie Frederick Murphy and Dorothy Enid Cole Wedderburn to hold office respectively for a term of two years from the First day of August, 1974 and to be eligible for re-appointment on the expiry thereof; and to inquire into, and report on, any such matters as may be referred to you by the Government as aforesaid:

AND for the better effecting the purpose of this Our Commission We do by these Presents give and grant unto you, or any three or more of you, full power to call before you such persons as you shall judge likely to afford you any information upon the subject of this Our Commission; to call for information in writing; and also to call for, have access to and examine all such books, documents, registers and records as may afford you the fullest information on the subject and to inquire of and concerning the premises by all other lawful ways and means whatsoever:

AND We do by these Presents will and ordain that this Our Commission shall continue in full force and virtue, and that you, Our said Commissioners, or any three or more of you may from time to time proceed in the execution thereof, and of every matter and thing therein contained, although the same be not continued from time to time by adjournment:

AND We do by these Presents will and ordain that you, or any three or more of you, do report to Us on any matter referred to you by the Government as aforesaid, so, however, that no such report shall disclose information which would enable persons whose income or wealth has been inquired into to be identified, or would in your opinion damage the legitimate business interests of any person.

GIVEN at Our Court at Balmoral the twenty-third day of August 1974;

In the Twenty-third Year of Our Reign.

By Her Majesty's Command.

Roy Jenkins.

Note: Professor Sir Henry Phelps Brown was created a Knight Bachelor in January 1976.

ELIZABETH R.

ELIZABETH THE SECOND by the Grace of God of the United Kingdom of Great Britain and Northern Ireland and of Our other Realms and Territories QUEEN, Head of the Commonwealth, Defender of the Faith, to Our Trusty and Well-beloved:

Sir Ernest Henry Phelps Brown, Knight, Member of Our Most Excellent Order of the British Empire;

Sir George Neville Butterworth, Knight;

Roy Arthur Cox, Esquire;

George Henry Doughty, Esquire;

John Greve, Esquire;

David Edward Lea, Esquire;

Leslie Frederick Murphy, Esquire;

Dorothy Enid Cole Wedderburn,

Greeting!

WHEREAS by Warrant under Our Royal Sign Manual bearing date the Twenty-third day of August 1974 the Royal Commission on the Distribution of Income and Wealth was constituted:

AND WHEREAS by the said Warrant you the said Sir Ernest Henry Phelps Brown, Sir George Neville Butterworth, Roy Arthur Cox, George Henry Doughty, John Greve, David Edward Lea, Leslie Frederick Murphy and Dorothy Enid Cole Wedderburn were appointed to be members of the said Commission to hold office for a term of two years from the First day of August 1974 and to be eligible for re-appointment on the expiry thereof:

NOW KNOW YE that We reposing great confidence in your knowledge and ability have re-appointed and do by these Presents re-appoint you the said Sir George Neville Butterworth, John Greve, David Edward Lea and Dorothy Enid Cole Wedderburn to be members of the said Commission for a further period of two years commencing on and from the First day of August 1976; you the said Sir Ernest Henry Phelps Brown, Roy Arthur Cox and George Henry Doughty to be members of the said Commission for a further period of one year commencing on and from the First day of August 1976; and you the said Leslie Frederick Murphy to be a member of the said Commission for a further period commencing on and from the First day of August 1976 until the Thirty-first day of December 1976.

GIVEN at Our Court at Balmoral the twentieth day of August 1976:

In the Twenty-fifth Year of Our Reign.

By Her Majesty's Command.

Merlyn Rees.

Note: David Edward Lea was created an Officer of the Most Excellent Order of the British Empire in January 1978.

v

ELIZABETH R. } Signed on
ANNE } behalf of
  } Her Majesty

ELIZABETH THE SECOND, by the Grace of God of the United Kingdom of Great Britain and Northern Ireland and of Our other Realms and Territories QUEEN, Head of the Commonwealth, Defender of the Faith, to Our Trusty and Well-beloved Deryk Vander Weyer, Esquire,

Greeting!

WHEREAS by Warrant under Our Royal Sign Manual bearing date the Twenty-third day of August 1974 the Royal Commission on the Distribution of Income and Wealth was constituted:

NOW KNOW YE that We reposing great confidence in your knowledge and ability have appointed and do by these Presents appoint you the said Deryk Vander Weyer to be a member of the said Commission for a period commencing on and from the First day of January 1977 until and including the Thirty-first day of July 1978, in the room of Our Trusty and Well-beloved Leslie Frederick Murphy, Esquire, whose term of office has expired.

GIVEN at Our Court at Saint James's the fifteenth day of February 1977;

In the Twenty-sixth Year of Our Reign.

By Her Majesty's Command.

Merlyn Rees.

ELIZABETH R.

ELIZABETH THE SECOND by the Grace of God of the United Kingdom of Great Britain and Northern Ireland and of Our other Realms and Territories QUEEN, Head of the Commonwealth, Defender of the Faith, to:

Our Right Trusty and Well-beloved Counsellor John, Baron Diamond;

Our Trusty and Well-beloved:

Sir Ernest Henry Phelps Brown, Knight, Member of Our Most Excellent Order of the British Empire;

Roy Arthur Cox, Esquire;

George Henry Doughty, Esquire;

Greeting!

WHEREAS by Warrant under Our Royal Sign Manual bearing date the Twenty-third day of August 1974 the Royal Commission on the Distribution of Income and Wealth was constituted:

AND WHEREAS by the said Warrant you the said John, Baron Diamond, were appointed to be Chairman of the said Commission, to hold office for a term of three years commencing on and from the First day of August 1974 and to be eligible for re-appointment on the expiry thereof; and you the said Sir Ernest Henry Phelps Brown, Roy Arthur Cox and George Henry Doughty were appointed to be members of the said Commission to hold office for a term of two years from the First day of August 1974 and to be eligible for re-appointment on the expiry thereof:

AND WHEREAS by a Warrant under Our Royal Sign Manual bearing date the Twentieth day of August 1976 you the said Sir Ernest Henry Phelps Brown, Roy Arthur Cox and George Henry Doughty were re-appointed to be members of the said Commission for a further period of one year commencing on and from the First day of August 1976:

NOW KNOW YE that We reposing great confidence in your knowledge and ability have re-appointed and do by these Presents re-appoint you the said John, Baron Diamond, to be Chairman of the said Commission for a further period of one year commencing on and from the First day of August 1977; and have re-appointed and do by these Presents re-appoint you the said Sir Ernest Henry Phelps Brown, Roy Arthur Cox and George Edward Doughty to be members of the said Commission for a further period commencing on and from the First day of August 1977 until and including the Thirty-first day of March 1978.

GIVEN at Our Court at Balmoral the twenty-seventh day of August 1977;

In the Twenty-sixth Year of Our Reign.

By Her Majesty's Command.

Merlyn Rees.

ELIZABETH R.

ELIZABETH THE SECOND, by the Grace of God of the United Kingdom of Great Britain and Northern Ireland and of Our other Realms and Territories QUEEN, Head of the Commonwealth, Defender of the Faith, to Our Trusty and Well-beloved Anthony Barnes Atkinson, and Our Trusty and Well-beloved Anthony Martin Grosvenor Christopher,

Greeting!

WHEREAS by Warrant under Our Royal Sign Manual bearing date the twenty-third day of August 1974 the Royal Commission on the Distribution of Income and Wealth was constituted:

NOW KNOW YE that We reposing great confidence in your knowledge and ability have appointed and do by these Presents appoint you the said Anthony Barnes Atkinson and Anthony Martin Grosvenor Christopher to be members of the said Commission for a period commencing on and from the first day of May 1978 until and including the thirty-first day of July 1979.

GIVEN at Our Court at Saint James's the twenty-third day of June 1978;

In the Twenty-seventh Year of Our Reign.

By Her Majesty's Command.

Merlyn Rees.

ELIZABETH R.

ELIZABETH THE SECOND, by the Grace of God of the United Kingdom of Great Britain and Northern Ireland and of Our other Realms and Territories QUEEN, Head of the Commonwealth, Defender of the Faith, to:

Our Right Trusty and Well-beloved Counsellor John, Baron Diamond;

Our Trusty and Well-beloved:

Sir George Neville Butterworth, Knight;

David Edward Lea, Officer of Our Most Excellent Order of the British Empire;

John Greve, Esquire;

Deryk Vander Weyer, Esquire,

Greeting!

WHEREAS by Warrant under Our Royal Sign Manual bearing date the twenty-third day of August 1974 the Royal Commission on the Distribution of Income and Wealth was constituted:

AND WHEREAS by a Warrant under Our Royal Sign Manual bearing date the twenty-seventh day of August 1977 you the said John, Baron Diamond were re-appointed to be Chairman of the said Commission, to hold office for a further period of one year commencing on and from the first day of August 1977:

AND WHEREAS by a Warrant under Our Royal Sign Manual bearing date the twentieth day of August 1976 you the said Sir George Neville Butterworth, David Edward Lea and John Greve were re-appointed to be members of the said Commission for a further period of two years commencing on and from the first day of August 1976:

AND WHEREAS by a Warrant under Our Royal Sign Manual bearing date the fifteenth day of February 1977 you the said Deryk Vander Weyer were appointed to be a member of the said Commission on and from the first day of January 1977 until and including the thirty-first day of July 1978:

NOW KNOW YE that We reposing great confidence in your knowledge and ability have re-appointed and do by these Presents re-appoint you the said John, Baron Diamond, to be Chairman of the said Commission for a further period of one year commencing on and from the first day of August 1978; and have re-appointed and do by these Presents re-appoint you the said Sir George Neville Butterworth, David Edward Lea, John Greve and Deryk Vander Weyer to be members of the said Commission for a further period of one year commencing on and from the first day of August 1978.

GIVEN at Our Court at Balmoral the fifth day of September 1978;

In the Twenty-seventh Year of Our Reign.

By Her Majesty's Command.

Merlyn Rees.

Note: David Edward Lea was created an Officer of the Most Excellent Order of the British Empire in January 1978.

ELIZABETH R.

ELIZABETH THE SECOND, by the Grace of God of the United Kingdom of Great Britain and Northern Ireland and of Our other Realms and Territories QUEEN, Head of the Commonwealth, Defender of the Faith, to:

Our Right Trusty and Well-beloved Counsellor John, Baron Diamond;

Our Trusty and Well-beloved:

Sir George Neville Butterworth, Knight;

David Edward Lea, Officer of Our Most Excellent Order of the British Empire;

Anthony Barnes Atkinson;

Anthony Martin Grosvenor Christopher;

John Greve;

Deryk Vander Weyer,

Greeting!

WHEREAS by Warrant under Our Royal Sign Manual bearing date the twenty-third day of August 1974 Commissioners were appointed to inquire into, and report on, such matters concerning the distribution of personal incomes, both earned and unearned, and wealth, as might be referred to the Commission by the Government:

AND WHEREAS by Warrant under Our Royal Sign Manual bearing date the fifth day of September 1978 you the said John, Baron Diamond were re-appointed to be Chairman of the said Commission, and you the said Sir George Neville Butterworth, David Edward Lea, John Greve and Deryk Vander Weyer were re-appointed to be members of the said Commission until and including the thirty-first day of July 1979;

AND WHEREAS by Warrant under Our Royal Sign Manual bearing date the twenty-third day of June 1978 you the said Anthony Barnes Atkinson and Anthony Martin Grosvenor Christopher were appointed members of the said Commission until and including the thirty-first day of July 1979 in the room of Commissioners who had retired:

AND WHEREAS it has been represented to Us that there is no continuing need for a standing commission to consider matters within the terms of Our said Warrant of the twenty-third day of August 1974:

NOW THEREFORE We do by these Presents will and ordain that Our said Warrant dated the twenty-third day of August 1974 shall cease to have effect on and from the first day of August 1979.

GIVEN at Our Court at Saint James's the twelfth day of July 1979;

In the Twenty-eighth Year of Our Reign.

By Her Majesty's Command.

W Whitelaw.

TERMS OF THE STANDING REFERENCE

Royal Commission on the
Distribution of Income & Wealth

Standing Reference on the
Distribution of Income & Wealth

To help to secure a fairer distribution of income and wealth in the community there is a need for a thorough and comprehensive enquiry into the existing distribution of income and wealth. There is also a need for a study of past trends in that distribution and for regular assessments of the subsequent changes.

The Government therefore ask the Commission to undertake an analysis of the current distribution of personal income and wealth and of available information on past trends in that distribution and would welcome an initial report on this as early as possible during the first year of the Commission's operation, and subsequent reports from time to time.

These reports should cover personal incomes at all levels; earned income of all kinds (including fringe and non-monetary benefits), unearned income of all kinds; capital gains; and all forms of personal wealth. They should take into account the incidence of taxation and any other factor which the Commission may consider relevant.

The Commission are invited to consult with the Government Statistical Service Service on any changes in the official collection of statistics which would help them in their task.

29 August, 1974.

Table of Contents

for more detailed Key to Chapters see following pages.

PART I

Chapter 1   Introduction

Chapter 2   The Growth of the Labour Force and Changes in its Composition

Chapter 3   Theoretical Background and Practical Approaches to the Analysis of Earnings

Chapter 4   Sources of Data

PART II

Chapter 5   Differences in Earnings between Occupations and between Industries

Chapter 6   Occupational Structure and Trends in Earnings

Chapter 7   Earnings in Selected Occupations

Chapter 8   Age-earnings Relationships and Fluctuations in the Earnings of Individuals

Chapter 9   Earnings and Other Employee Benefits

PART III

Chapter 10 Self-employed and Employees Compared

Chapter 11 Incomes of the Self-employed by Trade Group

Chapter 12 Assets, Income and Tax: Distinctive Features of Self-employment

Chapter 13 Self-employment Incomes in Eleven Countries

PART IV

Chapter 14   The Main Findings

Appendices

List of Tables

xix

List of Figures

Royal Commission on the Distribution of Income and Wealth

Report

To the Queen's Most Excellent Majesty

MAY IT PLEASE YOUR MAJESTY

We, the undersigned Commissioners, having been appointed "to inquire into, and report on, such matters concerning the distribution of personal incomes, both earned and unearned, and wealth, as may be referred to it by the Government" and having been asked by the Government to analyse and to report from time to time on the current distribution of personal income and wealth and on available information on past trends in that distribution

HUMBLY SUBMIT TO YOUR MAJESTY THE FOLLOWING REPORT.

PART I

CHAPTER 1

Introduction

The terms of our standing reference

1.1   We were appointed on 23 August 1974 to inquire into, and report on, such matters concerning the distribution of personal incomes, both earned and unearned, and wealth, as may be referred to us by Government; and, under the terms of our standing reference, were given the continuing task of reporting on the current distribution of personal income and wealth, and of available information on past trends in that distribution. Our terms of reference call upon us to cover personal incomes at all levels, earned income of all kinds (including fringe and non-monetary benefits), unearned income of all kinds, capital gains, and all forms of personal wealth; and to take into account the incidence of taxation and any other factor which we may consider relevant. The terms of the Royal Warrant by which we were appointed and of our standing reference are set out in full at pages iii to xi.

1.2   In this report we depart from the format of our earlier standing reference reports in that we concentrate on a particular aspect of the distribution of income: namely income from employment and self-employment which, in 1977, accounted for almost 80 per cent of total personal income. The Central Statistical Office's national income and expenditure figures for that year reveal that 68.6 per cent and 9.3 per cent of total personal income were derived from employment and self-employment, respectively.[1]

1.3   The latest available statistics on the current distribution of income and wealth were covered in our previous standing reference report. That report was the fourth in our standing reference series and was published in July 1979. Details of all our previous publications are given at the inside back cover of this report.

Origins of this report

1.4   In discussing major subjects for future work, in our first report on our standing reference (published in July 1975) we said that we intended to investigate the distribution of income between and within occupations. In addition, we said that a special study of self-employment would be necessary if its place within the total distribution of income was to be properly understood. In the

---

[1] See Table 2.1 in our Report No 7, *Fourth report on the standing reference*, Cmnd 7595, HMSO, July 1979.

1

relevant studies which we subsequently carried out we aimed to examine how earnings from employment vary from job to job, and to compare incomes from self-employment and from employment. We would emphasise, however, that while both studies examine aspects of income from employment, they involve separate examinations of data taken largely from different sources: our study of variations in earnings from employment mainly uses data from the Department of Employment's New Earnings Survey (which does not cover self-employment), while the comparison of incomes from self-employment and from employment draws on the Inland Revenue Survey of Personal Incomes and on a special survey we carried out of the incomes of proprietors of close companies.

Structure of this report

1.5   In Part II, Chapters 5 to 9, of this report we present the results of our studies of how earnings vary from job to job, and in Part III, Chapters 10 to 13, the results of our study of self-employment and comparison of incomes of the self-employed and employees.

1.6   We preface these with three introductory chapters to provide the context for the detailed studies. In Chapter 2 we summarise information on the changing structure of this country's labour force. Here we are concerned not with levels of earnings or incomes (which are examined in considerable detail in the main body of the report), but with the basic composition of the labour force in Great Britain in terms of sex, age, occupation and industry. Chapter 3 provides the analytical background to the main questions to which our studies were addressed. Chapter 4 contains a discussion of the sources used, including an account of two comparative international studies. A report on international comparisons of industrial earnings of employees prepared for us by Professor C T Saunders and Mr D Marsden is being published separately as a background paper,[1] but we draw on their material at appropriate places in this Report. The work on income from self-employment in other countries carried out for us by Dr T Stark is included in Chapter 13. The scope of these pieces of work is set out in Chapter 4.

1.7   Finally Chapter 14 provides a summary of the main findings and conclusions to be drawn from our studies.

---

[1] *Background Paper No 8: A six country comparison of the distribution of industrial earnings in the 1970s.* C T Saunders and D Marsden.

CHAPTER 2

The Growth of the Labour Force and Changes in its Composition

Introduction

2.1   In this Chapter we outline the way in which the composition of the labour force in terms of industries and occupations has changed, and the way in which industries and occupations are related, in order to set in context our analysis in Part II, Chapters 5 to 9, of the structure and variations in incomes from employment, and our analysis in Part III, Chapters 10 to 13, of incomes of the self-employed. We use the term 'labour force' to refer to those members of the population in employment (including self-employment) or seeking employment. The different definitions of the labour force that are used, in particular the 'working' population, the 'economically active' population, and (in 1951 and earlier) the 'occupied' population, are explained in the notes to the tables, and more fully in Appendix A. So that the geographical coverage of the figures we use shall be consistent throughout, we present figures for Great Britain rather than for the United Kingdom.

2.2   We begin by considering the age structure of the labour force—for earnings are linked to age—and the proportion of men, non-married (ie single, widowed and divorced) women, and married women; for not only are the earnings of men and women different but the changing proportions of men, non-married women, and married women are key aspects of the way in which the growth of the labour force has differed from the growth of the whole population. We then outline the way in which the labour force is distributed between occupations and how this distribution has changed through time. We next consider the changing distribution of the labour force between industries (in the broadest sense of the term, including services). Chapter 6 will attempt to analyse the separate effects of changes in occupational and industrial structure on the distribution of earnings from employment, so we have outlined here the relationship between occupation and industry. The composition of the labour force in terms of industries and its composition in terms of occupations are related but distinct[1]. In the final section of this Chapter we outline the changes in the number of self-employed men and women, and the occupations and industries in which they work.

2.3   The time-span and detail of the analysis of the changes is limited by the extent to which there are sufficiently comparable data. These limits are most severe for industrial structure, where changes in classification preclude com-

---

[1] These questions have been considered in greater detail in *The Changing Structure of the Labour Force* (Unit for Manpower Studies, Department of Employment, 1976).

Table 2.1 Age Structure of the Population of Great Britain; 1881 to 1976

	Aged 0–14	Aged 15–64	Aged 65 and Over	All Ages	Total Population
	%	%	%	%	'000
			Persons		
1881	36·5	58·9	4·6	100·0	29,710
1891	35·1	60·1	4·8	100·0	33,028
1901	32·5	62·8	4·7	100·0	37,000
1911	30·8	63·9	5·2	100·0	40,831
1921	27·9	66·0	6·0	100·0	42,770
1931	24·2	68·4	7·4	100·0	44,795
1951	22·4	66·7	10·9	100·0	48,854
1961	23·3	65·0	11·8	100·0	51,284
1971	24·0	62·8	13·2	100·0	53,979
1976	22·8	62·9	14·3	100·0	54,347
			Men		
1881	37·5	58·2	4·2	100·0	14,439
1891	36·2	59·4	4·3	100.0	15,996
1901	33·6	62·2	4·2	100·0	17,902
1911	31·9	63·5	4·6	100·0	19,754
1921	29·4	65·2	5·4	100·0	20,423
1931	25·5	67·9	6·6	100·0	21,459
1951	23·8	66·8	9·3	100·0	23,450
1961	24·6	66·0	9·3	100·0	24,787
1971	25.3	64·2	10·4	100·0	26,198
1976	24·1	64·5	11·4	100·0	26,435
			Women		
1881	35·5	59·6	5·0	100·0	15,271
1891	34·1	60·7	5·2	100·0	17,033
1901	31·5	63·3	5·2	100·0	19,098
1911	29·8	64·4	5·8	100·0	21,077
1921	26·5	66·8	6·6	100·0	22,346
1931	23·0	68·9	8·1	100·0	23,337
1951	21·1	66·5	12·4	100·0	25,404
1961	21·9	64·0	14·1	100·0	26,497
1971	22·7	61·5	15·9	100·0	27,781
1976	21·6	61·4	17·0	100·0	27,912

Source: 1881–1971: Censuses of Population.
1976: Office of Population Censuses and Surveys' estimate for June 1976.

Note: The population figures for Census years are the 'enumerated' populations. The 1976 figures relate to the estimated 'home' population, which is equal to the 'enumerated' population *less* members of the Armed Forces of other countries stationed here *plus* British Forces stationed overseas and British Seamen on the high seas.

parisons bridging 1961 except in very broad terms. The structure of the population in terms of age, sex and marital status, on the other hand, can be shown in a wholly consistent way back to 1921—or even further if need be, though for our purposes a half century's perspective will generally suffice.

Size and composition of the labour force

2.4 As a starting point, we show the growth of the population, with an indication of its changing age structure. There is no uniquely correct age structure to

4

use, owing for instance to the raising of the school leaving age in 1918, 1947 and 1972, and the changing age of retirement. But to give an outline of long term trends, a division into ages 0 to 14, 15 to 64, and 65 and over is appropriate. In this instance we go back before 1921 to show the extent to which trends evident since then are of longer standing.

2.5 The proportion of young people (under age 15) in the population fell continuously until 1931 as a result of the fall in the birth rate that began in the 1870s, and the lengthening of the expectation of life. The post-1945 "bulge" in births did not prevent a further fall between 1931 and 1951 in the proportion of the population that was under age 15; and the large rise in births between the mid-1950s and the mid-1960s produced no more than a small reversal of the previous downward trend in the proportion of the population that was under 15 years of age.

Table 2.2   Share of Labour Force in Total Population; 1881 to 1976

Great Britain

Year			Population	Labour[1] [2] Force	Share of Labour Force in Population
			'000	'000	%
1881..	..	..	29,710	12,795	43·1
1891..	..	..	33,028	14,676	44·4
1901..	..	..	37,000	16,312	44·1
1911..	..	..	40,831	18,351	44·9
1921..	..	..	42,769	19,357	45·3
1931..	..	..	44,795	21,055	47·0
1951..	..	..	48,854	22,610	46·3
1961..	..	..	51,284	23,810[3]	46·4
1971..	..	..	53,979	25,103	46·5
1976..	..	..	54,347	25,487[4]	46·9

Sources: Labour Force: 1881 from B R Mitchell and P Deane, *Abstract of British Historical Statistics*.

1891 and later from *Department of Employment Gazette*, July 1975, pp. 658–9 (this updates and revises data for 1891–1921 given in *British Labour Statistics, Historical Abstract, 1886–1968*, Table 109).

Notes:

[1] For 1951 and the earlier years the figures for the labour force refer to the 'occupied' population, which consisted of those normally occupied. For 1961 and 1971 the figures are those of the 'economically active' population, ie those in work or actively seeking work in the week before the Census. Students were excluded even if they were in temporary work. For 1881 to 1911 the lower age limit for the occupied population was 10 years, in 1921 12 years; in 1931 14 years, in 1951 15 years. For the 'economically active' and 'working' populations the lower age limit is determined by the school leaving age; 15 in 1961 and 1971 and 16 years in 1976.

[2] Includes part-time as well as full-time workers, all counted alike.

[3] 1961 Census figures for economically active population corrected by published bias factors.

[4] The figure is for the working population in June 1976. This estimate is based on the Department of Employment estimates of civilian employees in employment derived from the annual censuses of employment, and the self-employed, plus H M Forces and the *registered* unemployed. It is therefore not directly comparable with estimates of the economically active population derived from the Census of Population. See Table 2.6 for the change between 1971 and 1976 on a comparable basis, and Appendix A for a more detailed discussion of the differences in coverage and definition between the Census of Population figures of the economically active population and the Department of Employment's estimate of the working population.

2.6   Up to the 1930s the population aged 15 to 64 grew as a proportion of the total; for up to the decade 1901 to 1911 the number of births (as distinct from the birth *rate*) rose, increasing the working-age population when they reached adulthood (which more of them did, owing to a falling death rate). But by the 1930s the numbers reaching adulthood began to fall, with the result that the growth of the working-age population slowed in absolute terms, and declined as a proportion of the total. And as men and women born in the late nineteenth and early twentieth centuries began to reach old age, the proportion of the population aged 65 and over rose fast. Among women, the rise in the proportion over 65 rose also, due to greater longevity; but among men, the expectation of life at age 65 was little greater in the 1960s than in the 1860s, although in the intervening century the probability of getting to age 65 had increased enormously.

2.7   Notwithstanding these shifts in the age structure of the population, the labour force changed remarkably little as a proportion of the whole population, as Table 2.2 and Figure 2.1 show.

2.8   The relationship between the growth of the labour force and the growth of the whole population may be analysed in terms of *activity rates*. An activity rate measures the proportion of a specified group, usually defined in terms of age, sex and—for women—marital status, who are members of the labour force. Table 2.3 shows in summary form the changes in activity rates in Great Britain between 1921 and 1976.

2.9   Three major trends are evident: (1) a large decrease in activity rates in the lower age groups owing to the statutory school leaving age being raised, voluntary later school leaving, and the growth of full-time higher and further education; (2) a large decrease in activity rates among older men, owing to extension of coverage of State retirement pensions and then of occupational pensions; and (3) working in the opposite direction, a very large increase in activity rates among married women in all age groups.

2.10   In 1921 under 10 per cent of married women were in the labour force, very similar indeed to the proportion in 1911. The increase in women's employment in World War I was not permanent, unlike the increase in World War II, probably because by 1921 the British economy was in the depths of the post-war slump. But after World War II, the proportion of married women in paid employment rose steeply and continuously. By 1971 the largest increase in activity rates was among married women aged 45 to 64—who are likely to be women whose children have reached secondary school or have entered paid employment, or become students; but since 1971 the largest increases have been among younger married women, which suggests a tendency to return to paid employment after a shorter interval than hitherto.

2.11   A substantial part of the increase in numbers in employment, especially of married women, has consisted of part-time employment[1]. To that extent the labour force totals, which include both full-time and part-time workers counted equally, overstate the growth of actual labour input. The Unit for Manpower

---

[1] See also paragraph 2.18 below.

Figure 2.1 Age Composition and Labour Force Participation of Total Population; 1881 to 1971

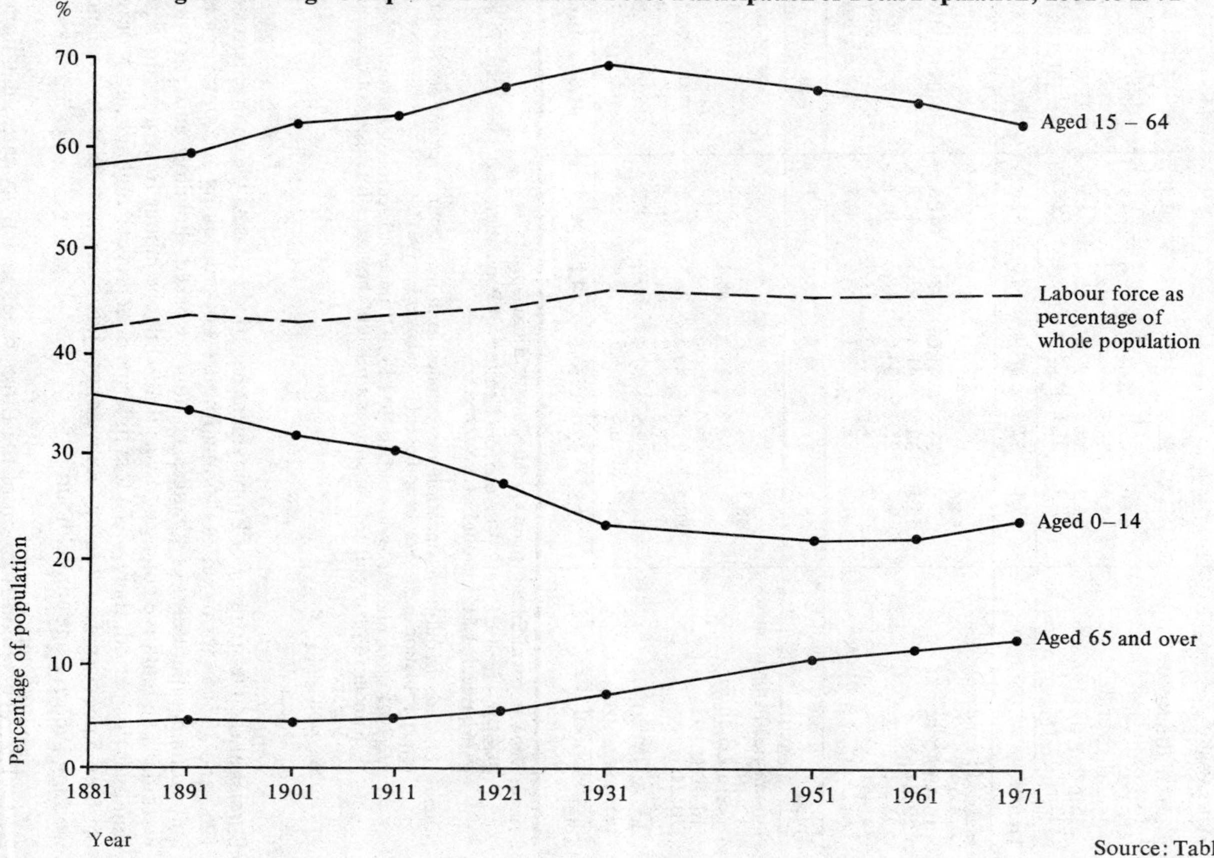

Aged 15 – 64

Labour force as
percentage of
whole population

Aged 0–14

Aged 65 and over

%

70

60

50

40

30

20

10

0

1881   1891   1901   1911   1921   1931   1951   1961   1971

Year

Percentage of population

Source: Tables 2.1 and 2.2.

7

Table 2.3 Economic Activity Rates by Age and Sex; 1921 to 1976[1]

Great Britain   Percentages

	1921	1951	1961	1966	1971	1975	1976P
Males aged							
12–19 ⎫	63.2						
15–19 ⎬ Under 20²		83.8	74.6	70.6	60.9		
16–19 ⎭						65.8	64.7
20–24	97.0	94.9	91.9	92.6	89.9	88.9	88.5
25–44	97.9	98.3	98.2	98.2	97.9	97.7	97.9
45–64	94.9	95.2	97.6	95.1	94.5	93.9	94.4
65+	58.9	31.1	25.0	23.5	19.4	15.3	15.9
Total	87.1	87.6	86.0	84.0	81.4	80.6	80.6
Married Females aged							
15–19 ⎫	14.6						
16–19 ⎬ Under 20²		38.1	41.0	43.6	41.6	51.9	51.9
20–24	12.5	36.5	41.3	43.5	45.7	54.3	54.6
25–44	9.1	25.1	33.6	41.8	46.4	55.1	56.3
45–64	8.0	19.0	29.6	41.4	47.5	52.4	53.9
65+	4.2	2.7	3.3	5.5	6.5	5.2	5.4
Total	8.7	21.7	29.7	38.1	42.2	47.9	49.0
Non-married Females aged							
12–19 ⎫	48.8						
15–19 ⎬ Under 20²		80.7	73.2	68.4	57.2		
16–19 ⎭						60.2	58.8
20–24	80.5	91.0	89.4	86.7	81.2	77.0	76.7
25–44	69.3	81.2	84.2	84.2	80.4	79.2	79.0
45–64	44.3	50.5	57.4	60.0	58.7	57.9	57.8
65+	12.7	6.6	6.5	7.4	6.3	4.5	4.5
Total	53.8	55.0	50.6	49.2	43.7	41.8	41.6

Source: Department of Employment Gazette July 1975 and April 1978.
Estimates for 1921 to 1971 taken from Censuses of Population: estimates for 1975 and 1976 based on EEC Labour Force Survey.

Notes: [1] Students in full-time education are excluded from the labour force but not from the total population aged 15 or 16 and over (12 and over for 1921).

[2] In 1921 those under 12 years old, in 1951 to 1971 under 15 years old, and in 1975 and 1976 under 16 years old, are excluded as a result of the successive raising of the school leaving age.

P Provisional.

Studies at the Department of Employment has tried to assess the change between 1961 and 1971 in terms of total annual hours worked, taking account, for men and women separately, of changes in hours worked, holidays and part-time working. The tentative conclusion was that while the labour force grew by 5 per cent over this period, there was a loss in terms of aggregate annual hours worked of about 5 per cent. This loss was equivalent to just over one million manual men working 1961 average annual hours[1].

2.12   The relative contribution of the three trends in activity rates, mentioned in paragraph 2.9, to the change in the size of the labour force may be shown by

[1] *The Changing Structure of the Labour Force, op cit*, pp. 11–12.

Figure 2.2 Economic Activity Rates by Age and Sex; 1921 to 1975

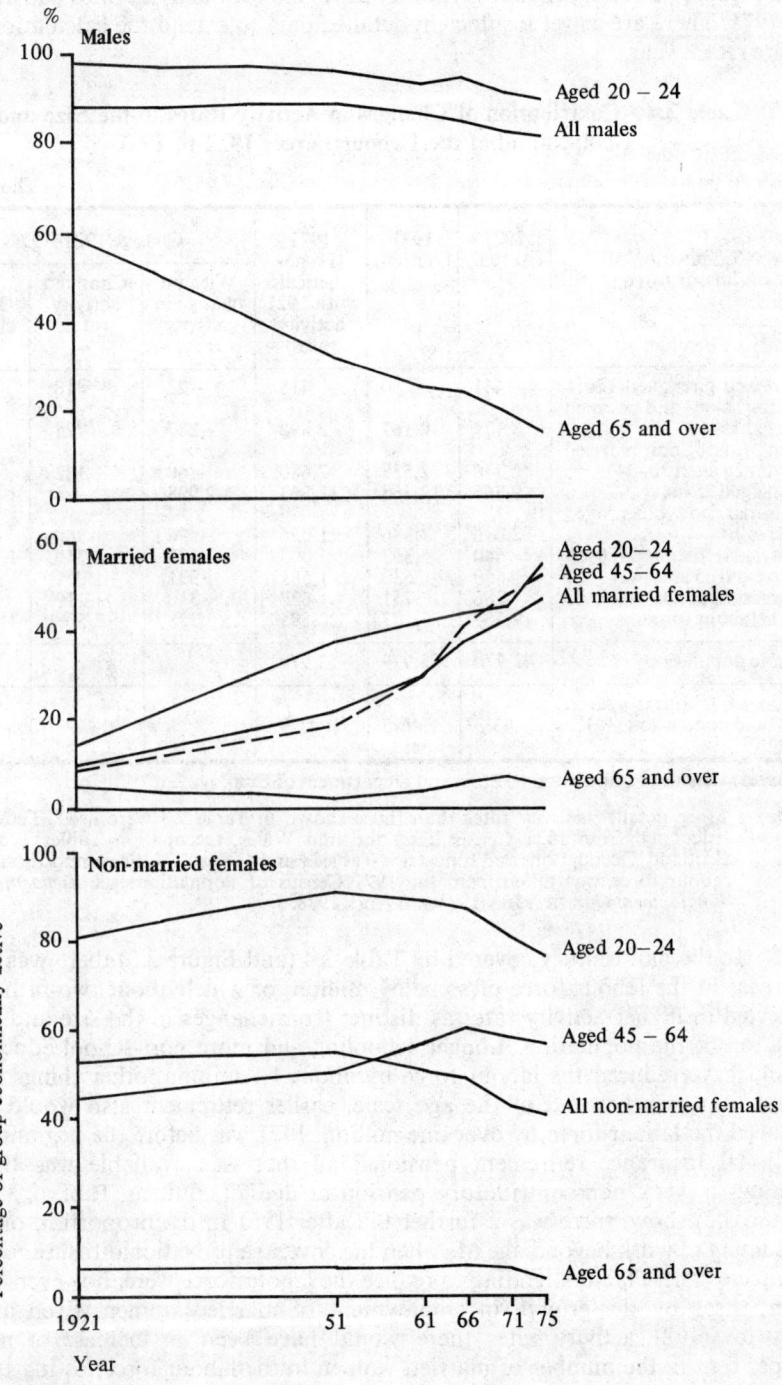

Source: Table 2.3.

comparing the actual change in the labour force between 1921 and 1971 with what would have happened if (hypothetically) the 1921 activity rates had applied in 1971. There are as yet insufficient detailed data to extend the calculation to a more recent year.

Table 2.4   Contribution of Changes in Activity Rates to the Size and Composition of the Labour Force; 1921 to 1971

Great Britain   Thousands

Composition of labour force	1921 (Actual)	1971 (Actual)	1971 (Hypo-thetical, with 1921 activity rates)	Change 1921–1971		
				With no change in activity rates	Changed activity rates	Total change
Boys and girls aged 12–14	441	0	418	−23	−418	−441
Young men and women aged 15–19	3,179	2,167	2,892	−287	−725	−1,012
Men and non-married women aged 20–24 ..	2,740	2,538	2,680	−60	−142	−202
Men aged 25–64	9,365	12,368	12,363	+2,998	+5	+3,003
Non-married women aged 25–59	2,016	1,386	1,026	−990	+360	−630
Married women aged 20–59	680	5,362	1,003	+323	+4,359	+4,682
Men aged 65 and over ..	650	530	1,581	+931	−1,051	−120
Women aged 60 and over	286	751	632	+346	+119	+465
Total labour force ..	19,357	25,103	22,595	+3,238	+2,508	+5,746
Whole population ..	42,770	53,979	53,979			
Ratio of labour force to whole population (%)..	45·3	46·5	41·9			

Sources: Census of Population (OPCS) and Department of Employment.

Note: More detailed activity rates than those shown in Table 2.3 were used. They were calculated from 1921 Census, England and Wales, Occupation Tables 1 and 4; Scotland, Occupations and Industries, Tables 1 and 4. For 1971 the composition of the labour force was taken from the 1971 Census of Population; see *Department of Employment Gazettes*, July 1975 and April 1978.

2.13   In the half century covered by Table 2.4 (and Figure 2.3) there was a net increase in the labour force of some 5¾ million, of which about two-fifths was reflected in higher activity rates as distinct from changes in the size and composition of the population. Longer schooling and more post-school education would have reduced the labour force by about 1.1 million, other things being equal. At the other end of the age scale, earlier retirement also would have reduced the labour force by over one million. 1921 was before the beginning of National Insurance retirement pensions; all that was available was the 10 shillings a week non-contributory pension at age 70. But, as Table 2.3 (and Figure 2.2) show, there was a further fall after 1961 in the proportion of men remaining at work beyond age 65, when the coverage of National Insurance was complete. These factors tending to reduce the labour force were, however, more than offset by the growth in employment of married women. Even at the very low 1921 activity rates there would have been an increase of nearly 50 per cent in the number of married women in the labour force, owing to the rise in the number of women of marriageable age, earlier marriage, and a much

10

Figure 2.3   The Influence of Activity Rates on Changes in Size and Composition of Labour Force; 1921 to 1971

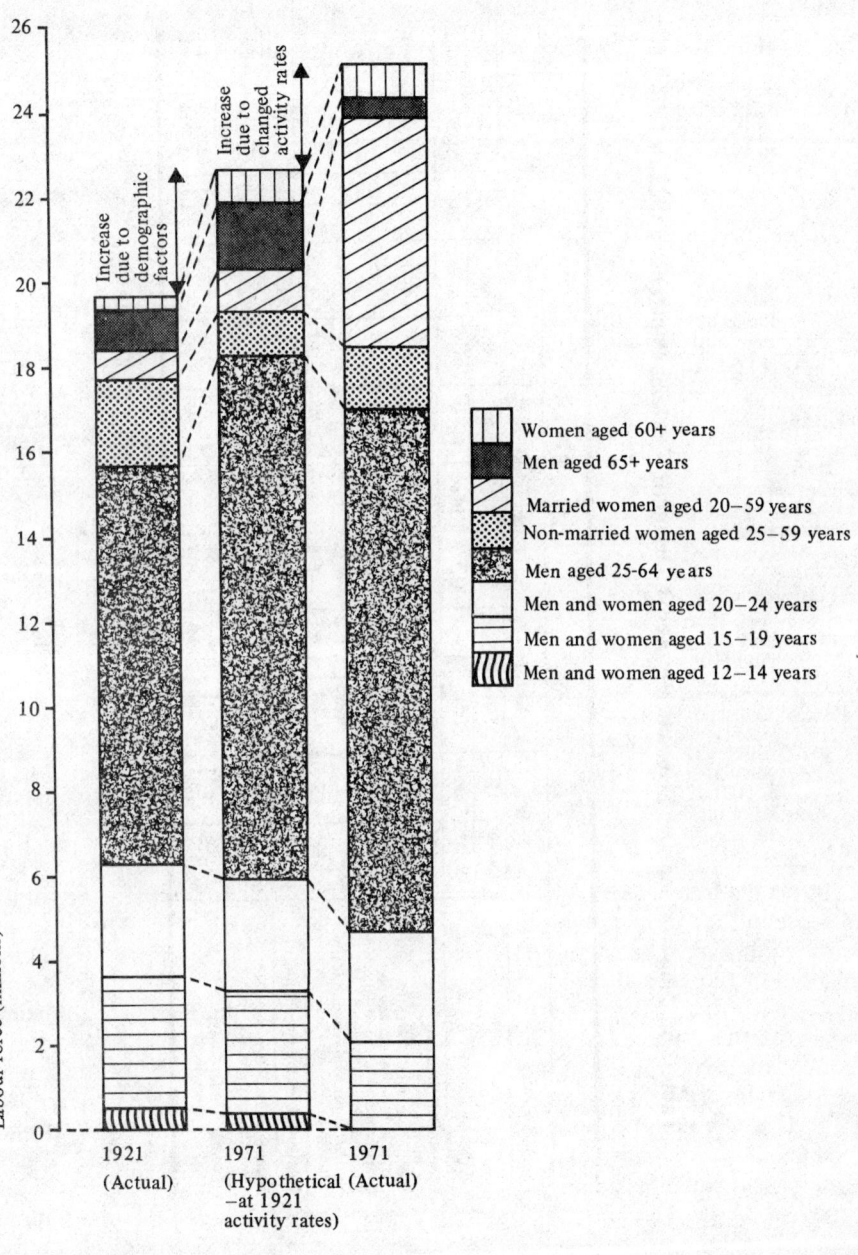

Source: Table 2.3.

Table 2.5 Non-working and Economically Active/Occupied/Working Population; 1921 to 1976

Great Britain

Year	1921						1961					
	Males		Females		Total		Males		Females		Total	
Population category	'000	%	'000	%	'000	%	'000	%	'000	%	'000	%
Whole population	20,423	100·0	22,347	100·0	42,770	100·0	24,787	100·0	26,497	100·0	51,284	100·0
Economically inactive:												
Children under 14/15/16 ..	5,553	27·2	5,490	24·6	11,043	25·8	6,109	24·6	5,814	21·9	11,923	23·2
Number aged 14/15/16 and over in full-time education	297	1·5	279	1·2	576	1·3	540	2·2	454	1·7	994	1·9
Others aged 14/15/16 to 60 or 65 not economically active	464	2·3	8,916	39·9	9,380	21·9	314	1·3	7,761	29·3	8,075	15·7
Numbers over 60/65 economically inactive..	453	2·2	1,961	8·8	2,414	5·6	1,753	7·1	4,728	17·8	6,481	12·6
Total non-working population ..	6,767	33·1	16,646	74·5	23,413	54·7	8,716	35·2	18,757	70·8	27,473	53·6
Economically active/occupied/ working population	13,656	66·9	5,701	25·5	19,357	45·3	16,071	64·8	7,740	29·2	23,811	46·4
Of which: Under 60/65 .. .. Over 60/65	13,006 650	63·7 3·2	5,415 286	24·2 1·3	18,421 936	43·1 2·2	15,506 565	62·5 2·3	7,232 508	27·3 1·9	22,738 1,073	44·3 2·1

Table 2.5 (continued) Non-working and Economically Active/Occupied/Working Population; 1921 to 1976

Great Britain

Year	1971						1976[1]					
	Males		Females		Total		Males		Females		Total	
Population category	'000	%	'000	%	'000	%	'000	%	'000	%	'000	%
Whole population	26,197	100·0	27,782	100·0	53,979	100·0	26,435	100·0	27,912	100·0	54,347	100·0
Economically inactive:												
Children under 14/15/16 ..	6,638	25·3	6,293	22·7	12,931	24·0	6,809	25·8	6,448	23·1	13,257	24·4
Number aged 14/15/16 and over in full-time education	954	3·6	831	3·0	1,785	3·3	771[2]	2·9	669[2]	2·4	1,440[2]	2·6
Others aged 14/15/16 to 60 or 65 not economically active	481	1·8	6,150	22·1	6,631	12·3	463	1·8	5,486	19·7	5,949	11·0
Numbers over 60/65 economically inactive	2,207	8·5	5,322	19·1	7,529	13·9	2,546	9·6	5,668	20·3	8,214	15·1
Total non-working population ..	10,280	39·2	18,596	66·9	28,876	53·5	10,589	40·1	18,271	65·5	28,860	53·1
Economically active/occupied/ working population	15,917	60·8	9,186	33·1	25,103	46·5	15,846	59·9	9,641	34·5	25,487	46·9
Of which: Under 60/65	15,387	58·7	8,435	30·4	23,822	44·1	15,382	58·1	8,954	32·1	24,336	44·7
Over 60/65	530	2·1	751	2·7	1,281	2·4	464	1·8	687	2·4	1,151	2·2

Sources: Censuses of Population, 1921, 1961, 1971: Annual Abstract of Statistics, 1977; *Department of Employment Gazette*, July 1975 and April 1978.

Notes:

[1] 1976 figures based on mid-year estimates of whole population by OPCS, and of working population by Department of Employment. The 1921 figures include all persons (other than retired) stating an occupation, whatever their employment status at the time of the Census, whereas the 1961 and 1971 figures include only those persons economically active at the time of the Census.

[2] 1976 estimates of persons aged 16 or over in full-time education supplied by Department of Education and Science. Estimates for earlier years were derived directly from the Censuses of Population. DES estimates might cover a smaller percentage of the population since they only include students (full-time and sandwich) in educational establishments (school, higher education and non-advanced further education). On the other hand, the estimates refer to January 1976 and so include the Easter school-leavers which would be excluded from an April estimate.

13

lower proportion of women remaining unmarried. But the rise in activity rates added some 4.36 million married women to the labour force. Demographic changes between 1921 and 1971—the rise in the proportion of older men and women in the population (see Table 2.1) and the increase in the proportion of women aged 20 to 59 who were married (63 per cent in 1921, 81 per cent in 1971) —would have produced a considerable fall in the labour force relative to the whole population, ie from 45·3 per cent to 41·9 per cent (Table 2.4). That the ratio of the labour force to total population did not fall—indeed rose slightly—was due to the massive rise in the proportion of married women in paid employment.

2.14   Although calculations cannot be made in the same detail as for 1921 to 1971, the available evidence (the annual employment census—which analyses employees by sex, though not marital status—and the 1975 Labour Force Survey) suggests that the trends described above continued from 1971 to 1976. The raising of the school leaving age in 1972 and an increase in the proportion of school leavers entering full-time higher or further education reduced still further the proportion of the population below age 25 in the labour force, and the fall in the proportion of men remaining at work beyond age 65 continued after 1971. Married women's activity rates, in contrast, continued to rise (see Table 2.3 and Figure 2.2).

2.15   The way in which over a long run of years the components of the labour force and their relationship to the whole population have changed is summarised in Table 2.5 and Figure 2.4. The 1976 figures are less precise than those for the other years, since in the absence of a Census the figures were drawn from three separate sources—the estimates of the whole population by OPCS; the Department of Employment's estimates of the working population; and the Department of Education and Science's estimates of numbers in full-time education at age 16 and above.

2.16   Table 2.5 and Figure 2.4 show in a different way the remarkable stability of the labour force as a proportion of the whole population, and even more so of the population below retirement age, and how this stability in the aggregate was the consequence of divergent trends for men and women. The change in the employment status of women was dramatic; in 1921 some 40 per cent of the female population were under age 60 and not in full-time education (or too young to go to school) but outside the labour force; by 1961 the proportion had dropped to just under 30 per cent; and in 1976 was down to 20 per cent. There was a sharp change, in the other direction, in the proportion of the male population who had left the labour force owing to age; between 1921 and 1961 the proportion more than trebled; and by 1976 it was four and a half times as great as in 1921. The fall between 1971 and 1976 in the percentage of young men and women in full-time education beyond the school leaving age was the consequence of the raising of the statutory minimum school leaving age from 15 to 16 in 1972. About 300,000 boys and girls aged 15, who in 1971 would have been counted among the population in full-time education beyond the school leaving age were thereby transferred to the school age population.

2.17   The composition and growth of the whole labour force is summarised in Table 2.6 and Figure 2.5. The estimate for the labour force in 1976 is derived

Figure 2.4 Economically Active and Non-working Population; 1921 and 1976

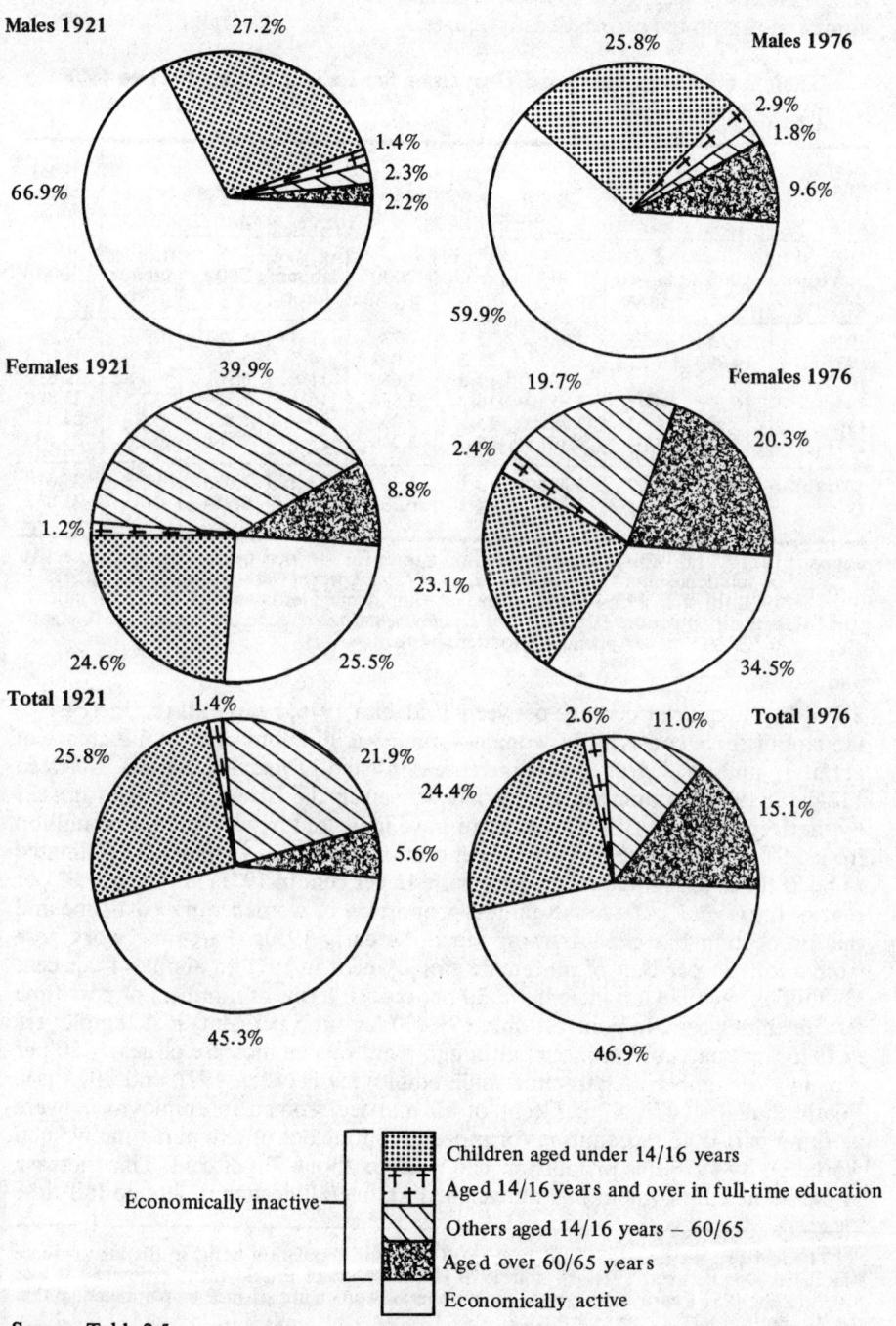

Males 1921   27.2%

1.4%
2.3%
2.2%

66.9%

25.8%   Males 1976

2.9%
1.8%

9.6%

59.9%

Females 1921   39.9%

19.7%   Females 1976

2.4%

20.3%

8.8%

1.2%

23.1%

24.6%   25.5%

34.5%

Total 1921   1.4%

25.8%   21.9%

2.6%   11.0%   Total 1976

24.4%

15.1%

5.6%

45.3%

46.9%

Economically inactive
- Children aged under 14/16 years
- Aged 14/16 years and over in full-time education
- Others aged 14/16 years – 60/65
- Aged over 60/65 years

Economically active

Source: Table 2.5.

15

from the Department of Employment working population figure, adjusted to bring it in line with the Census of Population definition of the economically active labour force. A comparable estimate is given for 1971 for purposes of comparison with the earlier Census figures.

Table 2.6   Composition and Growth of the Labour Force; 1921 to 1976

Great Britain

Year	Men '000	Men As % of labour force	Non-married women '000	Non-married women As % of labour force	Married women '000	Married women As % of labour force	Total women '000	Total women As % of labour force	Total labour force '000
1921	13,656	70·5	4,968	25·7	733	3·8	5,701	29·5	19,357
1931	14,790	70·2	5,312	25·3	953	4·5	6,265	29·8	21,055
1951	15,649	69·2	4,303	19·0	2,658	11·8	6,961	30·8	22,610
1961	16,071	67·5	3,853	16·2	3,886	16·3	7,739	32·5	23,810
1966	15,994	64·3	3,799	15·3	5,063	20·4	8,862	35·7	24,857
1971 (a)	15,917	63·4	3,387	13·5	5,799	23·1	9,186	36·6	25,103
1971 (b)	15,933	63·7	3,286	13·1	5,799	23·2	9,085	36·3	25,018
1976	15,914	61·5	3,223	12·5	6,731	26·0	9,954	38·5	25,868

Sources: 1921–71 (a)—Censuses of Population figures for the 'occupied'/'economically active' population, summarised in *Department of Employment Gazette*, July 1975 , pp. 658–9; 1971 (b) and 1976—Department of Employment estimates of the 'economically active' population, *Department of Employment Gazette*, June 1977, p.587. See footnotes to Table 2.2 and Appendix A for definitions.

2.18   In the quarter century between 1951 and 1976, nearly all the increase in the labour force consisted of women—some 3 million out of a total increase of about $3\frac{1}{4}$ million[1]. Most of this increase consisted of married women. Between 1971 and 1976 the number of married women in the labour force is estimated by the Department of Employment to have increased by just under one million from 5·8 to 6·7 million[2]. By 1976, 49 per cent of all married women were estimated to be in the labour force (compared with 42 per cent in 1971) and nearly 60 per cent of those under 60. A substantial proportion of women work part-time and this proportion has been growing since the early 1950s. Part-time work rose from about 36 per cent of all female employment in 1971 to about 44 per cent ($3\frac{1}{2}$ million) in 1976 (an increase of 30 per cent in terms of numbers of part-time female employees). In contrast only 699,000 (about 5 per cent) male employees in 1976 were part-time workers, although there was an increase of nearly 20 per cent in the number of part-time male employees between 1971 and 1976 (see Figure 2.6). In 1971, 47 per cent of all married women in employment were working part-time (accounting for more than four out of five part-time women workers). By 1976 this proportion had risen to about 53 per cent. This increase in part-time employment has outweighed an overall decline in female full-time

---

[1] The increase between 1951 and 1971 (a) (Census of Population basis) in the labour force was 2,493,000; between 1971 (b) and 1976 (Department of Employment estimates) it was 850,000. The 1951 Census understated the number of women in part-time employment, so that the 1951 to 1971 increase was overstated.
[2] 'New projections of future labour force', *Department of Employment Gazette*, June 1977.

16

Figure 2.5   Composition of Labour Force; 1921, 1951 and 1971

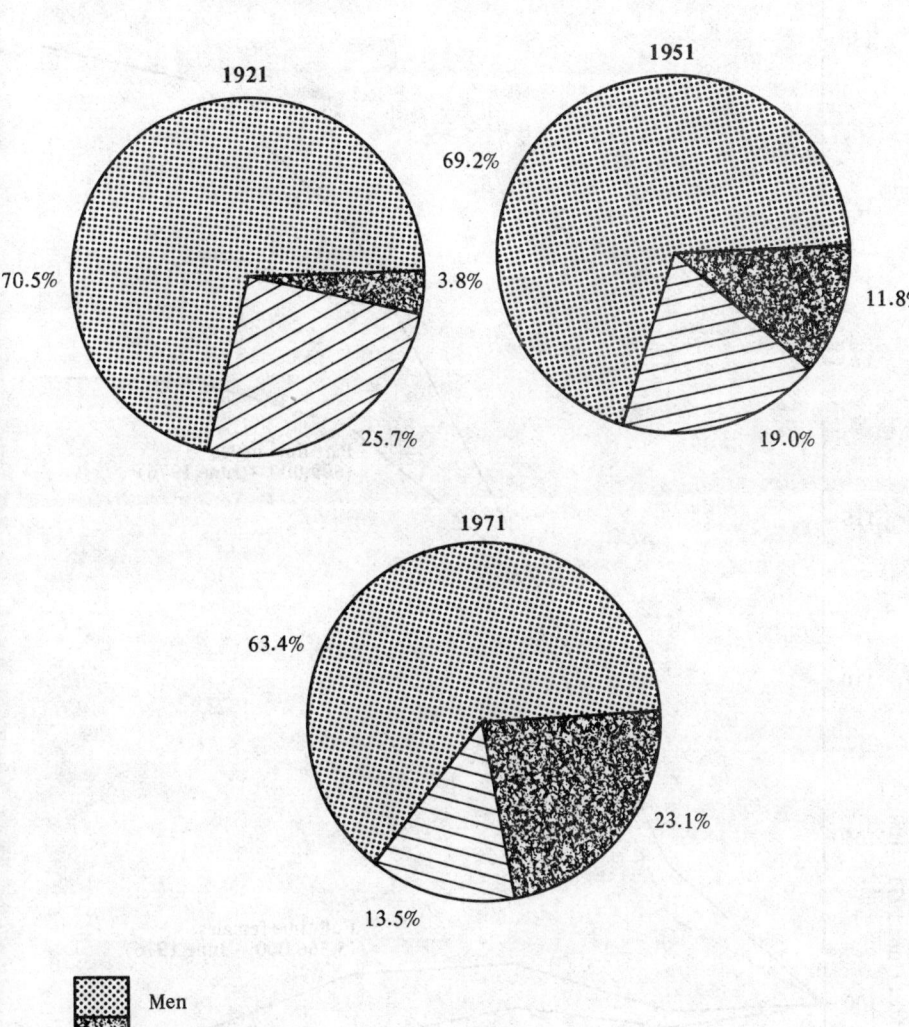

Source: Table 2.6.

17

Figure 2.6   The Growth of Part-time Work; 1971 to 1976

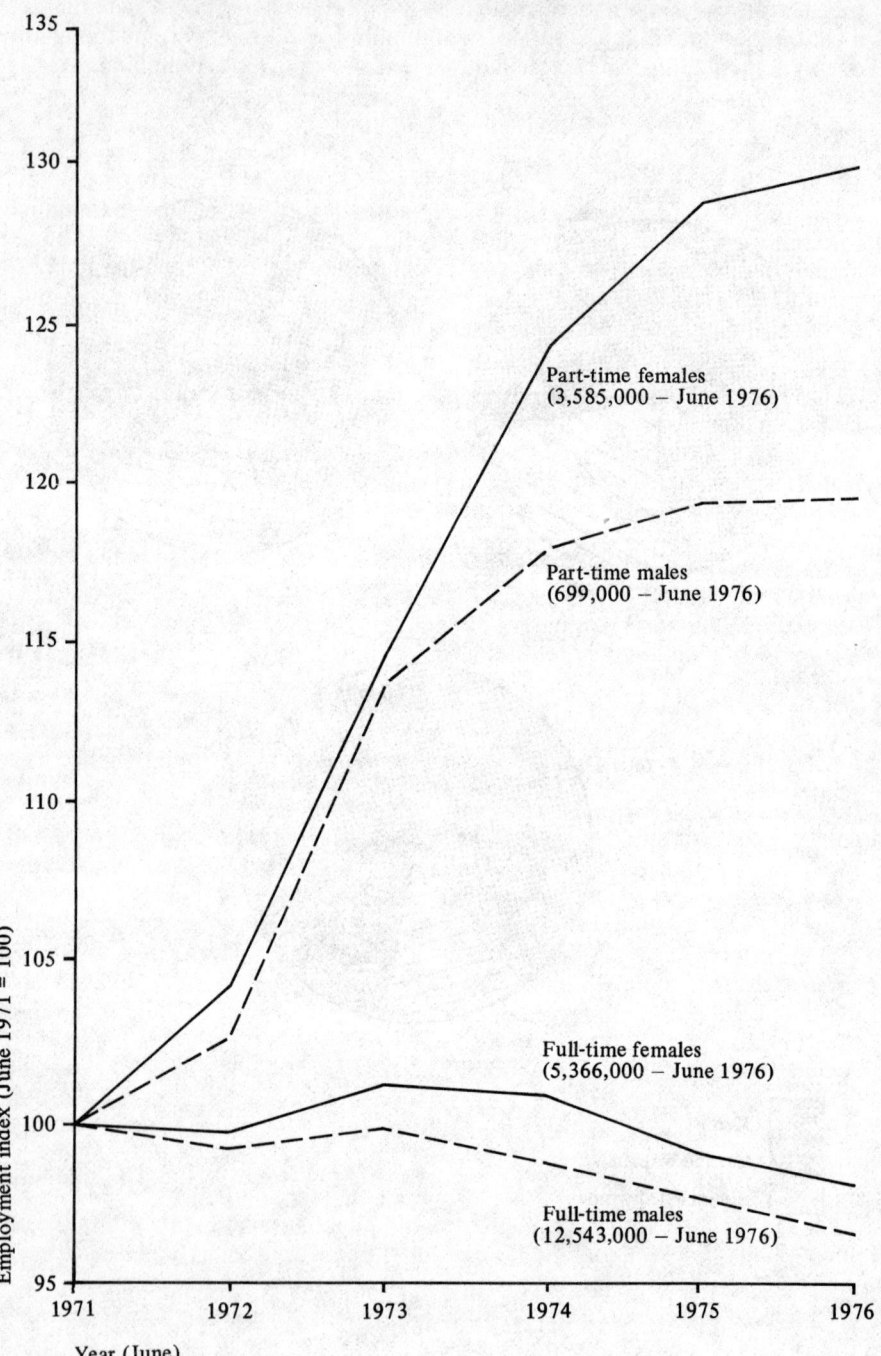

Part-time females
(3,585,000 – June 1976)

Part-time males
(699,000 – June 1976)

Full-time females
(5,366,000 – June 1976)

Full-time males
(12,543,000 – June 1976)

Employment index (June 1971 = 100)

Year (June)

Source: Census of Employment, 1971–76.

employment. Between 1961 and 1971, for example, the number of female full-time employees in manufacturing fell by 16 per cent[1]. Since 1951 there has been a continuous decline in the numbers of non-married women in the labour force due to demographic factors (see paragraph 2.13 above, and Table 2.6).

Occupational distribution of the employed labour force

2.19   In this section we show the way in which the distribution of the labour force between occupations has changed. The detail in which this can be done is limited by the major revisions to the classification of occupational groups according to which the statistics are analysed—revisions that were necessitated by the changing nature of the jobs themselves.

2.20   There are several ways in which occupations can be grouped together and classified. The Census of Population's classification of occupations is based on "the kind of work done" and "the nature of the operation performed". In some instances the work is fairly specific to particular industries—for instance farming or coal mining; in other instances the work is done in a very wide range of industries—clerical work, for example. The occupational classification is in this respect something of a hybrid, as it has been since it was originally devised. The main 'Order' headings (see Table 2.8 for examples) are, however, sub-divided in ways that enable finer distinctions to be drawn; in addition, a cross-classification is made by employment status—ie employers, employees, working on own account.

2.21   There have been too many major changes in the main classification of occupations for long-term comparisons to be made on the basis of groups of the kind shown in Table 2.8. Instead, we draw on the work of Dr G Routh in which he re-classified the Census data on occupations into what may conveniently be termed 'occupational classes'. These are broad groups distinguished according to the nature of the work and the degree of skill. How to classify occupations according to skill is a difficult and somewhat contentious matter; but such a classification is made by the Registrar-General, in the Census analysis, into five "social classes", one of which (III) is further divided into manual and non-manual. Dr Routh's allocation of manual occupations into skilled, semi-skilled and unskilled closely follows the Registrar-General's classification into III (manual), IV and V, though with a number of defined exceptions.[2] For example, actors and nurses are classified by Dr Routh as lower professional (1B) and shop assistants as semi-skilled manual (6), whereas they are all in Social Class III in the Registrar-General's classification.

2.22   Table 2.7 summarises figures for changes in occupational distribution since 1921, using Dr Routh's classification. They relate to employees, as opposed

---

[1] 'Part-time women workers, 1950-1972', *Department of Employment Gazette*, November 1973.

[2] For a full description reference should be made to G Routh, *Occupation and Pay in Great Britain, 1906–1960*. Cambridge: Cambridge University Press, 1965, Appendix A. See also Appendix G to this Report.

19

Table 2.7 Distribution of Employees by Occupational Class; 1921 to 1978[1]

Great Britain

Occupational Class	1921		1931		1951		1961[2]		1971[2]		1978[4]	
	'000	As % of total	'000	As % of total	'000	As % of total	'000	As % of total	'000	As % of total	'000	As % of total
Men:												
1A Higher professional	126	1·0	144	1·1	326	2·3	494	3·5	603	4·6	606	4·9
1B Lower professional	242	2·0	270	2·1	463	3·3	636	4·5	853	6·5	940	7·6
2B Managers and administrators	557	4·6	642	4·9	1,029	7·2	1,386	9·8	1,710	13·0	2,423	19·4
3 Clerks	735	6·1	815	6·2	988	6·9	1,049	7·4	890	6·7	653	5·3
4 Foremen	261	2·1	295	2·2	511	3·6	726	5·1	772	5·9	960	7·8
5 Skilled manual	4,200	34·6	4,223	32·1	4,519	31·7	5,095	35·9	4,303	32·6	3,985	32·2
6 Semi-skilled manual	3,789	31·2	4,181	31·8	4,279	30·0	3,501	24·7	3,046	23·1	2,182	17·7
7 Unskilled manual	2,232	18·4	2,580	19·6	2,129	15·0	1,284	9·1	998	7·6	636	5·1
Total	12,142	100·0	13,150	100·0	14,244	100·0	14,171[3]	100·0	13,175	100·0	12,385	100·0
Women:												
1A Higher professional	8	0·2	15	0·3	31	0·5	37	0·7	45	0·8	74	1·3
1B Lower professional	357	6·8	373	6·4	544	8·2	557	10·4	705	12·9	709	12·5
2B Managers and administrators	118	2·2	98	1·7	186	2·8	248	4·6	273	5·0	703	12·4[5]
3 Clerks	564	10·8	648	11·1	1,413	21·3	1,666	31·1	1,875	34·1	1,730	30·5
4 Foremen	18	0·3	28	0·5	79	1·2	122	2·3	150	2·7	272	4·8
5 Skilled manual	1,080	20·6	1,128	19·3	847	12·8	663	12·4	532	9·7	550	9·7
6 Semi-skilled manual	2,656	50·6	3,084	52·9	2,978	44·9	1,894	35·3	1,778	32·4	1,610	28·4
7 Unskilled manual	446	8·5	454	7·8	547	8·3	169	3·2	134	2·4	23	0·4
Total	5,247	100·0	5,828	100·0	6,625	100·0	5,356[3]	100·0	5,492	100·0	5,671	100·0

Sources: 1921–1951, G Routh, *Occupation and Pay in Great Britain. 1906–1960*, Cambridge University Press, 1965. 1961–1971, Chapter 6, Table 6.4. The figures for 1978 are projections (see Note 4 below).

Notes:
[1] For a fuller description of the methods and sources of material for this table see Chapter 6.
[2] Figures for 1961 and 1971 are not strictly comparable with those for 1921–1951, due to the change in occupational classification in the 1961 Census of Population.
[3] The total numbers in 1961 differ from those in Table 2.5 because part-timers and the self-employed are excluded.
[4] Figures for 1978 are projections, based on 1978 NES data reweighted by the quotient of the 1971 Census estimate and the 1971 estimate based on NES data (see Chapter 6).
[5] This figure is rather tentative, due to the small number of women in Class 2B in 1971.

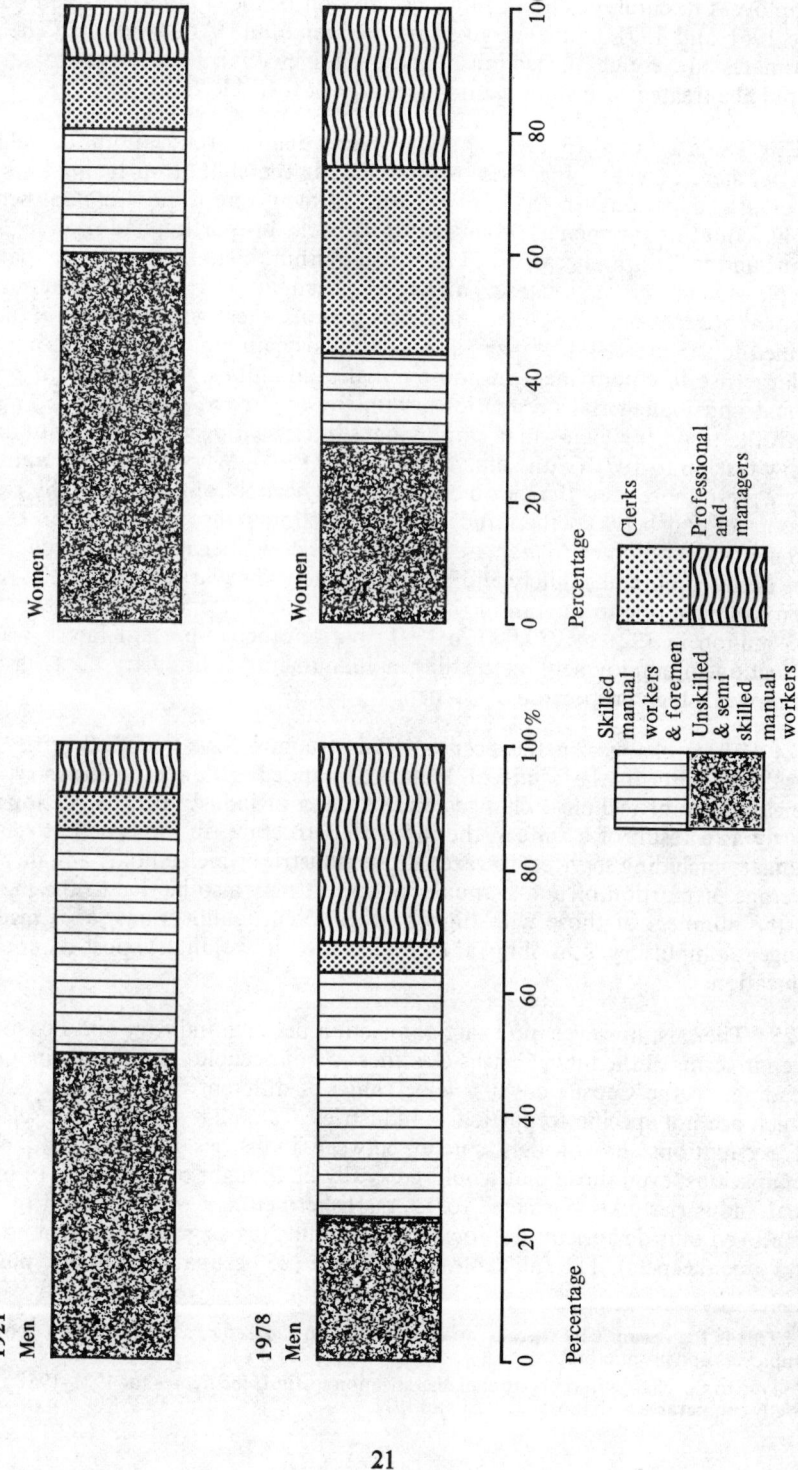

Figure 2.7 Occupational Distribution of Employees; 1921 and 1978

Source: Table 2.7.

21

to the whole labour force including the self-employed[1]; and refer to full-time employees in employment. A fuller description of the sources and methods for the 1961 and 1971 figures is given in Chapter 6 and Appendix G[2]. The 1978 estimates are rough projections, based on New Earnings Survey data, and should be treated with some caution (see Note 4 to Table 2.7).

2.23   Table 2.7 (and Figure 2.7) show several distinct trends, both for men and for women, of which the most pronounced is the shift from manual to non-manual occupations. In 1921, 14 per cent of men were in non-manual occupations (counting foremen as 'manual'); in 1951 the proportion had risen to 20 per cent; and in 1971 had reached 31 per cent. Within the non-manual occupations, employment in professional and managerial occupations rose much faster than in clerical occupations. Among manual occupations, there was a shift from the less skilled to the more skilled occupations. Similarly among women there has been a large rise in employment in non-manual occupations, particularly in professional and managerial occupations, with the important difference—compared with the trend for men—that employment in clerical occupations continued to grow fast up to 1971 (with some decline since then). Whereas in 1921 and 1931 there were more men than women in clerical occupations, by 1951 the reverse was true, and between then and 1971 the predominance of women in clerical occupations continued to increase. The number of women in manual occupations has declined both absolutely and proportionately. The largest part of the reduction has been due to the fall in the numbers employed in domestic service from 1·3 million in 1921 to 239,000 in 1971; but another important factor was the reduction in employment in textiles, a manufacturing industry that has long employed a high proportion of women.

2.24   These changes in the occupational structure have occurred partly as a result of shifts in the kinds of labour demanded within each industry, as a consequence of technical changes and changes in industrial organisation; and partly as a result of a shift in the industrial structure (in the broadest sense of industry including services) towards those industries which employ a higher than average proportion of non-manual workers. It may also be due to the increase in the numbers of those with higher educational qualifications, as a result of longer compulsory schooling and an increase in voluntary post-compulsory education.

2.25   There is, however, no exact connection between industry and occupation even in terms of the main Census classification of occupations. The main 'Order' headings in the Census cover a wide range of different occupations, many of which are not specific to particular industries. Table 2.8 shows, for a selection of occupations, how widely spread between industries are workers in most occupations, even those that would generally be thought of as specific to individual industries like 'farmers, foresters, fishermen', of whom one-fifth were employed outside agriculture, forestry and fishing (eg as gardeners, groundsmen and greenkeepers). The full table is very large (25 occupation 'Orders' plus the

---

[1] This is the reason why there is no category 2A in the Table, as this category comprises 'employers and proprietors'.

[2] Due to the change in occupational classification in 1961, the figures for 1921–1951 are not strictly comparable with those for 1961 and 1971.

Table 2.8 Employment by Industry, Occupation and Sex; 1971

Great Britain

Industries	MALES IN SELECTED OCCUPATIONS									FEMALES IN SELECTED OCCUPATIONS			
	I Farmers, foresters, fishermen	VI Electrical and electronic workers	VII Engineering and allied workers nec	XVII Drivers of stationary engines, cranes, etc	XVIII Labourers nec	XX Warehousemen storekeepers etc	XXI Clerical workers	XXIV Administrators and managers	XXV Professional and technical workers, artists	XXI Clerical workers	XXII Sales workers	XXIV Administrators and managers	XXV Professional and technical workers, artists
	%	%	%	%	%	%	%	%	%	%	%	%	%
I Agriculture, forestry, fishing	76.5	0.1	0.2	0.5	0.3	0.2	0.3	0.2	0.2	0.5	0.1	0.1	0.1
VI Metal manufacture	0.1	2.4	5.7	10.9	7.1	2.8	2.4	2.4	1.8	1.3	Neg	0.6	0.3
VII Mechanical engineering	0.1	3.7	20.1	6.8	4.3	7.4	4.7	7.6	6.1	3.8	0.1	3.3	0.5
IX Electrical engineering	0.1	13.6	6.4	2.3	2.0	5.0	3.3	4.7	5.8	3.1	0.1	2.6	0.9
XI Vehicles	0.1	3.0	15.2	5.7	3.2	6.0	3.9	2.9	4.2	1.8	Neg	0.8	0.3
XX Construction	0.4	19.1	8.0	18.6	19.9	2.2	3.0	10.0	4.7	2.9	0.2	3.8	0.3
XXII Transport and communications	0.1	20.9	3.3	4.4	5.0	5.6	11.3	5.7	2.2	5.3	0.5	3.9	0.4
XXIII Distributive trades	0.5	7.2	1.8	3.1	4.7	20.4	7.2	5.5	2.7	14.9	88.9	8.0	2.5
XXIV Insurance, banking, finance and business services	0.6	0.3	0.2	0.2	0.7	0.4	13.9	7.4	3.1	14.9	1.9	7.9	0.9
XXV Professional and scientific services	3.7	1.6	0.8	2.3	1.1	1.5	6.2	3.4	41.2	13.1	0.1	16.8	79.9
XXVI Miscellaneous services	7.2	3.0	7.8	0.9	2.8	6.1	5.2	7.2	3.7	8.0	4.1	10.4	4.9
XXVII Public administration and defence	6.1	1.9	1.2	4.5	9.0	3.4	16.5	9.1	7.0	11.1	Neg	14.7	2.8
Other industries[1]	1.4	20.6	25.4	34.7	27.5	34.2	19.2	31.9	15.4	17.9	2.0	26.0	4.3
Out of employment	3.1	2.8	3.8	5.3	12.6	4.9	2.9	1.9	1.9	1.4	1.9	1.1	1.9
All industries[2] (Total numbers)	100.0 (643,040)	100.0 (529,140)	100.0 (2,501,040)	100.0 (307,320)	100.0 (1,103,630)	100.0 (502,900)	100.0 (1,073,300)	100.0 (846,310)	100.0 (1,683,340)	100.0 (2,485,340)	100.0 (1,064,470)	100.0 (78,110)	100.0 (1,066,520)

Source: Census of Population 1971, Economic Activity Tables, 10% sample, Tables 4 and 19.

Notes:

[1] Includes inadequately described industries and those with workplace outside United Kingdom.
[2] Percentages do not add to 100.0 in all cases because of rounding.
Neg—negligible (ie less than 0.1).
Nec—not elsewhere categorised.

23

Armed Forces by 27 'Orders' of the Standard Industrial Classification), so only extracts for selected occupations and industries can be shown here.

2.26 The fast-growing Census occupational orders—among men, administrators and managers, professional, technical workers and artists, and among women, professional, technical workers and artists and clerical workers—are so widely distributed across so many industries that changes in the industrial structure do not go very far in explaining the growth in the numbers in these orders. This is plainly so for clerical occupations and administrators and managers, who are to be found in all industries and services; but as Table 2.8 shows, it applies to professional and technical workers as well. Only just over 40 per cent of men in this occupational order were employed in the 'industry' category termed 'professional and scientific services'. Only women employed as professional and technical workers constitute a partial exception to this generalisation, as just under 80 per cent were employed in 'professional and scientific services'. Nor are the manual occupational orders very specific to individual industries, as Table 2.8 also shows. 'Engineering and allied workers', for instance, were to be found in a very wide range of industries; only 27 per cent were employed in mechanical and electrical engineering; even including vehicles and metal manufacture raises the proportion to no more than 47 per cent. On the other hand, there are a few occupations which are very highly concentrated in particular industries, eg miners, train drivers, and dustmen, and whose earnings may be directly related to changes in industrial structure.

2.27 The description of trends in the numbers employed in the broad categories of occupations, and of the relationship between occupation and industries, has been based on the Censuses of Population. The Census of Population is the principal source of data on occupations—indeed the Census has recorded occupations for far longer than it has recorded industries. The sources from which the annual estimates of the working population are compiled—since 1971 the Department of Employment's employment census and before then the count of National Insurance cards—provide detail on industry of employment, but not occupation. In Chapter 6 use is made of the composition of the New Earnings Survey sample of employees to provide an indication of change since 1971 in the occupational structure and of the corresponding NES earnings distribution. But, as noted there, changes in the classification of occupations limit the accuracy with which the change can be measured within the sample. The possibility of bias resulting from non-response limits the usefulness of the survey even further as a measure of the labour force generally. A large scale more frequent household survey, although not in full Census detail, is needed to improve our information on trends in occupations and other labour force statistics, since the Census of Population cannot be processed quickly (due to its size), and in any event the ten year gap between Censuses is rather large. The EEC Labour Force Survey (LFS), a biennial household survey in which the UK has taken part since 1973, with appropriate development, could be a suitable vehicle for the collection of the required data.

Distribution of employment between industries

2.28 We turn now to the distribution of the labour force between industries, in order to place in context the findings of our study of the way in which earnings

24

HMSO BOOKS

An important new publication from
Her Majesty's Stationery Office

available from 9 January 1980 at £1.25

an A to Z of
Income and Wealth

- How does your own income compare with other people's?
- How many really wealthy people are there in the United Kingdom – how many really poor?
- What about fringe benefits?
- How about people who work on their own account?
- How much do women get paid, compared with men?

The answers to these and many other questions can be found in
AN A TO Z OF INCOME AND WEALTH

AN A TO Z OF INCOME AND WEALTH

This is a fascinating new study which puts the complexities of money matters into simple language, free of technical jargon.

It draws upon work carried out by the Royal Commission on the Distribution of Income and Wealth over the past five years.

The key facts, chosen by the Commission from its massive main reports, have been written up in a concise form which makes ideal background reading for sixth formers or undergraduates studying economics, government and social sciences, etc. It is a must for all who want a clearer understanding of the kind of society we live in.

Everyday questions about income and wealth are answered in sections covering work and pay, income and taxation, categories of wealth, and how wealth is accumulated.

AN A TO Z OF INCOME AND WEALTH is copiously illustrated with colour diagrams. They make percentages and statistics easy to follow and to relate to each other.

We started by repeating typical questions from this invaluable aid to study and research. We only have one more to ask:

Can you afford to be without a copy?

HMSO BOOKS

ORDER FORM

To: HMSO, PM1C, FREEPOST*, London EC1B 1DD
*No stamp required

I wish to purchase_____copy/copies of

AN A TO Z OF INCOME AND WEALTH

ISBN 0 11 730118 3 Price £1.25 (by post £1.52)

I enclose a remittance of_____or:

Please charge to my HMSO Account No. _____

Name_____

Address_____

_____

_____

PLEASE USE BLOCK CAPITALS

Please note: We are sorry that we cannot extend credit to overseas customers who do not hold an account with HMSO.

differ as between industries (Chapter 5 of this Report). We show in Table 2.9 the long-term trends in civil employment in broad groups of industries (used in a broad sense to include services). There were major revisions to the classification of industries (the Standard Industrial Classification or SIC) in 1948, 1958 and 1968, so that it has been necessary to make approximations in order to carry the comparisons across these years. We have started with the 1931 distribution of civil employment between industries; and then show separately the estimated 1931 to 1951 change; then the change between 1951 and 1961; and finally the changes from 1961 to 1971 and 1971 to 1975. The last two are comparable, being taken from the Department of Employment's continuous series, and the break at 1971 is put in to show the way in which trends were changing. The 1931 to 1951 and 1951 to 1961 changes are shown separately as they are taken from different sources: the 1931 to 1951 change is taken from the Census of Population (reclassified by Buxton and Mackay)[1]; the 1951 to 1961 change is taken from estimates made by the Ministry of Labour from National Insurance cards.

2.29 Several features stand out from Table 2.9 (some of which are shown in Figure 2.8).

— The massive expansion of employment in services, both in absolute terms and as a proportion of total employment. The rate of increase has been accelerating throughout, apart from the distributive trades; in terms of annual average rates of change, the increases in the 1971 to 1975 period were greater than for 1961 to 1971, which in turn were greater than for the 1951 to 1961 period.

— The shift from rapid expansion of employment in manufacturing industry (other than the textiles and clothing group) between 1931 and 1951 and 1951 to 1961, to a small fall from 1961 to 1971 and a faster fall from 1971 to 1975.

Table 2.9   Changes in Civil Employment by Industry; 1931 to 1975

Great Britain   Thousands

		1931 Total	1931–51 Change	1951–61 Change	1961–71 Change	1971–75 Change	1975 Total
A.	Agriculture, forestry, fishing	1,195	−69	−191	−335	−65	622
B.	Mining and quarrying	1,062	−221	−128	−331	−44	350
C.	Engineering, vehicles, metal working	1,968	+1,726	+808	−115	−289	3,867
D.	Textiles and clothing	1,925	−192	−255	−310	−141	939
E.	Other manufacturing	1,900	+570	+331	−32	−123	2,646
	(Total of manufacturing)	(5,792)	(+2,105)	(+884)	(−477)	(−553)	(7,452)
F.	Construction	993	+410	+154	−69	+105	1,651
G.	Gas, water, electricity, transport, communications	1,657	+404	−50	−92	−69	1,915
H.	Distributive trades	2,763	−23	+503	−208	+111	3,134
I.	All other services	5,383	+665	+539	+1,527	+1,060	8,910
Total		18,845	+3,271	+1,711	+36	+548	24,038

Source: See Appendix B for definitions and sources.

Note: Owing to the changes in definitions and source referred to in paragraph 2.28, the sum of the changes does not exactly equal the difference between 1931 and 1975.

---

[1] N K Buxton and D I Mackay, *British Employment Statistics*, Blackwell, Oxford, 1977.

25

Figure 2.8   Changes in Civil Employment by Industrial Sector; 1931, 1951 and 1975

Chart A
Civil Employment by Sector

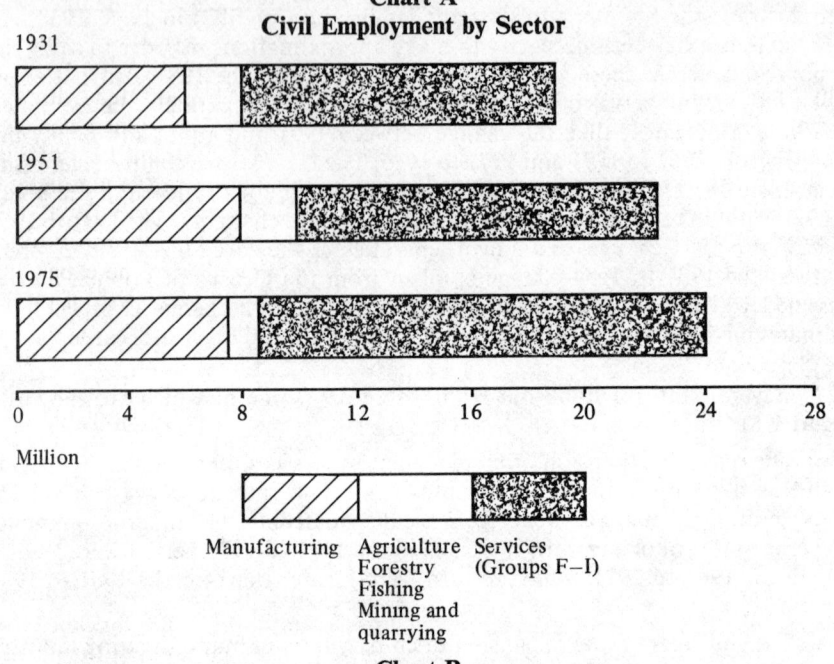

Million

Manufacturing   Agriculture   Services
                 Forestry   (Groups F–I)
                 Fishing
                 Mining and
                 quarrying

Chart B
Percentage Composition of Civil Employment

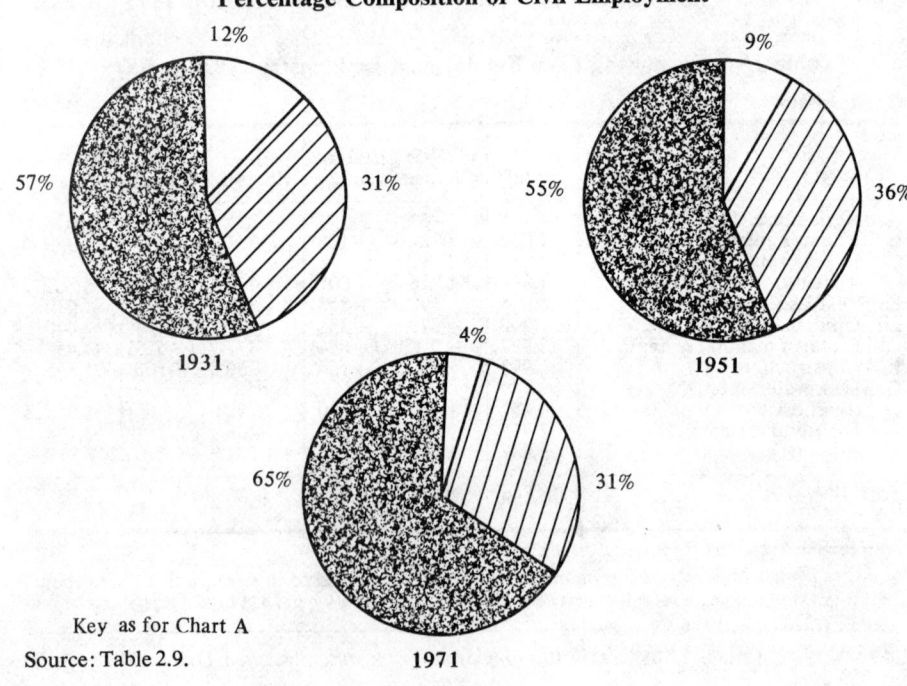

Key as for Chart A

Source: Table 2.9.

26

— The continuous decline in employment in agriculture (apart from the war-time halt, which explains why the net change between 1931 and 1951 was very small), mining, and textiles and clothing. The first of these trends goes back to well into the nineteenth century; and the second and third to the inter-war years.

2.30   The rapid expansion in employment in services is associated with the growth of women's employment, in particular that of part-time women workers. According to the Department of Employment: "Between 1961 and 1971 almost all the growth in service employment was due to the growth in the numbers of female workers by nearly 1.2 million, and the indications are that almost all this growth has been in part-timers"[1]. The rapid growth in the proportion of employment in non-manual occupations has also contributed to the expansion of employment in services. Part of the explanation lies in the growth of public service employment[2].

2.31   The way in which the growth of employment in services has been associated with the growth of public sector employment is outlined in Table 2.10 which shows the changes since 1961 and, in less detail, between 1951 and 1961. A distinction is shown between central and local government on the one hand, and the public corporations on the other. The latter comprise the nationalised industries, the Post Office (since 1961) and certain other trading bodies; the number employed in this part of the sector has varied through time as a result of the de-nationalisation of steel and road haulage in the 1950s, and partial re-nationalisation in the 1960s, as well as by the reduced demand for labour by certain of the industries that have remained nationalised throughout the period. We have used UK figures, as it is not possible to distinguish Northern Ireland separately in the figures for employment by public corporations. 1975 is taken as the terminal year because more recent figures for self-employment are not available (see paragraph 2.34 below).

2.32   The growth of public employment has not been the only reason for the growth of employment in services, but it has been a very important one. Of the total increase in employment in services between 1961 and 1975, 71 per cent was in the central and local government sectors. In the former, the National Health Service was especially important; in the latter, education. After 1975, however, the rise in central and local government employment in services slowed down and then came to a virtual halt between 1976 and 1977.

Self-employment

2.33   We now give an outline of changes in the total of self-employed men and women, the industries in which they work and their occupations, to provide a starting point for considering the results of our studies of the incomes of the self-employed (Part III of this Report). We follow the Census of Population

---

[1] *Department of Employment Gazette*, October 1975, p. 984.

[2] For a further discussion of changes in the industrial and occupational structure of the labour force since 1921 see the Unit for Manpower Studies' report, *The Changing Structure of the Labour Force*, Department of Employment, 1976.

27

United Kingdom

Table 2.10 Employment in the Public Sector in Relation to Total Civil Employment; 1951 to 1975

Thousands

	1951	1951–61 change[3]	1961	1971	1975[6]	1961–71 change	1971–75 change
Total public sector[1]	5,340	−127	5,369	6,194	6,906	+825	+712
Public corporations	2,789	−361	2,200	1,986	2,003	−214	−17
Central and local government	2,551	+234	3,169	4,208	4,903	+1,039	+729
Of which: services[2]	—	—	2,774	3,846	4,597	+1,072	+753
Private sector (incl. self-employed)	16,874	+1,743	18,617	17,838	17,726[6]	−779	−112
Of which: services[2], [5]	—	—	6,878	7,191	7,626	+313	+435
All services[2]	—	—	9,652	11,037	12,223	+1,385	+1,188
Public sector as percentage of all employment in services[2]	—	—	28·7	34·8	37·6	—	—
Overall total employment	22,214	+1,616	23,986	24,032	24,632	+46	+600
Public sector as percentage of overall total	24·0	—	22·4	25·8	28·0	—	—

Sources: *Economic Trends*, February 1976 and February 1977.

Notes: [1] Excludes HM Forces and Women's Services.

[2] Comprises distributive trades; insurance, banking, finance, business services; professional and scientific services; miscellaneous services; and public administration.

[3] Change does not equal difference between 1951 and 1961 totals because the 1951 figures were derived from National Insurance cards and refer to Great Britain, whereas 1961 and later figures refer to the United Kingdom and are based on the Census of Employment.

[4] Change between 1971 and 1975 does not equal the difference between the 1971 and 1975 figures owing to the transfer of about 34,000 employees in local authority water supply departments to Regional Water Authorities, which are classed as public corporations.

[5] Includes self-employed (from Table 2.14 below) as well as employees.

[6] Sum of public and private sector employment in 1975 exceeds total shown in Table 2.9 because that Table refers to Great Britain, not the United Kingdom.

definition (also that of the Department of Employment) of self-employed, which comprises men and women 'working on their own account with or without employees'. The self-employed include, in principle, home workers (ie people working in their own homes, eg taking in sewing), but thus far neither the Census nor other statistical sources provide even a moderately reliable estimate of their numbers, which are thought to amount to at least a quarter of a million. It is of course possible for a man or woman whose main source of income is wage or salary-earning employment to have an income from self-employment as well. The principal source of evidence about subsidiary self-employment is the Inland Revenue's Survey of Personal Incomes (SPI), and we discuss this aspect of self-employment in paragraphs 2.38 to 2.40 below. In the Census, however—the main source of evidence about self-employment—one cannot be both employed and self-employed; the Census is self-classificatory so it is up to the respondent to decide which is his main occupation, if he has more than one, and whether he is employed or self-employed, if he is both.

2.34 The statistics on the self-employed are rather deficient compared with those on employees in employment. The self-employed are not included in the Department of Employment's annual Census of Employment, so the prime sources of data are the Censuses of Population. Between 1966 and 1974 the estimates for self-employed men were updated annually, using the DHSS sample of Class 2 National Insurance cards, but this procedure could not be used for women, because many married self-employed women did not hold National Insurance cards. The estimates for women were therefore assumed to be unchanged at their 1971 Census of Population values between 1971 and 1974. Because the National Insurance card exchange system was discontinued, the estimates for 1975 were obtained by using information from the 1973 and 1975 EEC Labour Force Surveys to update the previously published 1973 estimates. There are no estimates for more recent years than 1975.

2.35 The EEC Labour Force Survey (LFS) was designed to provide information on the occupational and industrial distribution of both employees and the self-employed. It has already been noted (paragraph 2.27) that such information is needed to fill a present deficiency in the data on annual changes in the occupational structure of the labour force. The need is even greater for the self-employed, who are not covered by the New Earnings Survey. Unfortunately, the LFS uses a different occupational classification from that used in the Census of Population, and the data available from it are somewhat limited.

2.36 We therefore draw attention to the considerable room for improvement in the available annual statistics on the self-employed, which are now rather out of date and which do not provide adequate information on occupational and industrial distribution. We summarise here the information available about the self-employed, starting with their numbers in comparison with the total labour force; then their occupations in 1971 (no more recent figures are available); and then the industries in which they work, for which changes can be shown over the period from 1961 to 1975.

2.37 From 1921 to 1966 the trend of self-employment, as a proportion of the labour force, was downwards. Since a considerable part of the explanation lies

Great Britain

Table 2.11 Self-employed in Relation to Total Labour Force; 1921 to 1975

	Men			Women			Total		
	Self-employed	Labour force	Self-employed	Self-employed	Labour force	Self-employed	Self-employed	Labour force	Self-employed
	'000	'000	%	'000	'000	%	'000	'000	%
1921[1]	1,493	13,656	10·9	450	5,701	7·9	1,943	19,357	10·0
1951[1]	1,342	15,649	8·6	306	6,961	4·4	1,648	22,610	7·3
1961[2,3]	1,338	16,184	8·3	327	7,998	4·1	1,665	24,183	6·9
1966[2,3]	1,249	16,401	7·6	360	8,666	4·2	1,609	25,066	6·4
1971[2,3]	1,471	15,837	9·3	371	8,708	4·3	1,842	24,545	7·5
1975[2,3]	1,456	15,698	9·3	369	9,506	3·9	1,825	25,202	7·2

Sources: Censuses of Population (OPCS) and Department of Employment.

Notes: [1] 1921 and 1951 figures, both for the labour force and the self-employed, are from the Census of Population and compare the self-employed with the occupied population.

[2] The 1961, 1966, 1971 and 1975 labour force figures are the Department of Employment's June estimates for the working population, from their continuous series based on the Census of Employment.

[3] The 1961, 1966, 1971 and 1975 figures of the self-employed are the Department of Employment's estimates based on the Census of Population (1961, 1966, 1971) and Labour Force Survey (1975).

Figure 2.9   The Self-employed In Relation to the Total Labour Force; 1921 and 1975

Chart A
Percentage Self-employed, by Sex

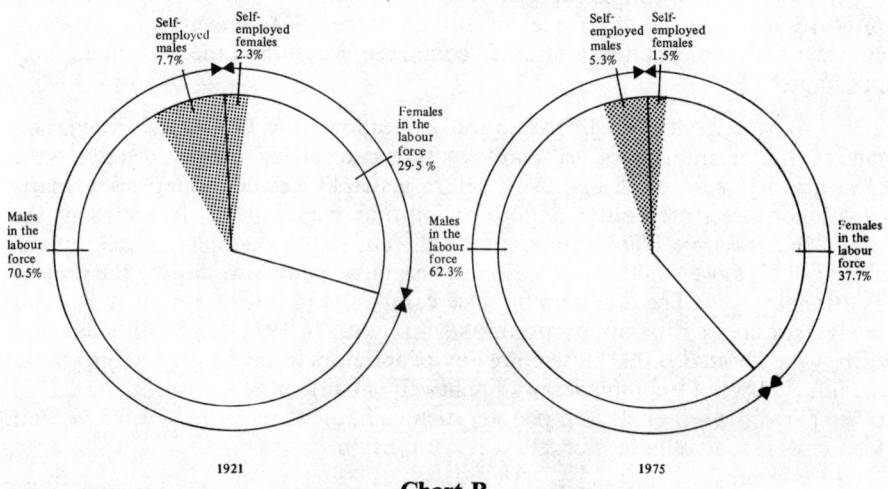

1921   1975

Chart B
Numbers Self-employed, by Sex

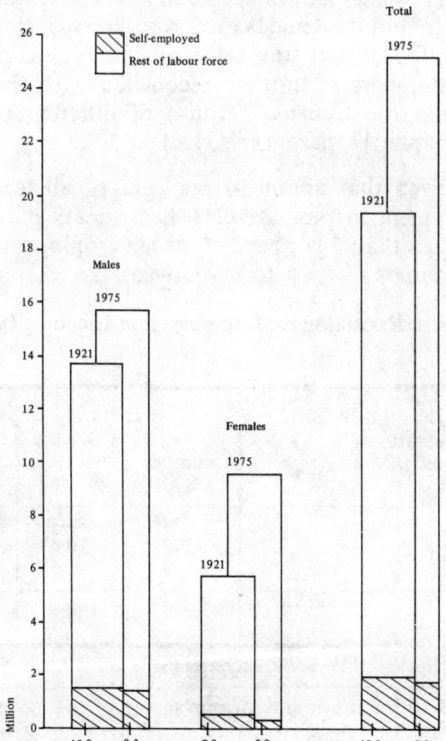

Source: Table 2.11.

31

in a reduction of the size of the sectors where self-employment is relatively large in relation to total employment, we discuss the reasons in paragraph 2.52 after outlining the occupational and industrial structure of self-employment in paragraphs 2.41 to 2.51. Between 1966 and 1971 the self-employment ratio increased again, and the numbers of self-employed are estimated to have reached a peak of 1,884,000 in 1973. The relative stability of self-employment, as a proportion of the labour force, in Britain since 1961, however, is in sharp contrast with the experience of other countries. We discuss the reasons for this in Chapter 13.

2.38 As was mentioned in paragraph 2.33 above, the Census of Population figures for the number of self-employed are determined on a subjective 'self-classificatory' basis. The figures therefore generally exclude independent part-time enterprise (for profit) of those in full-time employment. In addition, the coverage of people like close company directors, for example, is incomplete, since not all close company proprietors or similar people would see themselves as self-employed. The directors of close companies (4 out of 5 of all UK companies) are treated for tax purposes as employees; in 1974–5 we estimated that there were about 309,000 close company proprietors (excluding directors whose income from close companies was relatively small)[1]. The Census coverage of other part-time self-employed people, such as housewives selling cosmetics and kitchenware, and of homeworkers is also uncertain.

2.39 For reasons given in Chapter 10 we concentrate our attention on the incomes of those who are primarily self-employed. However, estimates of numbers of people receiving main or subsidiary source self-employment income can be derived from Inland Revenue tax returns. An analysis of the total number of tax units receiving full or part-time self-employment income is given in Table 2.12 below. These numbers cannot be reconciled with the numbers of self-employed recorded in the Census, because of differences in definition and coverage (see also Chapter 11, paragraph 11.6).

2.40 Table 2.12 shows that about 10 per cent of all tax units recorded as receiving self-employment income are classified for tax purposes as employees under Schedule E. Less than 5 per cent of all self-employment income recorded by the Inland Revenue accrues to employees, so the average amount of

Table 2.12   Tax Units Receiving Self-employment Income; 1974–75 and 1975–76

United Kingdom

Employment status of head of tax unit	1974–75		1975–76	
	Number ('000)	Per cent of total	Number ('000)	Per cent of total
Self-employed	1,728	89·1	1,664	90·3
Employees (Schedule E)	202	10·4	173	9·4
Other	9	0·5	6	0·3
Total	1,939	100·0	1,843	100·0

Source: Inland Revenue Survey of Personal Incomes (SPI).

[1] See Chapters 4 and 10 for the results of our survey of the incomes of close company directors.

Great Britain

Table 2.13 Distribution of Self-employed by Occupation; 1971

OCCUPATION	MALES				FEMALES			
	Employees in employment '000s	Self-employed '000s	Number in employment '000s	Self-employed as a % of number in employment %	Employees in employment '000s	Self-employed '000s	Number in employment '000s	Self-employed as % of number in employment %
All economically active	13,560	1,471	15,031	9·8	8,330	371	8,701	4·3
I Farmers, foresters, fishermen	378	246	623	39·4	62	33	95	34·4
II Miners and quarrymen	233	(a)	234	0·2	(a)	(a)	(a)	(a)
III Gas, coke and chemical makers	122	(a)	122	0·2	13	(a)	13	0·2
IV Glass and ceramic makers	60	1	61	1·8	28	(a)	28	1·6
V Furnace, forge, foundry, rolling mill workers	148	3	152	2·1	9	(a)	9	0·5
VI Electrical and electronic workers	488	27	515	5·2	86	1	86	0·4
VII Engineering and allied workers nec	2,307	98	2,405	4·1	287	(a)	288	0·4
VIII Woodworkers	335	63	398	15·8	12	1	12	1·2
IX Leather workers	49	7	55	12·2	55	(a)	56	1·4
X Textile workers	134	2	135	1·4	160	1	161	0·8
XI Clothing workers	63	13	75	16·6	308	13	321	4·1
XII Food, drink and tobacco workers	217	34	250	13·4	107	3	110	3·1
XIII Paper and printing workers	208	6	214	2·9	92	(a)	93	1·0
XIV Makers of other products	187	11	198	5·4	105	2	106	1·5
XV Construction workers	364	154	517	29·7	1	(a)	2	25·5
XVI Painters and decorators	198	62	260	23·9	8	(a)	8	2·8
XVII Drivers of stationary engines, cranes etc	288	3	291	1·0				
XVIII Labourers nec	942	22	964	2·3	4	(a)	4	0·3
XIX Transport and communications	1,141	68	1,209	5·6	133	2	133	1·3
XX Warehousemen, storekeepers etc	477	(a)	478	0·2	151	(a)	153	0·2
XXI Clerical workers	1,035	7	1,043	0·7	2,426	23	2,449	0·9
XXII Sales workers	833	313	1,147	27·3	897	147	1,044	14·1
XXIII Service, sports, recreation	717	148	865	17·1	1,899	98	1,997	4·9
XXIV Administrators, managers	830	(a)	830		77	(a)	77	
XXV Professional, technical workers	1,472	180	1,651	10·9	1,006	40	1,047	3·8
XXVI Armed forces	240	—	240	—	12	—	12	—
XXVII Inadequately described	95	4	100	4·3	105	3	109	3·2

Source: 1971 Census of Population, 10% sample, Economic Activity Tables, Table 4. Figures are rounded to nearest thousand.

Notes:
Totals of self-employed differ from Table 2.14 through being from a 10% sample, and the difference between Census date and end June.
(a) Less than 1,000.

Great Britain

Table 2.14 Distribution of Self-employed by Industry; 1961 to 1975

Thousands

Industry	1961 Men	1961 Women	1966 Men	1966 Women	1971 Men	1971 Women	1975 Men	1975 Women
Agriculture, forestry, fishing	304	26	261	28	235	31	203	31
Manufacturing	73	22	70	35	100	21	100	19
Construction	168	1	215	2	322	2	376	2
Transport and communication	44	2	44	2	67	3	75	2
Distributive trades	366	160	303	154	317	151	285	140
Insurance, banking, finance, business services	25	7	23	9	34	15	38	14
Professional and scientific services	146	26	133	30	153	33	168	37
Miscellaneous services	212	83	199	101	243	116	211	124
Total	1,338	327	1,249	360	1,471	371	1,456	369

Source: *Department of Employment Gazette*, December 1976 and June 1977.

Note: Detail does not add to totals owing to rounding and omission of mining and quarrying.

Figure 2.10   Industrial Distribution of the Self-employed; 1961 and 1975

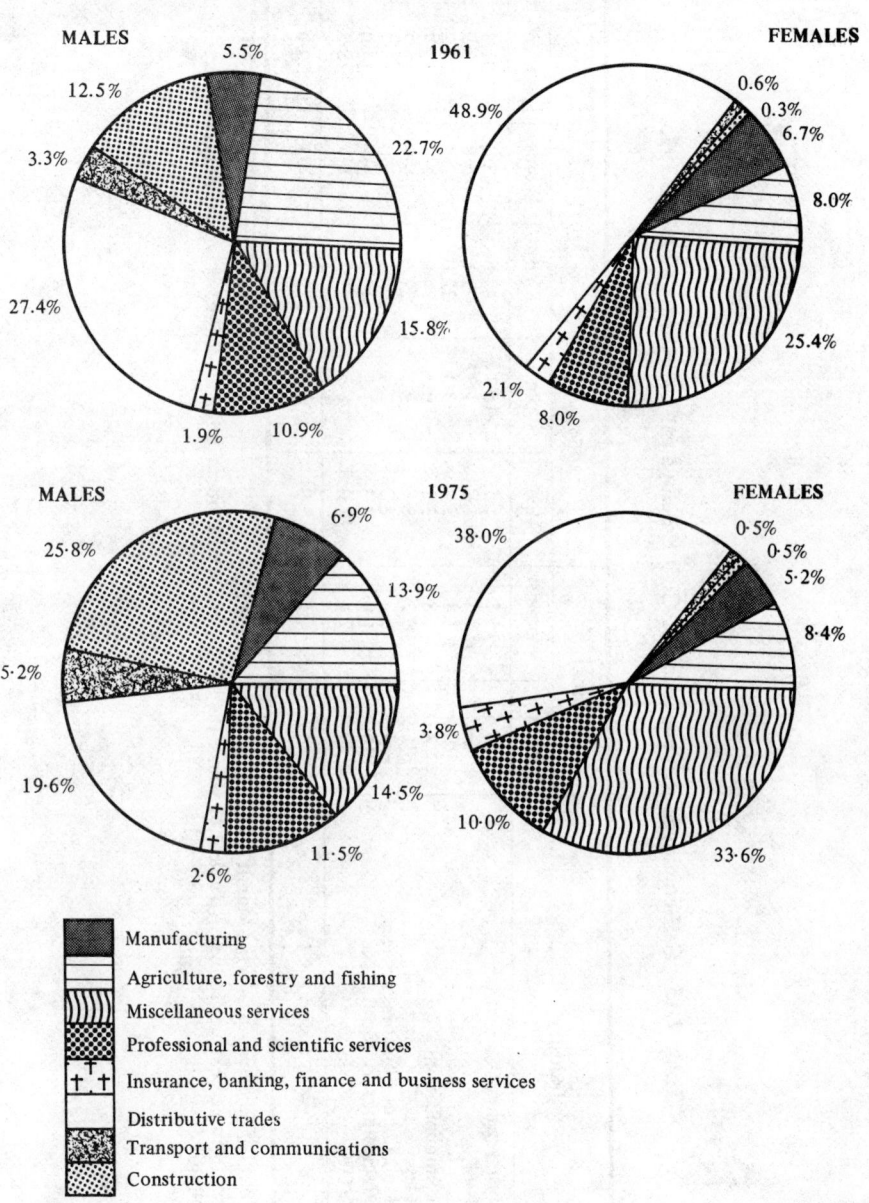

Source: Table 2.14.

35

Table 2.15 Self-employed as Proportion of Civil Employment by Industry; 1961 to 1975

Per cent.

Industry	1961		1966		1971		1975	
	Men	Women	Men	Women	Men	Women	Men	Women
Agriculture, forestry, fishing .. : : : :	35·6	15·7	31·3	18·1	42·6	23·0	41·4	23·5
Manufacturing.. : : : :	1·3	0·8	1·2	1·3	1·8	0·9	1·9	0·9
Construction .. :: : :	10·9	1·4	12·4	2·3	22·0	2·4	24·2	2·0
Transport and communication : :	3·0	0·8	3·1	0·8	4·9	1·2	5·7	0·7
Distributive trades : : : :	21·9	10·2	18·6	9·1	21·6	9·7	19·2	8·5
Insurance, banking, finance, business services : :	6·3	2·3	5·2	2·3	6·7	3·0	6·7	2·4
Professional and scientific services : :	16·8	1·9	13·3	1·8	13·5	1·7	13·0	1·6
Miscellaneous services : : : :	20·9	7·8	17·4	8·5	21·7	10·7	18·5	9·2
Total[1] : : : : : :	8·6	4·1	7·9	4·2	9·9	4·3	9·9	3·9

Source: *Department of Employment Gazette*, March 1975, December 1976, June 1977.

Note: [1] Differs from percentages shown in Table 2.11 where the basis is the whole labour force (ie civil employment plus HM Forces plus registered unemployed).

subsidiary self-employment income earned by employees is very small (less than 0.5 per cent of total net income in 1974–75)[1]. However, as explained in later Chapters, there are reasons for believing that only a small part of the income in this category is reported on tax forms and the classification of income recipients between self-employed and employees is at best imprecise.

2.41   The occupations (in the sense of the 'Orders' of the Census classification) of the self-employed are shown in Table 2.13 for 1971, the most recent year for which the information is available (from the Census of Population). The principal feature shown by the table is how unevenly distributed between occupations they are. The numerical importance of farmers, construction workers, sales workers, and professional and other services among self-employed men stands out. Among self-employed women the concentration in a small number of occupations is even greater.

2.42   This concentration is to be seen just as clearly in the distribution of the self-employed between industries (Tables 2.14 and 2.15 and Figure 2.10).

2.43   An indication of the range of activities included under "miscellaneous services" in Tables 2.14 and 2.15 and the number of self-employed men and women in the larger sub-categories is given in Table 2.16.

Table 2.16   Self-employment in Selected Services; 1971

Great Britain   (Figures in thousands)

	Men	Women	Total
Hotels, snack bars, cafes, public houses	78·6	52·8	131·4
Motor repairs, garages	61·0	3·6	64·6
Hairdressing..	20·9	29·9	50·8

Source: Census 1971, Great Britain, Economic Activity Tables, Table 16.

2.44   As we noted in paragraph 2.21, changes in the way in which occupations are classified in the Census limit the comparisons that can be made over time, and this applies of course to the self-employed as much as to employees. But for some of the professions, defined in terms of qualifications, the data from successive Censuses are likely to be comparable; so changes in the number of men and women engaged in these professions can be shown, and so can the way in which they are divided between the self-employed and employees (generally salaried). Table 2.17 shows a comparison between 1951 and 1971. Regard should be had to the fact that National Health Service general medical practitioners and general dental practitioners are 'self-employed', in that they are independent contractors paid by fees from public funds. Hospital doctors are for the most part salaried, and therefore are classified as employees. The changes in the numbers of salaried and self-employed medical practitioners, therefore, do not show anything about the numbers in private practice. What they do show is the more rapid increase in the number of doctors employed in hospitals than in general practice.

2.45   Table 2.17 shows that out of the six professional groups included, in five the proportion that were self-employed fell between 1951 and 1971. Since the

---
[1] See Chapter 10 for a more detailed discussion.

total numbers in all the professions rose, the absolute numbers of self-employed men and women rose; but since, with the exception of surveyors, the number working as employees rose even faster, there has clearly been a tendency for salaried employment to grow relative to self-employment.

2.46 In the professions many of the "employees" in fact work in private practices, but on a salaried basis, in contrast to the self-employed principals. In Table 2.17, employees of this kind are grouped together with those in salaried employment with, for instance, commercial firms or central and local government. To illustrate the significance of these distinctions we consider in more detail the employment structure of architects and solicitors, professions where there are contrasting trends. The statistics relating to both professions are defined in terms of professional qualifications. For architects they cover those registered with the Architects' Registration Council of the United Kingdom, and for solicitors those with practising certificates issued by the Law Society. The coverage is therefore narrower than that of the Census categories in Table 2.17, where barristers and judges are grouped with solicitors, and town planners with architects. The coverage is different also from that of the "trade groups" for which Inland Revenue data on incomes are shown in Chapter 11, which include some people who are not professionally qualified.

2.47 The distinction between salaried employment in private practice and salaried employment with central and local government and commercial and industrial firms is of significance in the context of the structure of earnings and the factors that influence it. While the main business risk in private practice is borne by the self-employed principals, in those professions where demand is variable and at risk to swings in the national volume of work (eg architects), it is probably true to say that there is more risk to employment as an assistant in private practice than to salaried employment elsewhere. In other professions, however, where the flow of work is steadier, the opposite is probably the case; employment in private practice is more secure but less well-rewarded than salaried employment in a commercial or industrial firm. We return to this theme in Chapter 3.

2.48 Of the fields of employment shown in Table 2.18, only principals in private practice are self-employed; all the others are employees—some of them salaried employees of private practices. The figures in Table 2.18 are not directly comparable with those in Table 2.17, where town planners are grouped with architects. A high proportion of town planners are employed by local authorities and this sector of employment has grown rapidly since 1951. The 1964, 1970 and 1973 RIBA surveys showed about one-half of all architects as being employed in private practice (either as principals or as salaried assistants), but the 1977 survey showed a rather lower proportion. The proportion of architects employed by public bodies—the next largest category after private practice—has tended to grow. Other kinds of salaried employment are not numerically important. There was less building work being done in 1977 than in 1973 (a boom year), which may help explain the fall in the proportion of architects employed in private practice, which illustrates the observations in the previous paragraph about business risk.

2.49 The proportion of solicitors who were self-employed (principals) fell between 1960–61 and 1977–78; but was largely offset by an increase in the

Table 2.17 Employment and Self-employment in Certain Professions; 1951 and 1971

Great Britain

	1951				1971			
	Employees	Self-employed	Out of work	Total "Occupied"	Employees	Self-employed	Out of work	Total "Economically active"
Medical practitioners (qualified)								
Number	27,060	20,426	739	48,225	41,360	23,630	720	65,710
Proportion (%)	56·1	42·4	1·5	100·0	62·9	36·0	1·1	100·0
Dental practitioners								
Number	3,270	9,555	88	12,913	3,780	10,390	140	14,310
Proportion (%)	25·3	74·0	0·7	100·0	26·4	72·6	1·0	100·0
Judges, barristers, advocates, solicitors								
Number	11,619	15,555	183	27,357	17,790	20,400	330	38,520
Proportion (%)	42·5	56·8	0·7	100·0	46·2	52·9	0·9	100·0
Accountants, professional								
Number	25,213	11,384	176	36,773	59,580	16,220	810	76,610
Proportion (%)	68·5	31·0	0·5	100·0	77·8	21·2	1·0	100·0
Surveyors								
Number	30,500	3,107	239	33,846	54,570	8,620	780	63,970
Proportion (%)	90·1	9·2	0·7	100·0	85·3	13·5	1·2	100·0
Architects, town planners								
Number	13,263	4,298	138	17,699	30,770	8,230	420	39,420
Proportion (%)	74·9	24·3	0·8	100·0	78·0	20·9	1·1	100·0

Source: 1951—Census of England and Wales, Occupation Tables, Table 1; Census of Scotland, Occupation and Industry Tables, Table 1.
1971—Census, Great Britain, Economic Activity Tables, Table 4.

Note: Nomenclature is as in 1971; in 1951 the titles were slightly different; in particular, the accountants were termed "qualified accountants".

Table 2.18   Architects in the UK: Fields of Employment; 1964, 1970, 1973 and 1977

Per cent

Category of employment	1964	1970	1973	1977
Private practice—principals	26·0	29·6	29·1	27·7
—assistants	24·1	19·2	20·5	17·5
Local government	28·6	27·3	31·5	31·3
Central government	} 10·5	} 11·9	5·6	6·8
Public corporations			4·2	7·5
Education	2·7	3·3	3·0	3·0
Others[1]	8·1	8·6	6·0	6·2
Total in full-time work	100·0	100·0	100·0	100·0

Source: Royal Institute of British Architects, *Earnings of Architects and their support staff*: *Report of RIBA survey 1970*, Table 3.7; Architects' Earnings *1977*, Table 18.

Notes: Estimates derived from 20 per cent sample (12½ per cent in 1970) of architects with UK addresses on the register of the Architects' Registration Council of the UK, with response rates of around 65 per cent in each survey. Exact totals to which the percentages apply are not known, but can be approximately estimated (from response detail) at about 19,500 in 1964, and 25,000 in 1977.

[1]Includes architects employed by contracting firms and other commercial and industrial firms.

number of salaried solicitors employed in private practice (consultants and assistant solicitors), so that the proportion of all solicitors in private practice has scarcely changed. Solicitors who are employees are more likely to be employees of other solicitors than to be employed by central or local government or business firms. The number of solicitors employed by business firms has, however, increased substantially, nearly trebling between 1960–61 and 1977–78, partly, no doubt, as a result of the increasing array of legal requirements to be complied with in many lines of business.

2.50   Comparison of Tables 2.18 and 2.19 shows a clear contrast between the way in which the structures of the architects' and solicitors' professions have changed. In the former, the proportion working in private practice as salaried employees has fallen while the proportion of self-employed principals has changed little; whereas, in the latter, the proportion of salaried employees in private practice has risen and the proportion of self-employed principals has declined, by approximately equal amounts. It is not for this Commission to investigate in any detail the reasons for these differences; but we note that the factors influencing the opportunities for and the choice between self-employment and salaried employment evidently vary considerably between the two professions.

2.51   The divergent trends shown for architects and solicitors indicate that to generalise about the reasons for the changing balance between employment and self-employment in the different professions would be unsound. There are important distinctions within the professions; the professional bodies in accountancy, for example, differ widely in the structure of employment of their members. Private practice is common among members of the Institute of Chartered Accountants, whereas members of the Institute of Cost and Management Accountants are far more likely to be employees of industrial and commercial firms, and most members of the Chartered Institute of Public Finance and Accountancy work for local authorities and other public bodies. Doctors and

Table 2.19 Solicitors in England and Wales: Fields of Employment; 1960–61 to 1977–78

Category of employment	1960–61		1970–71		1977–78		Change 1960–61—1977–78	
	Number	(%)	Number	(%)	Number	(%)	Number	(%)
1 Principals (own account and partnerships)[1]	13,792	(71·3)	16,744	(66·2)	19,908	(59·0)	+6,116	(44·3)
2 Consultants	147	(0·8)	385	(1·5)	1,382	(4·1)	+1,235	(840·1)
3 Assistant solicitors	3,044	(15·7)	5,015	(19·8)	7,645	(22·7)	+4,601	(151·1)
Total in private practice	16,983	(87·8)	22,144	(87·6)	28,935	(85·8)	+11,952	(70·4)
4 Government service	57	(0·3)	48	(0·2)	258	(0·8)	+201	(352·6)
5 Local government	1,507	(7·8)	1,785	(7·1)	2,520	(7·5)	+1,013	(67·2)
6 Commerce and industry[2]	470	(2·4)	822	(3·3)	1,238	(3·7)	+768	(163·4)
7 Other whole-time employment	310	(1·6)	475	(1·9)	771	(2·3)	+461	(148·7)
Total[3]	19,349	(100·0)	25,286	(100·0)	33,728	(100·0)	+14,379	(74·3)

Source: Law Society.

Notes: [1] Solicitors recorded as practising on their own account or as partners as well as being employed in other capacities are included here.
[2] Includes nationalised industries.
[3] Includes minor categories not shown separately, and excludes solicitors not in active practice, retired or abroad. Separate items in the table do not therefore sum to the total shown.

dentists are a special case because of their relationship to the National Health Service (see paragraph 2.44 above). All that can be safely said is that self-employment is important in parts at least of all the main professions, but that the factors influencing the choice between self-employment and salaried employment are heterogeneous.

2.52   The principal features of the changes in self-employment appear to be:
   i   The decline in employment of all kinds in agriculture (see also Table 2.9 above), which has led to a decline in the number of farmers—from 327,000 self-employed men in "agricultural employments" in 1921 to 304,000 in "agriculture, forestry, and fishing" in 1961 and 203,000 in 1975; though self-employment has diminished more slowly than total agricultural employment, and so the self-employment ratio has risen slightly since 1961.
   ii The reduction in the number of small shops and with it the number of self-employed shopkeepers. In 1921, self-employed "proprietors of whole-sale and retail businesses" numbered 363,000 men and 149,000 women, 512,000 in all. In 1975, self-employment in the "distributive trades"—a somewhat wider classification—numbered 285,000 men and 140,000 women, 425,000 in all.
   iii In the other direction, a growth in self-employment in the professions, even though in most of them the increase in the numbers in salaried employment rose faster still. It is impossible to generalise about the reasons for the changing balance between employment and self-employment in the different professions.
   iv A distinctive feature of the 1960s and early 1970s was the growth of self-employment in the construction industry, from 169,000 in 1961 to 324,000 in 1971, with a peak of 435,000 in 1973. The main increase took place after 1966, when self-employment amounted to 217,000. There was no other change in self-employment on anything like this scale. Much of the increase is widely attributed to a growth of "labour only" sub-contracting to take advantage of the fiscal benefits considered to be obtainable from self-employment—exemption from Selective Employment Tax when it was in force from 1966 to 1971; taxation under Schedule D; and—for a time—opportunities for tax evasion until counter-measures were taken in 1974 and 1975 (in other words the advantages of "the lump", ie labour-only sub-contracting in the construction industry).

Summary
2.53   In paragraphs 2.4 to 2.18 we describe changes in the size and age and sex composition of the labour force. We show first of all the growth in the population of Great Britain from 1881 (when it was just under 30 million) to 1976 (when it was over 54 million) and its changing age structure. The proportion of the population under 15 has fallen since 1881, because of the fall in the birth rate, while the proportion of the population aged 65 and over has risen over the same period. The population of working age (15–64) grew as a proportion of total population up to the 1930s and then declined. In spite of these shifts in the age structure of the population, the labour force has changed remarkably little as a proportion of the population over the period since 1881. Longer schooling and more post-school education has tended to reduce the proportion of the lower age groups in the labour force. At the other end of the age scale, earlier retire-

ment has also reduced the labour force. These reductions have been more than offset, however, by the large rise in the employment of married women, particularly as part-time workers. Considering only the ageing population and the rise in the proportion of women who are married, we would have expected the labour force to have fallen in relation to the whole population in the last 50 years. Because of the massive rise in the proportion of married women in (largely part-time) paid employment, the ratio of the labour force to total population, in fact, has actually risen slightly.

2.54   In paragraphs 2.19 to 2.27 we show that there has been a shift in the occupational distribution of the employed labour force from manual to non-manual occupations for both men and women. For men, employment in professional and managerial occupations has risen much faster than in clerical occupations. Among manual occupations there has been a shift from the less skilled to the more skilled occupations. For women, the increase in employment in non-manual occupations has occurred mainly in clerical occupations while the number of women in manual occupations (in particular, domestic service) has declined considerably. Workers in many occupations are widely spread between industries, although there are some categories, eg miners, which are specific to particular industries.

2.55   In paragraphs 2.28 to 2.32 we show that there has been a massive and continuous expansion in employment in services since 1931; a shift from rapid expansion of employment in manufacturing industry between 1931 and 1961 to an accelerating rate of decline since 1961; and a continuous decline in employment in agriculture, mining and textiles since 1931. The rapid expansion in employment in services, particularly in public services, is associated with the growth of part-time women's employment and with the rapid growth in employment in non-manual occupations. Of the total increase in employment in services between 1961 and 1975, 71 per cent was in the central and local government sector; after 1975 the rate of growth in employment in public services slackened off.

2.56   In paragraphs 2.33 to 2.52 we describe recent trends in self-employment. From 1921 to 1966 the trend of self-employment as a proportion of the labour force was downwards (from 10 per cent to 6.4 per cent). Between 1966 and 1971 self-employment increased again, reaching a peak in 1973. This was mainly due to the growth of labour-only subcontracting in the construction industry (ie the "lump"). There has been a growth in self-employed professional workers but not as great as the growth in the number of professional employees. A detailed study of employment in two of the professions, architects and solicitors, shows that in the former the proportion working in private practice as salaried employees has fallen while the proportion of self-employed principals has scarcely changed; whereas in the latter the proportion of salaried employees in private practice has risen and the proportion of self-employed principals has declined by approximately equal amounts. The factors influencing the structure of self-employment and salaried employment therefore must differ considerably between different professions. The downward trend in self-employment from 1921 to 1966 may be partly attributed to the continuous decline in agriculture, and the reduction in the number of small shops and with it the number of self-employed shopkeepers.

CHAPTER 3

Theoretical Background and Practical Approaches to the Analysis of Earnings

Introduction

3.1 The factors that influence the structure and distribution of earnings are many and various, and the amount of detailed information available is vast. Without some clues as to what to look for among the facts and how to organise them, description would be difficult and interpretation impossible. To provide such clues we begin by a brief review of the body of theory bearing on the determinants of the distribution of earnings. No attempt will be made to give a full review of the theory of earnings, which would be outside the scope of this Report.

3.2 We are concerned both with earnings (in the sense of income from employment) and with self-employment incomes. The latter can appropriately be regarded as consisting partly of earnings for labour services (to which the same body of theory applies as to employees' earnings), partly of a return on capital employed, and partly of a return (sometimes positive, sometimes negative) to the bearer of business risk. The relative importance of these three elements differs considerably between different categories of self-employment.

3.3 The distribution of earnings amongst the twenty-two million employees in the United Kingdom is now the dominant influence in shaping the total distribution of income. Self-employment, as we showed in Chapter 2, has tended to become numerically less important relative to working for an employer, even though in absolute terms self-employment is of very substantial significance.

3.4 When considering earnings from employment, the simplest way of analysing the distribution is in terms of the money wage or salary received, but for most purposes the "total reward" should ideally be taken into account, and from it deducted the total costs borne by the employee as a consequence of his particular employment. Total reward is defined here as the sum of: (i) money wages or salaries; (ii) other financial rewards; and (iii) non-cash benefits. The costs which an employee incurs include not only the time and effort put into the job and expenses incurred (eg travel) but also time and money spent on education or training, any personal risks incurred in doing the job, and any adverse conditions under which the work is done. Needless to say, most of the benefits other than wages and salaries, and many of the costs, are difficult to measure even in principle, let alone in practice with the data we have. Nevertheless, to ignore these complications would be unjustifiable.

44

Theories of wage and salary structure

3.5   The branch of economic theory that is relevant to this Report is that which relates to the structure of earnings, as distinct from the theory of the share of earnings in gross domestic product. Three strands can usefully be distinguished: (i) 'labour market' theories, which treat the structure of wages and salaries as being determined by market processes, ie that there is a market for labour services in which prices are set for those services in a way which is not intrinsically different from the setting of prices in other markets; (ii) 'human capital' theories, which regard the acquisition of knowledge and skills as an investment on which a return can be earned, and subject to the same influences as the supply of other kinds of investment; and (iii) what for want of a better term may be called 'institutional' theories, which regard the influence of customary relativities, collective agreements, and Government regulation as so pervasive that they transform the nature of the labour market. The differences from an ordinary market are considered to be so great as to make the concepts and techniques derived from other markets of little or no use for analysing the determination of wages and salaries.

3.6   These theories are not mutually exclusive. 'Human capital' theories highlight a particular aspect of the working of a market—the interaction between the cost of obtaining skills and knowledge, the extra income obtainable from possession of such skills and knowledge, and their supply. The importance attached to institutions is again a matter of degree; collective bargaining, minimum wages legislation, legislation on equal pay, and (from time to time since 1948) incomes policies are facts of life about the British economy, but how great their influence has been relative to other factors—in particular scarcities of particular kinds of labour—is open to dispute.

3.7   The 'market' theories start with the proposition that the demand for labour is derived from the demand for the goods or services that the labour in question can produce; so that the more productive the labour and the more valuable the product, the greater the price the employer is prepared to pay. On the supply side, people in work or seeking work have a very wide range of abilities and aptitudes; and consequently of possible alternative employments. The supply price facing a particular employer, or all employers in an industry together, is what the people they want to employ can get in alternative employments (assuming that such alternatives exist). This theoretical approach readily brings into account costs incurred by the employee, risk and danger, or disagreeable (but not dangerous) conditions. Given a choice at equal wages, most people would opt for the less risky or less unpleasant work; so to recruit enough workers and retain them, employers who have the less pleasant jobs to fill must offer higher pay.

3.8   'Market' theories thus focus attention on aspects of both demand and supply. On the demand side, industries that are expanding as a result of a growing demand for their products will usually be trying to add to their labour force and so are likely—other things being equal—to offer more pay than previously, in comparison with pay generally, for the kinds of worker they want. For industries with a shrinking market, the opposite is to be expected. Similarly,

45

technical changes increase the demand for some skills and abilities, and diminish the demand for others, with effect—in time—on earnings. The supply side is also relevant; a growth in the number of people with particular skills and qualifications can produce a change from a seller's to a buyer's market; and growth of alternative employment opportunities can reduce the supply of workers in particular occupations relative to the demand for their services.

3.9   "Human capital" theories concentrate on a particular aspect of labour supply, the supply of skills (in the widest sense) which must be acquired by training (including both on-the-job training and non-vocational training that develops the relevant aptitudes) and experience. These require an outlay of both time and money (including foregone earnings). The supply of such skills is seen by "human capital" theory as being determined by investment decisions that do not differ fundamentally from other investment decisions, in which the prospective return is compared with the cost of making the investment. The demand for the skills in question is determined by factors of the kind referred to above. The return on the investment comes from enhanced earnings, not just immediately but over a whole life-time. So "earnings profiles"—ie estimates of the amount an individual would earn in successive years in his career—are essential for assessing the rate of return obtained or in prospect.

3.10   The main difficulties with the "human capital" approach are of measurement and estimation, in particular the extent of the extra earnings of those with the relevant training and education, and how far the extra earnings are the consequence of the training or education as such, as distinct from innate ability. Owing to the length of human life, skills and abilities acquired or developed by education and training when young are assets with a very long useful life (unless made obsolete by technical change), so that the return on the investment is a very long term return, and estimating it is a very difficult problem.

3.11   We finally comment briefly on the 'institutional' approach, which emphasises stable—or only slowly changing— relativities based on custom or concepts of fairness; the effects of collective bargaining; and of government regulation, ranging from minimum wages to incomes policies. Custom and status tend to reinforce each other. Pay differentials which tend to persist through time often reflect differences in status, eg that of the skilled craftsmen relative to labourers (of which perhaps the most widely quoted example is that first cited by Phelps Brown[1], of the rate of pay of a mason being one and a half times that of a labourer in both 1412 and 1914), and of supervisors relative to the people they supervise. Such links between status and customary differentials appear to exist both within organisations and on a broader canvas—eg the proposition that the status of particular professions depends on their being relatively well paid. The distinctive feature of 'custom' as an influence on pay differentials is that it should produce, for some categories of employee, pay higher than would be strictly necessary to recruit and retain enough men and women of the abilities required. Pay rates set, for reasons of custom, below market levels could quickly come under pressure through there being too few recruits and too many departures. In other words, custom and the institutional frame-

---

[1] E H Phelps Brown, *The Economics of Labour*; Yale University Press, New Haven, Connecticut, 1962.

work of the professions are factors modifying market forces. 'Customary' differentials can persist even if they are greater than needed for 'market' reasons, because they ensure a minimum supply of labour.

3.12   One explanation of 'customary' differentials is that of the 'internal labour market'. If recruitment into an organisation is only a small proportion of the employment level within it, the argument runs, then employees at most levels are not in direct competition with people outside, and so are insulated from market pressures. Collective bargaining may work in the same direction. Pay increases negotiated in one industry may have a considerable influence on what unions in other industries will settle for; and there are several well known instances of recognised comparabilities between different occupations—the fire services and the police for instance, and electricity supply workers and surface workers in the coal industry.

3.13   Collective bargaining is a pervasive influence on wage and salary determination, but one exerted from the supply side; an effective trade union ensures that labour services are not on offer at rates below the union rate. Collective bargaining need not exclude market forces, but there is no doubt that it makes the process work quite differently from what happens if employees bargain individually. Just what effect collective bargaining by trade unions has had on the structure of pay is very difficult to determine. As we said in our Report on Lower Incomes (Report No 6) "Statistical studies indicate that differences in collective bargaining coverage are associated with differences in relative earnings but could explain only a limited part of the variation in earnings, and cause and effect are not clear"[1]. There have been far fewer attempts to estimate the effect of trade unions on wage levels in Britain than in the USA where non-union plants and firms are more numerous and comparisons can be more readily made.

3.14   Mention must finally be made of Government action. Historically, Government action to regulate wages began as a substitute for collective bargaining, to set minimum rates of pay in industries and trades where collective bargaining had not developed. In Britain the beginning was the Trade Boards Act of 1909, authorising the setting up of "trade boards" to determine minimum wages in "sweated" trades, but it has since been extended to cover such major industries as agriculture, and hotels and catering (the Catering Wages Act of 1943). Since the Second World War, however, Government has sought to influence pay in a totally different way, through incomes policies introduced to restrain inflation. Common to all incomes policies has been an attempt to apply limits that are of general application other than to (sometimes) defined special cases. Such policies should either 'freeze' differentials, if what is allowed is a percentage increase, or narrow them, if what is allowed is a flat sum (as in 1975), a flat sum plus a percentage (as in 1976), or a percentage with a maximum absolute amount (as in 1973). The Government has also sought to achieve equal pay for women through legislation (the Equal Pay Act, 1970, enforced from the end of 1975).

---

[1] Cmnd 7175, paragraph 3.81.

Earnings from self-employment

3.15 We noted in paragraph 3.2 that earnings from self-employment can be regarded as (in proportions that vary greatly between occupations and trades) earnings from labour services, returns on capital employed (in the ordinary sense, excluding human capital) and the profit or loss from the bearing of business risk. Such risk bearing carries with it the prospect of a high reward to compensate the bearer for the danger of loss of both capital and income. All three strands of the theories of the structure of earnings (the market for labour services, human capital and institutional factors) are relevant to earnings from self-employment. It may be argued that the particular institutional framework is important in explaining the distribution of earnings in some of the professions. Examples are specific legal or customary requirements that reserve certain categories of work for particular professions (eg conveyancing to solicitors, statutorily required audits to qualified accountants etc) accompanied by customary, or agreed, rather than competitively determined scales of charges. The incomes of the members of such professions are less affected by economic change, and can be expected to be correspondingly higher on average, than are those in professions or trades where competition is keener. Our analysis of incomes of the self-employed in separate trade groups (Chapter 11) illustrates this point. However, the earnings of the self-employed are not in general influenced directly by external institutional factors, such as Government regulations or collective bargaining. For example, the self-employed are not directly affected by incomes policies, though subject to some degree of price restraint; indeed, in some professions where charges are based on a fixed percentage, incomes are largely inflation-proofed.

3.16 Our description of the self-employed labour force in Chapter 2 suggests that there are very wide variations in the amount of human capital employed. The professions, indeed, may be taken as the extreme example of investment in human capital, because in many cases they require a long and exacting training, with low earnings (relative to future expectations) immediately following while experience is being gained. There are similarly large differences in the amount of ordinary capital required, ranging from the very small (for instance labour-only sub-contracting in the building industry) to the very large (for instance farming).

3.17 As we showed in Chapter 2, employment and self-employment are frequently found side by side in the same occupation. In many lines of business there are both salaried managers and self-employed proprietors; retailing provides many examples, as do the catering and hotel trades. So too in the professions there are both self-employed and employees. The main distinguishing features of self-employment compared with employment are: first, the degree of control over the organisation of the work, leading to a more immediate connection between the amount and quality of work done and earnings; second, the often considerable investment represented by the ownership of a business; and, third, the degree of risk involved (which is related to some extent to the owner's stake in the business). These distinctions are not, of course, absolute. In some forms of employment the amount of overtime worked is, within limits, voluntary; and payment-by-results schemes, piecework, and bonus schemes that relate pay partly to output are fairly common. Generally speaking, within the same line of business, the self-employed person is subject to a greater degree of variation in income than the employee (ultimately to the point of absolute loss of both capital and income) because he is more immediately affected by fluctuations in workload and trade and hence in cash flow. The employee is exposed to the risk of losing his employment, although variations in his earnings may be limited by the terms of his contract with his employer. There are some professions, on the other hand, where fluctuations in trade and cash flow are not great and the extra risk borne by the self-employed is not high; this may be due in part to the institutional factors mentioned in paragraph 3.15 above. There are other trades, such as building and construction, for example, which are subject to a high degree of risk for both employees and the self-employed; employees have little job security and there is considerable instability in the workload for small firms. Most forms of self-employment require investment of capital, sometimes very considerable, which constitutes a risk for the self-employed of losing all his assets, not just his invested capital. This is over and above the risk of loss of income from labour services that is borne in the same way by employees.

3.18   The pay that can be earned in salaried employment probably sets a standard against which the income prospects in self-employment can be assessed. There are some people who prefer to be their own masters, notwithstanding such extra risk as may be involved. Others, perhaps, will opt for self-employment only if the expected outcome (as they perceive it) will be a higher income than if they follow the less risky course of salaried employment.

3.19   We noted in Chapter 2 (paragraphs 2.44 to 2.51) that in the professions the proportion in salaried employment was tending to rise and the proportion in self-employment was tending to fall, though with exceptions. A rising demand for professional services leads more business and other organisations to employ their own full-time professional staff (eg accountants) rather than engage independent practitioners as and where needed. Moreover, when there are barriers to entry into independent practice because of the difficulty of obtaining business where advertising is not permitted and clients are firmly attached to established firms, salaried employment (for instance, working for established firms of self-employed principals) is a less risky way of acquiring an assured income than setting up in independent practice straight away.

3.20   Many of the occupations and trades where self-employment is common are subject to specific risks. Frequently the cause is the variability of public taste (for instance, as it affects the catering and fashion trades, entertainments, and arts and crafts) or competition from rivals with more resources behind them (especially important for retailers). It can also extend to the vagaries of the weather, which affects not just farming and market gardening but the holiday trades as well.

3.21   The greater incidence of risk in most cases, and the closer connection between amount and quality of work done and income, would be expected to lead to a wider dispersion of earnings from self-employment than of wage and salary earnings in the same occupations and trades. Especially is this so in terms of incomes measured in specific years. The various sources of risk are likely to lead to many self-employed people earning untypically high incomes in some years, and untypically low incomes in others. Over a run of years these will to some extent average out; but for a single year the dispersion of incomes is likely to be increased by the inclusion of those experiencing unusually "good" or "bad" years.

Our work on the structure of earnings

3.22   We have discussed above three sets of theories about the way in which the structure of earnings is determined, two of which (termed in paragraph 3.5 the 'labour market' and 'institutional' theories) are best regarded, except in extreme versions, as really differing only in the emphasis they place on different and particular features of the supply of, and demand for, labour services. The third, the 'human capital' theory, differs in concentrating on a particular aspect of the supply of skills. These three sets of theories are relevant here because they have different implications for what the structure of earnings should be like at a point in time, and how it might be expected to change through time.

3.23   It is not for the Royal Commission to arrive at a new judgement as to the validity of the theories outlined. Under the terms of our standing reference our main concern is with current and past trends in the distribution of personal income and wealth. The statistical evidence which we have produced in this Report may provide some background to the assessment of these theories by others. To place our work in perspective we formulate below the questions that we have set out to explore. This may serve as an introduction to the detailed work in the following chapters of this Report.

3.24   On the way to tackling these questions we necessarily devote much attention to assembling the statistical material with which to make the necessary comparisons. The sources (summarised in Chapter 4) have been combined wherever practicable to provide as complete a picture as possible.

3.25   We have identified eight main operational questions which are explored in the main body of this Report. They are:

  i   To what extent is the distribution of earnings related to differences in occupation and to differences in industry? (Chapters 5, 7, and 11)

 ii   How have the earnings of different occupational groups changed over time? (Chapter 6)

iii   What has been the relationship between changes in the occupational and industrial structure and the distribution of earnings? (Chapter 7)

 iv   What is the relationship between the age of employees and their earnings in different occupations, and how stable are the relative earnings of individuals through time? (Chapter 8)

  v   How have non-cash benefits grown in relation to earnings? (Chapter 9)

 vi   What is the relationship between institutional factors (eg equal pay legislation, incomes policies, and collective bargaining) and the structure of earnings? (Chapters 6 and 7)

vii On what basis is it possible to make legitimate comparisons between incomes of the self-employed and incomes of employees? (Chapter 12)

viii How does the structure of incomes from self-employment differ from the structure of incomes from employment? (Chapters 10 to 13).

Summary

3.26 We have discussed three strands to the theory of the structure of earnings: (i) 'labour market' theories, which treat the structure of wages and salaries as being determined by market processes, ie prices are regarded as being set for labour services in a way which is not intrinsically different from the setting of prices in other markets; (ii) 'human capital' theories, which regard the acquisition of knowledge and skills as an investment on which a return can be earned; and (iii) 'institutional' theories, which regard the influence of customary relativities, collective agreements, and Government regulations as so pervasive that they transform the nature of the labour market. These strands are not mutually exclusive, but their relative importance is a matter of disagreement, with implications for the structure of earnings.

3.27 Earnings from self-employment can be regarded as comprising earnings from labour services, returns on capital employed, and the profit or loss from the bearing of business risk. Institutional factors may reduce the degree of competition in certain professions, which is reflected in customary or agreed scales of charges rather than market-determined rates. This may explain in part why variations in incomes in some professions are lower, and average incomes higher, than in other professions or trades (Chapter 11). In many trades and professions both employment and self-employment are to be found, though in the professions in recent years the proportion of self-employed has fallen (Chapter 2). In those trades and professions where there are both employed and self-employed workers, the choice between employment and self-employment depends mainly on people's desire to control their own work and on their attitude to risk. Generally speaking, the self-employed person is subject to more risks than the employee in the same line of business, because of fluctuations in trade and cash flow. Most forms of self-employment require investment of capital, which contributes to the additional risk for the self-employed, as well as making it more difficult for new entrants to a trade or profession to set up their own business. These distinctive influences on the distribution of earnings from self-employment lead to the expectation that the dispersion of earnings from self-employment will be greater than the dispersion of employees' earnings.

3.28 From the consideration of the relevant theories, eight operational questions were identified, which are explored in Chapters 5 to 13 of the Report.

CHAPTER 4
Sources of Data

Introduction

4.1   The analyses of incomes in the following chapters rely heavily on two main data sources: the New Earnings Survey (NES) which is carried out annually by the Department of Employment (DE) and the Inland Revenue's Survey of Personal Incomes (SPI). The SPI data have been supplemented by a special survey of the incomes of close company directors which the Inland Revenue carried out for us. We also draw on the Family Expenditure Survey and on a variety of other sources.

New Earnings Survey

4.2   The NES is a rich source of data for the study of earnings by factors such as occupation and industry. It is a large annual survey (the sample consists of 1 per cent of the population in employment) which collects a wide range of employment-related information such as gross weekly and hourly earnings, overtime earnings, basic hours and paid overtime hours in a selected pay period in April each year.

4.3   An important feature of the survey is the relatively fast provision of results: the survey is carried out in April each year and the first results are generally available in the following October. The DE publish a large range of tables from the survey and hold an even wider and more comprehensive range of unpublished tabulations which we have been allowed to consult. The basic data are held on computer files but the main computing effort each year is directed towards the rapid production of the standard tabulations. There is very little flexibility in the annual programme of work associated with the survey but the Department did find scope to fit in a number of special analyses for us of the 1978 and earlier surveys.

4.4   The sampling method of the survey ensures that a substantial number of the same individuals are included in the sample in successive years, making possible analyses of matched samples from year to year. In general, about three quarters of the returns relate to employees for whom returns were obtained in the previous survey. The overlap between 1974 and 1975 samples was much smaller because of the changeover to a new sample design. The special tabulations which the Department produced for us included analyses of the data on a matched sample basis.

4.5   The detailed classification of employees by occupation and industry is invaluable. The NES provides the only existing series of data for studying the influence of these factors on the shape of the distribution of earnings. Occupations are divided into the two broad categories: "manual" and "non-manual". "Non-manual" occupations cover with a few exceptions all managerial, professional and related, literary, artistic and sports, clerical and related, selling, security and protective service occupations. Other occupations are classified as "manual". A different occupational classification was used for the 1972 and earlier Surveys but the manual/non-manual categories were similar.

4.6   The survey is of comparatively recent origin. The first full scale survey was carried out in April 1970[1]. For analyses of longer term changes, therefore, we draw on a variety of sources, but most heavily on the estimates of trends in earnings compiled by Dr G Routh[2].

4.7   The DE publish extensive analyses of the NES data: these are widely used by employers and trade unions in collective bargaining, by journalists and other commentators on economic developments and in economic studies generally. Despite the large volume of tables published, there is still a considerable need among a variety of users for further analyses of the data.

4.8   The Department rightly gives higher priority to maintaining the regular publication timetable than to producing tabulations to meet special requirements of individual users. However, we consider that such an invaluable source should be exploited as fully as possible. We have had considerable co-operation from the Department in preparing special analyses for the present Report but we recognise that such a facility is not widely available. The Department should give serious consideration to the possibility of making the data available, on a basis which protects confidentiality, to users to carry out their own analyses. If this should not prove possible, then the Department might consider developing the facility to respond readily and flexibly to requests for analyses from *bona fide* users of their data.

Survey of Personal Incomes

4.9   The NES is of course restricted in coverage to income from employment. For comparisons of the incomes of employees and the self-employed we turn to the SPI. This annual survey is based on the income tax records held by the Inland Revenue. The sample consists of some 120,000 cases. The survey covers all personal incomes reviewed for income tax purposes including those that were found not to be liable to tax through the operation of allowances and deductions.

4.10   The basis on which the SPI treats various types of income is summarised in Table 4.1. Income from employment is assessed under Schedule E whereas self-employment income (as defined for tax purposes) is assessed under Cases 1 and 2 of Schedule D. The Inland Revenue have provided us with previously

---

[1] An earlier but smaller survey ($\frac{1}{2}$ per cent of the employed population) was carried out in September 1968.
[2] G Routh, *Occupation and Pay in Britain, 1906 to 1960*, Cambridge; Cambridge University Press, 1965.

Table 4.1 Types of Income Covered by the Inland Revenue's Survey of Personal Incomes

Type of Income/Outgoings	SPI Treatment	Whether included in SPI "Total Income"	Whether included in SPI "Total Net Income"
Earned Income Income from employment, including close company directors' salaries and fees. Benefits in kind and expenses payments[1]. Family allowance. Pensions.	Schedule E income.	Included net of employees' superannuation contributions. (a)	Included net of deductions.
Income from self-employment less losses, capital allowances and stock relief.	Schedule D income (Cases I and II).	Included.	
Unearned Income Dividends from UK companies. Other interest, annuities etc taxed at source. Building society interest received. Income under Schedule D Case III. Rents (Schedule A) less tax-allowable expenses. Income under Schedule D Cases IV to VI (except earned income Cases V and VI).	Total investment income (income taxed at source is grossed up).	Included.	Included net of deductions.
Deductions Building society interest payable. Retirement annuity premiums. Charges. Other deductions.	Total deductions.	Not deducted.	Deducted.
Employees' superannuation contributions.	Not notified to Inland Revenue—not covered by SPI.	Deducted (see (a) above).	
Expenses Schedule E expenses.	Schedule E expenses.[2]	Deducted.[2]	Deducted.[2]
Schedule D expenses (Cases I and II).	Not recorded—are part of operating costs of business and deducted in arriving at chargeable profits.	Excluded.	Excluded.
Other Schedule D losses, capital allowances and stock relief.	Allowed against Schedule D income but not included under "Total deductions".	Excluded.	Excluded.
Income tax.	Recorded separately.	Before tax.	Before tax.
Non-taxable Transfer Incomes Unemployment benefit and supplementary benefit etc.	Not covered.	Excluded.	Excluded.

Notes:
[1] Only included in SPI if they come within taxable income, whether or not they are subsequently allowable (see note 2).
[2] Allowable expenses which may be deducted for tax purposes are those incurred "wholly, exclusively and necessarily" in the performance of employee's duties. They are deducted from SPI Total Income and Total Net Income only if they are recorded.

unpublished analyses of the incomes of tax units whose principal source of income was assessed under Schedules D Cases 1 and 2, and E, respectively. These tabulations relate to the years 1972–73 to 1975–76. The Schedule E main source tables include a number of income recipients whose main source is pension rather than current earnings from employment, thus distorting comparisons of employment and self-employment income based on these tables. However, we have estimated the effects of the inclusion of pensioners in the comparisons in Chapter 10.

4.11 The Inland Revenue have also provided us with special analyses of self-employment income by trade group for 1976–77. The main source tables referred to in paragraph 4.10 above are by range of total net income or total income. The trade group analyses show the spread of income of each group over ranges of self-employment income (see Chapter 11).

Survey of close company directors

4.12 For income tax purposes the incomes of close company directors are treated as employment incomes and, as such, are taxed under Schedule E. However, in our view this group have more in common with the self-employed than employees. They fit within our definition of the self-employed as those who own and control the enterprises in which they work. The data available from the SPI did not enable us to segregate the incomes of close company directors from those of other Schedule E cases; a special sample survey of close company directors' incomes was therefore necessary.

4.13 Our special survey was carried out in conjunction with the Inland Revenue and provided detailed information on the total incomes in 1974–75 of a sample of 1,000 close company directors. Income from close companies was not the main source for some 200 of these directors. The remaining 800, for whom close companies' income was the main source, we refer to as close company proprietors, to distinguish them from other directors whose incomes from their companies are of relatively small amounts.

4.14 For the one year 1974–75, by grossing-up the results of our special survey, we were able to subtract the total incomes of close company proprietors from the SPI main source Schedule E income distribution, thus deriving a more precise income distribution for employees for that year together with a combined distribution of the incomes of the self-employed who were assessed for tax under Schedule D and of close company proprietors. A description of the survey and the adjustments to the SPI is to be found at Appendix C.

4.15 From our special survey we estimated that there were about 309,000 close company proprietor tax units in 1974–75. The available data on the numbers of tax units recorded in the SPI over the period 1973–74 to 1975–76 is as follows:

				Main source Schedule D tax units	Close company proprietor tax units	Total tax units recorded in SPI
				'000	'000	'000
1973–74	..	..	..	—	—	22,900
1974–75	..	..	..	1,731	309	23,400
1975–76	..	..	..	1,660	—	23,500

55

Family Expenditure Survey

4.16 The other source of data used in our study of self-employment incomes was the FES, which is a continuous sample survey conducted by the Office of Population Censuses and Surveys on behalf of the Department of Employment. For our purposes, however, this survey poses problems as, in the 1975 FES, fewer than 500 of the 7,203 households covered by the survey had their heads of household classified as self-employed. We can use it therefore only to present broad aggregate income distributions.

4.17 The FES definition of income differs from that of the SPI in that it includes important non-taxable social security payments such as supplementary benefit and National Insurance unemployment benefit. It also provides a better coverage of low income recipients than the SPI. It can also be used to link the income levels of both employees and the self-employed to the possession of certain 'visible' assets. The results of an exploratory attempt to do this are presented in Chapter 10.

Time lags in the data

4.18 There is, however, a serious statistical problem which affects our use of the SPI and the FES: the self-employment income recorded for any year usually relates to an accounting period some year or more previously, whilst the employment income recorded normally relates to the current year. Ideally, any comparisons between the two types of income therefore require some kind of adjustment to allow for this lag.

4.19 The problem which this poses for our use of the SPI stems from the position that income assessed for tax under Schedule D for any fiscal year (and, therefore, included in the SPI of that year) is usually income earned in an accounting period ending sometime in the previous fiscal year. Since unincorporated businesses are free to choose whatever accounting period they like, the SPI statistics for any one year relate to accounting periods which vary considerably in terms of when they end. Table D.1 of Appendix D illustrates this. It gives the results of a sampling exercise undertaken by the Inland Revenue to ascertain when these accounting periods actually ended. This enabled an estimate to be made of the average time lag required to compare Schedule D income with Schedule E income. The average lag was found to be 15 months.

4.20 There are, however, two further considerations. First, the estimated average time lag does not take into account the possibility of any bias arising within the income distribution. This could happen as the result of, for example, Schedule D taxpayers with high incomes having the maximum possible time lag (approximately 24 months) and those with low incomes having the minimum time lag (approximately 12 months). The converse is also possible, of course. In periods of rapid inflation, such a bias would significantly understate the extent of inequality in the income distribution. Unfortunately, since we cannot relate information on time lags to individual incomes, we do not know whether such bias exists.

4.21 Second, a problem arises because the total income of a main source Schedule D tax unit is not solely composed of Schedule D income. Some may be

Schedule E income, so that, if the full time lag of 15 months was applied to our main source Schedule D income distribution, the result would be an over-compensation. However, in practice this is somewhat fortunate in that we only have the choice of lagging the data by either 12 or 24 months. That is, for example, of comparing the 1975–76 main source Schedule D distribution with either the 1974–75 or 1973–74 main source Schedule E distribution. The best approximation is obviously to take a 12 months lag.[1]

4.22   There is a similar problem with the FES. That survey asks respondents for information about income from self-employment for the last complete account-ing year. However, an exercise carried out by the Central Statistical Office has shown that the income data recorded in the survey can relate to periods several years in the past. The results are summarised in Appendix D. They indicate that the median time lag (compared with employment income recorded in the survey) is 15 months.

Other data sources

4.23   In preparing this report we have drawn on a large number of other sources to support the evidence from these three sources. We have used Census data and other labour force statistics in preparing our estimates of the composition of the labour force in Chapter 2, and in Chapter 9 a variety of sources are pressed into service to provide partial information on the incidence of non-cash benefits from employment. We cannot fully describe all of these sources here: references, when available, are given in the appropriate chapters.

International comparisons

4.24   The data sources described above are restricted to income in Britain. International comparisons of employment and self-employment incomes and of earnings distributions are of interest in themselves and also can provide ad-ditional insights into the processes of wage determination. However, inter-national comparisons in this area are fraught with problems of comparability of data sources. In the study of the distribution of income in a number of countries undertaken for the Commission by Dr T Stark[2], the solution adopted was to examine the coverage of the various data sources and to compare the inequality in each country with that in Britain, using the most comparable distributions. The comparisons of higher incomes from employment in our Report No 3 were derived from data collected in a number of countries on a consistent basis by a firm of management consultants. In those two earlier studies, the areas of concern were different from those in the present Report: Stark's study covered income from all sources; the Report No 3 comparisons were restricted to income from employment but were further restricted to cover earnings of managers only. They are of limited value, therefore, for our present purposes, but we draw on them where appropriate.

---

[1] For self-employment income, all dates quoted in this Report relate to financial years when the self-employment income concerned was assessed for tax and *not* to the period when that income was earned.

[2] Background paper No 4: *The distribution of income in eight countries*, T Stark, HMSO, 1977.

4.25 A special study of the importance of self-employment income and comparisons of the characteristics of the income distributions of the self-employed in a number of different countries was carried out for us by Dr T. Stark. We present the results of this study in Chapter 13. We also draw on the results of a new research project on industrial earnings in a number of European countries carried out by Professor Saunders and Mr David Marsden at the Sussex European Research Centre, University of Sussex. A paper[1] setting out some preliminary results of this project has been prepared for the Commission by the researchers and is being published as a background paper to this report.

4.26 This project covered industrial earnings in Britain and in five other European countries: West Germany, the Netherlands, France, Italy and Belgium. The main data source, the EEC's "Structure of Earnings in Industry" survey for 1972 (SEI) provided figures on a reasonably comparable basis for the 5 continental countries; the British NES figures were adjusted to conform as closely as possible with SEI coverage. Inevitably, however, a number of problems of comparability remain between all the countries but, most markedly, between Britain and the rest. These are set out in the background paper and are referred to in the present report only where they are of special relevance to particular findings.

4.27 Most of the analysis is restricted to 1972 but some partial information on changes since 1972 is presented. The industrial coverage corresponds approximately to the index of production industries in Britain.

Proportion of the Employed Population employed in Industry in 1975

	West Germany	France	Italy	Netherlands	Belgium	UK
Males ..	58	52	56	48	54	55
Females ..	35	29	41	18	33	28
Total ..	50	43	52	41	47	44

Source: Labour Force Survey, Eurostat, 1976.

4.28 The proportions of all employees employed in industry varied from 52 per cent in Italy to 41 per cent in the Netherlands. There was much greater variation between countries in the proportions of females than of males, suggesting that the distribution of industrial earnings would be closer to the overall distribution for men than for women. This was not the case, however, in Britain in 1978 as Table 4.2 demonstrates. For all groups there were significant differences between the earnings distributions of those employed in industry ("All index of production industries" in the table) and of all employees ("All industries and services"): the dispersion of industrial earnings was narrower for all groups and, apart from non-manual women, the median earnings in industry were higher than in all industries and services. There are no comparable overall figures for the other countries included in the comparisons in the background

---

[1] Background paper No 8: *A six country comparison of the distribution of industrial earnings in the 1970s*, C T Saunders and D Marsden.

paper but it is pointed out that an EEC survey of earnings in the distribution and finance sectors (1974) also shows for most countries a wider dispersion than that in industry.

Table 4.2   Dispersion of Gross Weekly Earnings of Full-time Men and Women; 1978[1]

Great Britain

	Median	As percentages of their respective medians				
		Lowest decile	Lower quartile	Median	Upper quartile	Highest decile
Manual men	£pw	%	%	%	%	%
All industries and services ..	76·8	69·5	82·4	100·0	121·2	146·1
All index of production industries	80·3	71·7	83·7	100·0	119·9	143·6
Non-manual men						
All industries and services ..	91·8	62·9	78·4	100·0	127·9	163·8
All index of production industries	93·0	67·4	81·2	100·0	126·8	162·2
Manual women						
All industries and services ..	47·6	70·8	83·2	100·0	119·7	141·0
All index of production industries	49·5	72·1	84·8	100·0	118·0	138·0
Non-manual women						
All industries and services ..	53·9	68·8	82·0	100·0	127·5	164·7
All index of production industries	52·3	74·4	86·4	100·0	117·6	139·8

Source: NES 1978.
Note: [1] Unaffected by absence.

4.29   The paper examines the trends in average industrial earnings over the period from 1967 to 1977 and notes that all countries experienced an acceleration of pay increases around 1970 and continued to have large increases throughout the 1970s. In 1972, the overall dispersion of industrial earnings was wider in Britain than in most of the other countries; it was narrowest in West Germany. This was also true of the dispersions within each of the four groups described as labour markets: manual men, non-manual men, manual women and non-manual women; and within more narrowly defined occupational groups. On the other hand, the differences between these groups in average earnings were in general less in Britain than in most of the other countries; in Germany, however, the occupational differences were similar to those in Britain. The difference in earnings between men and women was greater in Britain than it was in the other countries in 1972 (the only year for which a full comparison is possible). And even by 1978 the British difference was still greater than it was in other countries in 1972. The background paper concludes with a tentative assessment of the relative importance of factors such as age, length of service, occupation, industry of employment etc on the earnings distribution. We draw attention to the most relevant results of this work in later chapters.

Summary

4.30   The two main data sources used in this report are the New Earnings Survey (NES) and the Survey of Personal Incomes (SPI). The SPI has been supplemented by a special survey of the incomes of close company directors in 1974–75. A number of other sources are also used including the Population Census and the Family Expenditure Survey.

4.31   The NES is a large annual survey (the sample consists of 1 per cent of the population in employment) which collects information on earnings and a wide range of other employment related variables. A large proportion of the same individuals is included in the sample from year to year making analyses on a matched sample basis possible. The survey is of course restricted in coverage to income from employment.

4.32   The SPI is also a large annual survey but it is drawn from the administrative records held by the Inland Revenue. It covers all personal income reviewed for income tax purposes. A large variety of analyses of the data are possible. The most important ones used in this report show separately the incomes of main source Schedule D and Schedule E tax payers and breakdown the distribution of self-employment income over a number of trade groups. The supplementary survey of the incomes of close company directors is used to adjust the SPI distribution to combine this group with the self-employed.

4.33   For international comparisons of earnings we draw on Background Paper No 8 which presents a six country comparison of the distribution of industrial earnings in the 1970s prepared for us by Professor C T Saunders and Mr David Marsden. In Chapter 13 we present the results of a special study carried out by Dr T Stark of income distributions of the self-employed in a number of different countries.

PART II

CHAPTER 5

Differences in Earnings between Occupations and between Industries

Introduction

5.1   That earnings depend on occupation few would deny. The main purpose of this chapter is to measure the extent of the dependence or, putting it another way, to establish how much of the dispersion of earnings can be explained by differences in earnings between occupations. The answer will vary according to the fineness of the grid by which occupations are classified: we take for this purpose the classification into 441 occupations used by the New Earnings Survey (NES). As will be seen, the amount of dispersion explained is not very great, even using this fine classification, especially for manual workers; and international comparisons will be quoted to support the view that occupation is a less important factor in this country than in some other European countries.

5.2   Having examined 'occupation', we make a similar analysis of 'industry' as an explanatory factor. Here we restrict our analysis to the 27 industry orders of the Standard Industrial Classification (SIC) and, not surprisingly, we find that differences between industries explain even less of the dispersion of earnings than differences between occupations. The two factors are not, of course, entirely independent, and we briefly investigate the combined effect of occupation *and* industry.

5.3   In this Chapter the results are presented in quite general terms. In Chapter 7 we give some illustrations to show how earnings can vary within a particular occupation and thus account for that large part of the dispersion of earnings that is not attributable to differences between occupations.

The overall dispersion of earnings

5.4   There are significant differences in the dispersion of earnings for men and for women, and again for manual and for non-manual employees. We therefore take as our starting point the separate dispersions for all men and for all women in 1978; and break each of these down further into its manual and non-manual components. Table 5.1 illustrates the dispersions in terms of quantile points, and also gives the quantile points expressed as percentages of the median for each of these six distributions separately (all men, all women, and non-manual and manual for each sex). It shows the wide spread of earnings for all groups; for example, a male manual worker at the highest decile point earns £111 per week (147 per cent of the median) while a man at the lowest decile point earns £51 per week (68 per cent of the median). The dispersions are even wider for non-manual employees, particularly non-manual men; a man at the highest decile point earns 165 per cent of the median compared with the man at the lowest decile point who earns 60 per cent. The dispersion of women's earnings is in each case less than that of men's.

5.5 The differences between manual and non-manual employees, and between men and women, are borne out by comparing the Gini coefficients of the various distributions (see bottom line of the Table). The Gini coefficient is a useful summary measure of dispersion that we have used in previous reports. From it

Table 5.1 Dispersion of Earnings for All Men, Manual Men, Non-manual Men, All Women, Manual Women and Non-manual Women; 1978

Great Britain

Quantile group (men)	All men		Manual men		Non-manual men	
	% of median	£pw	% of median	£pw	% of median	£pw
Lowest decile	64·6	52·0	67·6	51·0	60·2	54·3
Lower quartile	79·5	64·0	81·5	61·5	77·2	69·6
Median	100·0	80·4	100·0	75·4	100·0	90·1
Upper quartile	125·6	101·1	121·8	91·9	128·9	116·2
Highest decile	158·8	127·8	147·2	111·0	165·0	148·8
Highest percentile	270·4	217·8	213·5	161·0	286·1	257·8
Mean £pw		87·1		79·1		98·5
Gini coefficient %	20·9		17·5		23·1	

Quantile group (women)	All women		Manual women		Non-manual women	
	% of median	£pw	% of median	£pw	% of median	£pw
Lowest decile	69·1	35·8	70·8	33·7	68·8	37·1
Lower quartile	82·2	42·6	83·2	39·6	81·9	44·2
Median	100·0	51·8	100·0	47·6	100·0	53·9
Upper quartile	125·3	65·0	119·6	57·0	127·4	68·7
Highest decile	161·4	83·6	140·9	67·1	164·7	88·8
Highest percentile	242·0	125·4	196·3	93·5	241·4	130·2
Mean £pw		56·4		49·4		59·1
Gini coefficient %	19·3		15·8		19·7	

Source: 1978 New Earnings Survey.
Note: Table refers to full-time employees aged over 18 whose pay was unaffected by absence in the survey pay period.

can easily be derived[1] an estimate of the expected difference in earnings between any two individuals in the population: for example, if two men are taken at random the expected difference between their weekly earnings will be £36. We return to this example later to consider by how much the expected difference is reduced if we are told that the two men have the same occupation. Useful though the Gini coefficient is in illustrating the differences between distributions,

---

[1] The Gini coefficient is equal to one half of the average of the differences (taken positively) between the earnings of any two employees in the distribution, divided by the average earnings. Therefore the expected difference = 2 × mean earnings × Gini. For the all-men distribution in Table 5.1, this = 2 × £87·1 × 0·209 = £36·4.

it is not convenient when it is a question of determining the contribution of component factors such as occupation to the overall spread of a distribution. For the main part of our analysis, we turn therefore to another measure of dispersion—the variance[1]. Discussion of the technical statistical issues will be found in Appendix E.

5.6   We start by estimating for each of the six distributions in Table 5.1 the overall variance in earnings. Next we set up hypothetical 'between-occupations' distributions where each person is represented not by his actual earnings but by the mean earnings of his occupation: eg all male bricklayers are assumed to have earnings of £77.04 per week and all female telephonists are assumed to have earnings of £49.70 per week. The variance of this distribution can be taken as the 'between-occupations' component in each of the six cases. The difference between this and the overall variance must be due to the differences in earnings within each occupation—the 'within-occupations' component.

5.7   The method of calculating variances, which is described in Appendix E, is an approximate one. For this reason it is desirable to have some check on the results, and a convenient way of doing this is to estimate the 'within-occupations' variance directly. For this purpose we set up another hypothetical distribution, this time assuming that all occupations have the same median earnings ($=100$) and that any variance arose from the dispersion around the median within each occupation. Taken together, the directly calculated 'between-occupations' and 'within-occupations' variances should add up to 100%; any difference will illustrate the margin of error in the method. In presenting the results in this chapter the numbers have been rounded to the nearest 5 per cent: the unrounded figures are given in Appendix E.

Occupation and earnings

5.8   The results are shown in Table 5.2.

Table 5.2   Components of Variance in Earnings Attributable to Differences Between Occupations and Differences Within Occupations; 1978

Great Britain   Percentages

	Between-occupations component	Within-occupation component	
		Residual derived from (1)	Directly estimated
	(1)	(2)	(3)
Men			
All men	35	65	65
Manual	15	85	—
Non-manual ..	40	60	—
Women			
All women ..	55	45	45
Manual	15	85	—
Non-manual ..	50	50	—

Source: NES 1978.
Note: Method of calculation of components is described in Appendix E. Figures rounded to the nearest 5 per cent.

[1] This is found by squaring the difference for each individual between his earnings and average earnings, summing these over all individuals and taking the mean. Its major advantage in the present context is that it can be conveniently decomposed to measure the relative contribution to the overall dispersion of particular sources of variation.

63

It can be seen that earnings differences between occupations explain a greater proportion of the variance for women (55 per cent) than for men (35 per cent). It is worth recalling from Table 5.1, however, that the spread of earnings, and therefore the amount of overall variance, is greater for men than for women. The between-occupations effect includes the effect of differences in earnings between manual and non-manual employees, and we have already seen that non-manual employees' earnings are more dispersed than manual employees'; when manual men and non-manual men are considered separately, 40 per cent of the variance in non-manual men's earnings can be attributed to differences between occupations but only 15 per cent of the variance in manual men's earnings. This leaves 60 per cent of the variance for non-manual men, and no less than 85 per cent of the variance for manual men, to be explained by differences in earnings within individual occupations. Similar findings apply to non-manual and manual women. The greater dispersion in non-manual earnings, therefore, can be attributed in part to greater differences between occupations in this category.

5.9   The alternative approach of measuring directly the proportion of the variance attributable to differences within occupations produced estimates of 66 per cent of the overall variance for men and 46 per cent for women, compared with 63 per cent and 47 per cent, respectively, derived from the estimate of the between-occupations effect. This confirms the general order of magnitude of the estimates. The small differences due to the method of calculation used do not show up in the rounded figures given in Table 5.2.

5.10   It can be seen therefore that much less than half of the dispersion of men's earnings, measured in terms of the variance, can be accounted for by occupation, and just about half in the case of women. For both sexes most of the explanation lies in the non-manual sector: if we are considering manual workers separately (male or female), occupation counts for very little. The weakness of the correlation overall can be seen in a different way by reverting to our example of the expected difference between the weekly earnings of two men, if they were taken at random from the distribution. In paragraph 5.5 we saw that the difference was £36. It can now be estimated that if we know they have the same occupation, the expected difference is reduced to £33. Between two women, the expected difference initially is £22; and with the added information that they have the same occupation the expected difference is reduced to £18. These not very striking reductions illustrate that when as much as 35 per cent and 55 per cent of the variance for men and women, respectively, is removed from the distribution very substantial differences between individuals remain.

Industry and earnings

5.11   We carried out a similar analysis to establish the proportion of the variance attributable to differences in earnings between the 27 industry orders of the SIC. The results are given in Table 5.3. Compared with occupation, for all groups, industry is a much less important factor. Only 5 per cent of the variance in men's earnings can be attributed to differences in earnings between industries compared with 35 per cent for differences between occupations. It is noteworthy that both the 'occupation' effect and the 'industry' effect are higher for women than for men. When manual and non-manual employees are considered separately, the pattern is somewhat different for women than for men but the proportions are still low all round.

Table 5.3   Components of Variance in Earnings Attributable to Differences Between Industries and Differences Within Industries; 1978

Great Britain   Percentages

	Between-industries component	Within-industry component	
		Residual derived from (1)	Directly esitmated
	(1)	(2)	(3)
Men			
All men	5	95	90
Manual	10	90	—
Non-manual ..	5	95	—
Women			
All women ..	20	80	75
Manual	10	90	—
Non-manual ..	10	90	—

Source: NES 1978.

Note: Method of calculating components is described in Appendix E. Figures rounded to the nearest 5 per cent.

5.12   Again we checked the method by making a direct estimate of the within-industry effect. The resulting figures—92 per cent for men and 74 per cent for women compared with 95 per cent and 82 per cent, respectively, derived as residuals from the between-industries figures—show that the approximation error is larger than for the occupational estimates but the estimates are sufficiently good to give reasonable confidence in the method.

5.13   As a final step in the analysis we calculated how much of the variance could be explained by occupation and industry combined. Special NES tabulations provided by the Department of Employment gave the mean earnings of each occupation by industry, for men and women separately. This information (which is of course voluminous) is not published in the normal series of reports on the NES. In some cases where an occupation is virtually confined to one industry (coal miners in 'mining and quarrying', train drivers in 'transport and communication') the combination of the two factors adds no new information: but these are the exceptions. Generally one would expect the combination of the two factors to be more powerful than either factor by itself. It turns out (see Table 5.4) that for women's earnings considerably more of the overall variance is explained. For men occupation-and-industry does not explain much more than occupation by itself. This is hardly surprising: for manuals, neither effect by itself is strong; and, for non-manuals, the occupation effect is strong and the industry effect negligible. A deeper analysis treating non-manual and manual employees separately might throw more light on the question but the data did not permit this.

Table 5.4 Components of Variance in Earnings Attributable to Occupation and Industry; 1978

Great Britain   Percentages

	Men	Women
	%	%
Occupation effect	35	55
Industry effect	5	20
Occupation-and-industry effect	45	70

Source: NES 1978.

Note: Method of calculating components is described in Appendix E. Figures rounded to the nearest 5 per cent.

Other factors

5.14 Our analysis is restricted to gross weekly earnings of full-time workers aged over 18 whose pay in the survey period was not affected by absence. This being so, the validity of our findings is unaffected by differences in part-time working between occupations and industries. However, part of the variance could be attributed to short-term fluctuations in weekly earnings. The size of this effect varies by occupation and industry; furthermore it tends to be greater for manual men, particularly the less skilled and less well paid, than for other groups. The effects of short term fluctuations in earnings, therefore, will be felt in both the between-occupation and within-occupation components of the variance and likewise for industry.

5.15 Part of the variance in earnings can be attributed to differences in age and hours worked. The nature of our data precluded the inclusion of such factors in one multivariate analysis but we discuss these influences on earnings separately in Chapters 8 and 9. Length of service is another factor, akin to age, which could be considered separately, although we have not done so.

5.16 What we have identified as 'occupation' and 'industry' may to some extent be proxies for underlying factors such as collective agreements and government legislation. Were we able to include these latter factors in our analysis, it is possible that the significance of occupation and industry would be reduced at least for manual workers and lower paid non-manual workers. Nevertheless, our evidence suggests that 'occupation' would still remain a significant factor in explaining the dispersion of earnings in that part of the labour force where the dispersion is the greatest: ie the higher paid non-manual sector.

5.17 As explained in Chapter 4, Saunders and Marsden have attempted to measure, for a number of European countries including Britain, the contribution to overall variation of a wide range of variables[1]. They found that age, region, establishment size and length of service, as well as occupation and industry, all made a contribution to the overall variance in earnings: the relative importance

---

[1] Background paper No 8.

66

of the various components differed between countries. Occupation was a much more important factor for non-manual employees than for manual employees in all countries. In general, occupation was a more important factor in France and Italy than in Britain.

Summary

5.18 Statistics derived from the NES show that in 1978 the earnings of all categories of employees were widely dispersed but that the degree of dispersion was greater for non-manual than manual employees, and somewhat greater for men than for women. Factors such as differences in age, length of service, and hours worked contribute to the overall dispersion in earnings, but we concentrate here on the effects of differences between occupations and between industries.

5.19 Occupational differences were found to be rather more important for women than for men, accounting for 55 per cent as opposed to 35 per cent of the overall variance, and much more important for non-manual employees than for manual employees. The greater dispersion in non-manual employees' earnings, therefore, can be attributed in part to greater differences in earnings between occupations. This latter finding is consistent with the results of a study of earnings in other countries published as a background paper.

5.20 Differences in earnings between industries are less significant than those between occupations. Industrial differences are largest for non-manual women and smallest for non-manual men. That part of the dispersion attributable to the combined effect of occupation and industry is, for men, not much greater than that attributable to occupation alone, but is considerably greater for women, amounting to 70 per cent of the total variance.

CHAPTER 6
Occupational Structure and Trends in Earnings

Introduction

6.1 In Chapter 5 above, we discussed the patterns of earnings for men and women in the four main labour markets in 1978, and the way in which these were affected by variations in occupation and industry. Now, instead of confining ourselves to looking at the current position (1978), we turn to changes over time in earnings, and occupational and industrial structure.

Trends in the overall distribution of earnings

6.2 All four Commission reports to date on the standing reference have carried tables showing trends in the distribution of earnings. A feature of the trends was the overall stability in the shape of the distribution while earnings at all levels grew in real and money terms. The changes which have occurred in the fortunes of individuals or particular groups of employees are masked in the overall distribution and the only trend to emerge has been a gradual decline in the earnings of the highest groups relative to those in the middle and lower half of the distribution. Table 6.1 below shows that the most marked change in dispersion over the period 1970 to 1978 was the decline in the top decile, and even more the top percentile, relative to the median for all groups except manual men. The distribution for manual men showed relatively little change over the period. This remarkable stability over the period 1970 to 1978 may be seen as the continuation of much longer term stability. Table 6.2 shows that the spread of earnings of manual men was not very different in 1978 from what it was in 1886 and that this pattern held for most of the years in between for which there are figures.

6.3 There are no consistent series of figures on earnings for the other groups over such a long period but the evidence from the *income* distributions presented in our previous reports suggests that, while there has been a significant trend towards equality over the long term, the changes have tended to be concentrated at the top of the distribution. How far trends in the income distribution reflect those in the earnings distribution is not known precisely but the evidence suggests a strong possibility of a relative decline in the earnings of higher paid non-manual employees. See, for example, Table 6.3 (taken from Report No 3) which shows that the decline of the highest percentile (and higher quantiles) relative to the median was continuous over the longer period 1959–60 to 1973–74. However, there was no significant fall in the highest decile, suggesting that the distribution below the top decile remained stable over this longer period.

Table 6.1 Dispersion of Earnings—New Earnings Survey; 1970 to 1978

Gross weekly earnings of full-time male employees aged 21 and over, and of full-time female employees aged 18 and over[1], whose pay for the survey pay-period was not affected by absence: median earnings, and deciles, quartiles and highest percentiles as precentages of the median; 1970 to 1978

Great Britain

	Median earnings	Lowest decile	Lower quartile	Median	Upper quartile	Highest decile	Highest percentile
	£ per week	%	%	%	%	%	%
Manual men							
1970	25·6	67·3	81·1	100·0	122·3	147·2	207·3
1971	28·1	68·2	81·8	100·0	122·1	146·5	209·5
1972	31·3	67·6	81·3	100·0	122·3	146·6	207·1
1973	36·6	67·3	81·4	100·0	121·6	145·3	206·7
1974	41·8	68·6	82·2	100·0	121·0	144·1	205·6
1975	53·2	69·2	82·8	100·0	121·3	144·4	208·1
1976	62·1	70·2	83·4	100·0	120·8	144·9	205·1
1977	68·2	70·6	83·1	100·0	120·3	144·4	207·4
1978	76·8	69·4	82·4	100·0	121·2	146·0	211·7
Non-manual men							
1970	31·4	61·8	77·1	100·0	130·8	175·1	349·6
1971	34·4	61·7	76·5	100·0	131·2	174·4	349·1
1972	38·5	61·7	76·8	100·0	131·3	173·7	340·4
1973	42·8	61·6	76·7	100·0	130·9	172·7	336·5
1974	48·5	62·9	77·6	100·0	130·2	171·6	327·1
1975	61·8	62·6	77·5	100·0	129·6	166·7	297·5
1976	73·9	62·5	77·8	100·0	130·5	167·5	291·9
1977	81·1	63·6	78·4	100·0	128·8	164·5	283·9
1978	91·8	62·9	78·4	100·0	127·9	163·9	283.5
All men							
1970	27·2	65·4	79·7	100·0	126·7	160·6	303·5
1971	29·8	66·1	80·3	100·0	126·5	160·7	298·8
1972	33·4	65·5	79·7	100·0	126·4	160·9	292·7
1973	38·4	65·6	79·9	100·0	125·3	158·5	286·4
1974	43·8	66·8	80·7	100·0	124·6	157·0	279·6
1975	55·9	67·0	81·0	100·0	125·3	157·6	264·4
1976	65·8	67·6	81·3	100·0	125·6	159·5	265·5
1977	72·3	68·1	81·4	100·0	125·1	157·7	264·1
1978	82·0	66·8	80·6	100·0	125·1	157·9	268·3
Manual women							
1970	12·8	69·0	83·0	100·0	120·1	144·8	214·0
1971	14·6	70·2	83·6	100·0	120·4	143·0	211·9
1972	16·4	68·9	82·5	100·0	121·6	145·9	209·2
1973	18·9	69·2	82·8	100·0	121·4	144·4	208·0
1974	22·7	69·1	83·0	100·0	119·8	143·4	202·8
1975	31·0	68·4	83·3	100·0	119·6	141·4	200·4
1976	38·4	67·8	82·6	100·0	119·6	140·6	190·7
1977	42·6	70·3	83·3	100·0	118·3	137·8	188·8
1978	47·6	70·8	83·2	100·0	119·6	140·9	196·3
Non-manual women							
1970	15·9	64·2	78·3	100·0	129·4	173·7	294·9
1971	18·0	65·0	78·8	100·0	128·2	169·9	270·4
1972	20·1	64·0	78·2	100·0	129·1	170·9	276·9
1973	22·3	65·6	79·2	100·0	129·0	169·5	280·7
1974	26·1	66·5	79·4	100·0	127·9	162·0	270·3
1975	35·9	66·5	80·3	100·0	127·2	171·5	262·5
1976	44·2	65·1	79·9	100·0	128·6	172·9	264·6
1977	49·2	68·1	81·7	100·0	126·8	165·6	243·9
1978	53·9	68·8	81·9	100·0	127·4	164·7	241·4

Table 6.1 (*continued*) **Dispersion of Earnings—New Earnings Survey; 1970 to 1978**

Great Britain

	Median earnings	Lowest decile	Lower quartile	Median	Upper quartile	Highest decile	Highest percentile
	£ per week	%	%	%	%	%	%
All women							
1970	14·6	66·4	79·8	100·0	129·3	170·4	295·7
1971	16·6	66·6	80·2	100·0	127·3	165·8	272·5
1972	18·6	65·6	79·6	100·0	128·6	167·1	278·9
1973	20·9	67·4	80·7	100·0	127·6	164·7	276·9
1974	24·7	67·7	81·0	100·0	126·4	159·1	263·1
1975	34·1	67·4	81·5	100·0	125·2	164·5	264·1
1976	42·4	66·1	80·2	100·0	125·9	165·9	260·2
1977	46·9	68·6	82·1	100·0	124·7	162·1	245·9
1978	51·8	69·1	82·2	100·0	125·3	161·4	242·0

Source: NES 1978, Table 15 and Department of Employment.

Note: [1] Age was recorded as at 1 January from 1974; previously age was taken as at April.

6.4 Although the distribution of earnings around the average remained stable, the level of average earnings rose dramatically between the early 1960s and the late 1970s as the figures below demonstrate:

	1963	1971	1978
Index of Retail Prices	100	148	365
Index of Average Earnings (older series)	100	183	508
Index of Average Earnings in real terms	100	124	139

In this chapter we examine the contribution of changes in occupational and industrial structure to both the level and overall distribution of earnings.

Table 6.2 Dispersion of Earnings of Male Manual Workers from 1886

Earnings of full-time male manual employees reported in censuses of earnings: median earnings and deciles and quartiles as percentages of the median; at dates from 1886 to 1978

Great Britain

Year	Median earnings	Lowest decile	Lower quartile	Median	Upper quartile	Highest decile
	£ per week	%	%	%	%	%
1886	1·2	68·6	82·8	100·0	121·7	143·1
1906	1·5	66·5	79·5	100·0	126·7	156·8
1938	3·4	67·7	82·1	100·0	118·5	139·9
1960	14·2	70·6	82·6	100·0	121·7	145·2
1970	25·6	67·3	81·1	100·0	122·3	147·2
1978	76·8	69·4	82·4	100·0	121·2	146·0

Source: *British Labour Statistics Historical Abstract* (*1886–1968*) and NES.

Table 6.3 Quantiles of Employment Income before Tax; 1959–60 to 1973–74

PART A

Quantiles of employment income from one or more sources of males, females and all recipients in the United Kingdom in 1959–60 and in each of the tax years from 1964–65 to 1973–74 inclusive. (Part B: The quantiles expressed as a percentage of the median.)

United Kingdom

Income unit: persons

Quantile	1959–60	1964–65	1965–66	1966–67	1967–68	1968–69	1969–70[1]	1970–71[1]	1971–72[1]	1972–73	1973–74[1]
	£	£	£	£	£		£	£	£	£	£
Males											
Median	612	836	902	945	1,001	1,046	1,120	1,269	1,412	1,608	1,836
Highest decile	1,016	1,385	1,495	1,567	1,658	1,768	1,920	2,227	2,409	2,679	3,017
Highest percentile	2,345	3,196	3,370	3,500	3,647	3,829	4,093	4,713	5,041	5,665	6,192
Highest millile	5,854	7,671	7,874	7,998	8,406	8,955	8,887	9,621	10,802	12,590	13,598
Highest decimillile	13,134	16,416	16,177	16,316	16,435	17,982	17,670	17,305	19,658	24,072	25,925
Females											
Median	260	364	386	399	415	427	467	529	599	685	778
Highest decile	526	711	758	771	806	849	947	1,091	1,256	1,400	1,578
Highest percentile	1,036	1,450	1,589	1,611	1,670	1,777	1,875	2,069	2,305	2,472	2,741
Highest millile	1,826	2,745	2,921	3,064	3,167	3,452	3,423	3,511	3,821	4,192	5,104
Highest decimillile	3,424	5,280	5,476	5,368	6,172	7,104	6,673	6,182	7,294	8,405	9,180
All recipients											
Median	485	671	721	748	788	824	876	967	1,076	1,257	1,421
Highest decile	922	1,265	1,369	1,425	1,513	1,605	1,739	1,974	2,160	2,414	2,711
Highest percentile	1,981	2,739	2,925	3,037	3,163	3,357	3,545	4,024	4,339	4,801	5,360
Highest millile	5,033	6,651	6,917	6,928	7,305	7,725	7,785	8,545	9,388	11,026	11,757
Highest decimillile	11,526	14,543	14,490	14,535	14,624	16,128	15,794	15,721	17,843	21,208	22,996

(Tax year)

Table 6.3 (continued)   Quantiles of Employment Income before Tax; 1959–60 to 1973–74

PART B
The quantiles as percentages of the corresponding median

Percentages

Quantile		Tax year										
		1959–60	1964–65	1965–66	1966–67	1967–68	1968–69	1969–70[1]	1970–71[1]	1971–72[1]	1972–73	1973–74[1]
Males		%	%	%	%	%	%	%	%	%	%	%
Highest decile	::	166	166	166	166	166	169	171	175	171	167	164
Highest percentile	::	383	382	374	370	364	366	366	371	357	352	337
Highest millile	::	957	918	873	846	840	856	794	758	765	783	741
Highest decimillile	::	2,146	1,964	1,794	1,727	1,642	1,719	1,578	1,364	1,392	1,497	1,412
Females												
Highest decile	::	202	195	196	193	194	199	203	206	210	204	203
Highest percentile	::	398	398	412	404	402	416	401	391	385	361	352
Highest millile	::	702	754	757	768	763	808	733	664	638	612	656
Highest decimillile	::	1,317	1,451	1,419	1,345	1,487	1,664	1,429	1,169	1,218	1,227	1,180
All recipients												
Highest decile	::	190	189	190	191	192	195	199	204	201	192	191
Highest percentile	::	408	408	406	406	401	407	405	416	403	382	377
Highest millile	::	1,038	991	959	926	927	938	889	884	872	877	827
Highest decimillile	::	2,376	2,167	2,010	1,943	1,856	1,957	1,803	1,626	1,658	1,687	1,618

Source: SPI.

Note:[1] The definition of tax deduction card employment income differed in 1969–70, 1970–71, 1971–72 and 1973–74 from the other years.

Occupational structure of employed population

6.5 The Census of Population is the main source of data on changes in the occupational structure. However, differences between the occupational classification systems between Censuses create difficulties in direct comparisons over time. A similar difficulty arises with the NES, the main source of data on recent trends in earnings by occupation; the classification system was changed for 1973 and subsequent surveys. In order to facilitate comparisons over time we have reclassified the Census data for 1961 and 1971 and the NES data for 1971 and 1978 into the broad occupational classes adopted by G Routh in his study of occupation and pay between 1906 and 1960[1] (see paragraph 2.21).

6.6 The NES provides detailed analyses of earnings by occupation for each year from 1970 to 1978. For the 1970, 1971 and 1972 surveys the occupational classification can be used to allocate, with considerable confidence, the individual occupations to Routh's occupational classes. In the classification system used in the 1973 and subsequent surveys, the status of an occupation, particularly among manual groups, is not clearly defined and the task of allocating individual occupations to the broader classes was much more difficult. Appendix F describes the two NES occupational classification systems and indicates the occupational class to which each individual occupation was allocated.

6.7 As noted above, the most satisfactory sources of data on changes in occupational structure were the population censuses. They are more suitable, however, for showing longer term changes than more recent trends and the latest Census was of course in 1971. To compare changes between 1971 and 1978, therefore, the sample numbers of those employed in each occupational class given in the NES, rather than the population figures of the Census were used. The NES is not an ideal source for measuring changes in occupational structure generally, but in the context of analyses of earnings data from the survey, the occupational structure implied by the NES sample is wholly appropriate. In order to set the more recent changes in the context of longer term changes, the occupational structures in 1961 and 1971 were also compared using Census data. The results of both sets of comparisons, 1961 with 1971 and 1971 with 1978, are shown in Table 6.4. Appendix G gives lists of the Census occupations which were allocated to each of the broader occupational classes.

6.8 Both the Census and the NES refer to full-time employees but there are some differences in coverage and bases:

 i the Census estimates cover all full-time employees; the NES figures are restricted to employees whose pay in the survey week was unaffected by absence;

 ii in the NES employers allocate employees in the sample to particular occupations. The Census is self-classificatory resulting perhaps in some bias in the results towards higher paid occupations; and

 iii the occupational classification systems are different.

---

[1] G Routh *Occupation and pay in Britain 1906–1960*, CUP, 1965

As a result the two sets of figures in Table 6.4 for 1971 differ significantly but the comparisons between 1961 and 1971 and between 1971 and 1978 are on internally consistent bases. Comparisons between 1961 and 1978 are not strictly valid. However, an estimate of the actual numbers in 1978 for each occupational class, derived by grossing up the numbers in the 1971 Census by the rates of growth implied by the NES, is given in Table 2.7 of Chapter 2 (right hand columns).

Table 6.4   Changes in Numbers in Occupational Classes in Britain; 1961 to 1971 and 1971 to 1978

Changes in Census numbers between 1961 and 1971

Great Britain

Occupational class	1961		1971	
	Nos '000	As percentage of total	Nos '000	As percentage of total
Men				
1A Higher professional	494	3·5	603	4·6
1B Lower professional ..	636	4·5	853	6·5
2B Managers and administrators	1,386	9·8	1,710	13·0
3 Clerks	1,049	7·4	890	6·7
4 Foremen	726	5·1	772	5·9
5 Skilled manual	5,095	35·9	4,303	32·6
6 Semi-skilled manual	3,501	24·7	3,046	23·1
7 Unskilled manual ..	1,284	9·1	998	7·6
Total	14,171	100·0	13,175	100·0
Women				
1A Higher professional	37	0·7	45	0·8
1B Lower professional ..	557	10·4	705	12·9
2B Managers and administrators	248	4·6	273	5·0
3 Clerks	1,666	31·1	1,875	34·1
4 Foremen	122	2·3	150	2·7
5 Skilled manual	663	12·4	532	9·7
6 Semi-skilled manual	1,894	35·3	1,778	32·4
7 Unskilled manual ..	169	3·2	134	2·4
Total	5,356	100·0	5,492	100·0

Source: Census.

Table 6.4 (contd)   Changes in Numbers in Occupational Classes in Britain; 1961 to 1971 and 1971 to 1978

Changes in NES sample numbers between 1971 and 1978

Great Britain

Occupational class	1971		1978	
	No in sample	As percentage of total	No in sample	As percentage of total
Men				
1A Higher professional	4,858	5·4	4,992	5·9
1B Lower professional ..	7,863	8·8	8,862	10·5
2B Managers and administrators	8,734	9·8	12,658	15·1
3 Clerks	6,875	7·7	5,163	6·1
4 Foremen	5,794	6·5	7,372	8·8
5 Skilled manual	24,101	26·9	22,827	27·1
6 Semi-skilled manual	23,138	25·8	16,957	20·2
7 Unskilled manual	8,147	9·1	5,314	6·3
Total	89,510	100·0	84,145	100·0
Women				
1A Higher professional	177	0·5	339	0·9
1B Lower professional ..	6,002	16·7	6,759	18·3
2B Managers and administrators	668	1·9	1,951	5·3
3 Clerks	13,962	38·9	14,402	38·9
4 Foremen	1,035	2·9	2,127	5·7
5 Skilled manual	2,247	6·3	2,578	7·0
6 Semi-skilled manual	7,907	22·0	7,979	21·5
7 Unskilled manual	3,865	10·8	895	2·4
Total	35,863	100·0	37,030	100·0

Source: NES.

6.9   Between 1961 and 1971, there was an increase in the proportions of the employed population in the higher paid classes and a fall in the proportions in manual occupations. The total number of managers and administrators increased over the 10 year period from 1.6 to 2·0 million, but the number of women in this class rose very slightly from 0·25 to 0·27 million. Also in the higher professional class, the total number increased over the 10 years from 0·53 to 0·65 million but the number of women in this case increased by only 8,000. There was substantial movement of women into the other non-manual classes, most notably into clerical occupations.

6.10   Between 1971 and 1978, the figures from the NES show that for men there is again a trend of rising proportions in higher paid classes and a fall in proportions in the manual classes. The most noticeable changes are the increases in the numbers of managers and administrators and foremen while the numbers of manual workers declined. However, a change in the NES sampling system in 1975 results in a slight overstatement of the increase in the numbers of managers and administrators. For women the trends are more marked but in a similar direction. The large increases in the proportions of women managers and administrators and higher professionals contrast with the small movement of women into these classes between 1961 and 1971. The large drop in the number of unskilled female workers may reflect the fact that a growing proportion of such jobs are now filled by part-time employees.

6.11 From the NES data for 1971 and 1978 average earnings figures were derived for each occupational group and these are compared in Table 6.5. As noted in Chapter 4, the first NES was in 1968 and there are no comparable figures in similar detail for 1961. The Inland Revenue's Survey of Personal Incomes (SPI) produces information on the distribution of earnings recorded on tax deduction cards. The surveys for 1959–60 and 1962–63 are the closest we can get to earnings in 1961, there having been no survey in the intervening years. The estimate below for 1961 was derived by interpolating between these two surveys after adjusting the figures to exclude part-year and part-time earnings. As a check on this methodology a comparison was made for three years where information is available from both the NES and SPI. As Table 6.6 shows there is considerable consistency for male average earnings, less so for average earnings of women, where the SPI figures, although for a slightly later period, are lower. Average earnings for the three years 1961, 1971 and 1978 are as follows:

	1961	1971	1978
	£pa	£pa	£pa
Men	850	1,721	4,638
Women	450	952	2,933

The increases in earnings in real terms (ie after adjusting for the increases in prices) were:

	1961 to 1971	1971 to 1978
	%	%
Men	31	9
Women	35	25

6.12 If we assume that average earnings for each occupation would have been the same irrespective of the occupational structure of employment then it is possible to estimate the effect that changes in occupational structure had on the overall level of earnings. This, however, is a purely statistical exercise and does not take account of any possible causal relationship between structural changes and earnings differences through the working of the labour market.

6.13 The overall average earnings figures in Table 6.5 have been reworked on the assumption that the numbers in each class did not change between 1971 and 1978 and these are included in the last line of Table 6.5 (average based on 1971 weights). The actual mean earnings for 1978 for both men and women were higher than the mean earnings for 1978 with 1971 weights.

6.14 A similar comparison was made between actual mean earnings in 1971, this time using the numbers in each occupational class given in the 1971 Census as weights and what these earnings would have been if the occupational structure had remained as it was in 1961. Again the actual mean earnings in 1971 were higher for both men and women than the mean earnings figures calculated with 1961 weights. It was not found possible to estimate directly the effect of changes in occupational structure over the whole period 1961 to 1978 since the structures implied by the NES and Census are not entirely consistent.

Table 6.5 Average Earnings for Eight Occupational Classes and Overall Averages on the Bases of Current and Constant Numbers in each Occupational Class; 1971 and 1978

Great Britain

	Men				Women			
			Change				Change	
	1971	1978			1971	1978		
	£	£	£	%	£	£	£	%
Non-manual								
1A Higher professional	2,408	6,046	3,638	151	2,049	4,743	2,694	131
1B Lower professional	2,023	5,259	3,236	160	1,300	3,764	2,464	190
2B Managers etc	2,480	5,774	3,294	133	1,394	3,745	2,351	169
3 Clerks	1,477	3,718	2,241	152	941	2,732	1,791	190
4 Foremen	1,856	4,714	2,858	154	1,165	3,169	2,004	172
Manual								
5 Skilled	1,648	4,350	2,702	164	827	2,550	1,723	208
6 Semi-skilled	1,446	4,006	2,560	177	764	2,435	1,671	219
7 Unskilled	1,331	3,636	2,305	173	733	2,356	1,623	221
Average based on NES weights								
Then current weights	1,721	4,638	2,917	169	952	2,933	1,981	208
1971 weights	1,721	4,481	2,760	160	952	2,829	1,877	197

Source: Derived from NES.

6.15   As the figures below show, the extent to which changes in occupational structure may have increased overall average earnings is small.

Percentage Increases in Real Average Earnings; 1961 to 1971 and 1971 to 1978

	1961 to 1971		1971 to 1978	
	Men	Women	Men	Women
	%	%	%	%
Percentage increase in real earnings	31	35	9	25
Percentage increase assuming no change in occupational structure	27	32	6	21
Difference	4	3	3	4

The first line shows the actual rise in earnings after adjusting for price changes. The second line shows what they would have been if the occupational structure had remained as it was in the earlier year and earnings in each occupation were as they were in the later year. The difference between these can be attributed to movement by the working population between occupations (or possibly to jobs being regraded).

6.16   From 1971 to 1978 the real growth in women's earnings was almost 3 times that of men's, possibly as a result of the implementation of the Equal Pay Act, and of this 16 per cent, on the assumptions outlined above, was the effect of structural changes. The real growth in men's earnings was relatively small but changes in structure accounted for one third of the growth. During both these periods, that is 1961 to 1971 and 1971 to 1978, nominal earnings increased rapidly. Carrying out the same analysis for nominal as for real earnings, the effect of structural change amounted to 5 per cent of the overall increase for both men and women, over each of the two periods.

Table 6.6   Average Annual Earnings of Men and Women; NES 1970 to 1972 and SPI 1970–71 to 1972–73

Great Britain NES
United Kingdom SPI

	1970/1970–71	1971/1971–72	1972/1972–73
	£ per annum	£ per annum	£ per annum
Men			
NES	1,564	1,716	1,914
SPI	1,594	1,723	1,963
Women			
NES	850	954	1,069
SPI	839	932	1,036

Source: SPI and NES.

6.17   To provide a longer time framework we make use of Routh's[1] estimates of earnings by occupational class, which go back to 1913. They are not directly

---

[1] G Routh, op cit.

78

comparable with later NES based estimates: specifically his earnings figures for Group 1A, "Higher professionals" relate to employees and self-employed and his estimates for Group 2B, "Managers and administrators etc" were derived from a variety of salary surveys, published rates etc. The coverage of these sources is unlikely to be consistent with the NES. In spite of these differences however his analysis provides a very useful historical background to the study of more recent trends in earnings.

Table 6.7   Average Earnings for Eight Occupational Classes and Overall Averages on the Bases of Current and Constant Numbers in each Occupational Class; 1961 and 1971

Great Britain

	Men		Women	
	1961	1971	1961	1971
	£	£	£	£
Professional				
1A Higher	—	2,408	—	2,049
1B Lower	—	2,023	—	1,300
2B Managers etc	—	2,480	—	1,394
3 Clerks	—	1,477	—	941
4 Foremen	—	1,856	—	1,165
Manual				
5 Skilled	—	1,648	—	827
6 Semi-skilled	—	1,446	—	764
7 Unskilled	—	1,331	—	733
Averages based on Census weights				
Then current weights	850	1,745	450	951
1961 weights	850	1,692	450	930

Source: 1961 average earnings derived from SPI, 1971 earnings figures for individual classes derived from NES, and weights derived from the 1961 and 1971 Censuses.

6.18   Dr Routh has provided us with an updated version of one of the more important tables in his book. It is reproduced as Table 6.8. This table takes the 1913 to 1960 analysis forward to 1978. A comparison of the 1978 figures in Tables 6.8 and 6.5 reveals, as expected, that the major differences are for Groups 1A and 2B. These arise from differences in coverage and definition. They do not affect the assessment of trends based on Table 6.8, which is reasonably consistent in coverage over time.

6.19   Average earnings increased over the period 1913–14 to 1960 by 802 per cent for men and 734 per cent for women. By comparing the differences in the current weighted averages and the 1911 weighted averages, Routh derived his estimate that, for both men and women, the move in numbers of employees from lower to higher classes accounted for 8 per cent of the total increase. This corresponds to the figure of 5 per cent derived in paragraph 6.16.

79

Great Britain

Table 6.8 Average Earnings for Eight Occupational Classes; 1913–14 to 1978

	1913–14 £	1922–24 £	1922–24 % of 1913–14	1935–36 £	1935–36 % of 1922–24	1955–56 £	1955–56 % of 1935–36	1960 £	1960 % of 1955–56	1970 £	1970 % of 1960	1978 £	1978 % of 1970	Multiple of 1913–14
Men														
1. Professional														
A. Higher	328	582	177	634	109	1,541	243	2,034	132	2,928	144	8,286	283	26
B. Lower	155	320	206	308	96	610	198	847	139	1,885	223	5,435	288	35
2B. Managers, etc.	200	480	240	440	92	1,480	336	1,850	125	3,400	184	8,050	237	40
3. Clerks	99	182	184	192	105	523	272	682	130	1,337	196	3,701	277	37
4. Foremen	123	268	218	273	102	784	287	1,015	129	1,669	164	4,685	280	38
Manual														
5. Skilled	106	180	171	195	108	622	319	796	128	1,440	181	4,354	302	41
6. Semi-skilled	69	126	183	134	106	469	350	581	124	1,289	222	3,827	297	55
7. Unskilled	63	128	203	129	101	435	337	535	123	1,154	216	3,390	294	54
Averages														
Current weights[1]	94	180	191	186	104	634	340	848[4]	134	1,707	201	4,786	280	51
1911 weights	94	177	188	185	104	590	319	746	126	1,445	194	4,241	293	45
Women														
1. Professional														
A. Higher	—	—	—	—	—	(1,080)	—	(1,425)	(138)	2,460	173	6,712	273	—
B. Lower	89[2]	214	240	211	99	438	208	606	138	1,224	202	3,892	318	44
2B. Managers etc.	(80)[2]	160	—	(168)	105	800	(524)	1,000	125	1,870	187	5,070	271	63
3. Clerks	45	106	235	99	93	317	320	427	135	839	196	2,730	325	61
4. Forewomen	57	154	270	156	101	477	306	602	126	1,014	168	3,214	317	56
Manual														
5. Skilled	44	87	198	86	99	317	369	395	125	677	171	2,246	332	51
6. Semi-skilled	50	98	196	100	102	269	270	339	126	645	190	2,356	365	47
7. Unskilled	28	73	261	73	100	227	280	283	125	610	215	2,275	373	81
Averages														
Current weights[1]	50	103	204	104	101	319	307	417[4]	131	824	198	2,691	327	54
1911 weights	50	103	205	104	101	307	295	402	131	731	182	2,516	344	50
Men and Women														
Current weighted average[3]	81	157	194	162	103	531	328	704	133	1,385	197	3,961	286	49

Source: Unpublished table prepared by Dr G Routh.
Notes: 1 According to number of men and women in relevant class in nearest population census year.
2 Included in weighted average. Their exclusion lowers the average fractionally.
3 According to proportions in occupational classes in nearest Census year until 1935–36; thereafter, proportion in total labour force.
4 Weights from G S Bain and R Price, *op. cit.*

Occupational structure and the dispersion of earnings

6.20 The NES provides estimates not only of average earnings by occupation but also of the distribution of earnings within each occupation. We have aggregated these to produce Table 6.9 which compares the earnings distributions of the various occupational classes in 1971 to 1978. Before examining these it should first be noted that there has been a decline over this period in the spread of average earnings between different occupational classes. This is shown by the fact that the earnings of lower paid groups (semi-skilled and unskilled manual workers) have increased faster than all the others, except women managers.

Percentage Change in Median Earnings; 1971 to 1978

	Men	Women
	%	%
Professional:		
Higher	161	146
Lower	170	202
Managers	150	226
Clerks	157	194
Foremen	152	183
Manual:		
Skilled	165	216
Semi-skilled	178	222
Unskilled	172	215

6.21 Earnings differences between occupations also narrowed considerably over the longer period covered by Table 6.8 but the trend of contracting earnings differences was not continuous as the following selected comparisons for men illustrate:

Average Male Earnings Expressed as a Percentage of Average Earnings of All Male Employees

	1913–14	1922–24	1935–36	1955–56	1960	1970	1978
	%	%	%	%	%	%	%
Unskilled manual	67	71	69	69	63	68	71
Skilled manual ..	113	100	105	98	94	84	91
Foremen..	131	149	147	124	120	98	98
Clerks ..	105	101	103	82	80	78	77
Managers	213	267	237	233	218	199	168
Higher profes-sional ..	349	323	341	243	240	172	173

There appear to have been some periods when earnings ratios were falling and others when they were increasing and, of course, some of the variations may be due to errors in the estimates. Nevertheless, over the whole period there was a substantial reduction in earnings ratios, most notably for higher professionals in relation to all other groups.

6.22 For the period 1971 to 1978 the reduction in differences in average earnings between occupational classes is accompanied by a reduction in the dispersion in the earnings of the more highly paid classes. The contraction is particularly marked at the top of the distribution and has contributed in part to the decline in average earnings differences.

Table 6.9 Dispersion of Earnings of Eight Occupational Classes and Overall Distribution on the Bases of Current and Constant Numbers in each Occupational Class; 1971 and 1978

Great Britain

Quantile points (£ per week)

	1971						1978					
	Lowest decile £pw	Lower quartile £pw	Median £pw	Upper quartile £pw	Highest decile £pw	Highest percentile £pw	Lowest decile £pw	Lower quartile £pw	Median £pw	Upper quartile £pw	Highest decile £pw	Highest percentile £pw
Men												
Professional:												
Higher ..	27.1	33.2	41.9	53.2	68.0	115.3	73.3	88.1	109.4	134.6	166.9	255.6
Lower ..	23.2	28.4	35.5	43.8	55.7	104.5	64.2	78.4	96.0	116.9	141.9	210.5
Managers ..	22.7	29.0	39.4	54.9	76.8	164.3	60.4	76.5	98.4	128.7	171.7	324.3
Clerks ..	18.7	22.1	26.3	32.5	40.2	59.0	50.4	57.8	67.6	80.9	97.2	139.7
Foremen ..	24.9	29.0	34.2	40.4	47.4	66.5	61.5	72.5	86.2	103.0	124.3	182.0
Manual:												
Skilled ..	21.4	25.1	30.0	36.2	43.4	62.5	56.8	66.5	79.4	95.3	144.3	167.6
Semi-skilled ..	18.2	21.5	26.4	32.2	38.7	53.7	50.4	59.6	73.3	89.3	107.4	154.1
Unskilled ..	17.1	19.8	24.2	29.6	35.9	50.5	47.3	54.8	65.9	80.6	97.2	142.5
All Groups												
Current weights ..	19.7	23.9	29.8	37.6	48.0	89.1	54.8	66.0	82.0	102.6	129.4	219.8
1971 NES weights ..	19.7	23.9	29.8	37.6	48.0	89.1	53.4	64.3	79.7	99.2	124.1	206.6
Women												
Professional:												
Higher ..	14.6	23.8	34.3	50.7	69.1	111.3	45.4	62.2	84.5	115.3	137.4	208.3
Lower ..	14.1	17.8	22.9	30.8	37.5	54.6	42.8	51.9	69.1	88.6	105.9	142.0
Managers ..	13.2	16.6	21.9	32.8	45.7	81.5	39.7	51.7	71.4	87.2	104.1	162.2
Clerks ..	12.1	14.3	17.3	20.9	25.0	35.1	37.3	43.5	50.9	59.8	69.0	94.2
Forewomen ..	13.9	16.6	20.7	26.6	33.4	44.2	41.5	48.8	58.5	70.6	85.2	108.7
Manual:												
Skilled ..	10.7	12.5	14.7	18.1	22.1	33.7	32.2	38.4	46.4	57.3	68.4	95.9
Semi-skilled ..	9.7	11.6	13.9	17.1	20.3	30.2	31.5	37.3	44.7	54.3	64.0	89.5
Unskilled ..	9.8	11.5	13.7	16.2	18.9	25.7	30.9	36.3	43.2	52.5	61.7	87.4
All Groups												
Current weights ..	11.0	13.3	16.6	21.1	27.5	45.1	35.8	42.6	51.8	65.0	83.6	125.0
1971 NES weights ..	11.0	13.3	16.6	21.1	27.5	45.1	35.0	41.6	50.5	62.3	79.2	120.5

Source: NES.

82

Table 6.9 (*continued*) **Dispersion of Earnings of Eight Occupational Classes and Overall Distribution on the Bases of Current and Constant Numbers in each Occupational Class; 1971 and 1978**

Great Britain

Quantile points as percentages of the median

	1971						1978					
	Lowest decile %	Lower quartile %	Median %	Upper quartile %	Highest decile %	Highest percentile %	Lowest decile %	Lower quartile %	Median %	Upper quartile %	Highest decile %	Highest percentile %
						Men						**Men**
Professional:												
Higher	64.7	79.4	100.0	127.0	162.4	275.5	67.0	80.5	100.0	123.1	152.6	233.7
Lower	65.4	80.2	100.0	123.7	157.0	294.7	66.8	81.7	100.0	121.7	147.7	219.2
Managers	57.7	73.5	100.0	139.4	195.2	417.2	61.4	77.8	100.0	130.8	174.5	329.6
Clerks	71.2	84.0	100.0	123.5	153.0	224.3	74.5	85.5	100.0	119.7	143.8	206.8
Foremen	72.6	84.6	100.0	117.9	138.5	194.1	71.4	84.1	100.0	119.6	144.3	211.3
Manual:												
Skilled	71.2	83.7	100.0	120.5	144.6	208.3	71.6	83.8	100.0	120.1	144.0	211.3
Semi-skilled	68.9	81.2	100.0	121.9	146.2	203.0	68.8	81.3	100.0	121.9	146.6	210.4
Unskilled	70.8	81.7	100.0	122.4	148.4	208.8	71.8	83.1	100.0	122.3	147.4	216.2
All Groups												
Current weights	66.0	80.3	100.0	126.1	161.0	298.5	66.8	80.6	100.0	125.2	157.9	268.2
1971 NES weights	66.0	80.3	100.0	126.1	161.0	298.5	67.0	80.7	100.0	124.4	155.7	259.1
						Women						**Women**
Professional:												
Higher	42.5	69.4	100.0	147.9	201.5	324.8	53.8	73.7	100.0	136.5	162.7	246.6
Lower	61.6	77.6	100.0	134.7	163.9	238.6	61.9	75.2	100.0	128.3	153.3	205.6
Managers	60.3	75.8	100.0	150.0	209.1	373.0	55.6	72.5	100.0	122.2	145.9	227.2
Clerks	69.8	82.7	100.0	120.9	144.1	202.9	73.3	85.5	100.0	117.6	135.5	185.2
Forewomen	67.3	80.4	100.0	128.7	161.5	213.6	70.9	83.4	100.0	120.8	145.7	185.9
Manual:												
Skilled	72.4	84.6	100.0	122.9	149.9	229.2	69.3	82.8	100.0	123.5	147.2	206.5
Semi-skilled	69.6	83.6	100.0	122.8	145.8	216.9	70.6	83.5	100.0	121.6	143.3	200.4
Unskilled	71.6	83.8	100.0	118.0	138.1	187.8	71.4	84.0	100.0	121.5	142.7	202.3
All Groups												
Current weights	66.7	80.2	100.0	127.2	166.0	272.4	69.0	82.1	100.0	125.3	161.2	241.2
1971 NES weights	66.7	80.2	100.0	127.2	166.0	272.4	69.3	82.2	100.0	123.3	156.7	238.5

Source: NES.

Note: The figures for all groups are not necessarily the weighted sum of the figures for the occupational classes. Those with current weights are taken directly from the NES distribution of earnings. Those with 1971 weights are derived by weighting together the range tables and then calculating the quantile shares.

6.23 The effect of changes in the occupational structure on the dispersion of earnings can be calculated in the same way as the effect on average earnings, with the same qualifications applying. The overall dispersion for 1978 has been calculated on the basis of the 1971 occupational structure (based on the NES figures) and, in the final two lines of each section of Table 6.9 is compared with the overall dispersion using the current structure. The 1978 dispersion of men's earnings calculated using 1971 weights has a slightly smaller interdecile range than the actual 1978 dispersion. There is little change in the lowest decile and quartile but the highest percentile, decile and upper quartile are all closer to the median. Thus, although the distribution for all men has become less unequal between 1971 and 1978, the effects of changes in the occupational structure were in the opposite direction. A similar pattern appears for women's earnings.

6.24 For years prior to 1968, the first year of the NES, there is no comprehensive set of data on the distribution of earnings by occupation. A different approach is, therefore, required for an assessment of the effect on the dispersion of occupational structure changes over the longer period from 1960 to 1971. The sparse and scattered evidence available on changes in the distribution of earnings from 1960 to 1971 suggests that there were no dramatic changes in dispersion over this period. Table 6.3 shows that the highest quantiles (ie those above the highest decile) moved gradually downwards but the highest decile may have moved slightly in the opposite direction in the later years of the period. This is probably only a temporary trend, however, since the highest decile seems to have reached a peak in 1971. Table 6.2 shows that the distribution of earnings for male manual workers changed little between 1960 and 1970 and Table 6.10, reproduced from Report No 1, reveals little change in the dispersion of the bottom half of the distribution between 1964/65 and 1972/73.

Table 6.10   Dispersion of Earnings—DHSS Statistics;
1964–65 to 1972–73

Annual earnings of men and women aged 18 and over in full or part-time employment through the year; median earnings, and deciles and quartiles as percentages of the median; 1964-65 to 1972-73

Great Britain

	Median earnings	Lowest decile	Lower quartile	Median	Upper quartile	Highest decile
	£ pa	%	%	%	%	%
Men						
1964–65	934	65·2	80·8	100·0	123·6	155·9
1968–69	1,198	64·3	80·2	100·0	125·0	159·1
1972–73	1,861	64·0	79·6	100·0	124·9	158·8
Women						
1964–65	466	55·7	76·5	100·0	131·6	177·8
1968–69	583	52·9	74·5	100·0	132·7	179·0
1972–73	907	53·4	73·1	100·0	134·4	178·3
Men and women						
1964–65	825	47·7	69·9	100·0	130·0	165·1
1968–69	1,034	45·3	68·0	100·0	132·3	168·8
1972–73	1,582	44·7	67·5	100·0	133·6	170·4

Source: derived from DHSS Statistics of Earnings.

6.25 In the absence of information on the spread of earnings within occupational groups for 1961 it was necessary to reweight the 1971 distribution with the 1961 Census figures for the numbers in each occupational group and again by the 1971 Census figures to provide a valid comparison. Table 6.11 compares the 1971 NES distribution weighted on two bases: with 1971 Census weights and with 1961 Census weights. Differences in general are small, especially at the lower end of the distribution, but the differences in the higher quantiles (closer to the median in the 1961 weighted distribution) suggest that over this period also the effect of change in occupational structure was to widen the dispersion.

Table 6.11   Dispersion of Earnings in 1971 and the Effect of the Change in Occupational Structure between 1961 and 1971

Great Britain

Quantile group	Men				Women			
	1971 (1971 weights)		1971 (1961 weights)		1971 (1971 weights)		1971 (1961 weights)	
	£ pw	Percentage of the median	£ pw	Percentage of the median	£ pw	Percentage of the median	£pw	Percentage of the median
Lowest decile	19·9	66·4	19·7	66·9	10·9	66·5	10·8	66·8
Lower quartile	24·2	80·4	23·8	80·9	13·2	80·1	13·0	80·5
Median ..	30·1	100·0	29·4	100·0	16·4	100·0	16·1	100·0
Upper quartile	37·9	126·1	36·9	125·3	20·9	127·2	20·4	126·6
Highest decile	48·7	162·0	46·7	158·5	27·4	166·9	26·5	164·4
Highest percentile ..	92·7	308·6	85·3	289·9	47·7	290·1	46·4	288·2
Gini coefficient % ..	22·0		21·1		21·8		21·4	

Sources: NES and Census.

6.26   The evidence, therefore, suggests that changes in occupational structure have tended to widen the dispersion of earnings. This may seem surprising given the apparent contraction in the differences in earnings between occupational classes. However, the summary figures below, and Figure 6.1, show that although the dispersion of earnings for the higher paid occupational classes has declined over time it is still greater than that for the lower paid occupational groups. Hence the movement from lower paid to higher paid occupations has widened the overall dispersion of earnings.

Industry structure

6.27   The changes in occupational structure are closely associated with changes in industry structure and, to complement the analysis of the effects of the former on the earnings distribution, a similar analysis was attempted for industry structure. Data from the NES for the industry groups of the Standard Industrial Classification (SIC) were used to compare the years 1971 and 1978. There are 27 industry groups in total, but from the published tables comprehensive data on earnings by industry group are available only for manual men. For non-manual

85

Figure 6.1   Dispersion within Occupational Groups; 1971 and 1978

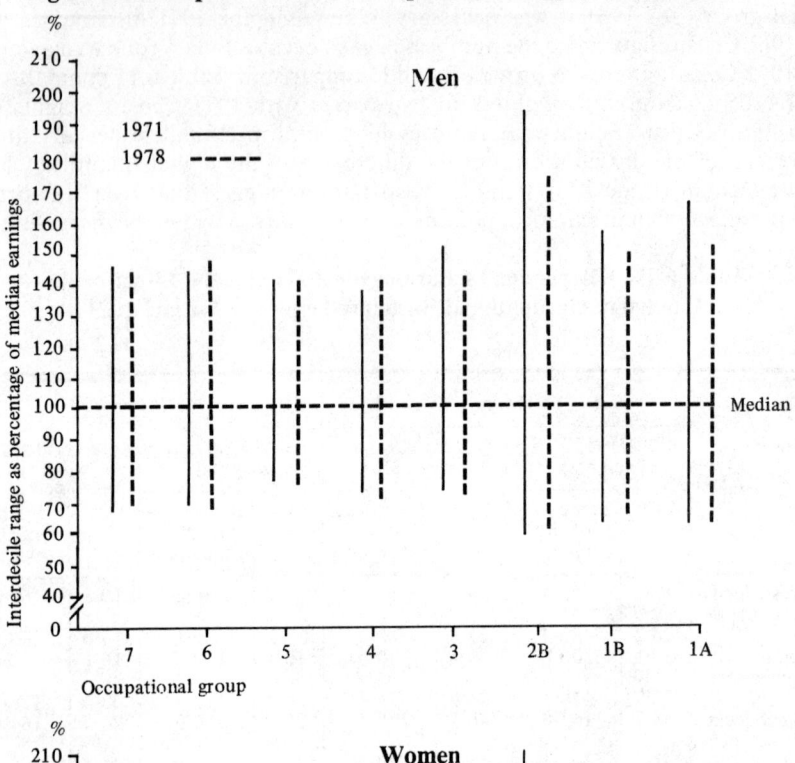

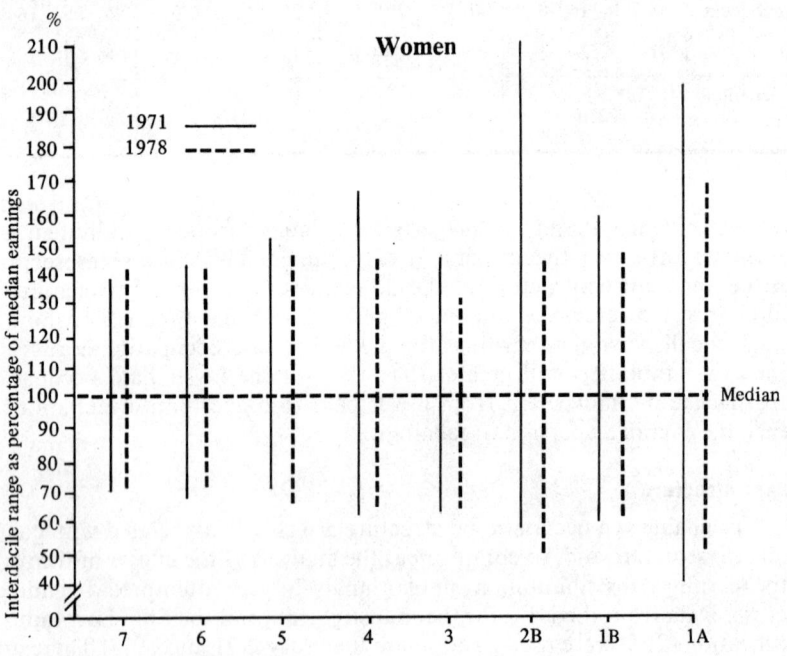

Source: New Earnings Survey.

Interquartile Range as Percentage of Median Earnings

	Men		Women	
	1971	1978	1971	1978
Professionals				
Higher	47·6	42·6	78·5	62·8
Lower	43·5	40·0	57·1	53·1
Managers	65·9	53·0	74·2	49·7
Foremen	33·3	35·5	48·3	37·4
Manuals				
Skilled	36·8	36·3	38·3	40·7
Semi-skilled	40·7	40·6	39·2	38·1
Unskilled	40·7	39·2	34·2	37·5
Clerks	39·5	34·2	38·2	32·1

men complete details are available for 14 groups. Analysis was considered possible for these two categories; no attempt was made to examine the effect of industry structure change on women's earnings.

6.28 Table 6.12 shows that there is little evidence of dramatic change in the spread of sample numbers over industry groups between 1971 and 1978. Not surprisingly therefore, Table 6.13 shows that the 1978 distribution of earnings was not much different from the 1978 distribution based on the 1971 industry structure.

6.29 It is unlikely that any dramatic change in earnings as a result of industry structure change could be observed over a period as short as 7 years but it should be noted that, in the preceding analyses, it proved possible to allocate a greater share of the change to the occupational structure effect. This suggests, therefore, that the occupational structure change between 1971 and 1978 tended to be concentrated within industry groups.

6.30 It has not proved possible to examine the effects of industry structure change over a longer period because of changes in the classification system and the lack of suitable earnings data. For the present, therefore, any interpretation of the results in this chapter has to concentrate on the effects of changes in occupational structure.

Summary
6.31 In order to study changes over time in occupational structure we have looked at eight broad classifications, higher and lower professionals, managers, foremen, clerks and three grades of manual workers (skilled, semi-skilled and unskilled).

6.32 Work done by Dr Routh and not published before shows the movements of average earnings in the various classes over the last 65 years. The tendency has been for the spread of these earnings to diminish with most of the contraction coming from a fall in professional earnings relative to the mean. This general contraction in the spread of earnings between occupational classes is also evident when comparing 1971 and 1978 using NES data.

Table 6.12 Distribution of Full-time Men between Industrial Groups; 1971 and 1978

Great Britain

Industry group	Manual men				Non-manual men			
	No. in NES sample		As percentage of total		No. in NES sample		As percentage of total	
	1971	1978	1971	1978	1971	1978	1971	1978
	No.	No.	%	%	No.	No.	%	%
Agriculture, forestry and fishing	1,019	1,205	1.8	2.5	—	177	—	0.5
Mining and quarrying	2,530	1,573	4.4	3.2	294	349	0.9	1.0
Food, drink and tobacco	2,547	1,906	4.5	3.9	944	816	2.9	2.3
Coal and petroleum products	226	211	0.4	0.4	110	114	0.3	0.3
Chemicals and allied industries	1,644	1,378	2.9	2.8	962	902	3.0	2.6
Metal manufacture	2,855	2,253	5.0	4.6	674	592	2.1	1.7
Mechanical engineering	4,283	3,548	7.5	7.3	1,903	1,513	5.9	4.3
Instrument engineering	388	380	0.7	0.8	257	343	0.8	1.0
Electrical engineering	2,192	1,791	3.8	3.7	1,618	1,333	5.0	3.8
Shipbuilding and marine engineering	872	773	1.5	1.6	224	147	0.7	0.4
Vehicles	3,641	3,354	6.4	6.9	1,403	1,095	4.3	3.1
Metal goods not elsewhere specified	1,990	1,755	3.5	3.6	580	521	1.8	1.5
Textiles	1,744	1,378	3.1	2.8	433	364	1.3	1.0
Leather, leather goods and fur	108	—	0.2	—	—	—	—	—
Clothing and footwear	544	378	1.0	0.8	190	126	0.6	0.4
Bricks, pottery, glass, cement, etc.	1,398	998	2.4	2.0	300	284	0.9	0.8
Timber, furniture, etc.	941	869	1.6	1.8	245	261	0.8	0.7
Paper, printing and publishing	2,022	1,631	3.5	3.3	843	884	2.6	2.5
Other manufacturing industries	1,071	986	1.9	2.0	380	322	1.2	0.9
Construction	6,128	5,667	10.7	11.6	1,174	1,702	3.6	4.8
Gas, electricity and water	1,635	1,139	2.9	2.3	842	870	2.6	2.5
Transport and communication	6,766	6,140	11.9	12.6	2,160	2,819	6.7	8.0
Distributive trades	3,064	2,979	5.4	6.1	3,197	3,656	9.9	10.4
Insurance, banking, finance and business services	576	479	1.0	1.0	2,831	3,287	8.7	9.3
Professional and scientific services	1,745	1,668	3.1	3.4	4,913	5,928	15.2	16.9
Miscellaneous services	2,300	2,686	4.0	5.5	1,313	1,968	4.1	5.6
Public administration	2,789	1,711	4.9	3.5	4,582	4,811	14.1	13.7
Total	57,018	48,836	100.0	100.0	32,372	35,184	100.0	100.0

Source: NES.

Note: Figures are not included where the sample is not sufficiently large.

Table 6.13 Distribution of Earnings for Manual and Non-manual Men on the Bases of Current and Constant Industrial Structure; 1971 and 1978

Great Britain

	No. in sample	Mean	Median	Lowest decile	Lower quartile	Upper quartile	Highest decile	Highest percentile	As percentage of median					Gini coefficient
									Lowest decile	Lower quartile	Upper quartile	Highest decile	Highest percentile	
		£ pw	£ pw	£ pw	£ pw	£ pw	£ pw	£ pw	%	%	%	%	%	%
Non-manual men 1971 ..	32,372	38·9	34·3	20·9	26·2	44·8	60·0	116·8	60·8	76·3	130·4	174·8	339·9	25·1
Non-manual men 1978 ..	35,184	100·8	91·7	57·3	71·8	116·9	150·4	267·8	62·5	78·3	127·6	164·1	292·2	23·0
Non-manual men 1978 based on 1971 structure ..	32,372	101·2	91·9	58·1	72·2	117·0	150·5	268·5	63·2	78·6	127·4	163·8	292·2	22·8
Manual men 1971 ..	57,018	29·4	27·8	18·9	22·4	34·2	41·2	58·7	68·1	80·8	123·1	148·1	211·1	17·6
Manual men 1978 ..	48,836	80·5	76·5	52·5	62·8	92·9	111·6	164·1	68·6	82·0	121·4	145·9	214·4	17·9
Manual men 1978 based on 1971 structure ..	57,018	81·1	77·0	52·9	63·2	93·5	112·4	164·8	68·6	82·1	121·3	145·8	213·8	17·8

Source: NES.

Note: These overall distributions cover all those in the sample about whom information on earnings by industry was published. Therefore, the quantile points differ slightly from those shown elsewhere in this chapter.

6.33   There has also been a tendency for people to move towards jobs in higher paid occupational classes. The effect of this change in occupational structure on the overall level and dispersion of earnings can be calculated, in a purely statistical fashion, by taking the occupational structure in the base year given by the proportions employed in each occupation and multiplying that by average earnings (or the dispersion of earnings) in each occupation in the current year. This effectively ignores any causal relationship between the level of earnings and the changes in structure. On this basis, between 1971 and 1978 changes in occupational structure accounted for one third of the growth in men's earnings, adjusted for the increase in prices, and less than one fifth of the growth in women's earnings.

6.34   The dispersion of earnings of the more highly paid occupational classes has declined over time but the dispersion still remains greater than that of lower paid occupational classes. Assuming that this reduction in dispersion is not related to the changes in occupational structure, then the movement towards higher paid occupations would have caused the overall dispersion to widen.

6.35   Information on the effect of changes in industrial structure is available for manual men and to a lesser extent for non-manual men. Between 1971 and 1978 there was very little evidence of a change in industry structure. The effect on the distribution of earnings of such changes is correspondingly small.

CHAPTER 7

Earnings in Selected Occupations

Introduction

7.1 In Chapters 5 and 6 we looked at the relationships between occupational and industrial structure and the overall earnings distribution. Those Chapters were concerned with the broad general effects and the overall trends. In this Chapter we look at the distribution of earnings and trends in earnings of a number of individual occupations as identified in the NES. The aim is to illustrate the differences in earnings between occupations and the range of earnings experienced in individual occupations and to show some examples of the variety of changes which combined to produce the overall effects.

7.2 The NES analyses make it possible to present earnings distributions for individual occupations classified according to the NES system; but, owing to the change of system between 1972 and 1973, the detailed occupational analyses are not consistent over the whole period for which the survey results are available. The NES can be used, therefore, for an analysis of changes in the earnings distributions of individual occupations only for the relatively short period from 1973 to 1978.

Selected occupations

7.3 The selected occupations are listed in Tables 7.1 and 7.2. There are 59 in total; for 24 of these, earnings figures are available for both men and women. The occupations considered for selection were limited to those for which information was available on a consistent basis from 1973 to 1978. In selecting from these we sought to include as many as possible of those occupations in which substantial numbers of both men and women were employed; but a number of other occupations where earnings and trends in earnings are of general interest were also included. The numbers included in the selected occupations amount to 29 and 74 per cent, respectively, of all full-time men and all full-time women included in the NES. The selection was not designed to produce a representative sub-sample.

7.4 Detailed tables showing trends in the earnings distributions of the selected occupations are in Appendix H; more summary figures are reproduced in Tables 7.1, 7.2 and 7.3. In Tables 7.1 and 7.2 the occupations are arranged in descending order of median earnings in 1978. It should be noted that the NES figures relate to one week in April each year; the timing of major pay settlements, therefore, can have a substantial effect on comparisons of pay levels of particular occupa-

Table 7.1 Median Earnings and Interdecile Ranges for Men in Selected Occupations; 1973 to 1978

Gross weekly earnings of 48 selected out of 441 occupations, arranged in descending order of median earnings in 1978, medians and interdecile ranges 1973 to 1978

Great Britain

Weekly earnings £

Occupation	Median						Interdecile range as percentage of median					
	1973	1974	1975	1976	1977	1978	1973	1974	1975	1976	1977	1978
Medical practitioners	60.0	71.0	92.0	123.3	145.0	154.2	144.5	142.1	122.8	124.0	92.1	90.1
University academic staff	73.4	82.2	97.3	120.4	125.6	135.7	101.0	81.0	85.5	77.9	79.3	75.1
Police inspectors and above, fire service officers	—	68.8	85.8	103.7	105.9	121.6	—	64.4	80.1	88.4	69.8	70.4
Teachers in establishments for further education	56.5	63.3	85.5	105.6	111.9	118.8	62.9	63.5	64.1	57.7	54.8	57.7
Engineers—electrical, electronic	51.4	58.5	79.6	95.0	101.9	112.3	72.6	73.9	66.3	67.9	66.5	74.0
Mechanical engineers	—	58.1	78.2	96.1	101.7	110.8	—	74.4	70.9	74.1	63.9	66.1
Production and works managers, works foremen	49.7	55.7	67.6	83.7	92.0	104.4	85.0	81.8	90.9	84.8	82.4	76.9
Face-trained coalminers	38.2	47.6	69.2	74.8	78.6	103.4	50.4	46.5	54.7	58.7	54.1	64.4
Accountants	48.7	55.1	69.0	80.6	88.3	102.1	115.1	121.2	96.7	108.6	100.7	102.4
Secondary teachers	47.0	53.1	71.2	88.1	92.2	101.0	75.1	68.4	69.8	65.3	61.7	60.3
Primary teachers	45.3	50.6	70.8	86.3	91.9	99.5	66.5	69.4	66.5	65.7	61.9	63.3
Foremen, electricians, installation and maintenance	47.9	51.1	64.6	80.3	86.5	88.4	55.4	56.8	73.1	75.3	47.2	83.8
Electricians, installation and maintenance plant, etc.	41.8	47.0	59.7	69.6	76.3	88.2	74.8	78.3	76.8	75.8	77.2	77.4
Policemen	42.4	44.7	60.0	73.2	74.9	86.1	74.7	80.2	65.4	72.0	72.1	59.6
Bus and coach drivers	39.4	46.0	63.5	71.1	76.4	85.8	58.3	61.1	59.8	61.4	61.2	64.3
Supervisors of clerks	40.6	49.3	58.2	72.4	76.5	84.6	65.2	60.5	64.0	54.4	49.5	52.2
Welders—skilled	40.5	46.6	59.2	68.0	73.8	82.0	73.9	66.9	72.6	69.5	72.4	74.3
Inspectors and testers (metal and electrical)	39.1	43.7	56.4	65.7	72.0	81.8	59.2	55.4	60.1	57.2	56.5	59.8
Press and stamping machine operators	38.8	44.4	50.6	63.6	69.6	80.8	71.5	64.2	61.9	64.4	62.5	66.5
Supervisors/foremen—caretaking, cleaning, etc.	35.0	41.8	54.8	68.0	71.0	80.5	71.5	65.5	78.0	83.3	71.0	84.3
Welfare workers	37.4	40.0	51.3	64.1	72.1	79.9	89.7	94.0	87.0	89.3	84.4	73.9
Machine tool operators (not setting up)	38.4	44.3	53.7	62.3	69.8	78.9	66.1	62.5	60.8	61.6	59.5	65.0
Bus conductors	36.1	38.9	60.2	65.3	71.0	78.8	55.8	61.9	53.1	68.9	64.5	58.0
Firemen	39.5	47.2	59.1	65.0	69.6	78.1	43.6	46.6	45.5	34.5	32.6	41.2

Table 7.1 (continued) Median Earnings and Interdecile Ranges for Men in Selected Occupations; 1973 to 1978

Gross weekly earnings of 48 selected out of 441 occupations, arranged in descending order of median earnings in 1978, medians and interdecile ranges 1973 to 1978

Great Britain

Weekly earnings £

Occupation	Median						Interdecile range as percentage of median					
	1973	1974	1975	1976	1977	1978	1973	1974	1975	1976	1977	1978
Repetitive assemblers (metal and electrical)	36.9	41.7	50.0	60.5	66.2	74.7	66.4	61.5	66.3	60.1	61.6	67.8
Railway guards	34.8	38.1	54.3	64.2	68.2	74.6	62.4	58.1	60.3	57.5	48.2	54.0
Plumbers, pipe fitters	37.1	42.3	52.4	60.2	64.5	74.4	67.0	71.2	85.4	79.8	84.0	82.5
Laboratory technicians	35.0	37.8	52.6	61.6	67.4	73.7	97.7	86.6	88.6	85.4	83.8	85.9
Packers, bottlers, canners, fillers	33.0	37.4	47.0	56.8	61.8	72.4	81.7	82.8	71.3	74.9	81.9	73.0
Bricklayers	38.2	42.3	51.8	57.8	64.7	71.8	73.2	74.6	76.3	75.5	60.7	76.4
Finance, insurance etc, clerks	35.5	40.6	50.0	58.2	62.5	71.6	87.6	90.6	79.9	78.0	75.9	88.5
Motor vehicle mechanics, skilled	33.1	38.7	48.6	56.0	62.3	70.7	90.6	79.1	80.2	80.9	79.9	82.1
Sales supervisors	38.0	42.7	54.1	63.2	69.9	70.3	94.0	82.7	79.9	78.8	80.1	80.7
Telephonists	30.1	37.4	49.8	59.3	69.4	68.1	86.0	111.5	74.8	55.2	75.2	72.3
Refuse collectors, dustmen	30.3	34.5	47.7	56.1	62.9	67.5	56.5	56.1	51.7	43.5	47.3	46.8
Records and library clerks	30.9	33.5	45.9	52.4	58.3	67.3	77.8	74.1	72.5	70.5	68.6	76.5
Shipping and travel clerks	32.6	37.4	46.6	54.8	59.6	67.1	97.9	79.5	101.0	89.8	96.7	80.5
Production and materials controlling clerks	31.8	36.9	45.4	54.5	59.1	67.1	74.5	69.8	66.8	63.2	61.2	64.4
Cash handling clerks	32.7	36.7	48.4	56.8	60.7	65.9	78.7	79.8	93.6	73.7	74.6	75.9
Footwear workers	—	41.8	42.5	53.0	57.3	65.3	—	80.1	81.3	72.8	84.6	81.5
Other motor vehicle mechanics	34.3	39.9	40.8	53.8	52.0	64.8	89.3	89.5	104.0	91.4	90.0	76.6
Storekeepers etc	30.1	34.4	43.5	51.8	56.6	64.6	75.1	73.0	72.8	73.6	73.6	78.2
Costing and accounting clerks	30.5	34.3	44.6	52.8	58.0	63.6	84.3	80.5	76.1	67.4	65.7	69.1
General clerks and clerks nec	28.1	34.0	41.2	52.7	57.5	62.4	83.1	70.2	74.7	72.7	68.7	72.7
Chefs/cooks	29.6	35.7	45.9	50.9	54.6	60.2	90.7	89.6	93.7	90.9	101.0	111.5
Tailors, cutters, dressmakers etc...	—	35.2	42.1	48.4	55.3	59.8	—	73.9	70.4	60.5	62.0	75.9
Registered and enrolled nurses and midwives	24.2	30.9	49.0	53.6	56.9	58.4	87.3	78.5	90.1	69.0	73.4	85.4
General farm workers	23.6	29.4	34.0	43.1	46.9	52.8	58.3	86.3	64.6	55.4	62.2	58.3

Source: NES.
Note: Data include some benefits in kind for a few occupations.

93

Table 7.2 Median Earnings and Interdecile Ranges for Women in Selected Occupations; 1973 to 1978

Gross weekly earnings of 35 selected out of 441 occupations, arranged in descending order of median earnings in 1978, medians and interdecile ranges 1973 to 1978

Occupation	Median						Interdecile range as percentage of median					
	1973	1974	1975	1976	1977	1978	1973	1974	1975	1976	1977	1978
Teachers in establishments for further education	48.7	53.5	75.0	91.8	94.8	99.1	73.1	80.6	76.2	65.0	61.2	58.5
Secondary teachers	37.2	43.3	62.0	76.8	79.8	88.1	84.2	74.2	71.7	68.1	64.8	63.3
Primary teachers	33.8	39.4	55.0	72.0	76.2	84.4	63.8	67.8	66.4	59.7	56.4	54.1
Nurse administrators and executives	36.0	38.0	65.5	76.1	80.4	82.0	50.6	56.0	66.5	56.2	40.5	37.9
Supervisors of clerks	28.6	35.9	44.3	55.7	60.4	66.9	80.2	81.6	69.4	72.0	68.7	64.6
Welfare workers	29.1	31.8	43.4	51.8	58.0	62.6	85.0	79.2	85.7	90.7	83.9	79.5
Laboratory technicians	24.4	27.0	39.6	47.4	53.5	59.5	83.8	85.6	70.2	73.7	68.9	65.7
Inspectors and testers	21.3	24.9	35.3	45.7	49.5	56.6	58.2	58.1	59.6	49.4	41.6	51.1
Secretaries, shorthand typists	23.8	28.1	36.1	44.0	49.9	55.6	70.9	66.8	66.1	67.4	62.3	62.5
Machine tool operators (not setting up)	22.3	24.9	35.5	45.6	53.7	54.8	60.8	54.0	50.7	60.0	55.7	62.0
Repetitive assemblers (metal and electrical)	20.8	24.6	33.0	42.6	46.0	52.8	56.3	57.5	56.1	52.0	50.8	52.8
Press and stamping machine operators	19.5	23.3	30.5	41.0	44.3	52.0	56.3	56.4	65.8	59.4	67.3	65.8
Shipping and travel clerks	21.6	26.5	33.9	42.8	45.5	51.4	95.8	81.8	99.2	75.3	80.5	78.8
Finance, insurance etc, clerks	23.2	26.3	34.9	42.2	45.2	51.4	86.0	76.1	84.2	66.0	68.2	74.6
Records and library clerks	20.1	23.7	33.7	41.4	46.8	51.3	72.7	67.7	65.8	63.9	61.2	61.5
Registered and enrolled nurses and midwives	21.2	24.5	39.4	46.4	49.7	51.2	91.7	86.4	87.6	75.1	63.5	70.4
Cash handling clerks	21.0	24.8	32.5	40.2	45.2	51.0	78.2	76.9	72.9	71.2	62.0	65.4
General clerks and clerks nec	21.2	26.6	34.0	42.6	46.6	50.7	68.6	67.6	59.8	63.9	59.4	59.1
Costing and accounting clerks	19.9	23.4	31.5	38.9	44.9	49.8	75.4	72.7	64.7	66.4	59.6	59.1
Other typists	19.8	23.5	31.7	39.1	43.6	49.4	62.1	60.9	55.7	62.4	53.0	52.3
Production and materials controlling clerks	21.4	22.8	30.5	41.8	47.0	49.1	72.6	64.0	62.8	62.0	61.5	59.5
Telephonists	19.4	25.0	34.7	38.6	43.8	48.8	57.6	57.5	62.3	60.6	59.5	55.8
Packers, bottlers, canners, fillers	20.0	22.2	30.8	38.5	43.2	48.5	64.5	63.5	65.2	64.9	58.2	57.2
Sales supervisors	18.9	23.3	32.5	37.6	41.9	47.3	74.3	66.3	66.8	63.0	61.8	72.2
Storekeepers etc.	18.6	22.7	30.8	43.1	46.5	47.1	61.8	58.5	68.7	69.8	57.6	69.5
Nursing auxiliaries and assistants	17.7	20.3	34.2	40.0	42.8	46.7	55.1	63.1	49.8	44.7	42.6	40.5
Home and domestic helpers, maids	—	21.9	32.0	37.6	40.6	46.6	—	79.2	72.2	62.8	59.5	58.9
Footwear workers	16.6	25.4	30.6	36.5	40.2	46.4	78.0	75.7	94.3	90.4	81.0	68.9
Other cleaners	18.4	21.4	30.7	36.6	39.4	44.7	74.7	69.3	72.1	76.6	65.9	72.6
Chefs/cooks	18.3	22.0	30.5	33.5	38.3	43.7	66.6	70.0	64.7	63.7	64.6	61.0
Sewing machinists, textiles	16.4	22.2	28.1	32.6	37.6	43.0	71.7	72.2	68.5	67.4	61.8	67.1
Counterhands	17.2	19.6	27.7	37.6	35.9	41.1	78.6	81.1	75.2	73.9	73.6	70.8
Receptionists	15.3	20.2	26.2	31.1	34.0	40.7	78.1	69.8	72.0	72.4	71.4	61.2
Salesmen, shop assistants and shelf fillers	14.6	18.1	24.5	29.1	32.6	37.3	61.7	59.9	58.2	51.8	48.1	52.4
Waiters		17.7	25.2	30.8		35.6	94.4	98.3	98.8	105.6	91.2	89.5

Table 7.3   Increase in Average Weekly Earnings of Men and Women in Selected Occupations; 1973 to 1978

Great Britain

Weekly earnings £

Occupation	Men				Women			
	Mean earnings		Increase 1973 to 1978		Mean earnings		Increase 1973 to 1978	
	1973	1978	£	%	1973	1978	£	%
Medical practitioners	82.9	163.3	80.4	97.0	60.3	126.9	66.6	110.4
Teachers in establishments for FE ..	59.2	121.8	62.6	105.7	49.9	102.3	52.4	105.0
Secondary teachers	47.5	102.7	55.2	116.2	39.8	90.1	50.3	126.4
Primary teachers	44.4	99.8	55.4	124.8	36.0	86.0	50.0	138.9
Inspectors and testers (metal and electrical)	40.5	85.2	44.7	110.4	22.2	56.6	34.4	154.9
Supervisors of clerks	41.6	84.8	43.2	103.8	30.3	69.3	39.0	128.7
Machine tool operators (not setting up) ..	39.7	81.2	41.5	104.5	22.5	56.5	34.0	151.1
Repetitive assemblers (metal and electrical)	37.9	76.8	38.9	102.6	21.1	54.1	33.0	156.4
Finance, insurance, etc clerks	37.2	75.6	38.4	103.2	24.8	53.5	28.7	115.7
Packers, bottlers, canners, fillers ..	34.7	74.8	40.1	115.6	20.0	49.4	29.4	147.0
Records and library clerks	32.6	69.7	37.1	113.8	21.4	52.8	31.4	146.7
Production and materials controlling clerks	33.3	69.3	36.0	108.1	21.0	50.8	29.8	141.9
Cash handling clerks	33.9	68.6	34.7	102.4	22.1	52.9	30.8	139.4
Storekeepers etc	31.5	68.1	36.6	116.2	19.6	50.0	30.4	155.1
Costing and accounting clerks	31.4	66.1	34.7	110.5	21.1	51.2	30.1	142.6
General clerks and clerks nec	29.2	64.9	35.7	122.3	21.8	51.9	30.1	138.1
Salesmen, shop assistants and shelf fillers	30.6	61.2	30.6	100.0	16.0	38.4	22.4	140.0

Source: NES 1978.

tions. These effects are likely to be much more marked in individual occupations than in the broader classes considered in Chapter 6.

7.5 There is a relatively large dispersion around the median earnings figures for all of the selected occupations, as evidenced by the interdecile range figures quoted in Tables 7.1 and 7.2. This results in a very considerable overlap in the earnings of occupations with very different levels of median earnings, as Figure 7.1 illustrates. The difference in earnings between medical practitioners at the highest and lowest deciles of their distribution is considerably larger than the differences between the median earnings of the highest and lowest paid occupations in Figure 7.1 The large interdecile ranges and the relatively small differences in median earnings are in keeping with the finding in Chapter 5 that occupation accounts for a fairly small proportion of the overall variation in earnings.

7.6 In Table 7.1 the inter-decile range narrowed between 1973 and 1978 in the two occupations, medical practitioners and university academic staff, with median earnings above the highest decile of the all men distribution: the detailed tables in Appendix H reveal that this was largely the result of falls in the highest deciles relative to the median. For all occupations, however, the inter-decile ranges exhibit considerable volatility over the six year period and no more general patterns of changes can be detected.

7.7 In Table 7.2 it can be seen that there is a much more general tendency for the dispersion of earnings of women's occupations to fall. There are notable exceptions but the detailed tables in Appendix H reveal that the overall impression is of a decline in the higher quantiles relative to the median. The overall distribution of women's earnings in Table 6.1 does show a decline in the higher quantiles relative to the median but this decline is not as great as might be expected in view of the widespread contraction of dispersions within those selected occupations.

7.8 Changes in the dispersion of earnings are not the only way in which the employment situation has changed in a different way for women than for men. Three strands can be distinguished. The first is concerned with changes in employment levels, the second with changes in the level of earnings and the third with changes in job opportunities.

7.9 As Chapter 2 has shown, there has been a substantial increase in the number of women employed while the number of men has scarcely changed. Although the greatest increase in female employment has been in part-time workers, there has been some movement from part-time to full-time work as Table 8.6 in Chapter 8 indicates. Unfortunately, as the analyses in both the report and background paper[1] are based on the earnings of full-time employees, very little can be said about the effect of this increase in part-time workers on either the distribution of earnings for women or the level of earnings for full-time male and female employees.

---

[1] Background Paper No 8.

Figure 7.1 Median Levels of Earnings and Inter-decile Ranges for Men and Women in Ten Occupations; 1978

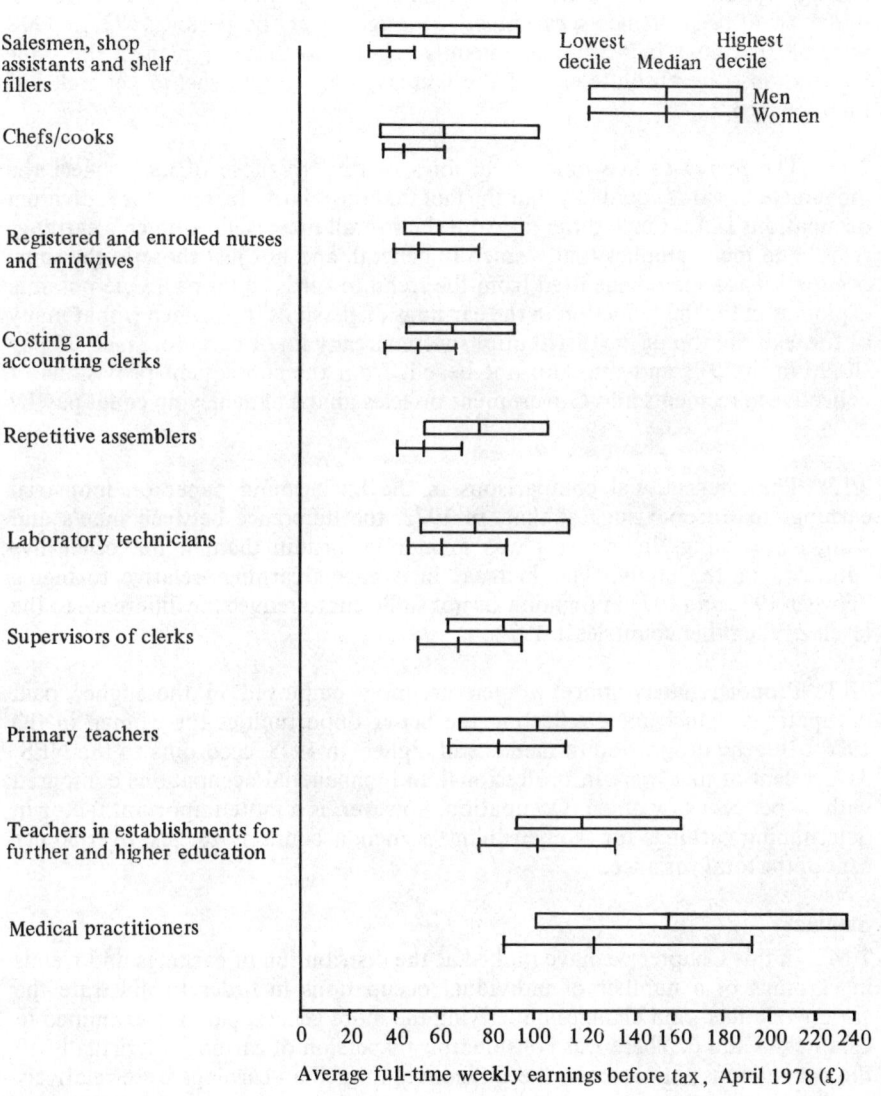

Average full-time weekly earnings before tax, April 1978 (£)

Source: New Earnings Survey 1978.

97

7.10   Women have seen their real earnings increase dramatically over the period 1971 to 1978 (25 per cent compared with an equivalent figure for men of 9 per cent). However, as Table 7.3 shows, in all of the selected occupations for which mean earnings figures were available for both men and women, women's earnings in 1978 are still substantially below the men's level. The differences, however, are not as great as the overall difference between men's and women's average earnings. In 1978 women's earnings for full-time employees were just under two-thirds of men's earnings. Although, over the period 1973 to 1978 women's earnings increased significantly relative to those of men in the same occupations, the absolute size of the increase for women was, in general, less than for men.

7.11   The increases in women's earnings relative to those of men reflect the movement towards equal pay, but the fact that the relative increase for individual occupations is not much different from the overall increase in women's earnings relative to men's implies that women in general, and not just those in the same occupations as men, benefitted from the trend towards equal pay. One possible explanation for the reduction in the earnings dispersions for women is that many of those at the top of the distributions were already in, or close to, an equal pay situation in 1973 and thus did not benefit from the subsequent provisions of collective agreements and Government policies aimed at achieving equal pay by 1975.

7.12   The international comparisons in the background paper on industrial earnings in Europe[1] suggest that, in 1972, the difference between men's and women's earnings in industry was greater in Britain than in the other five countries in the study. The increase in women's earnings relative to men's between 1972 and 1978 in Britain was not sufficient to reduce the difference to the levels of the other countries in 1972.

7.13   Proportionately more women are now employed in the higher paid occupations than before, reflecting the better opportunities for women in the 1970s. But the proportion of men is still higher. In 1978, according to the NES, 31 per cent of men were in professional and managerial occupations compared with 24 per cent of women. Occupation, however, is a more important factor in determining earnings for women than for men, accounting for just over 50 per cent of the total variance.

Summary

7.14   In this Chapter we have looked at the distribution of earnings and trends in earnings of a number of individual occupations in order to illustrate the variety of effects and changes underlying the more general patterns examined in Chapters 5 and 6. There was considerable dispersion of earnings in virtually all the occupations; in contrast, the differences in median earnings were relatively small.

7.15   Over the period 1973 to 1978, the gap between men's and women's earnings narrowed, both for the same occupations and overall, but women were

---

[1] Background Paper No 8.

still much worse off than men in 1978. In other countries this difference was found to be not so great. In fact, differences between men's and women's earnings in Britain in 1978 were still greater than those in the other countries studied in 1972. The introduction of equal pay legislation may account for both the relative rise in women's earnings and the reduction in the dispersions, as many of those women at the top of the distribution may already have been receiving equal pay.

CHAPTER 8

Age-earnings Relationships and Fluctuations in the Earnings of Individuals

Introduction

8.1 The inequality in the earnings distribution is typically measured in respect of earnings for a given week or year depending upon the data source. A possible cause of such inequality is to be found in the fact that earnings may vary over an employee's working life. If the earnings of all individuals follow a roughly similar life cycle pattern, then part of the observed inequality in the current earnings distribution can be attributed to the age structure of the population. On the other hand, if the life cycle patterns vary by occupation level, the differences in pay within one week or one year may tell us little about the different pay histories or expectations of individuals over a lifetime.

8.2 One approach to this problem is to collect data on the earnings of individuals over a period of years but there are generally considerable practical problems associated with longitudinal studies of this kind. There are few longitudinal data sets available. Matched sample data from the New Earnings Survey have been used by the Department of Employment[1] to chart the movement of an individual's earnings from year to year. The DE analyses were drawn upon in our examination of fluctuations in earnings, which was presented in Report No 5. We also made use of some additional tabulations which the Department produced for us, but all of these analyses covered a relatively short span of years. Professor Hart[2] analysed earnings data of a sample consisting of 3 separate age cohorts drawn from the records which were held by the DHSS in connection with the administration of the National Insurance scheme. Hart's analyses covered the annual earnings of the same individuals in 3 or 4 separate years over a 10 year period but the sample was small (approximately 2,100) and age was the only variable apart from earnings which was identified.

8.3 For the present report we have obtained some new longitudinal analyses of the New Earnings Survey data. These avoid some of the problems associated with previous analyses of the matched sample data but their usefulness is restricted in other ways and they highlight difficulties in the interpretation of these data which had not been identified so clearly in earlier studies. In particular, they show the extent to which the NES sample suffers from attrition and give an indication of the extent to which this attrition introduces bias into matched

---

[1] How individual people's earnings change, *DE Gazette*, January 1977.
[2] P E Hart, *A cohort analysis of changes in the distribution of incomes, United Kingdom 1963–1973*, University of Reading Discussion Papers in Economics, August 1975.

sample data. We present our analysis of these data in paragraphs 8.10 to 8.14 below.

Cross-section data

8.4 We consider initially an alternative approach which is to use cross-section data on earnings by age group to construct age-earnings profiles. In this section we present earnings profiles for broad occupational groups from the 1978 New Earnings Survey. Table 8.1 shows gross weekly average earnings by age group for manual and non-manual males, and manual and non-manul females and Figure 8.1 shows the age-earnings profiles constructed from this table for these four groups. The profiles follow the expected shape; for all groups there is a steep increase in average earnings in the first years of working life, followed by a plateau, and for all groups except non-manual females, a fall in the last years. The earnings of non-manual employees peak later and are higher than those of manual employees after about eight years of working life. There is a marked difference between the male and female earnings profiles. The women's average earnings do not rise as fast or to as high a level as men's and, apart from the first few years, show relatively little change over different age groups.

8.5 Figures 8.2 and 8.3 show similar patterns for narrower occupational groups.[1] Variation of earnings with age is far greater for higher paid occupational groups. The marked fall in male earnings in the oldest age group in occupations I to VI suggests that the mobility of individuals in these groups is substantial. The sample number is roughly halved, and apparently the higher paid members have either retired earlier or found other jobs more often than the lower paid members.

Table 8.1   Average Gross Weekly Earnings by Age Group; 1978

Great Britain

Age Group	Manual males	Non-manual males	Manual females	Non-manual females
	£ pw	£ pw	£ pw	£ pw
Under 18..	36·1	33·5	33·4	31·1
18–24	66·2	61·7	46·3	48·7
25–29	81·0	87·3	51·9	63·2
30–39	85·6	105·7	51·5	64·8
40–49	84·3	112·6	50·2	64·6
50–59	79·1	108·0	49·6	63·7
60–64	72·1	92·1	47·3	60·4
All ages	77·6	97·7	48·4	57·8

Source: NES 1978.

[1] The occupational groups in Figures 8.2 and 8.3 are as follows:

I   Managerial (general management).
II   Professional and related supporting management and administration.
III   Professional and related in education, welfare and health.
V   Professional and related in science, engineering, technology and similar fields.
VI   Managerial (excluding general management).
VII   Clerical and related.
VIII   Selling.
X   Catering, cleaning, hairdressing and other personal service.
XI   Farming, fishing and related.

101

Figure 8.1   Average Gross Weekly Earnings by Age Group for Four Groups of Employees; 1978

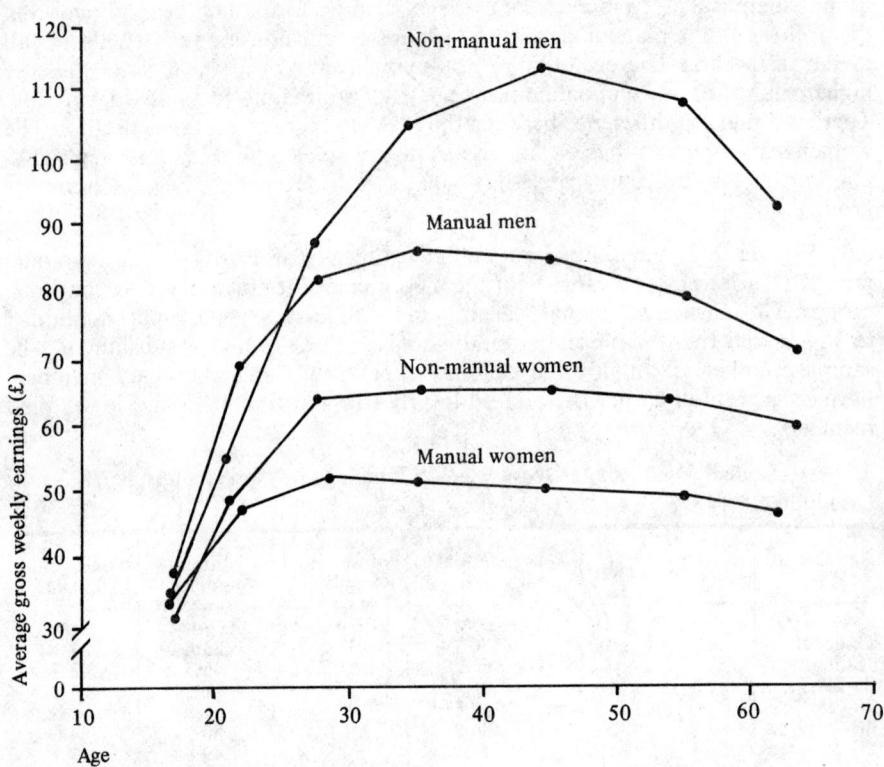

Source: New Earnings Survey 1978.

Figure 8.2 Average Gross Weekly Earnings by Age Group for Men in Nine Occupational Groups; 1978

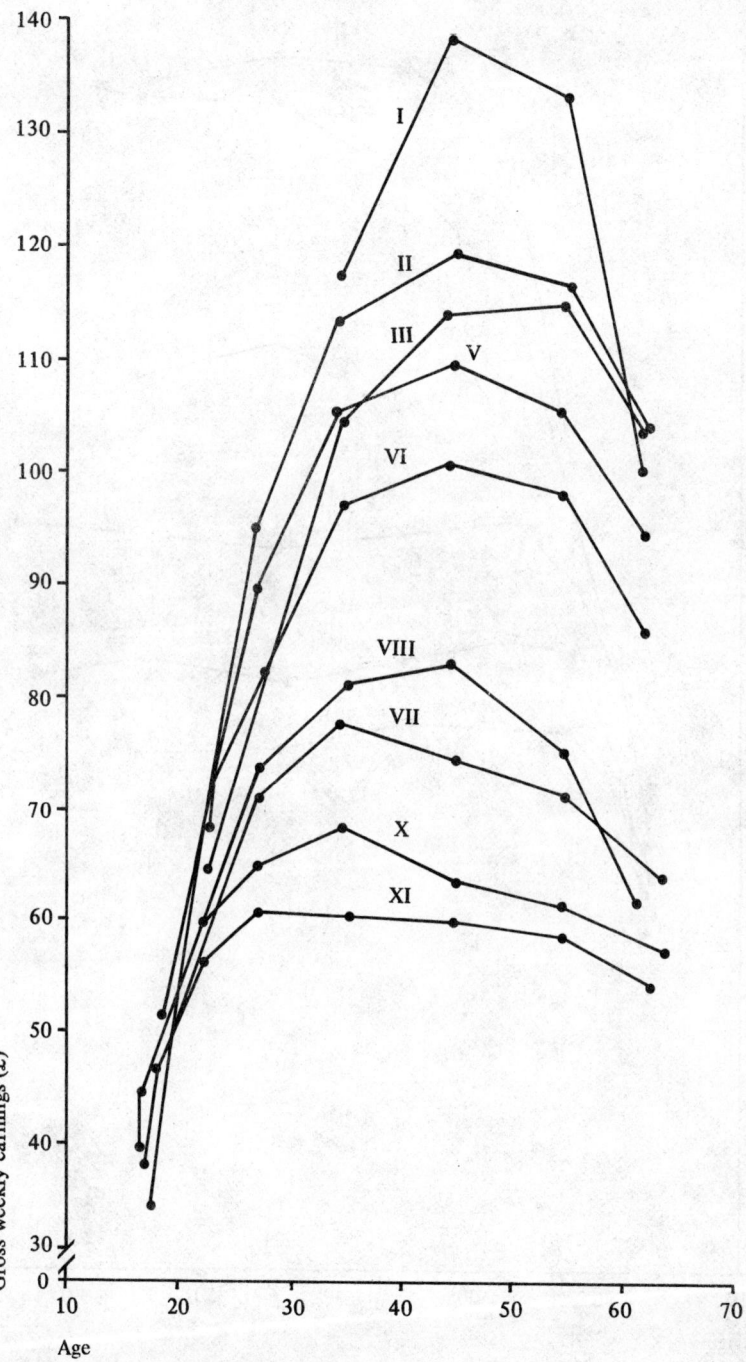

Source: New Earnings Survey 1978.

Figure 8.3 Average Gross Weekly Earnings by Age Group for Women in Five Occupational Groups; 1978

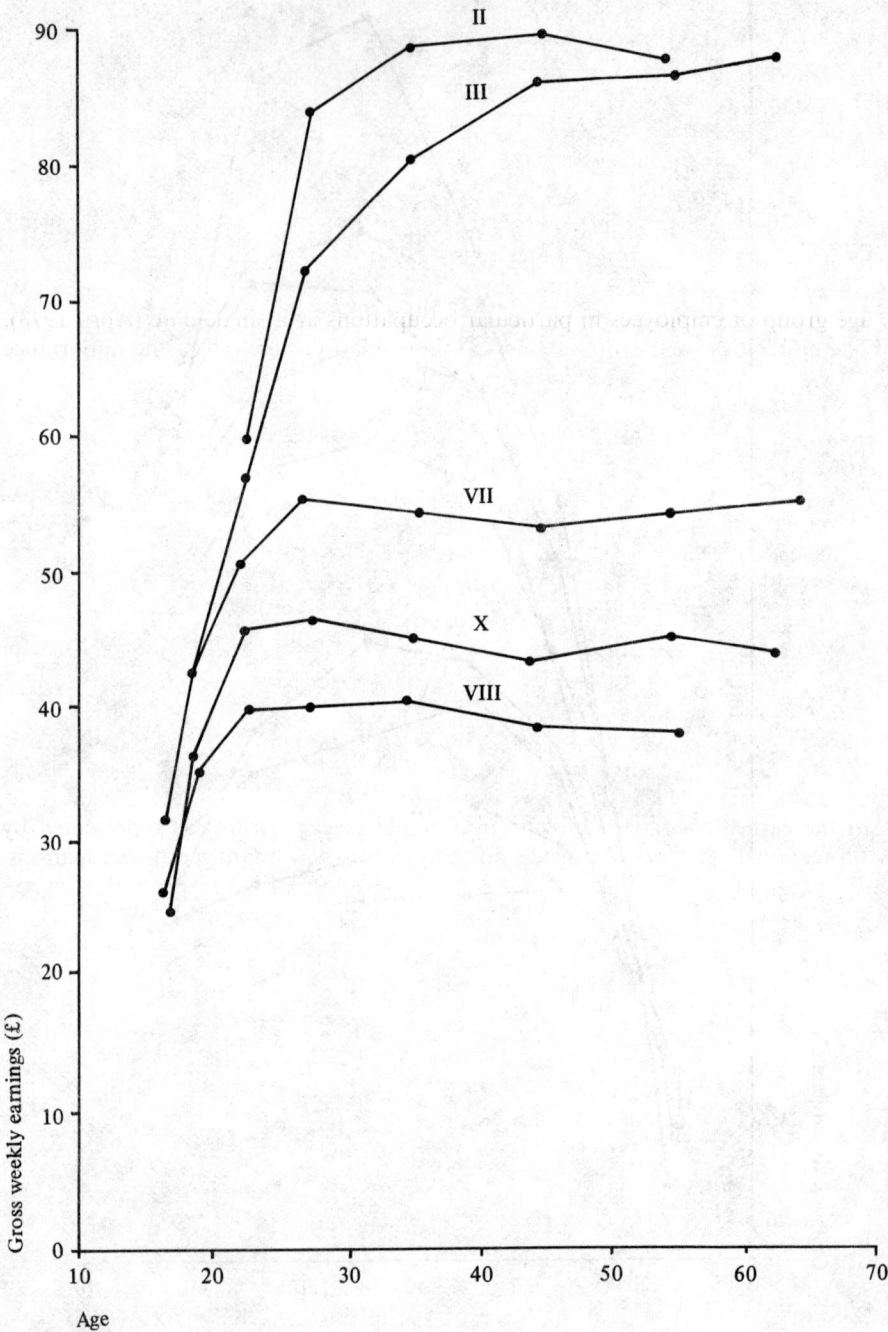

Source: New Earnings Survey 1978

8.6 The figures in Appendix I illustrate some of the characteristics commonly associated with professional and manual occupations: the dispersion of earnings is far wider for professional occupations, presumably because these have larger elements of discretion and responsibility. The earnings for women are noticeably lower than those for men. In particular, the highest decile of earnings of women aged 40–50 in professional occupations is about 72 per cent of the highest decile of the earnings of men aged 40–50 in professional occupations, whereas the ratio of the two lowest decile figures is only about 62 per cent. This situation is reversed in manual occupations such as catering, cleaning, hairdressing and other personal service.

8.7 It must be borne in mind, however, that these diagrams are not the age-earnings profiles of groups of individuals but are based on average earnings by age group of employees in particular occupations at a single date (April 1978). The difficulties in interpreting age-earnings relationships reflect the importance of information on occupational mobility. For example, the manual men profile in Figure 8.1 may flatten earlier than that for non-manual men because manual men on average are at their most productive in their mid-thirties. An equally plausible explanation, however, is that those manual men on highest earnings and on the fastest rising earnings paths in their twenties may become non-manual employees in their late twenties and thirties, thus adding to the continuing increase in the non-manual men cross-section profile and contributing to the differences in the profiles of manual and non-manual men.

8.8 Analyses of the data from the sample survey enquiry into occupational mobility carried out from Nuffield College, Oxford in 1972[1] provide an indication of the trends in occupational mobility during this century (the members of the first of the four cohorts in the Oxford sample were born between 1908 and 1917; those in the fourth cohort were born between 1938 and 1947). Respondents in the later cohorts appeared to have better chances than men of similar origins in the earlier cohorts of moving into higher level positions as represented by professional, higher technical, administrative and managerial occupations. This suggests a pattern of increasing mobility, against a background of movement at all levels and in all cohorts. Part of the mobility measured by Goldthorpe *et al* occurred or had already occurred at date of entry into the labour force but a significant proportion of it occurred between date of entry into the labour force and the date of the enquiry. The increase in mobility represented by the movement into higher level occupations was closely associated with structural changes (such as those noted in Chapter 6) and when the effect of these structural changes was allowed for, the evidence suggested that there was no change in mobility patterns.

8.9 The available information on mobility cannot be related directly to earnings data on which the above age-earnings relationships are based. However, it is possible to look more directly at the changes in earnings of individuals over time using the NES matched sample data.

---

[1] J H Goldthorpe, C Payne and C Llewellyn, Trends in class mobility, *Sociology*, Vol 12, September 1978.

Matched sample data

8.10 The new analyses of matched sample data cover the period 1971 to 1978 and separately 1975 to 1978. The change in the method of drawing the sample between 1974 and 1975 was accompanied by a major change in the composition of the sample. As a result, no more than one quarter of the 1974 sample was included in the survey in 1975 and subsequent years. It was because of this break that our previous analyses of these data were not carried beyond 1974[1]. Now, however, there is a run of four years of matched sample data available on the new basis and we have also obtained an analysis of the earnings of all those who were in the sample in both 1971 and 1978. The potential numbers in this eight-year matched sample were limited to a maximum of 25 per cent of the overall sample by the sampling procedures. This limitation in itself was unlikely to produce bias, but we show that movements in and out of the sample resulting from movements in and out of the employed population or from other reasons (eg non-response) were unlikely to be random over the eight-year period.

8.11 Table 8.2 shows the proportionate spread over quantile groups in 1975, 1976 and 1977 of manual men who were in specified quantile groups in 1978. The quantile points, which form the limits of the quantile groups, were determined with respect to the distributions for manual men using the whole sample in the relevant years. The table also shows the proportions in each quantile group (ranked according to the 1978 distribution) who in earlier years were not included in the sample. Tables 8.3, 8.4 and 8.5 show similar details for non-manual men, manual women and non-manual women, respectively. For all four labour markets a large proportion of those found in a particular quantile group in 1978 were to be found in other quantile groups in earlier years but the greatest number remained in the original quantile groups. The degree to which they are dispersed around the quantile group increases the earlier the year being compared with 1978. This is illustrated by the cumulative frequency distributions in Figures 8.4 and 8.5. There was not much difference in the degree of movement between quantile groups by manual and non-manual men at the bottom of the distribution, but the latter were considerably more stable at the top of the distribution. Non-manual women had moved less than manual women at both the top and bottom of the distribution. On the whole there was less movement among women than men at the top of the distribution and more at the bottom except in 1975 when more women are in the 'not included' column.

8.12 In Table 8.6 we present an analysis of what happened to those not included in Tables 8.2, 8.3, 8.4 and 8.5. It shows the percentage of those in the sample in 1978 who had a different status (ie non-manual), lost pay through absence during the survey week, were part-time or could not be traced in the sample files in 1975. It can be seen that a larger proportion of manual employees had suffered loss of pay in 1975, especially women (and they were concentrated surprisingly at the top of the distribution). A large proportion of non-manual men had changed status between 1975 and 1978, but very few non-manual women had. The much larger proportion of women part-timers is also an important feature.

---

[1] Report No 5: *Third report on the standing reference*, Cmnd 6999, HMSO 1977.

Table 8.2 Matched Samples of Manual Men Analysed by Quantile Groups of Full-time Earnings; 1971 to 1978

A 4-year matched sample of manual men; 1975, 1976, 1977 and 1978

Great Britain

Quantile group	Top 10	11–30	31–50	51–70	71–90	Bottom 10	Not included
	%	%	%	%	%	%	%
1978					1977		
Top 10 per cent..	31·9	21·9	9·1	4·4	1·6	0·4	30·7
11–30	10·6	29·6	16·5	7·7	3·3	0·8	31·5
31–50	3·7	16·2	25·5	15·1	6·0	1·2	32·3
51–70	1·7	6·6	15·2	27·2	13·6	2·5	33·2
71–90	0·8	2·8	5·0	13·6	34·8	8·0	35·0
Bottom 10 ..	0·2	0·5	0·8	1·8	11·3	42·3	43·1
1978					1976		
Top 10 per cent..	27·3	20·8	9·4	4·5	1·8	0·9	35·3
11–30	10·2	24·7	15·6	8·3	3·7	1·3	36·2
31–50	3·8	15·5	21·8	13·8	6·7	2·2	36·2
51–70	2·0	6·9	14·2	22·6	12·7	4·1	37·5
71–90	1·0	2·7	5·3	13·7	28·7	9·4	39·2
Bottom 10 ..	0·3	0·7	1·2	2·3	10·6	33·8	51·1
1978					1975		
Top 10 per cent..	22·3	19·1	8·8	5·3	2·8	1·1	40·6
11–30	9·4	22·1	13·6	7·8	4·2	1·9	41·0
31–50	3·5	14·4	18·2	12·2	7·1	2·7	41·9
51–70	1·7	6·7	13·5	19·0	11·9	4·3	42·9
71–90	0·9	2·8	5·0	11·6	23·6	9·4	46·7
Bottom 10 ..	0·5	1·0	1·8	2·6	9·2	23·1	61·8

An 8-year matched sample of manual men; 1971 and 1978

	Top 10	11–30	31–50	51–70	71–90	Bottom 10	Not included
1978					1971		
Top 10 per cent..	20·4	26·3	16·5	9·0	5·5	5·4	16·9
11–30	12·2	23·4	18·5	14·2	9·3	4·1	18·3
31–50	6·9	19·1	20·7	17·8	11·9	7·0	16·6
51–70	4·7	12·8	19·7	21·0	17·3	8·4	16·1
71–90	2·8	7·1	13·0	20·8	27·2	12·9	16·2
Bottom 10 ..	1·6	4·3	5·5	12·7	31·3	26·8	17·8

Source: NES.

Table 8.3 Matched Samples of Non-manual Men Analysed by Quantile Groups of Full-time Earnings; 1971 to 1978

A 4-year matched sample of non-manual men; 1975, 1976, 1977 and 1978

Great Britain

Quantile group	Top 10	11–30	31–50	51–70	71–90	Bottom 10	Not included
	%	%	%	%	%	%	%
1978				**1977**			
Top 10 per cent..	57·9	12·4	2·3	0·9	0·7	0·4	25·4
11–30	5·8	53·0	12·9	2·7	0·9	0·4	24·3
31–50	0·6	12·1	43·9	12·9	3·2	0·5	26·8
51–70	0·3	1·6	13·7	42·3	11·6	1·2	29·3
71–90	0·3	0·7	1·8	12·4	46·5	7·1	31·2
Bottom 10 ..	0·3	0·4	0·6	1·2	9·0	45·4	43·1
1978				**1976**			
Top 10 per cent..	49·4	14·4	3·0	1·5	0·9	0·7	30·1
11–30	6·8	46·3	13·3	4·0	1·5	0·4	27·7
31–50	0·7	12·8	35·1	14·3	4·1	0·9	32·1
51–70	0·3	2·0	13·6	34·2	12·6	2·1	35·2
71–90	0·3	0·8	1·8	12·0	36·1	8·9	40·1
Bottom 10 ..	0·5	0·6	0·9	1·5	8·3	34·0	54·2
1978				**1975**			
Top 10 per cent..	43·4	15·9	2·7	1·4	1·1	0·6	34·9
11–30	5·7	38·7	14·9	4·7	1·9	0·5	33·6
31–50	0·8	10·4	29·6	15·1	4·9	1·2	38·0
51–70	0·5	2·2	11·9	25·4	13·6	2·7	43·7
71–90	0·3	0·9	2·1	9·9	28·3	10·3	48·2
Bottom 10 ..	0·3	0·7	1·0	1·4	7·9	23·3	65·4

An 8-year matched sample of non-manual men; 1971 and 1978

Quantile group	Top 10	11–30	31–50	51–70	71–90	Bottom 10	Not included
1978				**1971**			
Top 10 per cent..	55·5	26·1	6·1	3·7	2·6	1·0	5·0
11–30	10·8	39·0	22·7	9·7	4·6	1·9	11·3
31–50	2·3	21·2	26·7	17·7	10·1	5·2	16·8
51–70	1·0	6·5	20·5	22·4	18·4	7·3	23·9
71–90	0·8	2·7	7·5	23·8	24·2	16·0	25·0
Bottom 10 ..	0·9	2·4	4·3	7·7	26·3	24·6	33·8

Source: NES.

Table 8.4 Matched Samples of Manual Women Analysed by Quantile Groups of Full-time Earnings; 1971 to 1978

A 4-year matched sample of manual women; 1975, 1976, 1977 and 1978

Great Britain

Quantile group	Top 10	11–30	31–50	51–70	71–90	Bottom 10	Not included
	%	%	%	%	%	%	%
1978				1977			
Top 10 per cent..	36·7	15·9	4·1	2·0	0·8	0·3	40·2
11–30	9·5	33·9	10·4	4·4	1·6	0·3	39·9
31–50	1·9	13·9	28·4	10·9	2·8	0·9	41·2
51–70	0·3	3·4	10·6	32·4	8·8	1·3	43·2
71–90	0·1	0·7	1·8	9·1	34·9	6·8	46·6
Bottom 10 ..	0·6	0·2	0·7	1·8	10·3	31·5	54·9
1978				1976			
Top 10 per cent..	29·4	16·1	4·6	1·6	1·1	0·7	46·5
11–30	8·1	27·3	10·6	3·7	1·3	1·1	47·9
31–50	1·8	11·9	22·6	9·9	3·3	1·3	49·2
51–70	0·7	4·0	10·7	23·6	8·7	2·2	50·1
71–90	0·1	0·6	2·1	9·0	24·4	7·2	56·6
Bottom 10 ..	0·3	0·3	1·3	1·6	9·2	20·6	66·7
1978				1975			
Top 10 per cent..	22·4	14·2	4·3	2·0	1·6	0·4	55·1
11–30	7·9	19·6	8·8	3·9	2·5	1·1	56·2
31–50	2·0	11·7	16·2	8·1	3·9	0·9	57·2
51–70	0·6	2·8	9·2	17·0	8·1	2·0	60·3
71–90	0·2	1·5	1·9	9·2	17·3	4·2	65·7
Bottom 10 ..	0·4	0·7	0·9	2·0	7·7	12·8	75·5

An 8-year matched sample of manual women; 1971 and 1978

	Top 10	11–30	31–50	51–70	71–90	Bottom 10	Not included
1978				1971			
Top 10 per cent..	26·2	18·7	8·2	5·5	2·8	3·4	35·2
11–30	5·9	20·0	20·4	7·8	5·9	3·0	37·0
31–50	5·3	11·1	24·5	13·1	5·0	4·3	36·7
51–70	1·4	6·5	21·6	20·5	11·2	4·3	34·5
71–90	1·5	4·7	10·6	12·8	18·6	6·6	45·2
Bottom 10 ..	2·3	3·7	3·9	8·4	13·0	23·7	45·0

Source: NES.

Table 8.5 Matched Samples of Non-manual Women Analysed by Quantile Groups of Full-time Earnings; 1971 to 1978

A 4-year matched sample of non-manual women; 1975, 1976, 1977 and 1978

Great Britain

Quantile group	Top 10	11–30	31–50	51–70	71–90	Bottom 10	Not included
	%	%	%	%	%	%	%
1978					1977		
Top 10 per cent ..	59·4	16·6	1·0	0·4	0·5	0·1	22·0
11–30	5·2	53·1	12·3	3·0	1·4	0·3	24·7
31–50	0·2	10·2	44·4	14·5	2·9	0·6	27·2
51–70	0·1	1·2	10·5	41·8	14·8	1·9	29·7
71–90	0·1	0·4	1·4	7·8	42·9	11·2	36·2
Bottom 10 ..	0·3	0·4	0·7	1·2	7·7	42·6	47·1
1978					1976		
Top 10 per cent ..	53·7	17·7	1·7	0·7	0·5	0·0	25·7
11–30	4·3	43·3	13·8	3·6	2·1	0·7	32·2
31–50	0·2	8·7	35·3	15·93	4·5	1·2	34·2
51–70	0·2	1·2	9·3	31·4	16·5	3·3	38·1
71–90	0·1	0·5	1·3	7·9	27·9	13·2	49·1
Bottom 10 ..	0·2	0·3	0·5	1·3	7·6	31·3	58·8
1978					1975		
Top 10 per cent ..	42·3	18·7	2·0	0·8	0·5	0·2	35·5
11–30	5·1	31·5	15·4	3·5	2·2	0·9	41·4
31–50	0·2	7·2	25·2	15·7	5·9	1·1	44·7
51–70	0·2	1·4	7·9	20·5	16·0	4·9	49·1
71–90	0·2	0·6	1·5	6·4	18·9	12·1	60·3
Bottom 10 ..	0·2	0·4	0·6	1·6	5·7	18·5	73·0

An 8-year matched sample of non-manual women; 1971 and 1978

	Top 10	11–30	31–50	51–70	71–90	Bottom 10	Not included
1978					1971		
Top 10 per cent ..	51·1	29·1	10·0	0·6	0·6	0·6	8·0
11–30	11·6	37·7	22·3	5·5	4·4	1·3	17·2
31–50	0·8	15·5	27·3	18·9	14·7	5·7	17·1
51–70	0·9	4·8	19·9	22·4	15·9	8·8	27·3
71–90	0·7	1·8	7·1	19·3	27·0	13·8	30·3
Bottom 10 ..	0·0	2·0	4·6	8·5	30·6	21·2	33·1

Source: NES.

Table 8.6   Classification of Those Excluded from the Matched Samples in 1975

Great Britain

	Change of status	Loss of pay	Part-time	No trace	Total
	%	%	%	%	%
1978		Manual men			
Top 10 per cent	4·5	8·8	0·2	27·1	40·6
11–30	3·9	8·5	0·1	28·4	40·9
31–50	3·8	8·5	0·1	29·5	41·9
51–70	3·5	7·2	0·3	31·9	42·9
71–90	3·7	6·5	0·2	36·3	46·7
Bottom 10 ..	4·2	4·3	0·7	52·6	61·8
1978		Non-manual men			
Top 10 per cent	2·1	1·5	0·9	30·4	34·9
11–30	5·1	1·4	0·3	26·8	33·6
31–50	9·3	1·3	0·5	26·9	38·0
51–70	9·4	1·6	0·4	32·3	43·7
71–90	8·9	1·5	0·4	37·4	48·2
Bottom 10 ..	7·8	1·0	0·6	56·0	65·4
1978		Manual women			
Top 10 per cent	5·4	12·1	2·9	34·7	55·1
11–30	5·6	10·2	4·5	35·9	56·2
31–50	5·1	10·1	4·0	38·0	57·2
51–70	5·0	8·9	5·0	41·4	60·3
71–90	4·8	6·9	6·3	47·7	65·7
Bottom 10 ..	4·3	5·6	8·1	57·5	75·5
1978		Non-manual women			
Top 10 per cent	0·9	1·9	2·6	30·1	35·5
11–30	1·5	2·2	2·4	35·3	41·4
31–50	2·0	2·6	2·5	37·6	44·7
51–70	2·9	1·9	3·4	40·9	49·1
71–90	3·7	1·8	3·6	51·2	60·3
Bottom 10 ..	3·2	1·6	4·9	63·3	73·0

Source: NES.

8.13   Surprisingly, large proportions of the 1978 sample were not traced in the earlier years and the proportions tended to be larger at the lower earnings levels and for women. Young people entering the labour force for the first time provide a partial explanation of these missing numbers. Other possible causes are unemployment or non-response (which is not generally a serious problem in the NES) in earlier years.

Numbers in the 1978 sample who could not be traced in earlier years

	Manual men	Non-manual men
	%	%
1977	23	22
1976	27	26
1975	33	33

The change in sampling methods means we could expect to trace back to 1971 no more than 25 per cent of the 1978 sample, even with no attrition; and with attrition the proportion is in fact reduced to about 10 per cent. Since the numbers

Figure 8.4 Quantile Position in 1975, 1976 and 1977 of Men belonging to certain Quantile Groups in 1978

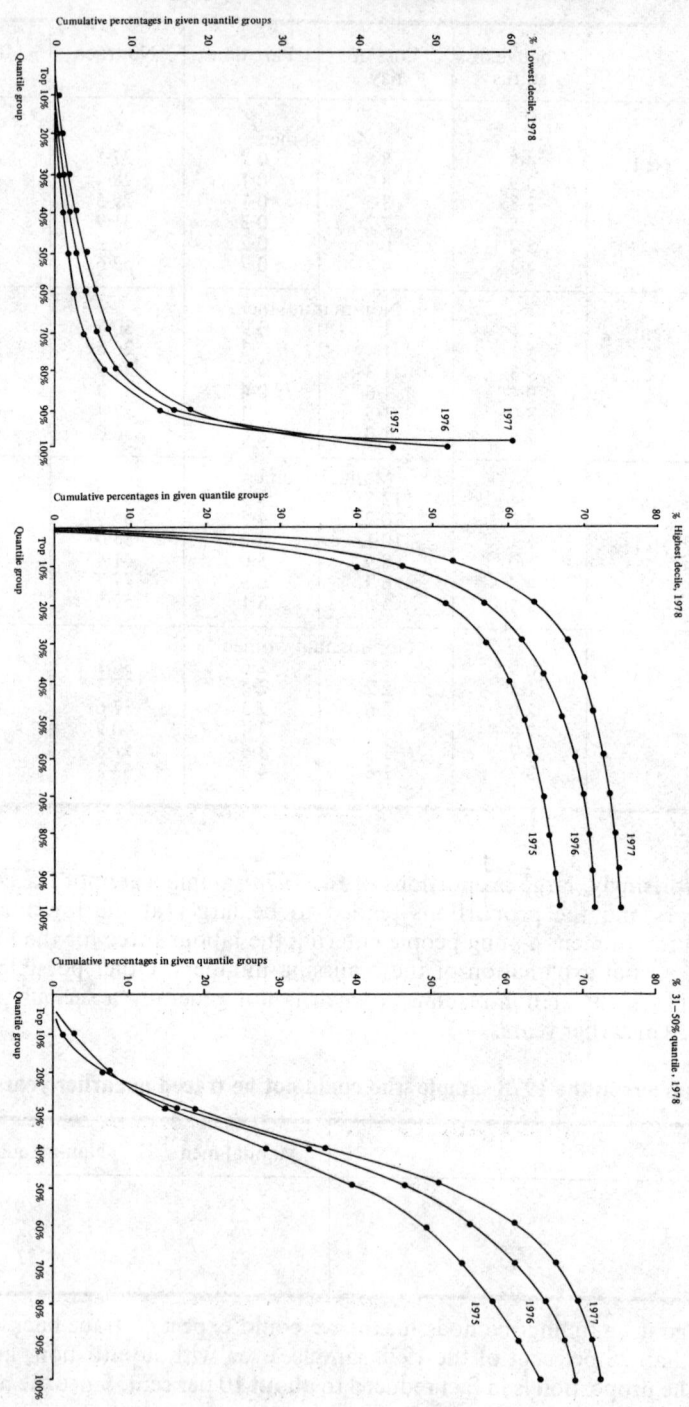

Source: New Earnings Survey.

Figure 8.5 Quantile Position in 1975, 1976 and 1977 of Women belonging to certain Quantile Groups in 1978

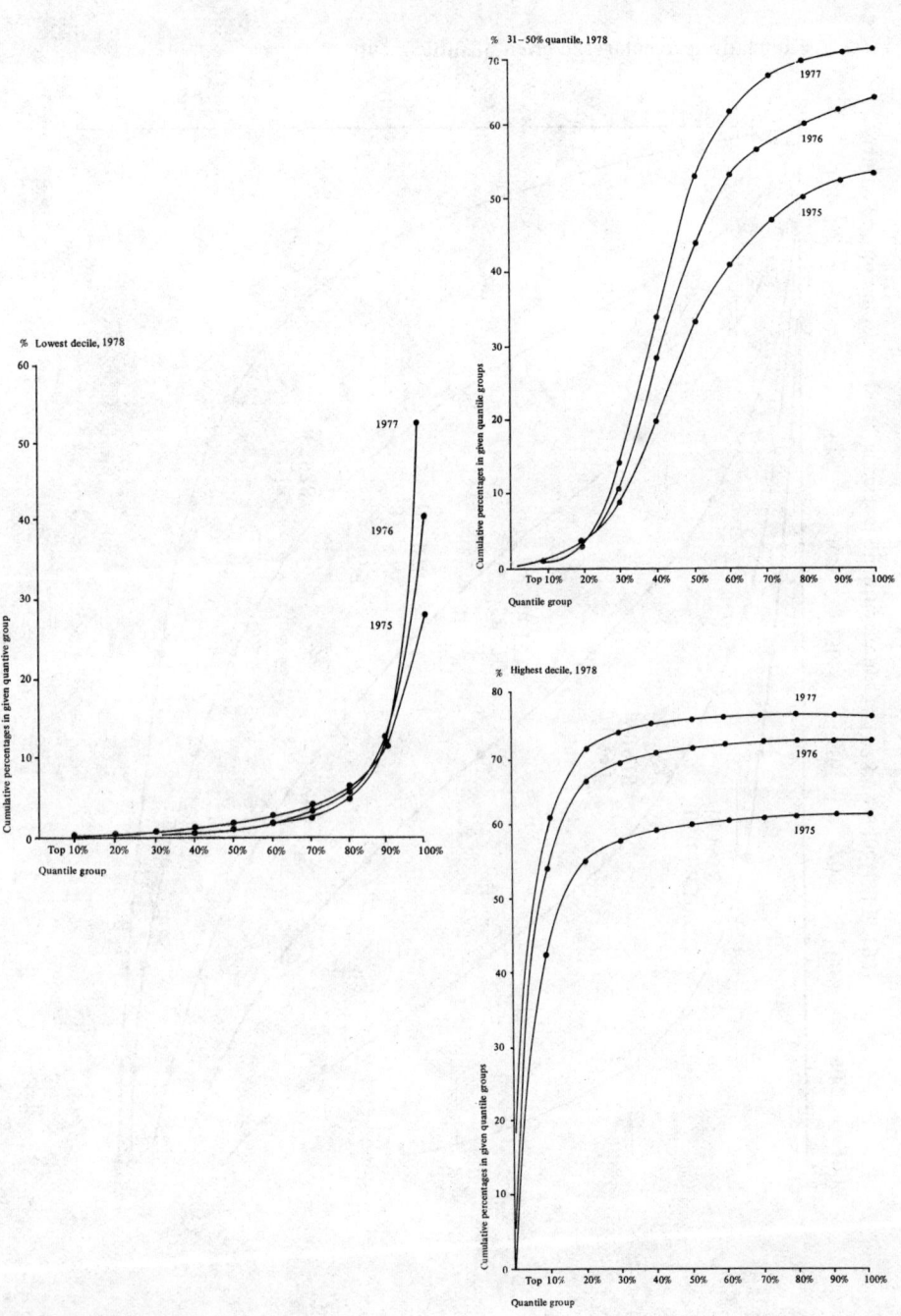

Figure 8.6   Quantile Position of Men in 1978 compared with 1975

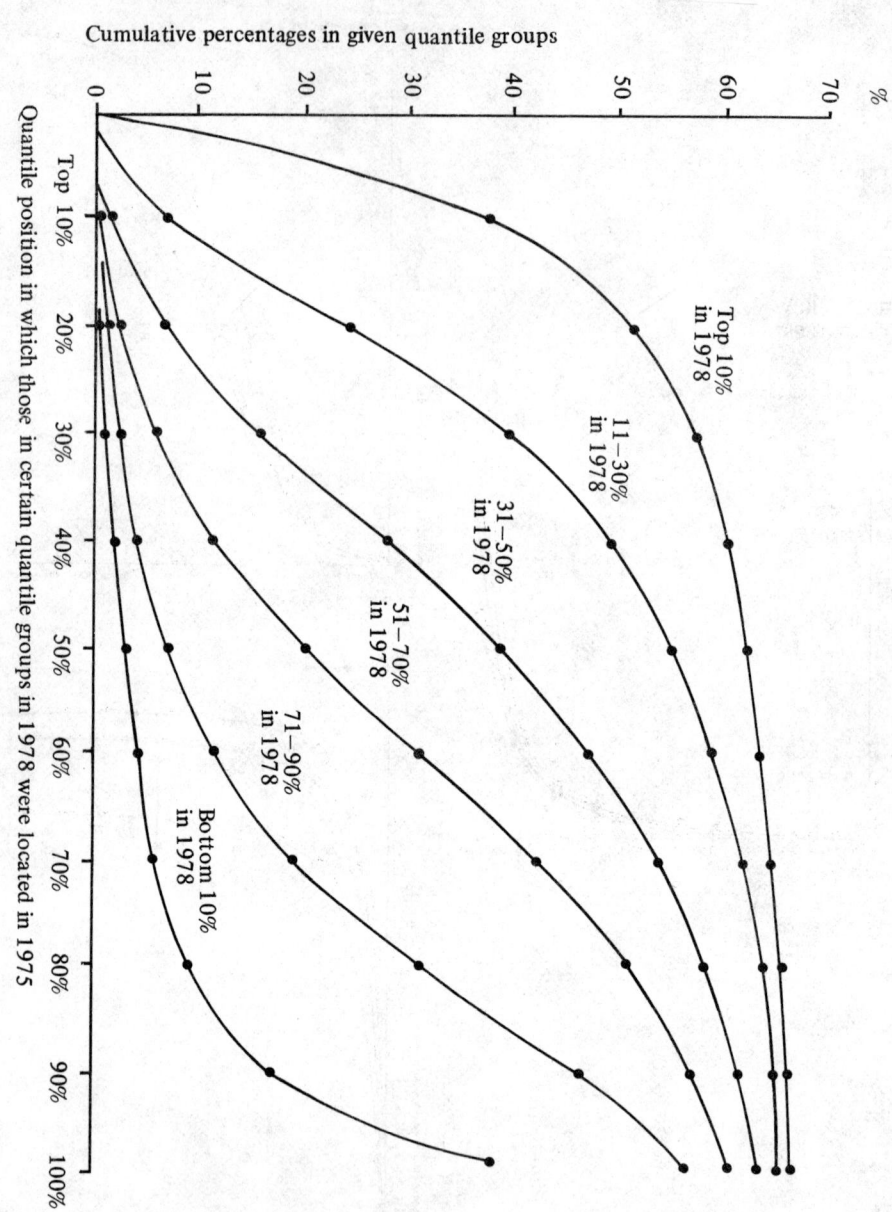

Source: New Earnings Survey.

Figure 8.7 Quantile Position of Women in 1978 compared with 1975

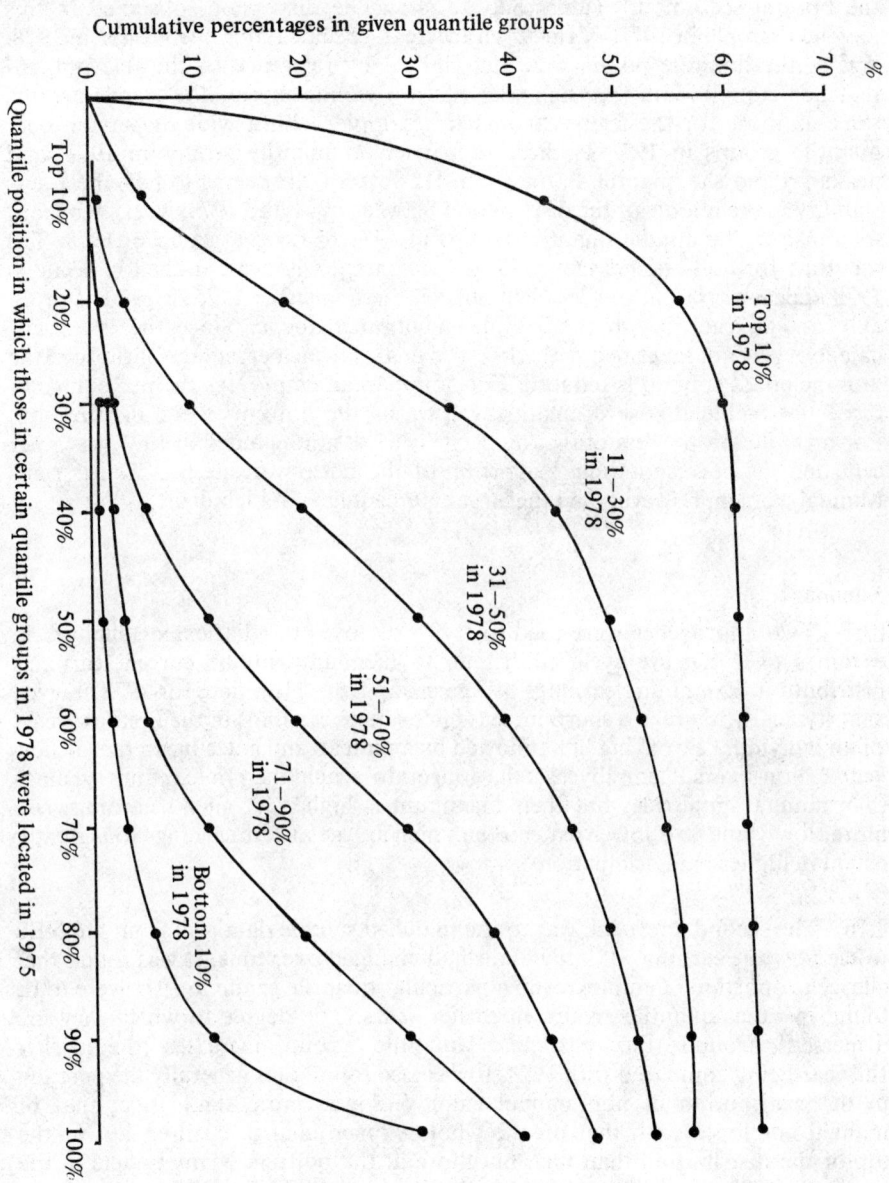

of 'no trace' elements are greatest when earnings are low, the 1971–1978 sample is likely to suffer from considerable bias.

8.14   If with these reservations we turn now to the eight-year matched sample, the bottom sections of Tables 8.2–8.5 show the dispersion, observed in this matched sample in 1971, of those who were in specified quantile groups in 1978. Again, the quantile points were determined by reference to the relevant un-matched sample data for each year. As we would expect, the trends are the same as those for the four-year matched sample, with a wide dispersion over quantile groups in 1971 of those in particular quantile groups in 1978, and peaks around the quantile in question. However, there seems to have been less stability in the middle of the distribution between 1971 and 1978, with a tendency for those in the middle quantile groups in 1971 to drop a group in 1978. The fact that, for non-manual men, a larger percentage who were in the top decile in 1978 appear also to have been there in 1971 than in either 1975 or 1976, is prob-ably due to the bias in the sample, mentioned above. Since the 'no trace' category was not identified in the 1971–78 analysis, the percentage of those in the 'not included' column is reduced. For non-manual employees the percentage of those not included rose dramatically towards the bottom of the distribution. For men, the proportion of the top decile in 1978 not included in 1971 was 5 per cent and the corresponding proportion of the bottom decile was 32 per cent. Manual women, however, had the largest percentage not included.

Summary

8.15   Two approaches were used to try to discover to what extent changes in earnings over the life cycle contribute to inequality in the current earnings distribution. Examining earnings by age group from NES data for 1978 showed that, typically, there is a sharp increase in average earnings in the first few years of an individual's working life, followed by a plateau and a decline in the last few years. Non-manual employees take longer to reach their maximum earnings than manual employees but their maximum is higher. Women's earnings rise more slowly and to a lower plateau than men's. Age affects earnings to a greater extent in higher paid occupations.

8.16   The second approach was to use matched sample data also from the NES to see how the earnings of individuals had changed over time. It was found that a large proportion of employees in a particular quantile group in 1978 were to be found in other quantile groups in earlier years. The degree to which they are dispersed around the particular quantile group increases the earlier the year being compared with 1978. It was also found that generally the position in the distribution of non-manual employees was more stable than that of manual employees and that on the whole women change position less at the top of the distribution than men but more at the bottom. Many people in the sample in 1978 could not be traced in earlier years, and this will bias the results which should therefore be treated with caution. The bias is likely to be more marked on the eight-year matched sample covering the period 1971 to 1978, but the general trends derived from the data are similar to those in the matched sample data covering the shorter period 1975 to 1978.

8.17   In conclusion, it should be pointed out that the variation in the earnings of individuals implied by the matched sample suggests that lifetime earnings patterns cannot be directly inferred from age-earnings profiles based on one year's cross-sectional data.

CHAPTER 9
Earnings and Other Employee Benefits

Introduction

9.1 We saw in Chapter 3 that when discussing the remuneration of employees, the "total advantages and disadvantages" of employment should be taken into account. Apart from cash earnings, which have been the main subject of Chapters 5 to 8, these include:

  i   the numbers of hours per week and days per year worked. These, and their relationship to hourly earnings, are discussed in paragraphs 9.3 to 9.14 below with supporting detail in Appendix J;

  ii   pensions and sick pay arrangements (paragraphs 9.15 to 9.20);

  iii   the goods and services of value to the employee which are provided by the employer, eg subsidised or free lunches, medical insurance, loans, rent-free housing, free produce, company cars (paragraphs 9.21 to 9.26); and

  iv   the other effects the job may have on the employee, for example on his health, contentment and future prospects in the labour market (paragraphs 9.27 to 9.35).

9.2 Throughout this Chapter, we try to assess the following:

  a   How are the advantages and disadvantages distributed among different employees? For example, are there clear distinctions between the benefits received by manual workers and those received by management?

  b   Is there a relationship between the level of earnings and the level of benefit received? Is it likely that low earnings in a job are accompanied by high benefits?

  c   Has the pattern of non-earnings entitlements, holidays, hours and conditions of work been changing?

  d   How do non-earnings factors in the UK compare with those prevalent elsewhere in the EEC?

Holidays

9.3 The development of holiday entitlements for manual workers has been a slow process extending over more than 50 years. By 1974, three weeks paid holiday had become almost standard for manual and non-manual employees alike, while approximately one in ten of male manual employees and one in three of male non-manual employees were entitled to more than four weeks.

Surveys show that women generally have lower entitlements than men and clerical and manual grades have lower entitlements than managerial staff. That the overall trend is still improving, is shown in the following Table 9.1 comparing figures drawn from the New Earnings Surveys for 1970 and 1974 in which years a specific question about holidays was asked.

9.4 Fuller supporting data are given in Appendix J, which also shows the result of comparisons, based on the 1974 NES, between average earnings in an occupation and the proportion of employees entitled to less than 4 weeks paid holiday a year. The relationship is found to be significant, the higher paid occupations being likely to have fewer employees below the 4 week level. This is another indication of the general tendency for better holiday entitlements to be enjoyed by the better paid occupations.

Table 9.1 Paid Holiday Entitlements of Manual and Non-manual Employees; 1970 and 1974

Great Britain

| Type of employee | Percentage of employees having holiday entitlement of | | | | | |
| | 2 weeks or less | | 3 weeks or less | | 4 weeks or less | |
	1970	1974	1970	1974	1970	1974
	%	%	%	%	%	%
Men						
Manual	14·8	4·4	79·0	45·6	96·2	90·1
Non-manual	3·8	2·5	34·0	25·4	69·1	67·1
Women						
Manual	15·0	7·1	84·5	49·1	96·9	96·8
Non-manual	8·6	5·1	48·5	40·9	75·8	76·9

Source: NES 1970, 1974.

9.5 Britain is somewhat below the EEC average both in general holiday entitlements and in public holidays. A continuing trend towards a higher minimum level for holidays can be attributed to the influence of EEC practice and to the pressure from trade unions for better employee benefits. This general improvement is tending to reduce the historic differences between non-manual and manual workers, and between the higher and lower grades of non-manual employees.

Hours

9.6 The subject of hours worked is less straightforward than that of holiday entitlements. One can be reasonably sure that longer holidays would be regarded by employees as a definite benefit; attitudes to hours of work may vary. For example, an employee may prefer to work just long enough to earn what he regards as a reasonable wage; or he may prefer to work as many hours as possible, especially if some are paid at a premium rate.

9.7 The question whether employees who work long hours do so from choice was raised by Layard *et al* in a study completed recently for the Royal Commis-

119

Figure 9.1   Annual Paid Holidays in the EEC; 1976

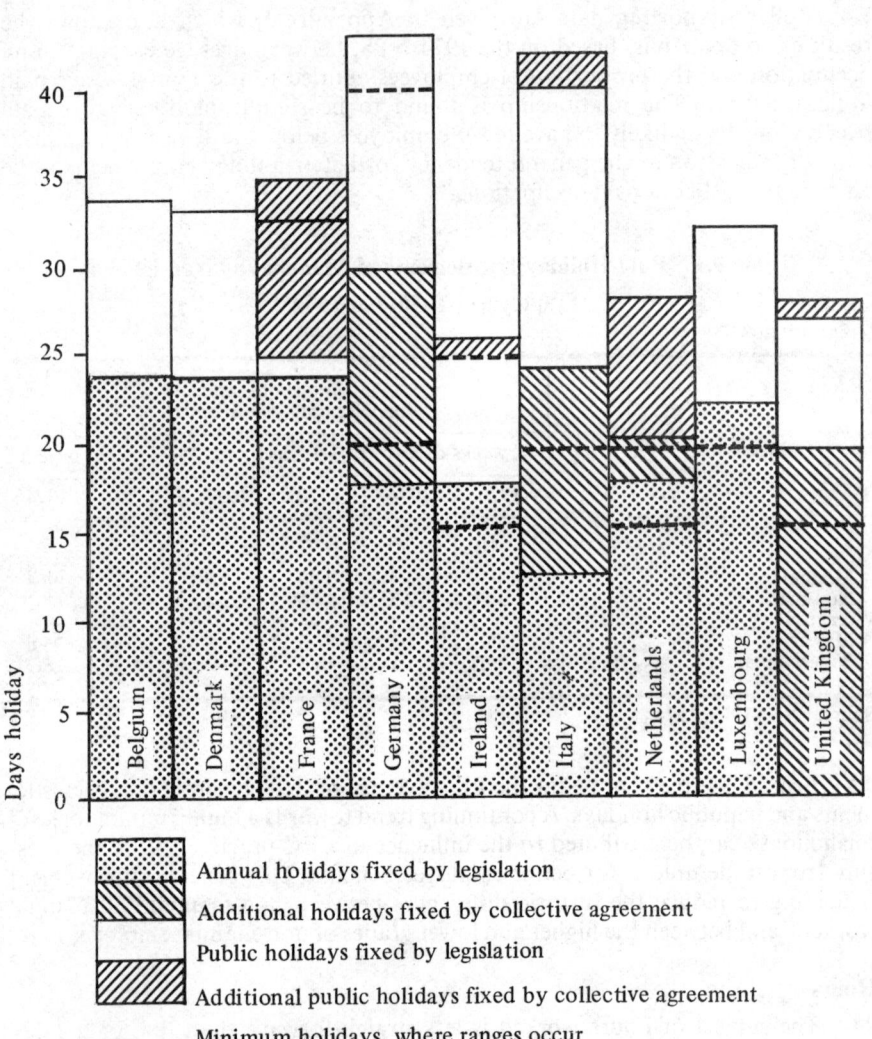

Source: Eurostat Social Indicators (Table 111/2).

sion[1]. They wrote: "with hours and weeks of work, there is an obvious problem: does the behaviour of an individual really reflect choice on his part, subject to the hourly earnings which he or she can command? Or are individuals essentially rationed in the hours and weeks that they can work? . . . It is of course true that to any one person in any particular job it may often appear that he has no freedom to vary his hours. Even if he does overtime this may not be really voluntary yet if he steps back and asks himself why he is doing his particular job, he is likely to conclude that he was influenced in his choice by the combination of earnings and hours of work which it offered. So in a more 'long run' sense, hours do reflect a process of choice". That there is considerable variation in the number of hours worked per week is shown by Table 9.2, taken from Layard *et al* and based on data from the General Household Survey. It gives the number of hours worked per week for different earnings ranges for married men, single men, married women and single women for the 1975 General Household Survey sample. Interesting features of this table are that in every earnings range married men work longer hours than single men; and that for married men there appears to be a clear relationship between the range of earnings and the number of hours worked, whereas there is no such strong correlation for single men.

Table 9.2   Average Hours Worked per Week by Hourly Earnings; 1975

Employees under 65 (men) or 60 (women)

Hours

	Hourly earnings (pence)						
	Under 62·5	62·5 —	75 —	87·5 —	100 —	125 —	150+
Average hours							
Married men (FT) ..	62	52	48	48	46	44	41
Single men (FT) ..	44	45	44	43	43	41	40
Single women (FT) ..	39	39	39	38	38	38	40
Married women (FT+ PT)	25	27	28	29	29	30	23
Number in sample							
Married men (FT) ..	70	118	264	432	1,150	845	1,339
Single men (FT) ..	153	104	122	145	241	144	119
Single women (FT) ..	117	103	106	84	104	47	44
Married women (FT+ PT)	611	467	498	328	387	138	225

Source: *Background Paper No 5*, Table 5.5.

Notes:

FT means 30 hours or more a week, PT means less than 30 hours a week.
The figures should be treated with care due to the small size of the sample.

9.8   We have used the 1977 NES to investigate further the relationship between earnings and hours. We plotted average earnings for all occupations for which figures were available against basic hours and against average hours worked, and the results are set out and analysed in Appendix J. Basic weekly hours for most occupations were in the range of $39\frac{1}{2}$–$40\frac{1}{2}$ regardless of wage levels. However, those in non-manual occupations tended to have both higher basic wages and

---

[1] The causes of poverty, *Background Paper No 5*, HMSO, 1978.

121

lower weekly hours. It may be that the concept of basic weekly hours is not wholly appropriate for some professions.

9.9   Average hours worked were more various, largely because of differences in overtime where the distinction between manual and non-manual occupations is quite marked, as the table shows. It should be noted in passing that for many forms of non-manual employment "hours worked" is not very meaningful and employers do not report hours or hourly earnings in the NES, so the figures for non-manual occupations are not fully representative.

Table 9.3   Average Weekly Hours and Average Hourly Earnings; 1977

Great Britain

	Average weekly hours			Average gross hourly earnings (excluding overtime) pence
	Normal basic	Overtime	Total	
Men				
All non-manual occupations	37·3	1·4	38·7	227·9
All manual occupations ..	39·9	5·8	45·7	154·3

Source: NES 1977, Table 86.

9.10   Comparison with other EEC countries shows no great differences in manual workers' hours. The detailed information is given in Appendix J.

"Real" rates of pay

9.11   In paragraphs 9.3–9.10, the variation in the number of weeks per year and hours per week worked has been discussed. If individual holiday entitlements were known, it would be possible to adjust the earnings for the total number of hours of work which are done in a year. The "real" hourly wage would then be:

$$£ \frac{\text{total weekly earnings} \times 52}{\text{total weekly hours} \times (52 - \text{weeks holiday entitlement})}$$

eg, for a man with gross weekly earnings of £85·50 per week, who works an average of 46 hours a week and has 17½ days (3½ weeks) paid holiday a year, the "real" hourly wage will be:

$$£ \frac{85.50 \times 52}{46 \times 48\frac{1}{2}} \text{ per hour}$$

= £1·99 per hour.

The hourly rate calculated simply by dividing weekly pay by weekly hours is:

$$£ \frac{85·50}{46} \text{ per hour}$$

= £1·86 per hour.

Details of average holiday entitlements for each of the 18 main occupation groups as recorded in the NES were provided by the Department of Employment. By combining these with information on average weekly hours and earnings, the average "real" hourly wage for each occupation group was estimated. These data are only available for the year 1974.

122

9.12 The results of the calculations (plus the various items of relevant information) are shown in Tables 9.4 and 9.5. Only 14 groups are identified in Table 9.5 as the numbers of women in the sample were rather small in the remaining four groups. The final two columns of the tables contrast the average gross hourly earnings as measured directly in the NES with the derived average "real" hourly wage. Inevitably, the differences are greatest in those groups with the greatest holiday entitlement. The contrast is particularly marked in group III which includes teachers and, in general, is less marked in the male manual groups (groups X to XVIII) such as catering, construction etc.

9.13 A characteristic of the male manual groups is the relatively large number of average hours worked per week. Overtime earnings are included in gross weekly earnings which, in the calculation of "real" hourly wages, are multiplied by 52 to give a notional annual earnings figure. Holiday pay is frequently restricted to basic earnings rather than gross earnings; thus the relatively small differences between gross hourly earnings and "real" hourly wages may be somewhat overstated for men in the manual occupation groups. It should be noted that the average weekly hours recorded in the survey for non-manual employees may represent the average length of the contractual working week, but may well understate the number of hours actually worked, particularly for professional groups and managers. This would result in some overstatement of the hourly earnings figure but is unlikely to alter substantially the contrast between hourly earnings and the "real" hourly wage, as the latter would also be reduced by an increase in the average weekly hours figure used in its calculation.

9.14 The comparisons of "real" hourly wage rates, as such, in Tables 9.4 and 9.5, therefore, are approximate. The occupational groupings are rather broad; the concept of "real" wage rates would perhaps be of greater value in more detailed comparisons. Nevertheless, the approach does illustrate a worthwhile alternative method of comparing earnings levels which in this instance results in some increase in the differences in average earnings between occupation groups.

Pensions and sick pay arrangements

9.15 An employee who retires or is sick is generally eligible for support from the State. Many employers make provision for pensions and sick pay themselves, however. Before the new earnings related State pension scheme was introduced, there was a considerable difference between the incomes of those with occupational pensions and those with only flat-rate State pensions (see Report No 6). In those firms which had an occupational pension scheme, white-collar employees were more likely to be entitled to join it than blue-collar workers, and were likely to be entitled to benefits of a greater value. In the survey of employee benefits in 1977 published recently by the British Institute of Management[1], it was found that 98 per cent of companies in the survey had a pension scheme, and of those 74 per cent provided cover for all employees. Most of the companies who restricted their pension schemes to some employee categories (mostly non-manual) were smaller organisations. As with earnings, large firms were more

---

[1] H Murlis, Employee benefits: a survey of practice in 400 companies, *Management Survey Report No 37*.

Great Britain

Table 9.4 Real Rates of Pay of Full-time Men; 1974[1]

Occupation	Average gross weekly earnings £	Average[2] weekly hours	Average holiday entitlement (days)	Average "real" hourly wage £	Average gross hourly earnings £
I Managerial (general management)	106·6	38·1	18	3·01	2·64
II Professional and related supporting management and administration	66·5	37·3	20	1·93	1·73
III Professional and related in education, welfare and health	57·1	32·9	34	2·00	1·69
IV Literary, artistic and sport	53·3	38·8	20	1·49	1·35
V Professional and related in science, engineering, technology and similar fields	56·3	38·6	21	1·59	1·40
VI Managerial (excluding general management)	54·9	39·9	18	1·48	1·40
VII Clerical and related	41·1	40·8	18	1·08	1·01
VIII Selling	43·3	40·6	16	1·14	1·03
IX Security and protective service	46·9	46·2	19	1·10	1·02
X Catering, cleaning, hairdressing and other personal services	35·2	46·5	15	0·80	0·76
XI Farming, fishing and related	35·6	46·6	15	0·81	0·74
XII Materials processing (excluding metal)	43·8	47·1	16	0·99	0·93
XIII Making and repairing (excluding metal and electrical)	45·3	45·1	16	1·07	1·01
XIV Processing, making, repairing and related (metal and electrical)	46·7	45·9	17	1·09	1·02
XV Painting, repetitive assembling, product inspecting, packaging and related	42·8	44·9	16	1·02	0·95
XVI Construction, mining and related not identified elsewhere	45·6	46·1	16	1·05	0·98
XVII Transport operating, materials moving and storing related	42·4	48·4	16	0·93	0·88
XVIII Miscellaneous	39·5	46·7	16	0·90	0·85
Total	47·7	43·7			1·08

Source: NES and Department of Employment.

Note: [1] Rates of pay for all full-time men with no loss of pay.

  [2] Average weekly hours includes overtime.

Great Britain

Table 9.5 Real Rates of Pay of Full-time Women; 1974[1]

Occupation	Average gross weekly earnings £	Average[2] weekly hours	Average holiday entitlement (days)	Average "real" hourly wage £	Average gross hourly earnings £
II Professional and related supporting management and administration	43·7	36·5	19	1·29	1·20
III Professional and related in education, welfare and health	35·1	34·1	31	1·17	1·07
IV Literary, artistic and sport	36·0	37·5	17	1·03	0·93
V Professional and related in science, engineering, technology and similar fields	32·5	37·4	18	0·93	0·85
VI Managerial (excluding general management)	30·4	38·5	16	0·84	0·81
VII Clerical and related	26·7	37·1	17	0·77	0·72
VIII Selling	19·9	39·0	14	0·54	0·51
X Catering, cleaning, hairdressing and other personal services	22·2	39·5	16	0·60	0·56
XII Materials processing (excluding metal)	23·6	40·3	15	0·62	0·59
XIII Making and repairing (excluding metal and electrical)	23·7	39·1	16	0·65	0·61
XIV Processing, making, repairing and related (metal and electrical)	25·5	40·3	16	0·67	0·63
XV Painting, repetitive assembling, product inspecting, packaging and related	24·3	40·1	16	0·65	0·61
XVII Transport operating, materials moving and storing related	26·2	42·2	15	0·66	0·62
XVIII Miscellaneous	24·2	40·4	15	0·64	0·59
Total	26·9	37·8			0·71

Source: NES and Department of Employment.

Note: [1] Rates of pay for all full-time women with no loss of pay.

[2] Average weekly hours includes overtime.

generous with benefits than small firms[1]. The survey comments: "Over a quarter of participants have improved their scheme since 1973 and manual employees are now much more likely to be included in company schemes. Pensions is an area in which manual and white-collar trade unions have recently shown considerable interest, both in terms of negotiating improved benefits and in participating in the management of pensions funds by the appointment of union-nominated trustees." In 1971 the total number of employees covered by occupational pension schemes was 11·1 million[2]. The Government Actuary's survey[3] in 1975 showed that there had been little change, the estimated total membership being 11·5 million. No information is available on total membership since 1975.

9.16 The differences in pension entitlement between different occupations have recently been reduced, because of trade union activity, incomes policy, and the introduction of the universal earnings-related pension scheme; all employees must be either members of the State scheme, or else members of an occupational scheme offering benefits at least as good as those offered in the State scheme. It is still the case that senior management may be offered "top hat" pensions well above general entitlement levels (see Table 9.9).

9.17 Occupational pension schemes are in general more sophisticated and highly developed in Great Britain than they are in other EEC countries. This is because in Europe pensions are closely tied or integrated into State social security provisions, and the level of State provision is high relative to the level in Britain. In general the provisions apply equally to all occupational groups.

9.18 State benefit paid during periods of sickness or injury, although earnings related, is usually at a level well below that of an employee's average earnings. Many firms, therefore, agree to give either full pay or a proportion of full pay for a limited number of weeks a year. However, not all employees are entitled to benefit from employers' sick pay schemes and within a scheme different employees may have different entitlements. Table 9.6 shows the proportion of full-time employees covered by sick-pay schemes in different occupations in 1974. The main features are that:

a   over 90 per cent of employees (male and female) in non-manual occupations were covered, compared with 74 per cent of men and about 56 per cent of women in manual occupations; and

b   in certain occupations, eg groups XII, XIII, XIV and XV, women were much less likely to be covered than men.

9.19   Table 9.7 shows that in 1974 those manual workers who were covered by sick pay schemes were likely to receive less favourable treatment than non-manual employees; only 50 per cent of manual employees who were covered by

---

[1] *Labour Cost Survey*, Department of Employment, 1977.

[2] *Fourth Survey on Occupational Pension Schemes*, Government Actuary, 1971.

[3] *Occupational pension schemes 1975: Fifth survey by the Government Actuary*, HMSO, 1978.

sick pay schemes would have received full pay, compared with 93 per cent of non-manual employees. The DHSS report also gave details of the length of qualifying period for which workers had to be employed before becoming eligible for sick pay. For full-time men, the proportions of those covered for whom there was no qualifying period varied from 80 per cent for "professional and related in education, welfare and health" workers to 21 per cent for "transport operating, materials moving and storing related" workers. Similarly, less than 3 per cent of the former group had to wait for more than a year before qualifying for sick pay, compared with over 40 per cent of the latter group.

Table 9.6 Proportions of All Full-time Employees Covered by Sick Pay Schemes in Different Occupations; 1974

Per cent

Occupations	Men	Married women	Other women
All occupations	80·1	76·7	79·4
I Managerial (general management)	90·9	100·0	0·0
II Professional and related supporting management and administration	95·6	100·0	100·0
III Professional and related in education, welfare and health	98·7	100·0	97·7
IV Literary, artistic and sport	90·3	50·0	100·0
V Professional and related in science, engineering, technology and similar fields	90·5	94·1	91·7
VI Managerial (excluding general management)	96·3	85·7	100·0
VII Clerical and related	94·1	92·4	95·7
VIII Selling	92·9	86·1	84·1
IX Security and protective service	95.9	100·0	100·0
X Catering, cleaning, hairdressing and other personal services	80·6	76·4	75·9
XI Farming, fishing and related	80·7	0·0	0·0
XII Materials processing (excluding metal) ..	71·9	49·3	38·1
XIII Making and repairing (excluding metal and electrical)	67·1	34·0	33·7
XIV Processing, making, repairing and related (metal and electrical)	67·6	36·4	40·7
XV Painting, repetitive assembling, product inspecting, packaging and related	70·7	61·8	58·3
XVI Construction, mining and related not identified elsewhere	91·2	0·0	100·0
XVII Transport operating, materials moving and storing related	79·3	82·7	88·2
XVIII Miscellaneous	68·8	68·7	47·1
All manual occupations	74·0	57·9	54·4
All non-manual occupations	94·2	92·8	94·9

Source: Report on a survey of occupational sick pay schemes, DHSS, 1977.

Generally, of those covered by sick pay schemes, 72 per cent of full-time men in manual jobs had to undergo a qualifying period, compared with 33 per cent of those in non-manual jobs. The qualifying period is one factor reducing the likelihood of coverage for manual workers, as it is in the case of occupational pension schemes coverage.

9.20 During the recent years of incomes policy, improvements in pensions and sickness provision have been one way of increasing employees' total income within the Government's regulations. As a result, in the last five years there have

127

Table 9.7   Proportion of Employees in each Occupation Covered by Sick Pay Schemes, by Amount of Sick Pay at Commencement of Payment; 1974

Occupation	Number of employees	Amount of sick pay at commencement of payment												
		Full pay			Half pay			£10 or more	Flat rate per week					Amount at employers' discretion
		Without deduction	Less all NI benefit	Less some NI benefit or other deduction	Without deduction	Less all NI benefit	Less some NI benefit or other deduction		£7 or more but less than £10	£5 or more but less than £7	£4 or more but less than £5	£3 or more but less than £4	Less than £3	
(MEN FULL-TIME)														
All Occupations	5,031	11.5	40.1	14.9	1.8	0.2	0.2	5.5	0.8	0.9	0.7	0.8	3.9	18.4
I Managerial (general management)	40	18.7	57.5	19.6	0.0	0.0	0.0	1.4	0.0	0.0	0.5	0.0	0.5	1.9
II Professional and related supporting management and administration	219	7.5	73.3	15.7	0.7	0.7	0.0	0.7	0.0	0.0	0.0	0.0	0.0	1.4
III Professional and related in education, welfare and health	151	13.3	60.5	17.5	0.5	0.3	0.0	0.8	0.0	0.0	0.3	0.0	0.3	2.8
IV Literary, artistic and sport	28	22.7	51.1	21.6	0.7	0.0	0.0	1.1	0.0	0.0	0.0	0.0	0.0	6.4
V Professional and related in science, engineering, technology and similar fields	392	21.8	51.0	22.3	0.2	0.5	0.0	1.0	0.0	0.4	0.0	0.4	0.0	3.2
VI Managerial (excluding general management)	286	16.7	40.3	24.1	0.4	0.0	0.0	7.5	0.4	0.4	0.4	0.4	1.3	7.9
VII Clerical and related	427	8.1	57.0	16.3	4.7	0.0	0.0	5.8	0.0	0.0	0.0	0.0	1.2	7.0
VIII Selling	250	7.6	47.5	22.0	2.5	0.0	0.0	3.4	0.0	0.8	0.0	1.7	0.8	13.5
IX Security and protective service	93	12.3	55.5	11.1	2.5	0.0	0.0	8.6	0.0	0.0	0.0	0.0	1.2	8.6
X Catering, cleaning, hairdressing and other personal service	141	9.1	34.5	13.2	3.0	0.0	0.5	12.7	0.5	2.0	0.5	1.5	2.0	20.3
XI Farming, fishing and related	92	15.0	23.5	9.4	3.3	0.5	0.5	3.7	0.5	2.3	2.3	0.5	14.5	23.9
XII Materials processing (excluding metal)	240	7.5	26.1	11.4	3.2	0.5	0.8	8.6	1.7	1.9	0.8	1.7	2.9	32.7
XIII Making and repairing (excluding metal and electrical)	245	8.6	27.7	10.6	1.2	0.4	0.0	6.9	1.6	1.6	1.2	0.4	6.9	32.7
XIV Processing, making, repairing and related (metal and electrical)	880	4.0	28.3	4.7	0.6	0.0	0.3	8.1	1.6	0.0	1.2	1.5	13.7	37.4
XV Painting, repetitive assembling, product inspecting, packaging and related	282	6.1	30.5	13.1	2.9	0.0	0.2	8.8	2.3	1.4	2.1	1.4	6.1	25.1
XVI Construction, mining and related not identified elsewhere	362	4.9	36.8	11.3	2.9	0.5	0.4	5.4	1.5	2.9	0.5	2.0	7.3	24.0
XVII Transport operating, materials moving and storing related	652													
XVIII Miscellaneous	251													
All manual occupations	3,233	7.7	30.6	11.7	2.5	0.3	0.4	8.0	1.3	1.5	1.1	1.3	6.2	27.3
All non-manual occupations	1,798	17.7	55.3	20.0	0.6	0.2	0.0	1.6	0.1	0.0	0.1	0.1	0.2	4.1
(WOMEN FULL-TIME)														
All Occupations	1,741	19.3	37.5	29.1	1.5	0.0	0.3	4.1	0.1	0.5	0.3	0.3	0.6	6.2
All manual occupations	543	13.0	27.0	27.2	2.8	0.0	0.4	9.1	0.5	1.6	0.5	1.2	2.1	15.1
All non-manual occupations	1,198	21.7	41.6	29.9	1.0	0.2	0.4	2.2	0.0	0.0	0.2	0.0	0.1	2.8

Source: *Report on a survey of occupational sick pay schemes*, DHSS, 1977.

Table 9.8 Company Cars by Jobs; 1973 to 1978

Job	Proportion of job holders having the full use of a company car in:					
	1973	1974	1975	1976	1977	1978
	%	%	%	%	%	%
1. Managing directors	94·2	95·0	97·0	96·0	95·2	98·1
2. General Managers	93·2	94·4	94·9	94·4	94·8	96·1
3. Company Secretaries:						
(i) Private Companies	67·1	71·8	76·7	69·7	68·7	74·7
(ii) Public Companies	70·8	77·7	77·1	84·7	81·0	87·9
(iii) All Company Secretaries	69·3	75·3	76·9	78·0	75·4	81·2
4. Personnel Executives	51·6	58·8	61·9	58·2	60·4	64·0
5. Training Executives	25·9	34·8	31·6	38·0	40·8	42·2
6. Financial Executives	55·8	60·0	60·9	62·9	67·0	66·9
7. Cost Accountants	16·4	26·3	24·1	24·2	24·0	24·0
8. Production Executives:						
(i) Single Works	58·4	63·7	64·7	65·1	64·6	69·1
(ii) Several Works	71·9	82·2	84·4	83·9	84·9	88·9
(iii) All Production Executives	61·8	68·4	69·1	69·1	69·2	73·4
9. Chief Engineers	33·1	39·1	38·7	39·2	36·5	41·6
10. Production Controllers	22·4	26·1	26·8	30·0	28·5	29·7
11. Heads of Work Study	18·6	19·4	17·7	20·3	17·6	25·6
12. Quality Control Executives	21·9	28·9	25·4	34·9	32·1	33·3
13. Distribution Executives	37·3	45·1	38·8	41·5	46·8	53·5
14. Purchasing Executives	31·6	50·0	39·5	44·5	41·6	46·2
15. Sales Executives:						
(i) All Sales	89·2	94·7	93·9	91·9	92·9	93·6
(ii) Home Sales only	90·5	89·2	83·9	84·9	91·9	90·7
(iii) All Sales Executives	89·9	91·6	88·2	87·6	92·3	91·7
16. Export Sales Executives	69·6	78·3	70·3	80·0	72·1	81·1
17. Marketing Executives	69·5	79·6	69·9	79·0	81·2	76·7
18. Heads of Research & Development:						
(i) Research only	60·8	73·8	71·7	54·2	47·8	66·7
(ii) Development only	42·7	49·2	46·2	58·8	55·7	66·9
(iii) Combined Research & Development	64·1	70·1	72·8	71·3	77·1	82·6
(iv) All Research and/or Development	56·2	62·4	63·1	63·8	63·2	73·4
19. Heads of Data Processing	37·0	47·5	40·7	41·6	47·6	52·9
All jobs listed	55·2	62·0	60·6	62·3	63·8	67·4

Source: Survey of executive salaries and fringe benefits, Inbucon, 1978.

been substantial improvements in sick pay arrangements. In the DHSS survey of occupational sick pay schemes nearly half the manual workers were entitled to less than 13 weeks sick pay a year in 1974[1]. However, an Incomes Data Services survey of companies in 1978[2] found that the entitlement had been increased to at least 13 weeks for most of the companies they contacted.

Other employee benefits

9.21 Employee benefits provided in kind and not as a necessary feature of a job are what are commonly referred to as "fringe benefits". By making employment conditions more attractive, they enable employers to retain and attract staff. If grouped according to the extent to which they are widespread, they fall naturally into two categories:

[1] Report on a Survey of Occupational Sick Pay Schemes, HMSO, 1977.
[2] IDS Study 165, March 1978, *Sick Pay Changes*.

i   "Welfare" benefits. These include free or subsidised meals, sports facilities and goods at discount prices, rent free housing and other benefits in kind.

ii "Other" benefits. These include a company car in cases where its use is not directly related to the job, free or cheap loans, bonuses and profit sharing.

The benefits in group (i) are generally available to all employees in a firm.Their structure was often a result of historical accident; their recent growth has been a result of negotiation between employers and unions. The benefits in group (ii) are provided to attract and retain staff, and have expanded considerably over the years of incomes policy, to combat the narrowing of the margin of executive rewards caused by the tax structure and pay restraint.[1] Examples of changes in executives' entitlement to fringe benefits over the last five years are given in Tables 9.8 and 9.9. The cost of benefits to employers and their value to employees are hard to assess, since most firms do not try to cost their benefit schemes. (In the BIM 1978 survey on fringe benefits, Helen Murlis found that only 22 per cent of the firms co-operating in the survey did so.) However, Figure 9.2 indicates the approximate proportions of labour costs which could be ascribed to wages and salaries, holidays and sick pay, National Insurance and redundancy payments and employee benefits, in 1960, 1973 and 1977. The proportion of labour costs accounted for by discretionary payments has risen sharply from around 10 per cent in 1960 to around 20 per cent in 1973 and 25 per cent in 1977.

Table 9.9   Fringe Benefits other than Retirement Pensions; 1973 to 1978

Benefit	Proportion of the sample receiving benefit in:					
	1973	1974	1975	1976	1977	1978
	%	%	%	%	%	%
Top hat pension	23·6	19·3	20·3	19·4	15·2	15·6
Full use of company car	55·2	62·0	60·6	62·3	63·8	67·4
Allowance for regular use of own car	14·5	12·3	12·8	10·7	8·6	8·3
Subsidised lunches	65·0	64·2	63·6	67·3	65·9	68·6
Subsidised housing	1·4	0·9	1·1	1·0	0·7	1·0
Assistance with house purchase	6·3	4·7	6·4	5·9	7·4	8·0
Life assurance ⎰ up to and incl. 3 × salary	—	53·1	57·9	58·8	61·6	62·4
⎱ exceeding 3 × salary	—	22·2	25·5	27·5	23·9	26·7
Free medical insurance	26·4	30·1	37·9	37·3	38·8	44·1
Share option scheme	2·5	4·2	4·3	5·3	3·7	6·0
Share purchase scheme	5·1	4·3	3·5	4·1	3·3	3·4
Low interest loans	—	—	—	7·2	9·7	9·6
Bonus	30·2	32·6	31·1	33·9	33·3	37·1

Source: Survey of executive salaries and fringe benefits, Inbucon, 1978.

9.22   There are no comprehensive data on the benefit entitlements of different employees at different earnings levels. Since the intention behind the benefits in group (ii) is that they will widen the distribution of earnings at the top end, this is presumably their effect, although somewhat offset by taxation and pay policy. One of the most popular of these special status benefits is the provision of a

---

[1] See, eg BIM Surveys of 1974, 1978, Alfred Marks Bureau, etc.

Figure 9.2   Composition of Total Labour Costs; 1960, 1973 and 1977

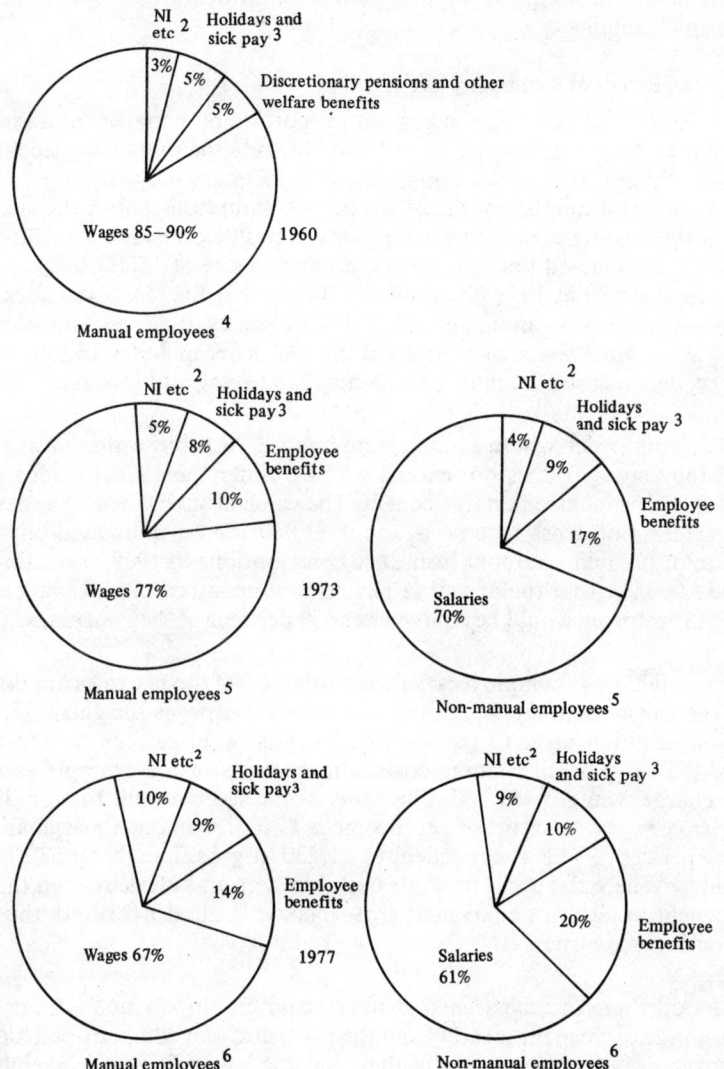

Notes:

[1] These charts are not meant to be precise. They indicate the possible situation in firms in different years.

[2] NI etc includes statutory National Insurance, Redundancy Fund and employers' liability insurance payments, plus repayments of SET in 1974.

[3] Holidays and sick pay includes other time off with pay and absence due to sickness and injury.

[4] The Department of Social and Economic Research at the University of Glasgow carried out a survey of the labour costs of manual employees. Expenditure on benefits apart from discretionary pension entitlements was almost negligible.

[5] Estimates of the make-up of total labour costs made using data from the DE Gazette labour cost survey (published November 1975) and BIM Survey on employee benefits, 1974.

[6] Estimates of the make-up of total labour costs, using data from the DE Gazette labour cost survey (published November 1977) and the BIM Survey of employee benefits, 1978.

company car, the value of which to employees is discussed below. There can, however, be no presumption as to the effect on the dispersion of income of the first group of benefits.

Value to employees of a company car

9.23   Table 9.8 shows that an increasing proportion of managers and executives have the use of a company car. In order to illustrate the monetary benefit of the provision of company cars to employees, it is necessary (as was done in Report No 3[1]) to adopt a number of fairly arbitrary assumptions about the size of car involved, the income of the recipient and his overall tax position. For illustrative purposes, it is assumed that the car has an engine size of 1500–2000 cc with an average capital cost at 1978 prices of £3,120 and that the employee does 10,000 miles per year private motoring. The AA estimates that the annual cost of running a car on these assumptions is £1,200. This includes car licence and insurance, depreciation, running costs other than petrol, and interest.

9.24   For employees whose salary (including the 'taxable' value of any fringe benefits they receive) does not exceed £7,500, under the 1976 Finance Act no taxable charge is incurred on this benefit. The value of such a benefit as described above in terms of gross income is about £1,960 for an individual paying the basic rate of tax and National Insurance contributions in 1978. Thus for someone on £5,000 per year the benefit of having a company car and using it entirely for private motoring would be equivalent to 39 per cent of their earnings.

9.25   For higher paid employees earning over £7,500 the tax rules are different. Where the car is used almost entirely for private purposes the Inland Revenue imposes a taxable charge to income on the basis of 20 per cent of the market value of the car plus all running costs. On the basis of the example above the taxable charge would be £1,150. The value of the same benefit to an individual on £10,000 per year in terms of net income is £740 (assuming a marginal rate of tax of 40 per cent). This is equivalent to £1,230 of gross income or 12.3 per cent of earnings. Where the car is used for both business and pleasure then the value of the benefit in terms of equivalent gross income is smaller for both the higher and lower income earners.

9.26   It can, therefore, be seen that lower paid employees not subject to any taxable charge can benefit greatly from the provision of a company car, although such provision is not widespread at these income levels. Higher paid employees are subject to a taxable charge but it is clear that this charge does not represent the full value of private usage and there is, therefore, a significant benefit in terms of equivalent income.

Other effects

9.27   There are several factors which affect the welfare of the employee apart from his earnings and benefits. The most obvious one is the nature of the job and the conditions under which it is done. Present data sources do not give information on the working conditions of people at different earnings levels; nor

[1] Appendix H, Report No 3, *Higher incomes from employment*, Cmnd 6383, January 1976.

is it obvious from observation that there is any definite correlation between earnings and conditions of work. North Sea divers and face-trained coalminers are highly paid compared with ordinary divers and open-cast coalminers, but dustmen and sewermen earn less than the average manual employee's hourly wage.

9.28 The Swedish Central Bureau of Statistics regularly carries out 'level of living' surveys. One of the aims of these surveys is to register, measure and describe conditions confronting workers in employment[1]. Table 9.10 shows the findings from the 1975 and 1976 surveys. Two groups of employees are shown; the first work in production and distribution industries, the second group are office workers, technicians etc. They are further classified by level of income.

9.29 The percentage of employees with 'bad' working conditions is greater for those in the production and distribution industries. While there is little difference in the degree to which physical strain is involved between those in high and lower incomes in these industries, it is noticeable that other unpleasant working conditions appear to be correlated with high pay. This suggests that employees receive compensation for these unpleasant or dangerous conditions in the form of higher pay. For those who work in offices, on the other hand, unpleasant working conditions and jobs involving physical strain appear to affect those with lower incomes more than others.

9.30 A worse measurement problem is confronted when the nature of the job itself is considered: a job which one employee enjoys because it is not demanding in any way, another employee will find monotonous and boring. Furthermore, satisfaction with a job will depend on what the employee expects from his job in the first place. Questions on job satisfaction are asked in the General Household Survey, but the answers need to be interpreted with care; they may be biased because respondents may give what appears to be the required answers. The answers are also very subjective, depending to some extent on the events of the day on which the question was asked. A serious drawback to using the GHS analysis for present purposes is that the income question relates to income including all earnings from all jobs (possibly more than one at a time) and income during spells of sickness or unemployment over the previous twelve months. A rate of pay for the job about which the satisfaction question is asked ("present job") cannot therefore be derived, and no correlation between work satisfaction and level of earnings can be sought.

9.31 Even if adequate data on people's views about their jobs were available, the problems of interpretation would be large. One important factor is the educational level achieved by employees; a man with high educational qualifications is likely to find less satisfaction in a job on a production line than a man with none, for example. The Department of Employment are at present engaged in analysing GHS data to discover whether there is any relation between age, sex, socio-economic group and so forth and the level of job satisfaction. However, Michael White found that various factors commonly used to

---

[1] *Level of living surveys in Sweden: some issues and findings*, Torkel Alfthan, International Labour Review, Vol 117 No 5, September-October 1978.

classify employees in surveys ie age, sex, level of seniority, pay level, length of service, function and geographical location, rarely account for as much as 15 per cent of the total statistical variation in satisfaction.[1] Moreover, any differences which are found are not consistent across surveys, with the exception of managers who are nearly always more satisfied with most aspects of their employment, including work content, than non-managers.

Table 9.10 Income from Work and Physical Working Environment of Full-time Employees—Sweden; 1975–76

Sweden   Per cent

	Employees in production and distribution industries		Office employees, technicians etc	
	Low income	High income	Low income	High income
Physical strain in work				
Heavy lifting	57·3	52·9	18·7	8·8
Repeated and one-sided movement ..	51·6	41·5	37·3	8·8
Unsuitable working postures	42·7	47·9	16·3	6·8
Violent shaking or vibration	9·2	26·4	1·7	2·0
Physically demanding in at least one aspect	84·1	82·2	53·7	20·3
Heating and lighting[1]				
Inadequate ventilation	32·7	37·0	30·7	23·2
Unsuitable lighting	11·6	24·7	11·6	9·6
Contact with dirty or dangerous material				
Dirty work	60·9	72·1	21·2	15·7
Gas, steam, smoke or haze[1]	35·5	59·0	12·3	10·2
Acids, or corrosive substances	11·4	26·3	10·0	9·9
Flammable or explosive substances ..	17·3	35·9	9·6	13·1
Noise				
Constant deafening noise	18·4	34·2	3·9	5·0
Not noisy	52·1	30·8	72·9	74·8
Accidents at work				
Regard work as hazardous	20·2	31·6	6·0	7·3

Source: Swedish Central Bureau of Statistics, *Living Conditions Report 16*, Low income families—which they are and how they live, 1975–76.
Note: [1] 1975 only.

9.32 Most employees spend a large proportion of their day at work. The job they do may, therefore, exert a considerable influence on their health, both mental and physical. Robert Karasak[2] used data from the 1968 and 1974 Swedish level of living surveys to examine the effect of the extent of "job demands" and "job discretion" on individuals' leisure behaviour, and found a relationship between job behaviour and leisure behaviour. Workers with "active" jobs were more likely to be "active" in their leisure time. Whether this is because naturally active people are more likely to be doing a more active job is not ascertained. There is more substantial evidence that the working environment affects physical health. While, in the past, differences in occupational mortality were determined

---

[1] Michael White, *Systematic Analysis of Employee Satisfaction*, SSRC, 1975.

[2] Robert A Karasak, Jr, *The impact of the work environment on life outside the job*, Stockholm, Institutet för Social Forskning, 1976.

to a great extent by the probability of having an accident, today they are more likely to result from differences in levels of exposure to dust, chemicals or other hazardous substances.

9.33 The recent OPCS supplement on occupational mortality gives details of death rates for 223 occupational units. In some cases there are clear links between occupation and cause of illness and death, while in some there are unexplained associations. The supplement stresses the importance of standardisation of death rates for social class before comparing the differences between rates for different occupational units. It notes, for example, that "less skilled workers have hardly reacted to advice given in relation to smoking, alcohol and diet; anti-smoking campaigns, in particular, have had far more effect in the higher social classes".[1] Apart from the difficulties of extracting occupational effects from those due to wider social class differences such as those of housing and education, there are additional data problems in this survey arising from the inaccuracy of occupation descriptions on death certificates, and the fact that the occupation registered, which is the one at time of death or retirement, might not be the one in which the individual was exposed to noxious substances or other hazards. Nevertheless, certain industrial diseases are clearly attributable to particular jobs. The people exposed to them are likely to be those engaged in the production process; where this is the case, there may be a link between earnings levels and certain illnesses.

9.34 A further disadvantage of employees at low earnings levels is that they are likely in many cases to be unskilled or semi-skilled workers, and therefore more vulnerable to unemployment and redundancy. Skilled workers are generally in short supply and less likely to suffer prolonged spells of unemployment. Evidence for this comes in data collected by the Department of Employment in June 1976. A sample survey of the unemployed aged eighteen and over registered at unemployment offices resulted, among other things, in information on duration of unemployment by broad occupational category. Table 9.11 shows that unemployed "general labourers" (48 per cent of whom were aged under 25) were more likely than any other group to be out of work for more than six months. The second group most likely to be unemployed were clerical workers; this is at least partly because nearly half the sample of unemployed clerical workers were aged between 60 and 64, many having been employed in managerial or clerical work before retiring at age 60. The unemployed skilled craftsmen were least likely to be out of work for a long time.

9.35 Table 9.11 reflects the value of different occupational groups in the labour market. Those with particular skills are least likely to have difficulty in finding work. Clerical workers and general labourers tend to remain unemployed longer and these groups are likely to have low incomes. An interesting feature of the sample of the unemployed is that, for all manual unemployed, 63 per cent overall were unemployed for more than 13 weeks and 43 per cent for

---

[1] *Occupational Mortality*, the Registrar General's decennial supplement for England & Wales, 1970–72 OPCS; HMSO, 1978.

more than 26 weeks; these figures are very similar to the 63 per cent and 41 per cent respectively for the aggregate non-manual group[1].

Table 9.11   Occupational Categories of Unemployed Men; 1976

Occupational group	Total of sample of unemployed	Percentage of sample unemployed for more than 13 weeks	Percentage of sample unemployed for more than 26 weeks
		%	%
Managerial and professional ..	1,168	61·4	38·2
Clerical and related	1,184	66·8	46·9
Other non-manual occupations ..	404	57·2	33·4
Craft and similar occupations ..	2,273	53·8	32·0
General labourers	5,767	68·3	51·4
Other manual occupations ..	3,498	59·4	38·8
Total	14,294	62·8	43·3

Source: *D E Gazette*, Sept 1977, p972.

Summary

9.36   The total advantages and disadvantages of employment should be taken into account when discussing the remuneration of employees. Besides cash earnings, discussed in previous chapters, occupational variations occur in other, mainly non-financial, conditions of employment: hours worked, holidays, pensions and sick pay arrangements, fringe benefits, etc.

9.37   There appears to be a significant relationship between the level of occupation and the number of weeks holiday to which employees are entitled. Surveys show that clerical and manual grades have lower entitlement than managerial staff, and women lower entitlement than men. However, it is possible that the influence of EEC practice and trade union pressure is reducing these differences.

9.38   On average, those in non-manual occupations tend to have shorter basic hours and to do less recorded overtime than those in manual occupations, possibly because their average earnings per hour are greater.

9.39   It is possible to adjust gross earnings to take account of differences in holiday entitlement and hours worked to get a measure of the "real" rates of pay in each of the 18 main occupational groups. Using this measure increases the differences in average earnings between occupational groups.

9.40   While recent years have seen an increase in the number of workers covered by occupational pensions and sick pay arrangements, it is still the case that a greater proportion of non-manual employees benefit from these than manual employees.

---

[1] Caution must always be exercised when analysing unemployment data. However, by considering the long term unemployed amongst the total of unemployed some problems, such as that of differential classification of skilled and unskilled workers, might be eliminated.

9.41   Two general types of fringe benefits can be distinguished. The first type, 'welfare' benefits, include free or subsidised meals, sports facilities and other benefits in kind and are generally available to all employees in a company. The second type are benefits given specifically to an individual such as a company car and free or cheap loans. While it is not possible to say what effect the former may have on the dispersion of income, the latter will almost certainly increase it.

9.42   There is no UK information on the working conditions of people at different earnings levels, nor is it obvious from observation that there is any definite correlation between earnings and conditions of work. Evidence from Sweden suggests that for workers in production and distributive industries high pay is correlated with unpleasant or dangerous working conditions while, for office employees and the like, it is the lower paid who are more likely to have unpleasant jobs than the higher paid.

9.43   The effect on the earnings distribution of the less direct aspects of re-muneration is therefore somewhat indeterminate. However, it is likely that pension entitlements and the other benefits less equally distributed are those of greatest value to employees. To this extent it may be possible to say that the dispersion of the earnings distribution is likely to be increased by the inclusion of non-cash aspects of remuneration. It is not apparent that employee benefits or working conditions will generally compensate for low earnings; on the contrary, it is more likely that these provide additional remuneration in cases where the labour market reveals shortages and inadequacies.

PART III

CHAPTER 10

Self-employed and Employees Compared

Introduction

10.1   We have shown in Chapter 2 that the 1·8 million self-employed persons in this country comprise about 7·2 per cent of the total labour force; that both self-employed men and women are strongly represented in agriculture, the distributive trades and miscellaneous and professional and scientific services; and that men are also strongly represented in the construction industry (the growth in the total number of the self-employed reached a peak in 1973 mainly by reason of the growth of self-employment in the construction industry).

10.2   In Chapter 3, in our discussion of the theoretical background and practical approaches to the analysis of earnings, we noted that self-employment incomes can appropriately be regarded as consisting partly of earnings, partly of a return on capital employed and partly of a return to the bearer of business risk; and that the relative importance of these three elements differs considerably between different categories of self-employment.

10.3   In this Chapter we use data from the SPI, from our special survey of the incomes of close company proprietors and from the FES to compare the incomes and standards of living of employees and the self-employed[1]. We concentrate on analyses of total incomes from all sources of the two groups rather than on analyses of self-employment income and of employment income as such. This means, for example, that when we examine the incomes of tax units whose main source of income is self-employment income taxed under Schedule D, we also examine their income from such subsidiary sources as employment, other investments etc.[2] Those tax units whose main source of income is from self-employment account for 95 per cent of all self-employment income recorded in the SPI, and about 75 per cent of their net incomes is from self-employment.

10.4   Distributions of self-employment incomes are generally less meaningful because they include large numbers of small subsidiary self-employment incomes which do not reflect the total incomes of the people concerned. This can be seen from Figure 10.1 where the distribution of self-employment income in terms of

---

[1] These data sources are described in Chapter 4.

[2] In the SPI, tax units consist of single persons and married couples (the incomes of husbands and wives are aggregated—even where they are separately taxed).

tax units by level of income is shown separately for main source and secondary source self-employed. The two distributions have nothing in common and we concentrate attention in this report on the incomes of main source self-employed persons.

10.5 If an individual taxpayer has several sources of income there may be several tax records relating to him. The source designated 'main' by the Inland Revenue is chosen for administrative convenience rather than for statistical purposes. It is usually, but not always, the largest source: if a taxpayer has two sources of income, one chargeable under Schedule E and the other under Case I or Case II of Schedule D[1], the Schedule D source will normally be designated as his main source, even though it may be his smaller source (the rules allow for certain exceptions and Schedule E income may be taken as the main source in certain circumstances, eg where profits are very small). This means that the distributions of Schedule D main source self-employment incomes derived from SPI data include a small proportion of cases where the taxpayers' employment incomes were the larger source; and that, in consequence, the amounts of subsidiary source employment incomes will be inflated. Similarly, the distributions of Schedule E main source employment incomes will exclude a small proportion of cases where employment incomes were the larger source and the amounts of subsidiary source self-employment income will be deflated. While we have no means of estimating the precise effect of these distortions, from our examination of the distributions themselves, including those of subsidiary source self-employment and employment incomes (including—for example— the distribution of subsidiary source 'employment and pensions' income in Table 10.9), we have concluded that they do not significantly distort the comparisons in this Chapter.

10.6 Our special survey of the incomes of close company proprietors, which we described in Chapter 4 (paragraphs 4.12–4.15), was necessary because we had decided that our study of self-employment incomes should cover their incomes, and because we could not otherwise segregate the SPI data on the incomes of close company proprietors from the SPI data on the incomes of other employees. The income data from this special survey—grossed up as appropriate—were used to derive new distributions of self-employment and employment incomes for 1975–76 and 1974–75, respectively. These new distributions were made by adding together the separate distributions of self-employment incomes taxed under Schedule D and of close company directors' incomes; and by subtracting from the distribution of all employees' incomes taxed under Schedule E the incomes of close company directors. In doing this we needed to make an adjustment for differences between the ways in which Schedules D and E incomes are assessed to tax: the self-employment income recorded for any year relates to an accounting period some year or more previously, while the employment income recorded normally relates to the current year. Any comparison between the two levels of income ideally requires some kind of adjustment to allow for the lag in the assessment of self-employment incomes.

---

[1] For convenience, we use the term Schedule D to mean Case I or Case II of Schedule D.

Figure 10.1   Numbers of Tax Units with Main Source and Subsidiary Source Income from Self-employment, by Level of Income; 1974–75

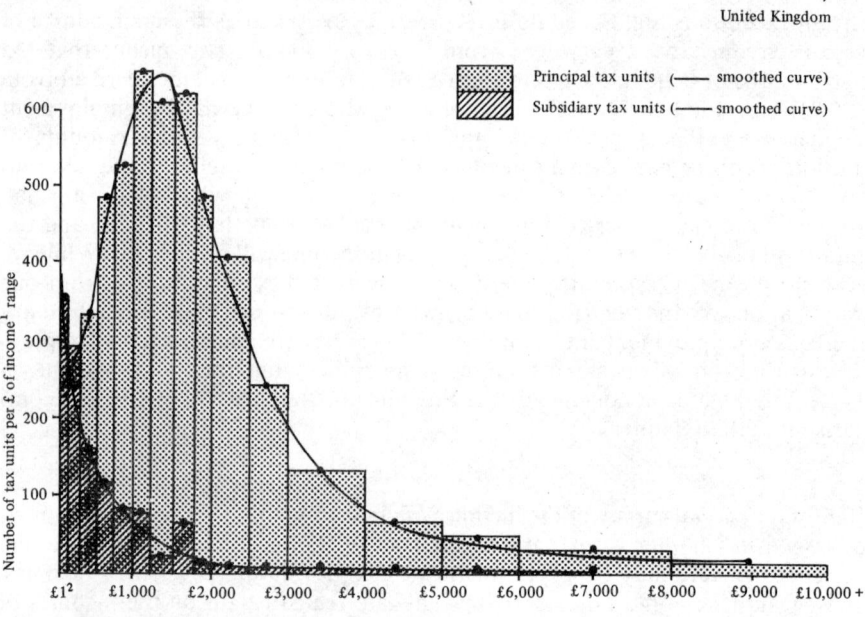

[1] Excluding wives' income in cases where the tax unit is a married couple.

[2] 53,588 principal and 8,684 subsidiary tax units with nil or negative income (representing 3 per cent and 4 per cent, respectively, of all such tax units) are excluded as the range in which they fall cannot be determined.

Source: Survey of Personal Incomes.

Differences between the available data on the incomes of the self-employed and employees

10.7   The main objective of this chapter being to compare the incomes of the self-employed with those of employees, it is necessary to sound a note of caution and explain why making such comparisons is not as straightforward as might appear at first sight. The difficulty arises from the difference in the nature of the incomes received by the two groups and, to a very large degree, from the differences between the income tax regime that applies to profits from a business (Schedule D) and the regime that applies to income from employment (Schedule E). These differences are described at length in Chapter 12 and only the main points will be given here.

10.8   The main factors that give rise to the differences may be briefly mentioned:
  (i) the system of capital allowances with its provisions for accelerated depreciation can give rise to large fluctuations from year to year in taxable self-employment incomes;
  (ii) many employees enjoy non-cash benefits that do not appear in the SPI and which would not be available to the self-employed;
  (iii) the retained profits of close companies do not appear as income in the SPI although they could be regarded as part of the total remuneration of close company proprietors; and
  (iv) opportunities for the under-reporting of income or (what comes to the same thing) the overstating of expenses to set against income are greater for the self-employed than for the employee.

10.9   It is not possible to give any estimate of the magnitude of these distortions, beyond saying that they could be quite considerable and that in general the net effect will be such as to cause the incomes of the self-employed to be understated relative to those of employees. It is hoped that enough has been said to show why it is necessary to approach the comparisons of income of the self-employed and of employees with some caution and to pay due regard to the essential differences between the two kinds of income.

Income distributions

10.10   In this part of our report, by using data from our sample survey of the incomes of close company directors, we present income distributions of the total self-employed population and, where possible, we compare these with distributions of the incomes of employees. Except in Table 10.8, the data we present in this Chapter on the distribution of the income of employees include the incomes of those tax units whose main source of income was pension (see paragraph 10.23 below).

10.11   Tables 10.1 and 10.2 use both SPI and FES data to present percentage shares of total income received by specified quantile groups of the self-employed and of employees, respectively. The different income receiving units and definitions of income used in SPI and FES may explain a large part of the differences between the distributions derived from each source. The FES distributions—which relate to households—are less unequal (as measured by their Gini coefficients) but the coverage of higher incomes in the FES is relatively poor.

141

10.12   For the one year 1975–76, by using data from our sample survey of the incomes of close company directors, Table 10.1 shows income distributions for the self-employed on two definitions of SPI data: basis (A) presents the distribution of tax units whose main source of income was assessed for tax under Schedule D, and basis (B) presents a joint distribution of those tax units plus company director tax units whose main source of income was from close companies (taxed under Schedule E). As measured by the Gini coefficient, the joint distribution is more unequal and mean income rises from £3,510 per annum on basis (A) to £4,043 per annum on basis (B). In moving from basis (A) to basis (B), the share of the top 1 per cent group fell from 8·9 per cent to 8·6 per cent but the share of the top 20 per cent group rose from 50·4 per cent to 52·4 per cent.

10.13   Similarly, Table 10.2 shows, for 1974–75 (and thus making due allowance for the time lag problem), the effect of removing the incomes of close company directors from the distribution of total income of employees. After removal, mean income falls from £2,464 to £2,396 and the distribution becomes more equal.

10.14   When Tables 10.1 and 10.2 are compared, however, one feature stands out: the much greater inequality of the distribution of self-employment income as measured by the income shares of the higher income groups and by the Gini coefficients of the distributions.

10.15·   Table 10.3, which has not been adjusted for time lags, shows the proportions of the total amounts of self-employment, employment and investment income recorded in the 1974–75 SPI received by each type of income recipient. The striking feature of the table is the high proportions of total income from each source received by those whose main source it was: 94·5 per cent of total self-employment income taxed under Schedule D was received by those tax units whose main source of income was self-employment taxed under Schedule D; 95·0 per cent of total income from close companies was received by close company proprietors; and 97·3 per cent of total employment income was received by employees. Since it was not possible to adjust Table 10.3 for time lags between Schedule D and other incomes, comparisons of the aggregate amounts of income should however be regarded with caution. Moreover, were it possible to exclude pensioners from the incomes of employees in Table 10.3, this might slightly reduce the proportions of investment income shown in the last column of the table.

10.16   Table 10.4 expresses the information in Table 10.3 in terms of average amounts of income received by individual tax units. However, because the incomes of Schedule D and E tax units have not been adjusted for time lags and pensioner tax units have not been separated out from other Schedule E tax units, comparisons between the incomes of the self-employed and employees should again be regarded with caution. Nevertheless, the Table does show that the average income recipient whose income was assessed for tax under Schedule D received only 75.7 per cent of his total income from the source 'self-employment'—a proportion which is low in comparison with that for employees (96·4 per cent from their main source) and that for close company proprietors (89·0 per cent).

Table 10.1 Distributions of the Total Income of the Self-Employed; 1973–74 to 1976

Percentage shares of total income received by specified quantile groups of the self-employed

United Kingdom

Income units: tax units and households

Year	Data source	Income unit	Basis[1]	Top 1 per cent	Top 5 per cent	Top 20 per cent	21–40 per cent	41–60 per cent	61–80 per cent	Bottom 20 per cent	Mean income	Gini coefficient[2]
				%	%	%	%	%	%	%	£	%
1973–74	SPI	Tax Units	(A)	9·5	24·9	51·1	19·7	13·9	10·0	5·4	2,642	44·7
1974	FES	Households	(C)	9·4	22·5	47·7	20·7	14·9	10·9	5·8	3,801	40·8
1974–75	SPI	Tax Units	(A)	9·5	24·6	51·2	20·1	14·0	9·8	4·9	3,043	45·1
1975	FES	Households	(C)	7·9	20·4	45·9	21·4	15·3	11·3	6·1	4,091	38·9
1975–76	SPI	Tax Units	(A)	8·9	23·7	50·4	20·3	14·1	10·1	5·1	3,510	44·2
1975–76	SPI	Tax Units	(B)	8·6	23·8	52·4	20·2	13·5	9·2	4·7	4,043	46·4
1976	FES	Households	(C)	6·8	18·8	44·9	22·4	15·6	11·0	6·0	5,238	38·8

Source: SPI and FES.

Notes: [1] Basis (A) = those tax units whose main source of income was Schedule D.
Basis (B) = basis A *plus* close company directors whose main source of income was from close companies.
Basis (C) = a broadly self-classificatory definition.

[2] The Gini coefficient measures the degree of inequality in a distribution: the larger (closer to 100 per cent) the coefficient, the greater the degree of inequality.

Table 10.2 Distributions of the Total Income of Employees; 1972–73 to 1976

Percentage shares of total income received by specified quantile groups of employees

Income units: tax units and households

Year	Data source	Income unit	Basis[1]	Top 1 per cent	Top 5 per cent	Top 20 per cent	21–40 per cent	41–60 per cent	61–80 per cent	Bottom 20 per cent	Mean income	Gini coefficient
				%	%	%	%	%	%	%	£	%
1972–73	SPI	Tax Units	(A)	5·3	15·0	39·1	24·1	18·3	12·7	5·8	1,776	33·6
1973–74	SPI	Tax Units	(A)	5·3	14·6	38·5	24·0	18·6	12·9	6·0	2,041	32·8
1974	FES	Households	(C)	3·6	12·2	34·9	23·1	18·2	14·4	9·4	3,622	25·6
1974–75	SPI	Tax Units	(A)	—	14·9	39·6	24·2	18·0	12·5	5·7	2,464	34·2
1974–75	SPI	Tax Units	(B)	4·2	13·6	38·3	24·7	18·4	12·7	5·9	2,396	32·9
1975	FES	Households	(C)	4·2	13·4	36·2	22·6	17·9	14·1	9·2	4,566	26·8
1975–76	SPI	Tax Units	(A)	4·7	14·3	38·9	24·3	18·3	12·7	5·8	3,096	33·6
1976	FES	Households	(C)	3·3	11·7	34·2	22·6	18·2	14·6	10·4	5,143	23·8

Source: SPI and FES.

Note: [1] Basis (A) = those tax units whose main source of income was Schedule E.
Basis (B) = basis A *minus* close company directors whose main source of income was from close companies.
Basis (C) = a broadly self-classificatory definition.

Table 10.3   Composition of Total Income from Each Source; 1974–75

Composition of total income from each source, by type of income recipient

United Kingdom   Income unit: tax unit

Type of income recipient	Compisition of total income from each source			
	Self-employment income		Employment income (including pensions)	Investment income (net)
	Schedule D income	Close company income		
	%	%	%	%
Self-employed—				
taxed under Schedule D	94·5	1·6	1·4	17·4
close company proprietors	0·6	95·0	0·2	4·8
Employees[1]	4·1	1·3	97·3	46·6
Other	0·8	2·1	1·1	31·2
Total	100·0	100·0	100·0	100·0

Source: SPI and Close Companies Survey.

Note: [1] This category includes some main source Schedule E tax units who were economically inactive but were receiving pensions of taxable amounts.

United Kingdom

Table 10.4   Average Amounts of Income by Type of Recipient and by Source; 1974–75

Income unit: tax unit

Type of income recipient	Composition of total income for an average tax unit				Total
	Schedule D income	Close company income	Employment income (including pensions)	Investment income (net)	
	£	£	£	£	£
Self-employed—					
taxed under Schedule D	2,447	21	416	345	3,229
close company proprietors	89	7,049	251	533	7,922
Employees[1]	9	2	2,392	78	2,481
Other	39	52	570	1,149	1,810
	%	%	%	%	%
Self-employed—					
taxed under Schedule D	75·7	0·7	12·9	10·7	100·0
close company proprietors	1·1	89·0	3·2	6·7	100·0
Employees[1]	0·4	0·1	96·4	3·1	100·0
Other	2·2	2·9	31·5	63·4	100·0

Source: SPI and Close Companies Survey.

Note: [1] This category includes some main source Schedule E tax units who were economically inactive but were receiving pensions of taxable amounts.

146

10.17 Table 10.5 takes the time lag between Schedule D and Schedule E incomes into account and, for 1974–75, compares the income distribution of employees with one for the self-employed which combines Schedule D and close company proprietors' incomes (the column showing the income distribution for 'all self-employed' is a combination of the incomes of Schedule D self-employed for 1975–76 and the incomes of close company proprietors for 1974–75).

10.18 As Figure 10.2 shows, the distributions reveal striking differences, especially in the top income ranges. For example, the average income of the top decile of the close company proprietors' distribution was £21,068, compared with £12,290 for main source Schedule D incomes and £5,482 for employees. The impact of these relatively high incomes from self-employment can most readily be appreciated by examining the effect of self-employment income on an aggregate distribution of all types of earned income. Tables 10.6 and 10.7 present a combined distribution of Schedule D and Schedule E incomes (lagging the former by one year) and, for specified quantile groups of the aggregate distribution, show the contribution made by the self-employed. Table 10.6 expresses this contribution in terms of the shares of total net income in each quantile that were attributable to the self-employed, while Table 10.7 expresses the contribution in terms of the proportion of total tax units in each quantile group who were self-employed.

10.19 Table 10.6 shows that the shape of the combined distribution of total net income (TNI) changed very little over the 3 year period 1972-73 to 1974–75 whether measured in terms of changes in the Gini coefficient (which varied around 35 per cent), or in terms of the share of TNI received by the top decile group (which decreased from 25·9 per cent to 25·7 per cent).

10.20 We have to use the narrower definition of self-employed tax units (ie basis (A) which excludes close company proprietors) to measure over time the share of total net income of the self-employed. On this basis, Table 10.6 shows it varied quite markedly, increasing from 8.5 per cent in 1972-73 to 12·1 per cent in 1973–74 and then falling back to 10·3 per cent in 1974–75. This variation is likely to reflect a number of factors including, for employees, the period of wage restraint (1973) followed by the period of rapid increase in wages (1974 and 1975); and, for the self-employed, changes in the proportions of the total numbers of tax units receiving self-employment incomes (see Table 10.7).

10.21 The dominance of the self-employed at the top of the combined distribution is clearly demonstrated in Table 10.6. For 1974–75, on the basis of the wider definition (basis (B) which includes close company proprietors within the definition of self-employed tax units), the table shows that their share of total net income was over one third (34·1 per cent) for the top decile and nearly three quarters (73·7 per cent) for the top 1 per cent. Table 10.7 shows that in 1974–75 the self-employed with main source incomes taxed under Schedule D together with close company proprietors taxed under Schedule E constituted 8·8 per cent of the total number of tax units (see also paragraph 4.15).

Table 10.5 Comparison between the Distributions of the Total Net Incomes of 'All Self-Employed' and Employees; 1974–75

United Kingdom

Income unit: tax unit

Income distributions (non-overlapping)

Quantile group	Main source Schedule D— self-employed 1975–76		Close company proprietors 1974–75		All self-employed 1974–75		Main source Schedule E— employees[1] 1974–75	
	Shares of TNI	Average income in range	Shares of TNI	Average income in range	Shares of TNI	Average income in range	Shares of TNI	Average income in range
	%	£	%	£	%	£	%	£
Top 1 per cent[2] ..	8·9	31,115	⎫ 19·4	⎫ 26,755	8·6	34,528	4·2	10,097
2–5 ,, ..	14·8	12,971	⎭	⎭	15·2	15,401	9·4	5,593
6–10 ,, ..	11·4	7,980	11·1	15,380	12·2	9,870	9·3	4,470
Top 10 per cent ..	35·1	12,290	30·5	21,068	36·0	14,548	22·9	5,482
11–20 ,, ..	15·4	5,388	17·4	12,017	16·4	6,612	15·4	3,696
21–30 ,, ..	11·2	3,932	12·6	8,726	11·4	4,597	13·3	3,189
31–40 ,, ..	9·1	3,206	10·1	6,989	8·8	3,566	11·4	2,741
41–50 ,, ..	7·7	2,695	8·4	5,837	7·4	2,985	9·8	2,341
51–60 ,, ..	6·4	2,260	6·7	4,649	6·1	2,464	8·6	2,065
61–70 ,, ..	5·6	1,943	5·3	3,686	5·1	2,072	7·1	1,710
71–80 ,, ..	4·5	1,586	4·3	2,976	4·1	1,677	5·6	1,333
81–90 ,, ..	3·4	1,193	3·1	2,137	3·1	1,267	4·1	975
91–100 ,, ..	1·7	603	1·6	1,105	1·6	644	1·8	429
Gini coefficient ..	44·2%		42·8%		46·4%		32·9%	
Overall average income	£3,510		£6,919		£4,043		£2,396	

Source: SPI and Close Companies Survey.

Notes: [1] In addition to wages and salaries from employment, this category includes pensions taxed under Schedule E (see paragraph 10.10). Close company proprietor tax units have been disaggregated from this distribution.

[2] The data did not enable the share of the top 1 per cent group of close company proprietors to be estimated.

Figure 10.2 **Average Total Net Incomes of 'All Self-employed' and Employees by Quantile Group; 1974–75**

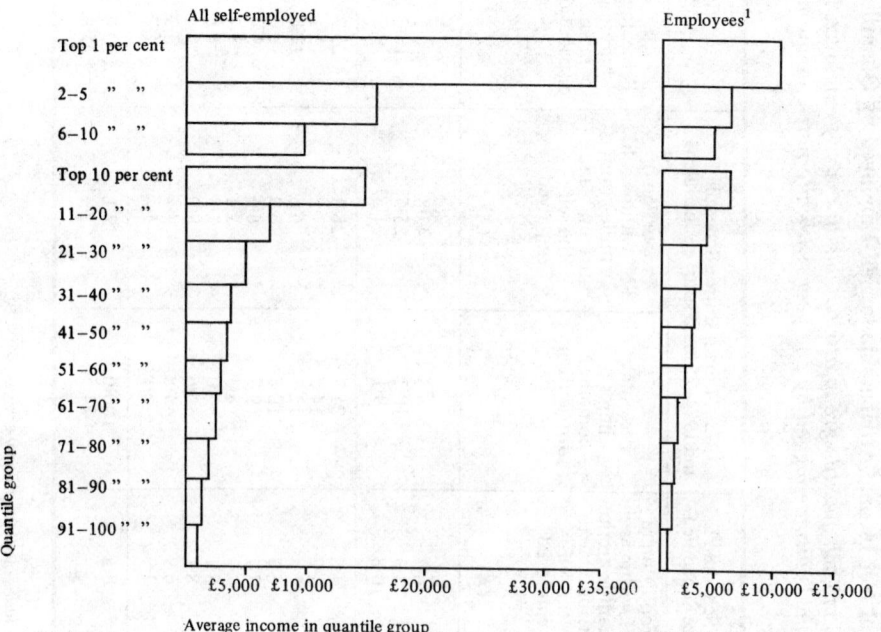

[1] This category includes pensioners (see footnote to Table 10.5).
Source: Table 10.5.

Table 10.6 Proportions of Total Net Income Attributable to Self-Employed by Quantile Groups; 1972–73 to 1975–76

Proportion of total net income (TNI) in each quantile group attributable to the self-employed in the combined distribution of self-employed and employees, with Schedule D income lagged by one year, with alternative definitions of the self-employed for 1975–76

United Kingdom

Income unit: tax unit

Quantile group of combined distribution of TNI	1972–73 main source Schedule E and 1973–74 main source Schedule D		1973–74 main source Schedule E and 1974–75 main source Schedule D		1974–75 main source Schedule E and 1975–76 main source Schedule D		
	Percentage shares of combined distribution	Proportion of TNI within each quantile group attributable to the self-employed (A)	Percentage shares of combined distribution	Proportion of TNI within each quantile group attributable to the self-employed (A)	Percentage shares of combined distribution	Proportion of TNI within each group attributable to the self-employed (A)	Proportion of TNI within each group attributable to the self-employed, including close company proprietors (B)
	%	%	%	%	%	%	%
Top 1 per cent ..	6·5	46·2	6·5	47·8	6·1	43·5	73·7
2–5 ,, ..	10·3	23·3	10·1	25·5	10·3	19·7	30·2
6–10 ,, ..	9·1	10·8	9·1	11·5	9·3	9·7	12·4
Top 10 per cent ..	25·9	24·6	25·7	26·3	25·7	21·7	34·1
11–20 ,, ..	14·8	7·2	14·5	7·9	15·1	7·3	8·7
21–30 ,, ..	12·5	7·4	12·5	6·6	12·8	6·0	6·8
31–40 ,, ..	10·9	6·7	10·8	6·9	10·9	6·1	6·9
41–50 ,, ..	9·5	7·1	9·7	6·6	9·4	6·3	6·9
51–60 ,, ..	8·3	7·9	8·3	7·4	8·3	6·1	6·7
61–70 ,, ..	6·9	8·1	7·0	7·8	6·8	6·5	7·1
71–80 ,, ..	5·4	8·1	5·6	8·0	5·4	6·1	6·6
81–90 ,, ..	3·9	6·9	3·8	7·4	3·9	5·7	6·1
91–100 ,, ..	1·9	3·9	2·1	5·4	1·7	3·9	4·0
Total ..	100·0	8·5	100·0	12·1	100·0	10·3	14·0
Gini coefficient ..	35·1	—	34·5	—	35·4	—	—

Source: SPI and Close Companies Survey.

Notes: (A) — definition of self-employed *excludes* close company proprietors.
(B) — definition of self-employed *includes* close company proprietors.

150

Table 10.7 Proportions of Self-Employed Tax Units by Quantile Groups; 1972–73 to 1975–76

Proportion of tax units in each quantile group who were self-employed in the combined distribution of total net income (TNI) of self-employed and employees, with Schedule D income lagged by one year, with alternative definitions of the self-employed for 1975–76

United Kingdom   Income unit: tax unit

Quantile group of combined distribution of TNI	1972–73 main source Schedule E and 1973–74 main source Schedule D		1973–74 main source Schedule E and 1974–75 main source Schedule D		1974–75 main source Schedule E and 1975–76 main source Schedule D		
	Lower limit of income range for the combined distribution	Proportion of tax units in each quantile group that were self-employed (A)	Lower limit of income range for the combined distribution	Proportion of tax units in each quantile group that were self-employed (A)	Lower limit of income range for the combined distribution	Proportion of tax units in each quantile group that were self-employed (A)	Proportion of tax units in each quantile group that were self-employed (definition of self-employed including close company proprietors) (B)
	£	%	£	%	£	%	%
Top 1 per cent	7,206	43·0	8,148	45·8	9,722	43·2	72·2
2–5 ,,	3,784	22·1	4,265	24·2	5,323	19·7	29·3
6–10 ,,	3,056	10·8	3,485	11·6	4,348	10·2	12·8
Top 10 per cent	3,056	18·5	3,485	20·1	4,348	17·4	25·3
11–20 ,,	2,498	7·2	2,845	7·9	3,472	7·7	9·1
21–30 ,,	2,134	7·5	2,480	6·7	3,010	6·3	7·1
31–40 ,,	1,877	6·8	2,158	7·0	2,592	6·5	7·2
41–50 ,,	1,637	7·1	1,900	6·7	2,219	6·7	7·3
51–60 ,,	1,393	8·0	1,619	7·5	1,901	6·5	7·1
61–70 ,,	1,132	8·2	1,326	7·8	1,552	6·8	7·4
71–80 ,,	856	8·1	1,016	8·1	1,180	6·4	6·9
81–90 ,,	571	6·8	694	7·3	762	5·9	6·2
91–100 ,,	—	4·2	—	5·7	—	4·2	4·5
Total ,,	—	8·2	—	8·5	—	7·4	8·8

Source: SPI and Close Companies Survey.

Notes: (A) — definition of self-employed *excludes* close company proprietors.
(B) — definition of self-employed *includes* close company proprietors.

151

10.22   The detail of Table 10.7 reveals a similar pattern over time to that of Table 10.6. And again the proportion of self-employed tax units in the top of the distribution was disproportionately high: they constituted over one-quarter (25·3 per cent) of the top decile group of tax units and nearly three-quarters (72·2 per cent) of the top 1 per cent group.

10.23   As noted above, a point that should be borne in mind in drawing comparisons between the incomes of the self-employed and of employees is that those income recipients classed as main source Schedule E taxpayers included pensioners (ie those whose main source of income was pension) whose income came to the attention of the Inland Revenue. In 1974–75 there were approximately 1·7 million pensioner tax units and around 18·7 million employee tax units. This may be expected to depress somewhat the average levels of the 'employee' incomes shown in the earlier tables in this Chapter, especially at the lower end of the distribution. It has not proved practicable to obtain employees-only Schedule E income distributions directly from the basic Inland Revenue data. However, using a number of different tables from the SPI, we have made an estimate for 1974–75 of the effect of excluding pensioners from the distribution. The estimate depended upon an assumption that, in each range of total net income, the average income of those whose main source was pension was the same as that of all income units with any pension income. The likely effect of this assumption is a slight overstatement of the amount of income received by pensioners and, therefore, a slight over-adjustment of the income distribution in arriving at our estimate of 'employees only' income.

10.24   Table 10.8 compares our estimated 'employees only' income distribution with the main source Schedule E distribution from Table 10.5. The Gini coefficient is significantly smaller in the 'employees only' distribution; the income share of the top 10 per cent is smaller and the shares of the bottom three decile groups are slightly higher. In spite of this difference in inequality, the average income of 'employees only' (£2,513) is still well below that shown for the self-employed in Table 10.5 (£4,043). This is also true for the average income of each quantile group identified in the tables. The exclusion of pensioners, therefore, while reducing the inequality and raising the average of the overall main source Schedule E distribution, does not substantially alter the comparisons of main source Schedule E and Schedule D incomes presented in this Chapter.

Sources of income

10.25   In analysing aggregate incomes we noted that, for each type of income recipient, main source income predominated as a proportion of total income. However, this was less so for the self-employed (especially Schedule D self-employed) who had significant amounts of income from sources other than self-employment (see Table 10.4). The following four tables show how these other sources of income vary in importance as a proportion of total net income for selected quantile groups. The tables follow the same format: they list the average total net income of each quantile group and show its composition.

10.26   Table 10.9 relates to 1975–76 and provides a breakdown of the distribution of the TNI of Schedule D self-employed tax units. It shows that self-employment income constituted only about three-quarters of total net income

Table 10.8 Distributions of Total Net Incomes of Main Source Schedule E Income Recipients Including and Excluding Pensioners;[1] 1974–75

Quantile group	Main source Schedule E		Main source Schedule E excluding pensioners	
	Shares of TNI	Average income in range	Shares of TNI	Average income range
	%	£	%	£
Top 1 per cent	4·2	10,097	4·0	10,162
2–5 ,, ...	9·4	5,593	9·0	5,656
6–10 ,, ..	9·3	4,470	9·0	4,538
Top 10 per cent	22·9	5,482	22·0	5,548
11–20 ,, ...	15·4	3,696	15·0	3,768
21–30 ,, ...	13·3	3,189	13·0	3,275
31–40 ,, ...	11·4	2,741	11·2	2,816
41–50 ,, ...	9·8	2,341	9·8	2,469
51–60 ,, ...	8·6	2,065	8·8	2,201
61–70 ,, ...	7·1	1,710	7·3	1,833
71–80 ,, ...	5·6	1,333	6·0	1,502
81–90 ,, ...	4·1	975	4·6	1,145
91–100 ,, ...	1·8	429	2·3	574
Mean	—	2,396	—	2,513
Gini coefficient % ..	32·9		30·7	
No. of tax units (million)	20·4		18·7	

Source: Derived from SPI.
Note: [1] Pensioners are defined as those whose main source of income is pension.

(the proportions being higher in the lower ranges of the distribution). It also shows that spouses' incomes were more important under Schedule E (employment and pensions) than Schedule D (self-employment); and that investment income was proportionately larger for the top decile group (the 5·1 per cent share of TNI from 'dividends from companies' represented an average annual income of £620 and the 13·7 per cent share from 'other investment' £1,680 for the top 10 per cent group).

10.27   In order to correct for time lags, while Table 10.9 relates to 1975–76, Tables 10.10 and 10.11 relate to 1974–75. Table 10.10 provides a breakdown of the TNI of employees excluding close company proprietors (the process of disaggregation limited subsequent analysis by source of income). It shows the paramount importance of Schedule E income (ie income from employment and pensions) to the joint incomes of husbands and wives (the bottom 90 per cent group receive less than 3 per cent of their TNI from other sources). Dividends from companies and 'other investment income' was only a significant source for the top decile group. If Tables 10.9 and 10.10 are compared it will be seen that employees in the top decile group received a lower proportion of their TNI from 'other' investments (4·6 per cent) than did the self-employed (13·7 per cent). This probably reflects the higher incomes of the self-employed and their need to make their own pension arrangements. The 3·1 per cent of TNI derived by the top decile group from company dividends represented—for employees—an

Table 10.9 Distribution of Total Net Income of the Self-Employed by Source of Income; 1975–76

Quantile group	Mean total net income for the group	Proportion of TNI derived from each source[1]						
		Schedule D		Employment and pensions		Investment		Total
		Husband	Wife	Husband	Wife	Dividends from companies	Other investment	
	£	%	%	%	%	%	%	%
Top 10 per cent ..	12,290	68·3	4·9	4·0	4·0	5·1	13·7	100
11–30 ,, ..	4,660	69·6	4·5	3·6	12·9	1·6	7·8	100
31–50 ,, ..	2,951	70·3	3·8	3·7	16·1	0·8	5·3	100
51–70 ,, ..	2,102	75·8	3·4	3·2	11·9	0·6	5·1	100
71–90 ,, ..	1,386	80·8	2·5	3·1	7·2	0·6	5·8	100
91–100 ,, ..	603	77·0	1·1	5·7	7·4	0·5	8·3	100
Total	3,510	70·9	4·2	3·7	9·6	2·5	9·1	100

Source: SPI.

Note: [1] The percentages given here are approximations: in deriving estimates from SPI data of net income by source it has not always been possible to distinguish between deductions made in respect of one source and those made in respect of another source.

154

Table 10.10 Distribution of Total Net Income of Employees (Excluding Close Company Proprietors) by Source of Income; 1974–75

United Kingdom

Income tax: tax unit

Quantile group	Mean total net income for the group	Proportion of TNI derived from each source[1]					
		All Schedule E income[2]	Of which, spouse's Schedule E income	Schedule D income	Dividends from companies	Other investment income	Total
	£	%	%	%	%	%	%
Top 10 per cent : : :	5,482	91·5	18·6	0·8	3·1	4·6	100
11–30 ,, : : :	3,443	97·9	16·4	0·2	0·4	1·5	100
31–50 ,, : : :	2,541	97·9	6·9	0·3	0·3	1·5	100
51–70 ,, : : :	1,888	98·0	3·2	0·3	0·1	1·6	100
71–90 ,, : : :	1,154	97·9	1·4	0·3	—	1·8	100
91–100 ,, : : :	429	99·6	0·6	0·2	—	0·2	100
Total .. : : :	2,396	96·5	11·1	0·4	0·9	2·2	100

Source: SPI and Close Companies Survey.

Notes: [1] See footnote to Table 10.9.
  [2] In addition to wages and salaries from employment, this category includes pensions taxed under Schedule E (see paragraph 10.10).

Table 10.11 Distribution of Total Net Income of Close Company Proprietors by Source of Income; 1974-75

United Kingdom

Income unit: tax unit

Quantile group	Mean total net income for the group	Proportion of TNI derived from each source[1]									
		Close company income					Other Schedule E income	Schedule D income	Other dividends	Other investment income	Total
		Emoluments	Wives' income	Dividends	Benefits and other allowances	Total					
	£	%	%	%	%	%	%	%	%	%	%
Top 10 per cent	21,068	57·7	13·6	6·7	8·0	86·0	1·4	0·6	1·4	10·6	100
11–30 ,,	10,372	64·3	12·9	1·6	5·4	84·2	3·2	1·3	2·0	9·2	100
31–50 ,,	6,431	72·1	8·9	0·3	8·2	89·5	3·5	1·2	1·2	4·6	100
51–70 ,,	4,168	69·6	10·0	0·4	7·2	87·2	5·3	1·7	0·9	4·9	100
71–90 ,,	2,557	68·3	10·9	—*	6·7	89·5	4·6	0·8	1·0	4·1	100
91–100 ,,	1,105	—*	6·9	—*	—*	78·8	2·9	1·1	1·9	—*	100
Total	6,919	64·5	11·7	3·0	7·1	86·3	3·1	1·1	1·5	8·0	100

Source: SPI and Close Companies Survey.

(*Because of the presence of some unrepresentative cases in the sample—where total deductions amounted to as much as, or even more than TNI—it was not possible to provide estimates of these proportions.)

Note:[1] See footnote to Table 10.9.

average income of £170 (their income from 'other investments' amounted to £250). Wives' incomes were only important in the higher income ranges. This is to be expected, however, as tax units with two earners are more likely to feature in the top parts of the distribution.

10.28   Table 10.11 was derived from the results of our special survey of the incomes of close company proprietors. It shows that the emoluments of close company proprietors formed a larger proportion of their TNI for groups in the lower ranges of the distribution and that spouses' close company incomes constituted an important proportion (13·6 per cent) of the TNI of the top decile group. Dividends from close companies were only an important proportion (6·7 per cent) for the top decile group. Since such dividends may attract the investment income surcharge if they are above a certain level, it is not surprising that they are generally an unimportant source of income from close companies.

10.29   The 'benefits and other allowances' included in Table 10.11 are shown at their values as assessed for tax. This may not always represent the full value to the recipient—a topic which we consider later in Chapter 12 (paragraphs 12.22–12.23).

Allowable tax deductions

10.30   The kinds of expenditures which may be set against total income for tax purposes include building society interest payable, retirement annuity premiums, charges, and employees' superannuation contributions and Schedule E allowable expenses (see Table 4.1). Comparison between figures for the three groups of income recipient in Table 10.12 discloses three interesting points:
   (i)   the relatively high level of deductions of the Schedule D self-employed on account of retirement annuity premiums;
   (ii) the comparatively high levels of total deductions of close company proprietors; and
   (iii) the comparatively low levels of the Schedule E allowable expenses of employees (it should be noted that the data for employees' allowable tax deductions exclude their superannuation contribution, as these contributions are excluded from the coverage of the SPI).
We examine this aspect of the UK tax system in Chapter 12 (paragraphs 12.18–12.21).

10.31   In Table 10.12 allowable tax deductions are shown as percentages of the average income in each range—this should be remembered when making comparisons with some of the high percentages shown in the lower parts of the distributions where both the levels of average income and the absolute value of the deductions will be low. While Table 10.12 shows that the total deductions of close company proprietors were greatly in excess of those of the other two types of income recipient, it should be noted, however, that total deductions of Schedule D self-employed are shown as proportions of their TNI after deduction of their Schedule D allowable expenses.

Income distributions after tax

10.32   Tables 10.13, 10.14 and 10.15 provide a comprehensive analysis of the effect of income tax on the incomes of the self-employed taxed under Schedule D (Table 10.13), the incomes of close company proprietors taxed under Schedule E

Table 10.12 Comparison between the Allowable Tax Deductions of the Self-Employed and of Employees; 1974–75

United Kingdom   Income unit: tax unit

Quantile group of TNI of combined distribution	Percentage share of TNI	Mean annual income of quantile group	Schedule D self-employed (1975–76)		Close company proprietors (1974–75)		Employees (1974–75)	
			Retirement annuity premiums as % of mean income of quantile group	Total deductions as % of mean income of quantile group	Schedule E allowable expenses as % of mean income of quantile group	Total deductions as % of mean income of quantile group	Schedule E allowable expenses as % of mean income[1] of quantile group	Total deductions as % of mean income[1] of quantile group
	%	£	%	%	%	%	%	%
Top 10 per cent ..	25·7	6,539	8·6	13·8	14·7	17·7	0·6	5·5
11–30 ,, :	27·9	3,240	5·6	12·5	18·1	27·3	0·7	9·4
31–50 ,, :	20·3	2,388	6·0	14·1	20·8	27·4	0·8	11·3
51–70 ,, :	15·1	1,734	7·1	16·9	25·4	34·7	1·0	14·3
71–90 ,, :	9·3	996	16·3	25·2	50·9	84·3	1·5	25·3
91–100 ,, :	1·7	441	7·0	75·8	—*	—*	1·5	53·1

Source: SPI and Close Companies Survey.

(*Because of the presence of some unrepresentative cases in the sample—where total deductions amounted to as much as, or even more than TNI—it was not possible to provide estimates of these proportions.)

Note: [1] See footnote 2 to Table 10.10.

158

(Table 10.14) and the incomes of employees taxed under Schedule E (Table 10.15). While Tables 10.14 and 10.15 relate to 1974–75, in order to adjust for time lags Table 10.13 relates to 1975–76.

10.33   The progressive nature of the income tax system is clearly evident from the figures in Tables 10.13, 10.14 and 10.15. They show, for example, that income tax had the following effect on percentage shares of total net income:

	Percentage share of TNI		
	Top 1 per cent group	Top 10 per cent group	Bottom 40 per cent group
	%	%	%
Self-employed (Table 10.13)—			
before tax	8·8	35·0	15·2
after tax	4·3	26·7	18·9
Close company proprietors (Table 10.14)—			
before tax	—	30·4	14·3
after tax	—	25·9	17·4
Employees (Table 10.15)—			
before tax	4·2	22·9	18·6
after tax	2·9	20·8	20·1

It is also evident from the figures in the penultimate columns of each of the tables, ie from the figure for average tax paid as a percentage of average income before tax.

10.34   On average, income tax in 1975–76 reduced the total incomes of the top 1 per cent group of Schedule D self-employed tax units from £31,115 to £11,363 (tax paid £19,752) (Table 10.13). In comparison, in 1974–75 it reduced the total incomes of the top 5 per cent group of close company proprietors assessed under Schedule E from £26,755 to £15,531 (tax paid £11,224) (Table 10.14) and those of the top 1 per cent of Schedule E employee tax units from £10,097 to £5,696 (tax paid £4,401) (Table 10.15).

Living standards

10.35   So far in this Chapter we have largely relied upon the SPI and our special sample survey of the incomes of close company proprietors to compare the incomes of the self-employed and employees. As we have already noted, by reason of the differences in the nature of the incomes received by the two groups and of differences in the ways they are assessed to tax, such comparisons are not straightforward.

10.36   Because it is not possible to establish income figures which are truly comparable, we have looked for other data which might enable us to compare the true economic position of the two groups. Accordingly, using FES data, we have attempted to compare the standards of living of households headed by self-employed persons with those of households headed by employees. For this purpose we have taken the possession of certain consumer durables and different types of housing tenure as indicators of the relative standards of living of the two population groups.

159

Table 10.13 Average Amounts of Income Tax Paid by Self-Employed Assessed under Schedule D; 1975–76

United Kingdom   Income unit: tax unit

Quantile group of TNI before tax	Average income before tax	Percentage share of income before tax	Average income after tax	Percentage share of income after tax	Average tax paid	Average tax paid as percentage of income before tax[1]	Percentage share of tax paid
	£	%	£	%	£	%	%
Top 1 per cent	31,115	8·8	11,363	4·3	19,752	63·5	21·7
2–5 ,, ...	12,971	14·8	7,579	11·7	5,392	41·6	23·6
6–10 ,, ...	7,980	11·4	5,575	10·7	2,405	30·1	13·2
Top 10 per cent	12,290	35·0	6,955	26·7	5,335	43·4	58·5
11–20 ,, ...	5,388	15·4	4,069	15·7	1,319	24·5	14·5
21–40 ,, ...	3,570	20·3	2,888	22·2	682	19·1	15·0
41–60 ,, ...	2,478	14·1	2,141	16·5	337	13·6	7·4
61–80 ,, ...	1,764	10·1	1,596	12·3	168	9·5	3·7
81–100 ,, ...	898	5·1	854	6·6	44	4·9	0·9
All groups	—	100·0	—	100·0	—	—	100·0

Source: SPI.

Note: [1] The figures in this column represent the levels of the average amounts of tax paid by income units within the specified quantile groups. They do not represent either the relevant marginal rates of tax paid or the amounts of tax paid on the levels of before tax incomes listed in column 2.

Table 10.14 Average Amounts of Income Tax Paid by Close Company Proprietors Assessed under Schedule E; 1974-75

United Kingdom

Income unit: tax unit

Quantile group of TNI before tax	Average income before tax £	Percentage share of income before tax %	Average income after tax £	Percentage share of income after tax %	Average tax paid £	Average tax paid as percentage of income before tax[1] %	Percentage share of tax paid %
Top 5 per cent	26,755	19·3	15,531	16·0	11,224	41·9	27·1
6-10 "	15,380	11·1	9,602	9·9	5,778	37·6	13·9
Top 10 per cent ..	21,068	30·4	12,567	25·9	8,501	40·4	41·0
11-20 "	12,017	17·4	7,869	16·3	4,148	34·5	20·0
21-40 "	7,858	22·7	5,682	23·4	2,176	27·7	21·0
41-60 "	5,243	15·2	4,112	17·0	1,131	21·6	10·9
61-80 "	3,331	9·6	2,768	11·4	563	16·9	5·4
81-100 "	1,621	4·7	1,439	6·0	182	11·2	1·7
All groups	—	100·0	—	100·0	—	—	100·0

Source: Close Companies Survey.

Note: [1] The figures in this column represent the levels of the average amounts of tax paid by income units within the specified quantile groups. They do not represent either the relevant marginal rates of tax paid or the amounts of tax paid on the levels of before tax incomes listed in column 2.

Table 10.15 Average Amounts of Income Tax Paid by Employees Assessed under Schedule E (Excluding Close Company Proprietors); 1974–75

United Kingdom — Income unit: tax unit

Quantile group of TNI before tax	Average income before tax £	Percentage share of income before tax %	Average income after tax £	Percentage share of income after tax %	Average tax paid £	Average tax paid as percentage of income before tax[1] %	Percentage share of tax paid %
Top 1 per cent : : :	10,097	4·2	5,696	2·9	4,401	43·6	9·5
2–5 ,, : : :	5,593	9·4	4,246	8·8	1,347	24·1	11·6
6–10 ,, : : :	4,470	9·3	3,503	9·1	967	21·6	10·5
Top 10 per cent : : :	5,482	22·9	4,020	20·8	1,462	26·7	31·6
11–20 ,, : : :	3,696	15·4	2,959	15·3	737	19·9	15·9
21–40 ,, : : :	2,965	24·7	2,416	25·0	549	18·5	23·7
41–60 ,, : : :	2,203	18·4	1,813	18·8	390	17·7	16·9
61–80 ,, : : :	1,522	12·7	1,290	13·3	232	15·2	10·0
81–100 ,, : : :	702	5·9	657	6·8	45	6·4	1·9
All groups : : :	—	100·0	—	100·0	—	—	100.0

Source: Close Companies Survey and SPI.

Note: [1] The figures in this column represent the levels of the average amounts of tax paid by income units within the specified quantile groups. They do not represent either the relevant marginal rates of tax paid or the amounts of tax paid on the levels of before tax incomes listed in column 2.

10.37 For this to be realistic, three factors needed to be taken into account. First, as in our analyses of SPI data, it was necessary that a time lag of one year be applied: we compared data from the 1975 FES for employees with data from the 1976 FES for the self-employed. Second, in order to allow for differences between the income distributions of the two types of households, we standardised the incomes of the self-employed to those of employees. Third, in order to allow for differences between their age distributions, we then standardised the ages of the self-employed to those of employees.

10.38 The results, presented in Table 10.16, show that after standardising for income and age, the proportions of self-employed households possessing television sets, washing machines etc increased and (except for television sets) were significantly higher than the proportions of employee households possessing such items. The data on housing indicate that proportionately more employees live in council housing and proportionately less own their houses outright than do self-employed households. Caution is needed in interpreting these results, however, as the numbers in the FES sample of heads of household who were self-employed were small (or even zero) for some income/age groups.

10.39 This approach, however, to assessing the differences between employees and the self-employed has considerable scope for development. It gives, at best, only an approximate guide to the differences but there are few viable alternative methods of measuring the extent of under-recording of self-employment relative to employment income. We would therefore encourage researchers in this field, either in Government Departments or in academic institutions, to develop this type of analysis.

Summary
10.40 Whether we look at the separate distributions of self-employment and employment incomes, or at the shares of the self-employed in the combined distributions of self-employment and employment incomes, one feature stands out, the much greater inequality of the distribution of self-employment income.

10.41 This greater inequality is clearly evident from a comparison of the Gini coefficients in Tables 10.1 and 10.2. Table 10.1 also shows that the effect of adding the total incomes of close company proprietors (taxed under Schedule E) to the total incomes of the self-employed (taxed under Schedule D) was to make the 1975–76 combined income distribution of self-employed tax units more unequal (the Gini coefficient rose from 44·2 to 46·4 per cent); and Table 10.2 shows that the effect of excluding the incomes of close company proprietors from the 1974–75 total income distribution of employees (taxed under Schedule E) was to make the distribution less unequal (the Gini coefficient fell from 34·2 per cent to 32·9 per cent).

10.42 Comparison of the income levels of the self-employed and of employees is not straightforward. Firstly, it has to be remembered that the incomes are of different kinds: self-employment income, as already noted in Chapter 3, represents not only a reward for work but also in varying degree a return on capital and a return to the bearer of business risk. Secondly, for a variety of

Table 10.16 Living Standards as Measured by Possession of Certain Consumer Durables and by Type of Housing: Households Headed by Self-Employed and Employees; 1975

United Kingdom
Unit: Households

Type of consumer durable/housing	Proportion of households possessing specified consumer durables or occupying housing of the specified type			
	Households headed by employees	Households headed by self-employed persons	Households headed by self-employed persons, data standardised by income	Households headed by self-employed persons, data standardised by income and age
	%	%	%	%
Consumer durable—				
television set	96·4	96·6	97·1	97·5
washing machine	81·6	84·3	87·3	88·7
central heating	53·5	57·1	59·7	61·0
car(s) (one or more)	71·8	85·8	90·9	91·0
cars (two or more)	13·2	26·0	28·1	29·7
Housing—				
council rented	29·0	13·3	11·7	12·3
other rented (unfurnished) ...	8·2	10·6	8·9	8·9
rented (furnished)	5·3	2·2	1·3	1·5
owned with mortgage	43·4	40·2	43·3	45·2
owned outright	11·2	30·1	31·2	28·7
rent free	2·9	3·6	3·6	3·4

Source: FES.

reasons, set out more fully in Chapter 12, largely arising from the different income tax regimes that apply, incomes of the self-employed as recorded in the SPI will tend to be understated relative to those of employees.

10.43   With these reservations in mind, the differences between the income levels for different groups are none the less striking. For example, when appropriately time-lagged distributions of total net incomes are compared, Table 10.5 shows that the average incomes within the top tenth of the individual distributions were:

		£
1975–76	Main source Schedule D self-employed	12,290
1974–75	Close company proprietors	21,068
1974–75	All self-employed	14,548
1974–75	Main source Schedule E employees (excluding close company proprietors)	5,482

10.44   When we look at the combined distribution of self-employment and employment incomes, we see that self-employed tax units were disproportionately represented at the top of the distributions. In 1974–75 the self-employed (including close company proprietors) constituted under 9 per cent of the total number of tax units but their share of total net income was over one-third for the top decile group and nearly three-quarters for the top 1 per cent group (Table 10.6). They also constituted over one-quarter of the number of tax units within the top decile group and nearly three-quarters within the top 1 per cent group (Table 10.7). However, while a disproportionately large number of income recipients in top income groups are self-employed, there are also substantial numbers of the self-employed in the lowest income groups.

10.45   While, for each type of income recipient, main source income predominated as a proportion of total income, the self-employed received significant amounts of income from sources other than self-employment (Tables 10.9, 10.10 and 10.11). For employees, dividends from companies and 'other investment income' were significant only for the top decile group: the bottom 90 per cent group derived less than 3 per cent of their total net income from sources other than employment.

10.46   Table 10.12 shows that, for 1975–76, Schedule D tax units had relatively high levels of tax deductions for retirement annuities, and that the total tax deductions of close company proprietors for 1974-75 were greatly in excess of those of the other types of income recipient. The progressive nature of income tax on the incomes of both the self-employed and employees is clearly evident from Tables 10.13, 10.14 and 10.15.

10.47   After standardising 1975 and 1976 FES data for income and age, the proportions of self-employed households possessing television sets, washing machines etc were significantly higher than the proportions of employees' households possessing such items (Table 10.16). The data also indicate that

165

proportionately more employees live in council housing and proportionately less own their houses outright than do self-employed households. Since the numbers of self-employed heads of households in the sample were relatively small (or zero) for some income/age groups, caution is needed in interpreting these results, though the broad conclusions stand.

CHAPTER 11

Incomes of the Self-employed by Trade Group

Introduction

11.1 Following an examination of how employees' earnings vary from job to job (Part II of this report) it is natural to ask whether any similar study is possible in relation to the self-employed. Fortunately the Survey of Personal Incomes, one of the two major data sources in relation to the self-employed, records the trade classification of those classified as self-employed and the first purpose of this Chapter is to compare the self-employment income distributions by trade group with that for all the self-employed. As far as possible we will try to differentiate between-group from within-group inequalities.

11.2 These trade groups, defined in the following section, do not, by and large, correspond to a great degree with those occupational and industrial classifications employed in Part II of this report. Moreover, certain comparisons would seem to be only of minor interest. For example, when one compares the incomes of the self-employed in agriculture with those of employees in this group, one cannot expect to learn much, bearing in mind that in this case the comparison is largely between farmers on the one hand and farm labourers on the other. However, in the case of say solicitors (and others of the professions) a better basis for comparison exists. Outside the professions, although the exact duties of those compared are unlikely to be similar, we have been able to match closely the areas of business concerned.

11.3 The second purpose of this Chapter, therefore, is to make comparisons of the incomes of the self-employed and employed within each "trade group", and thus the present Chapter is linked to the previous one, as well as to Part II of the report as described above. These comparisons are possible because, notwithstanding our previous remarks, some groupings of New Earnings Survey (NES) occupational and industrial classifications are similar to the SPI trade group definitions and therefore of value. This analysis appears in a later section of this Chapter.

11.4 The SPI data used in this Chapter are available only for the 1976–77 tax year. It should be mentioned at this stage that in neither the SPI nor the NES does the use of a professional label necessarily imply coverage of only professionally qualified persons (see paragraphs 2.46 to 2.51).

Definitions used in the trade group analyses

11.5   The twenty-two trade groups identified in tabulations of the income of the self-employed are listed below in Table 11.1 and analysed in the following paragraphs. Much fuller descriptions are given in Appendix K. These data form part of the Inland Revenue's Annual Income Survey (Survey of Personal Incomes) for the tax year 1976–77.

11.6   The tabulations cover the main source self-employment incomes (net of losses and capital allowances) of main source self-employment tax units, the incomes of wives being excluded in cases where the tax unit is a married couple. In these respects therefore it should be noted that the figures given in the analyses in this Chapter are on a different basis to that used elsewhere in this report. It should also be borne in mind that the distribution for each trade group is ranked by ranges of main source self-employment income (net of losses and capital allowances), enabling comparisons to be made between any two groups, and between any one group and the distribution of all self-employed.

Table 11.1   List of Trade Groups; 1976–77

Number of tax units in each group, number as percentage of total, and amount of main source self-employment income in each group as a percentage of total

United Kingdom

Serial number	Trade group	No. of tax units	No. of tax units as % of total self-employed	Amount of main source self-employ-ment income as % of total
1	Agriculture	246,561	14·9	12·6
2	Building and Contracting	375,433	22·6	18·7
3	Retail Distribution	224,183	13·5	12·3
4	Catering	64,685	3·9	3·6
5	Motor Repairs	47,719	2·9	2·7
6	Other Services	114,895	6·9	4·4
7	Barristers	3,612	0·2	0·5
8	Solicitors	19,742	1·2	4·3
9	Accountancy	16,258	1·0	2·7
10	Architecture	7,907	0.5	1·3
11	Engineering	5,976	0·4	0·6
12	Medicine	22,639	1·4	3·6
13	Dentistry	12,711	0·8	2·1
14	Manufacturing Industry	100,607	6·1	5·9
15	Wholesale Distribution	24,922	1·5	1·8
16	Road Transport	64,997	3·9	3·1
17	Entertainments and Gambling ..	39,045	2·3	1·7
18	Other Medical Services	8,354	0·5	0·5
19	Surveying	5,147	0·3	0·8
20	Advertising and Business Services ..	4,669	0·3	0·2
21	Insurance, Stockbrokers and Jobbers	9,815	0·6	1·1
22	All Other Trade Groups	237,824	14·3	15·4
	Total self-employed (all trade groups)	1,657,701	100·0	100·0

Source: SPI.

11.7   Some other components of income of the self-employed by trade group are identified and summary analyses of these are given in a later section. In the

168

following section (paragraphs 11.39 to 11.43) the dispersion of incomes by trade group is analysed, and in paragraphs 11.47 to 11.67 a comparison of the incomes of self-employed and employees within trade group is attempted. Paragraphs 11.68 *et seq* present a summary of this chapter.

11.8   For the purposes of the present Chapter the self-employed category embraces those Schedule D case I and II tax units whose trade classification is known, which does not exclude instances where profit was reported as "nil".

11.9   Provision was not made in the 1976–77 survey for recording main and subsidiary self-employment incomes separately[1]. In cases where more than one trade classification is involved, that used is generally the one which applies to the main source, which in the majority of cases is also the largest source.

11.10   Losses, stock relief and capital allowances (including those from other years) are included only to the extent that they are actually allowed against 1976–77 income.

Comparison of the incomes of the self-employed by trade group

11.11   The analysis enabling comparisons of self-employment income distributions to be made by and between trade groups is shown in Table 11.2, where the 22 trade groups are further grouped into professions, services, production groups and miscellaneous (see paragraph 11.16). It is important to remember that throughout this table the quantile groupings used are those of the self-employment income distribution for all trade groups (1 to 22) combined. In what follows we will simply use the term "the combined distribution" to refer to this.

11.12   The size of each trade group, ie the number of tax units[2] in each group, has already been noted in Table 11.1, where also this information is given in percentage terms, together with that concerning the amounts of main source self-employment income. The actual numbers given for each trade group, as is always the case in SPI analyses, are not the actual numbers surveyed, but are grossed up from the usable cases sampled. The sample is an adequate one for our purposes because the stratified sampling system of the SPI ensures sufficient representation at all levels.

11.13   Four groups each represent more than 10 per cent of the self-employed and together account for a total of 65.3 per cent of all tax units covered. Nine groups each comprise less than one per cent of the tax units analysed and together form only 4.5 per cent of the total. The smallest group (Barristers) make up just 0·2 per cent of the self-employed.

11.14   The distribution of all the self-employed, income ranges of which are shown in Table 11.2[2], shows that just over one per cent of the self-employed

---

[1] Subsidiary self-employment incomes are however recorded where the main source is Schedule E.
[2] Though the income unit shown on Table 11.2 and other tables in this Chapter is "tax unit" (because of the nature of the SPI database), the figures do in fact relate to individuals (main source), except where otherwise stated.

Table 11.2 Comparison of Self-employment Income Distributions

Percentage of self-employed in each trade group that fall into given quantile

United Kingdom

All Self-employed (all trade groups combined) Quantile group	Self-employment income range (lower limit)	7 Barristers	8 Solicitors	9 Accountancy
	£ pa	%	%	%
Top 1 per cent	17,496	6·4	13·5	8·5
Top 5 ,, ...	9,036	30·8	50·8	34·1
Top 10 ,, ...	6,244	51·6	70·3	50·6
Top 20 ,, ...	3,978	70·8	85·8	66·4
Top 50 ,, ...	2,053	76·4	94·4	84·8
Top 80 ,, ...	986	85·4	97·2	93·4
Total	—	100·0	100·0	100·0
No. in each group as % of total	100·0	0·2	1·2	1·0

All Self-employed (all trade groups combined) Quantile group	3 Retail Distribution	4 Catering	5 Motor Repairs	6 Other Services	15 Wholesale Distribution	16 Road Transport
	%	%	%	%	%	%
Top 1 per cent	0·4	0·1	0·4	0·1	2·3	0·2
Top 5 ,, ...	3·0	2·0	2·5	1·1	6·2	1·1
Top 10 ,, ...	7·7	7·6	7·3	2·8	13·8	4·3
Top 20 ,, ...	18·5	22·0	19·4	9·7	27·9	12·8
Top 50 ,, ...	48·1	54·7	53·2	32·3	53·5	43·6
Top 80 ,, ...	79·8	83·6	85·4	70·0	78·5	83·2
Total	100·0	100·0	100·0	100·0	100·0	100·0
No. in each group as % of total	13·5	3·9	2·9	6·9	1·5	3·9

The second section is headed (ii) Services.

Source: SPI.

Notes: [1] Schedule D cases I and II incomes excluding the incomes of wives.

[2] Though the income unit is shown as "tax unit" (because of the nature of the SPI database),
The total number in any given quantile group across all trade groups differs by less than discrepancy is an effect of the method of interpolation used.

of the Main Source Self-employed by Trade Groups; 1976–77

groups of the self-employment income distribution[1] for all trade groups; 1976–77

Income unit: tax unit[2]

(i) Professions

10 Architecture	11 Engineering	12 Medicine	13 Dentistry	19 Surveying	21 Insurance, Stockbrokers and Jobbers
%	%	%	%	%	%
10·5	4·2	1·0	4·6	8·2	8·8
31·4	13·3	31·2	34·8	27·4	15·3
46·6	24·0	70·2	62·3	46·1	23·2
63·2	37·3	85·6	82·1	60·8	33·5
76·6	65·4	92·2	94·6	78·7	59·7
87·9	84·0	96·0	96·6	87·7	75·7
100·0	100·0	100·0	100·0	100·0	100·0
0·5	0·4	1·4	0·8	0·3	0·6

			(iii) Production groups			(iv) Miscellaneous
17 Entertainments and Gambling	18 Other Medical Services	20 Advertising & Business Services	1 Agriculture	2 Building and Contracting	14 Manufacturing Industry	22 All Others Trade Groups
%	%	%	%	%	%	%
0·5	0·6	0·9	0·7	0·2	1·0	1·4
2·1	2·7	2·2	3·9	1·3	4·0	6·7
4·5	8·2	7·1	8·2	2·9	8·0	12·9
11·4	20·8	14·5	18·3	10·3	18·9	23·8
34·5	50·3	37·3	40·1	54·4	50·7	50·1
65·6	78·0	62·3	68·4	89·1	82·1	76·6
100·0	100·0	100·0	100·0	100·0	100·0	100·0
2·3	0·5	0·3	14·9	22·6	6·1	14·3

the figures do in fact relate to individuals (main source), except where otherwise stated.

0·6% from that obtained by taking the relevant proportion of the overall total number. This very minor

have self-employment income of £17,000 per annum or more and just over five per cent have £9,000 or more, while nearly half (48.4 per cent in fact) received less than £2,000 of income under Schedule D cases I and II, and over 20 per cent (20·3 per cent) less than £1,000. While the figures in this table relate to the 1976–77 tax year survey, the effects of time lags (see paragraph 4.18 *et seq*) should be borne in mind.

11.15   Turning to the main body of Table 11.2 our chief interest is in the comparison between the columns giving the numbers of tax units in the specified quantile groups of the combined distribution as percentages of the total for each trade group.

11.16   In making comparisons between trade groups, it is useful to arrange them as in Table 11.2 in four divisions:

    i   Professions (trade group numbers 7, 8, 9, 10, 11, 12, 13, 19 and 21);

    ii   Services (trade group numbers 3, 4, 5, 6, 15, 16, 17, 18 and 20);

    iii   Production groups (trade group numbers 1, 2 and 14); and

    iv   Miscellaneous (trade group number 22).

11.17   In the professions we find a large degree of concentration into the higher parts of the combined distribution. For seven of the professional trade groups we find that at least 27 per cent of the tax units in the group fall into the top five per cent of the combined distribution, at least 46 per cent in the top twenty per cent quantile group and at least 76 per cent above the median. The other two professional groups, namely 11—Engineering and 21—Insurance, Stockbrokers and Jobbers, are rather different in ways which will be described below.

11.18   The group whose members are most highly concentrated in the upper groups of self-employment income is 8—Solicitors, which has the greatest percentage figures in every row of Table 11.2 except the top 50 per cent where the percentage is just 0·2 per cent below that for Dentistry. The professional group (excluding the two special cases already mentioned) with the lowest representation in the top quintile (20 per cent) group is Surveying, although the representation of this group in the top one per cent of the combined distribution is typical of the professions.

11.19   Medicine and Dentistry show high concentrations in the top five and more especially in the top ten and top twenty per cent of the combined distribution. The proportion of those in Dentistry falling into the top percentile of the combined distribution is rather low at 4.6 per cent compared to other professional trade groups. Somewhat surprisingly, the corresponding figure for Medicine is 1.0 per cent, ie this group has no more and no less members of the top percentile than a representative sample of all trade groups combined.

11.20   While each of these seven professional trade groups is small and expected to be relatively homogeneous in character, the foregoing analysis shows that there are some within-group inequalities (it could theoretically have been the case that negligible numbers of those in these groups fell below the combined median, though in no case does this actually occur) and has also drawn out some dissimilarities between these groups.

11.21   It is important to note that these are comparisons, not across the whole of each profession, but across that part of each profession that is self-employed; thus we may be comparing almost all of one profession against only a part (that part that has moved from the salaried ranks into private practice) of another. It has been noted in Chapter 2 (paragraphs 2.46 to 2.51) that the professions differ widely in the opportunities offered for self-employment and salaried employment, respectively. For example, in 1977 self-employed architects in private practice accounted for only just over one-quarter of the total number of architects in full-time work, while for solicitors the equivalent figure was just under 60 per cent. It is very likely that if equivalent figures were available for barristers they would show that the great majority were self-employed. This wide difference in the opportunities for the two types of employment in the different professions must be borne in mind in studying the above comparisons.

11.22   There are two trade groups in the professions (i) and another in the services (ii) which are markedly dissimilar to the others in the relevant division, and are in some ways intermediate between the professions and the services. The first of these groups we will discuss is 21—Insurance, Stockbrokers and Jobbers. The position of this group is not surprising considering that, if it were possible to separate them, one would perhaps class those in Insurance as being in the services division and those in Stockbroking and Jobbing with the professional trade groups.

11.23   The Engineering trade group is also an intermediate one, in the sense that it does not exhibit the high concentration into upper ranges of self-employment income generally shown by the professions, but cannot be likened to a typical services trade group. In fact this group consists of a small number of Civil, Consulting, Inspecting and Mining Engineers in private practice. It is possible that some tax units in this group could more usefully, for our present purposes, have been included in the Manfuacturing Industry group.

11.24   The Wholesale Distribution group stands out within the services division by virtue of the fact that considerably greater proportions of its members fell into the quantile groups at all levels above the median. The degree of concentration, however, is much below those in even the two least well represented professional groups considered in the preceding two paragraphs.

11.25   Among the remaining 8 groups forming the main bulk of the services division (including Retail Distribution and the Other Services group) there is less variation between groups in concentration into the quantile groups of the combined distribution as compared to the differences between the professional groups. An exception must be made in the case of the bottom quintile where there is a notable lack of pattern in the figures.

11.26   Two groups in this division have the lowest concentration, over all trade groups, in the top half of the combined distribution. These are the Other Services group and Entertainments and Gambling. Together with Road Transport, these groups exhibit low concentration in the top ten and twenty per cent quantile groups, but are not atypical in terms of the top one per cent and top five per cent groups. The proportion of those in Other Services falling in the five to ten per cent group of the combined distribution is particularly low at 1.7 per cent.

11.27 Turning now to the production groups division (iii), we find that the concentration into overall quantile groups of the combined distribution is more or less comparable to a typical trade group in the services division. Building and Contracting has low concentration in the top twenty per cent ranges being comparable to Other Services. In the middle part of the combined distribution the percentages for Building and Contracting are similar to those for the services division while few tax units in this trade group fall in the bottom fifth of the combined distribution, as in the case of the professions.

11.28 The remaining two groups, Manufacturing Industry and the miscellaneous division All Other Trade Groups are both rather typical of the combined distribution of the self-employed. This is no surprise in the case of All Other Trade Groups which, by definition, has a very heterogeneous composition.

11.29 In attempting to assess further the degree to which inequalities in the combined distribution arise from within-group or between-group differences it is useful to look at the figures in Table 11.2 aggregated for the four disivisions of trade groups which we have been considering.

11.30 These figures are shown in Table 11.3 where we see that the professional trade groups clearly supply a major degree of inequality in the combined distribution, but each professional trade group contributes to this in varying ways as discussed earlier. Although there is heavy concentration into the upper ranges within the professional division it should not be forgotten that this division accounts for only slightly more than 6 per cent of the total number of self-employed tax units, which moderates the effect of the very high concentrations.

Table 11.3 Comparison of Self-employment Income Distributions[1] of the Main Source Self-employed by Trade Group Division; 1976–77

Percentage of self-employed in each trade group division that fall into given quantile groups of the self-employment income distribution for all trade groups; 1976–77

United Kingdom   Income unit: tax unit[2]

Quantile group of the combined self-employed distribution	(i) Professions	(ii) Services	(iii) Production groups	(iv) Miscellaneous
	%	%	%	%
Top 1 per cent	7·2	0·4	0·5	1·4
Top 5 „	33·1	2·3	2·5	6·7
Top 10 „	55·5	6·4	5·4	12·9
Top 20 „	71·0	16·5	14·3	23·8
Top 50 „	84·7	45·0	49·0	50·1
Top 80 „	91·9	78·0	81·1	76·6
Total no...	103,806	593,469	722,601	237,824
No. in each division as % of total	6·3	35·8	43·6	14·3

Source: derived from Table 11.2.

Notes: [1] Schedule D cases I and II incomes excluding the incomes of wives.
         [2] See footnote 2 to Table 11.2.

11.31 Concentration into various parts of the combined distribution is similar for the services and production groups divisions. The miscellaneous division is hard to comment upon further but it is worth reminding ourselves that, as shown in Appendix K, this group certainly includes a number of professional trades, and this fact appears to be reflected in the figures.

Summary analysis of other components of income

11.32 In relation to the self-employed, we are chiefly concerned in this Chapter with their main source self-employment income. However, some data are available which enable us to examine other components of income by trade group. We here present a summary analysis only of this information, the aim being to highlight the differences, if any, in the overall effect of a given

Table 11.4 Comparison of Incomes by Trade Group: Wives' Self-employment Incomes[1]; 1976–77

Numbers of wives with self-employment income as percentages of numbers of tax units with self-employment incomes, amounts of wives' incomes as percentages of tax units' incomes (excluding wives); 1976–77

United Kingdom   Income unit: **tax unit**[3]

Trade group[2]	Number of wives with self-employment income as % of number of tax units with self-employment incomes	Amount of wives' incomes as % of tax units' incomes (excluding wives)
	%	%
1 Agriculture	14·6	13·6
2 Building and Contracting	2·9	1·9
3 Retail Distribution	29·4	19·4
4 Catering	28·1	16·5
5 Motor Repairs	9·1	8·5
6 Other Services	25·5	16·4
7 Barristers	3·5	1·6
8 Solicitors	1·3	0·4
9 Accountancy	1·4	0·4
10 Architecture	3·7	1·7
11 Engineering	2·3	0·7
12 Medicine	9·9	4·5
13 Dentistry	14·8	3·4
14 Manufacturing Industry	8·9	7·1
15 Wholesale Distribution	11·8	9·6
16 Road Transport	8·0	3·9
17 Entertainments and Gambling	10·9	5·3
18 Other Medical Services	12·1	8·4
19 Surveying	2·0	0·8
20 Advertising and Business Services	7·1	4·4
21 Insurance, Stockbrokers and Jobbers	5·0	2·5
22 All other Trade Groups	7·8	4·7
All self-employed (all trade groups combined)	16·3	9·1

Source: SPI.

Notes: [1] Schedule D cases I and II incomes.
        [2] Trade group of husband (main source).
        [3] See footnote 2 to Table 11.2.

Table 11.5 Comparison of Incomes by Trade Group:
Employment Income of the Main Source Self-employed; 1976–77

Employment income as a percentage of main source self-employment income, excluding and including wives; 1976–77

United Kingdom   Income unit: tax unit[1]

| | Trade group | Employment income as a percentage of main source self-employment income (excluding wife) | |
		Excluding wives	Including wives
		%	%
1	Agriculture	2·9	3·3
2	Building and Contracting	2·7	2·9
3	Retail Distribution	3·0	5·1
4	Catering	3·8	4·1
5	Motor Repairs	7·9	8·5
6	Other Services	58·6	59·5
7	Barristers	3·7	4·4
8	Solicitors	0·6	0·7
9	Accountancy	3·6	3·6
10	Architecture	2·4	2·4
11	Engineering	17·3	17·3
12	Medicine	28·6	29·4
13	Dentistry	0·9	2·8
14	Manufacturing Industry	3·5	14·2
15	Wholesale Distribution	4·4	12·6
16	Road Transport	2·7	18·2
17	Entertainments and Gambling	6·1	22·0
18	Other Medical Services	5·8	18·0
19	Surveying	2·9	8·3
20	Advertising and Business Services	3·0	19·7
21	Insurance, Stockbrokers and Jobbers	7·9	15·3
22	All Other Trade Groups	4·9	16·0
	All self-employed (all trade groups combined)	6·9	10·8

Source: SPI.
Note: [1] See footnote 2 to Table 11.2.

component between trade groups. A possible refinement would be to break down this analysis by level of main source self-employment income.

11.33   The first additional component to be considered is wives' self-employment incomes. These are excluded from the main source incomes already considered in cases where the tax unit is a married couple. There will therefore be some instances where this component will be the largest source for a given tax unit. Table 11.4 shows that in three trade groups[1] namely Retail Distribution, Catering and Other Services, it is relatively common to find tax units which represent married couples where the wife has some income from self-employment. The proportions in this situation in the professional trade groups are small, except in the case of Medicine and Dentistry where the figures are more comparable with other trade groups. In all cases the mean income of wives for a

---

[1] The trade group here is that of the husband where the latter provides the main source. In many cases (ie partnerships) the wife's trade group will be the same as that of her spouse.

group of tax units in a given trade group is below the main source mean, generally considerably so, but only by a small amount in, for example, Agriculture and Motor Repairs.

11.34 Employment income does not play a large part in shaping the distribution of total income for most trade groups but exceptions to this occur in Engineering, Medicine and Other Services in which group employment income amounts to more than half of the figure for self-employment income. It is not possible here, of course, to pin-point any particular trades within the Other Services group which may be responsible for influencing the overall situation in that group. The effect of also including wives' employment income is relatively inconsequential as far as trade groups numbers 1 to 12 are concerned but significant in trade groups 13 to 22.

11.35 Subsidiary self-employment incomes generally are not separated from the main source (see paragraph 11.9) and thus no separate analysis of this component is presented. Some other data on various components of income are available but since they are incomplete in that they cover only trade groups numbers 14 to 22 the figures are not tabulated here but are shown in Appendix L. The following points, however, are worthy of note here.

11.36 Losses and capital allowances taken as a percentage of the main source self-employment income (excluding income of wife) gross of such losses and capital allowances as were actually allowed is certainly a major component for some trade groups. This component has important effects in the Road Transport group where it amounts to over 20 per cent of gross self-employment income and to a varying extent in the other groups for which figures are available, being over 9 per cent for the miscellaneous division of All Other Trade Groups and falling to only about 3 per cent for Surveying. The effect of including losses and capital allowances of the wife, however, is negligible.

11.37 Retirement annuity relief is a component which varies in incidence but is noticeably prevalent in the Surveying trade group affecting 47.5 per cent of tax units in that profession. It is speculated that a similar situation would be found in cases of other professional trade groups, were statistics available. The amount of this deduction is considerably less than that of other deductions, with the exception of the Surveying group just mentioned. Although the incidence of other deductions is high and variable (between 38 and 60 per cent of tax units are affected in the groups considered), the amount involved, taken as a percentage of total self-employment incomes (excluding wives') is fairly constant (7 to 9 per cent) across trade groups, being slightly greater though in the Insurance, Stockbrokers and Jobbers group, in which instance it amounts to nearly 12 per cent.

11.38 Other income includes Schedule D cases III to VI, Schedule A rents, Building Society interest, dividends from UK companies and any other income taxed before receipt, all of which may be considered as investment income. There is considerable variation in the figures for this component and little pattern, but it generally forms a substantial proportion of total income, being 19 per cent for

Table 11.6 Dispersion of Self-employment Income Distributions[1] of

Top percentile, highest and lowest deciles and upper and lower quartiles group;

United Kingdom

Quantile	Quantile point	Quantile as percentage of median	7 Barristers	8 Solicitors	9 Accountancy
	£ pa	%	%	%	%
Top percentile ..	17,496	852	430	416	593
Highest decile ..	6,244	304	243	213	261
Upper quartile ..	3,433	167	159	151	174
Lower quartile ..	1,162	57	41	62	48
Lowest decile ..	475	23	12	35	23
Median £ pa ..	2,053		6,411	9,143	6,331
Mean £ pa ..	2,961		7,352	10,658	8,126

All self-employed (all trade groups combined)   (ii) Services

Quantile	3 Retail Distribution	4 Catering	5 Motor Repairs	6 Other Services	15 Wholesale Distribution	16 Road Transport
	%	%	%	%	%	%
Top percentile	693	475	592	627	1,019	488
Highest decile	279	252	257	265	330	234
Upper quartile ..	169	164	161	164	191	152
Lower quartile.. ..	57	56	62	56	50	66
Lowest decile	26	28	37	20	13	35
Median £ pa	1,982	2,246	2,155	1,474	2,214	1,881
Mean £ pa	2,685	2,759	2,818	1,886	3,512	2,330

Source: SPI.

Notes: [1] Schedule D cases I and II incomes excluding the incomes of wives.

[2] See footnote 2 to Table 11.2.

the Main Source Self-employed Within Trade Groups; 1976–77

as percentages of the median; median and mean for each trade
1976–77

Income unit: tax unit[2]

(i) Professions

10 Architecture	11 Engineering	12 Medicine	13 Dentistry	19 Surveying	21 Insurance, Stockbrokers and Jobbers
%	%	%	%	%	%
611	1,068	216	357	653	1,746
311	356	144	196	278	555
185	194	119	145	169	222
38	48	73	68	43	40
13	13	35	41	11	18
5,721	3,145	8,011	7,244	5,638	2,568
7,901	4,995	7,715	8,095	7,586	5,562

			(iii) Production groups			(iv) Miscellaneous
17 Entertainments and Gambling	18 Other Medical Services	20 Advertising and Business Services	1 Agriculture	2 Building and Contracting	14 Manufacturing Industry	22 All other trade groups
%	%	%	%	%	%	%
975	628	866	966	473	860	953
292	268	339	348	187	267	353
179	170	197	192	138	162	185
46	54	51	44	71	60	51
13	19	22	17	43	27	23
1,447	2,067	1,381	1,632	2,149	2,077	2,058
2,121	2,773	2,329	2,515	2,448	2,897	3,185

All Other Trade Groups, over 15 per cent for Surveying and nearly 30 per cent in the case of the Advertising and Business Services group.

Dispersion of the incomes of the self-employed by trade group

11.39 The dispersion or spread of self-employment incomes varies considerably with trade groups as is shown by Table 11.6 (parts 1 to 3 covering the groups as in Table 11.2). This new table shows quantiles for each trade group and for all the self-employed as percentages of the median.

11.40 Table 11.6 also gives the mean self-employment income for each trade group, assisting in the comparison of overall levels of income between the groups. As previously, we consider the analysis in four divisions of trade groups. In the professional division, the mean income from self-employment varies from £7,352 per annum for Barristers to £10,658 per annum in the case of Solicitors. Here we are excluding Engineering and Insurance, Stockbrokers and Jobbers, which we have already identified as intermediate trade groups. Mean self-employment incomes in the services division range from a high of £3,512 (Wholesale Distribution) to £2,121 (Entertainments and Gambling) with that for the Other Services trade group being even lower (£1,886 per annum).

11.41 Comparing the mean with the median provides a simple way of assessing the shape of a distribution, and from Table 11.6 we see that the mean as a percentage of the median varies (with two exceptions) between 112 per cent and 169 per cent, though with little pattern in the figures within or between the divisions. The two exceptions are in the cases of the Insurance, Stockbrokers and Jobbers trade group where the mean is more than double the median (217 per cent) and in Medicine which is the only trade group where the mean is less than the median (96 per cent). This unusual feature of the shape of the self-employment income distribution for Medicine is consistent with what was noted about the concentration in the combined distribution for this group in paragraph 11.19.

11.42 Further reference to Table 11.6 again picks out the same trade groups as previously mentioned as being exceptional or remarkable. The distributions of self-employment incomes for the "hybrid" trade groups (Wholesale Distribution, Insurance, Stockbrokers and Jobbers, and Engineering) show high degrees of dispersion. The distribution for Building and Contracting shows a compression of self-employment income, especially from the bottom to the median of the distribution. That for Medicine shows even more compression, notably as viewed from the top.

11.43 Another way of comparing the spread of income within each trade group is to study the average income by quantile group of the distributions concerned. Table 11.7 presents such analysis for selected trade groups. The arrangement of this table is in accordance with the divisions used in earlier analyses. The particular combination of quantile groupings chosen was made so that comparison with Table 11.6 and the overall distribution of self-employment income shown in Table 11.2 could be made.

180

Table 11.7 Average Self-Employment Income[1] of the Main Source Self-employed by Quantile Group Within Selected Trade Groups; 1976-77

United Kingdom

Income unit: tax unit[2]

Quantile group	(i) Professions					(ii) Services			(iii) Production Groups		
	8 Solicitors	9 Accountancy	12 Medicine	13 Dentistry	21 Insurance, Stockbrokers and Jobbers	3 Retail Distribution	4 Catering	5 Motor Repairs	1 Agriculture	2 Building and Contracting	14 Manufacturing Industry
	£ pa	£ pa	£ pa	£ pa	£ pa	£ pa	£ pa	£ pa	£ pa	£ pa	£ pa
Top 1 per cent	56,200	52,500	23,700	29,500	65,300	19,360	13,520	21,000	23,000	15,160	27,000
2-5 „ „	} 23,900	25,200	14,480	18,980	} 24,800	9,387	8,196	8,961	10,670	6,452	11,110
6-10 „ „		18,210	11,920	15,200		6,349	6,166	6,191	6,587	4,391	6,482
Top 10 per cent	27,200	24,400	14,120	18,140	28,900	8,866	7,713	8,782	9,871	6,293	10,390
Top 25 „ „	20,600	17,810	11,840	14,370	16,540	6,040	5,738	6,059	6,449	4,507	6,657
26-50 „ „	11,180	8,483	8,846	8,707	3,639	2,571	2,852	2,697	2,234	2,483	2,609
51-75 „ „	7,456	4,605	6,961	6,320	1,812	1,532	1,742	1,738	1,189	1,853	1,674
76-100 „ „	3,439	1,610	3,218	2,987	251	595	706	780	187	949	648

Source: SPI.

Notes: Figures greater than £20,000 pa have been rounded to the nearest £100 and those between £10,000 pa and £20,000 pa to the nearest £10.

[1] Schedule D cases I and II incomes excluding the incomes of wives.

[2] See footnote 2 to Table 11.2.

Classification by reward, and other rankings of the trade groups

11.44 Nine of the trade groups stand out from the rest on almost every count—high medians, high means, high proportions in the upper quantiles of the combined distribution, low proportions in the lower quantiles. These nine are coincident with the nine groups identified in the professional division. Two of these groups—Engineering, and the group of Insurance, Stockbrokers and Jobbers—are less prominent than the others but are nevertheless well separated from the field. We class these nine together as Class I—Higher Reward. At the other end of the scale we find four groups which are weakly represented (less than $2\frac{1}{2}$ per cent) in the top 5 per cent of the combined distribution, *and* strongly represented (well over 50 per cent) in the bottom 50 per cent. These we call Class III—Lower Reward. The mean income of Class III is about a quarter of that of Class I (£2,065 pa vs £8,021 pa). The Higher Reward and Lower Reward trade groups between them cover only one-fifth of the total self-employed population, and so there remains an extensive intermediate class of trade groups to be accounted for. We can further distinguish, within this intermediate range, between (A) those groups that have a fair representation both in the top 5 per cent ($2\frac{1}{2}$–7 per cent) and in the bottom 50 per cent (45–50 per cent), and (B) those that are not so well favoured *either* at one end of the distribution *or* the other. This last class includes several of the largest groups: Retail Distribution and Agriculture which have more than the average proportion of low incomes and also Catering and Building and Contracting which have few high incomes. The partition of trade groups brought about in this way corresponds exactly to the ranking of distributions by means, though not to that by medians.

11.45 The distinction between Class I and the rest is extremely clearcut, but we think the further classification, based on purely statistical features of the distributions of each group, may be helpful. The groups in divisions other than the professions are distributed between classes IIA, IIB and III. The trade groups are listed in the four categories with supporting data in Table 11.8. Within each category they are listed in order of medians: this is only one of the many alternative rankings and should not be regarded as having any more general significance.

11.46 The preceding paragraphs gave one of many possible presentations of the results derived so far in this chapter. A more comprehensive view of the situation is afforded by Table 11.9, a summary rank table which shows, for instance, that the Manufacturing Industry trade group has the eleventh highest percentage of tax units falling in the top one per cent of the combined distribution, the twelfth highest mean self-employment income, the sixteenth greatest inter-quartile dispersion etc.

Comparison of the self-employed and employees within trade group

11.47 The New Earnings Survey (NES) analyses employees' earnings by both industrial and occupational classifications. As detailed tabulations of the relevant distributions were available, it was decided to attempt a comparison of the self-employed and employees within 'trade group' by selecting combinations of industrial or occupational categories which would closely match the definition of trade groups used thus far in this Chapter and defined in Appendix K.

Table 11.8 Trade Groups Arranged by Reward Class; 1976–77

United Kingdom

Class	Trade Group and serial number	Number as percentage of total	Median	Percentage falling in	
				Top 5%	Bottom 50% of the combined distribution
		%	£ pa	%	%
I HIGHER REWARD	8 Solicitors	1·2	9,143	50·8	5·6
	12 Medicine	1·4	8,011	31·2	7·8
	13 Dentistry	0·8	7,244	34·8	5·4
	7 Barristers	0·2	6,411	30·8	23·6
	9 Accountancy	1·0 ⎤ 6½%	6,331	34·1	15·2
	10 Architecture	0·5	5,721	31·4	23·4
	19 Surveying	0·3	5,638	27·4	21·3
	11 Engineering	0·4	3,145	13·3	34·6
	21 Insurance, Stock-brokers and Jobbers	0·6	2,568	15·3	40·3
IIA INTER-MEDIATE (A)	15 Wholesale Distribution	1·5	2,214	6·2	46·5
	5 Motor Repairs	2·9	2,155	2·5	46·8
	14 Manufacturing Industry	6·1 ⎬ 25%	2,077	4·0	49·3
	18 Other Medical Services	0·5	2,067	2·7	49·7
	22 All Other Trade Groups	14·3	2,058	6·7	49·9
IIB INTER-MEDIATE (B)	4 Catering	3·9	2,246	2·0	45·3
	2 Building and Contracting	22·6 ⎬ 55%	2,149	1·3	45·6
	3 Retail Distribution	13·5	1,982	3·0	51·9
	1 Agriculture	14·9	1,632	3·9	59·9
III LOWER REWARD	16 Road Transport	3·9	1,881	1·1	56·4
	6 Other Services	6·9	1,474	1·1	67·7
	17 Entertainments and Gambling	2·3 ⎬ 13½%	1,447	2·1	65·5
	20 Advertising and Business Services	0·3	1,381	2·2	62·7
All self-employed (all trade groups combined)		100·0	2,053	5·0	50·0

Source: derived from Tables 11.2 and 11.6.

11.48 We are comparing the self-employment incomes of those for whom this is the main source with the gross earnings of employees. This is a good basis for comparison but, unfortunately, this approach brings with it the many problems that can arise when we wish to compare data sources which differ as much from each other as do the SPI and the NES.

11.49 The NES data used are those for 1975. Use of the 1976–77 SPI data involves a time lag of the order of 18 months (see paragraphs 4.18 to 4.22) and spans a tax year (April to April) while the NES relates to a single week in April. Therefore use of the 1975 NES as a source is appropriate but the possibility of bias in the SPI data due to variations in time lag remains.

Table 11.9 Summary Rank Table by Self-employed Trade Group; 1976–77

United Kingdom

Trade group and serial number	POSITION AS RANKED[1] BY:						
	Percentage falling in top 1% of the combined self-employed distribution	Percentage falling in top 20% of the combined self-employed distribution	Percentage falling in top 50% of the combined self-employed distribution	Mean	Median	Interquartile range (as a percentage of the median)	Highest and lowest inter-decile range (as a percentage of the median)
PROFESSIONS							
7. Barristers	6	4	7	7	4	11	15
8. Solicitors	1	1	2	1	1	18	19
9. Accountancy	4	5	4	2	5	10	14
10. Architecture	2	6	6	4	6	3	7
11. Engineering	8	8	8	9	8	4	2
12. Medicine	12	2	3	5	2	22	22
13. Dentistry	7	3	1	3	3	20	20
19. Surveying	5	7	5	6	7	9	9
21. Insurance, Stockbrokers and Jobbers	3	9	9	8	9	1	1
SERVICES							
3. Retail Distribution	18	16	17	16	17	13	10
4. Catering	22	12	10	15	10	15	16
5. Motor Repairs	17	14	13	13	12	17	17
6. Other Services	21	22	22	22	20	14	12
15. Wholesale Distribution	9	10	12	10	11	6	6
16. Road Transport	19	19	18	19	18	19	18
17. Entertainments and Gambling	16	10	21	21	21	8	8
18. Other Medical Services	15	13	15	14	15	12	11
20. Advertising and Business Services	13	18	20	20	22	5	5
PRODUCTION GROUPS							
1. Agriculture	14	17	19	17	19	2	3
2. Building and Contracting	20	21	11	18	13	21	21
14. Manufacturing Industry	11	15	14	12	14	16	13
MISCELLANEOUS							
22. All Other Trade Groups	10	11	16	11	16	7	4

Source: Derived from Tables 11.2 and 11.6.

Note: [1] Greatest figures = rank 1, least figures = rank 22.

11.50 The actual NES data used relate to weekly earnings (basis D[1]) grossed up to annual figures for all full-time employees (men and women combined). The NES data cover Great Britain while the geographical extent of the SPI is the United Kingdom.

11.51 The effect on our results of all the incompatibilities in the two data sources which have been mentioned is hard to assess. Inevitably, more than usual caution must be exercised when interpreting the figures. The principal points to bear in mind are the components of income not covered here (see paragraph 11.32 *et seq* in relation to the self-employed), the differing effects of taxation upon the self-employed and employees (see paragraphs 10.30 and 10.31 and 12.18 to 12.21), and any bias towards higher self-employment incomes due to the time lags referred to in paragraph 11.49. There is also the question of non-cash benefits of employees to be considered.

11.52 An attempt was made to match every industrial and occupational group identified in the NES with one of the SPI trade groups to produce NES 'trade groups' which would be comparable in definition. As pointed out in paragraphs 11.2 to 11.4, this does not necessarily imply any correspondence between the type of duties carried out by the self-employed and employees under the same nominal heading.

11.53 Many of the occupational categories, unfortunately, could not be matched with any trade groups since some groups—eg 'purchasing officers and managers' and residual groups such as 'all other professional and related in education, welfare and health'—overlap several trade groups using the SPI definitions shown in Appendix K. Such groups were therefore omitted, though the effect of this is small in the case of those classes finally selected for analysis (see below). These remarks do not apply in the case of comparisons made on an industry basis, where all industry groups could be allocated.

11.54 From the 44 (22 each on an industrial and occupational basis respectively) potential distributions which could have been produced in this way, thirteen were selected after due consideration as being worthy of being analysed. These were as follows:

Industry basis	Occupation basis
1 Agriculture	7+8 Barristers and Solicitors
2 Building and Contracting	9 Accountancy
3 Retail Distribution	10 Architecture
4 Catering	12 Medicine
5 Motor Repairs	13 Dentistry
16 Road Transport	16 Road Transport
	19 Surveying

The definitions of these NES 'trade groups' are to be found in Appendix M. Comparisons of the latter with Appendix K will show how the definitions of trade groups in the SPI match up to those adopted for use in the NES comparative analysis.

---

[1] Pay for the survey pay period not affected by absence.

Table 11.10 Comparison of the Self-employed and Employees within Trade Groups: Agriculture (1), Building and Contracting (2); Industry Basis; 1976–77[4]

Percentage of self-employed and employees who fall into given quantile groups of the self-employment income distribution[1] for all trade groups. Quantiles as percentages of the median for the self-employed and employees. Mean incomes for the self-employed and employees.

United Kingdom (self-employed)
Great Britain (employees)

Income unit: tax unit[3] (self-employed),
Full-time men and women (employees)

Quantile group	Self-employment income[1] range (lower limit)	AGRICULTURE (1)		BUILDING AND CONTRACTING (2)	
		SELF-EMPLOYED	EMPLOYEES	SELF-EMPLOYED	EMPLOYEES
		Percentage with self-employment income[1] in the specified quantile group of the combined self-employed distribution	Percentage with employment income[2] in the specified quantile group of the combined self-employed distribution	Percentage with self-employment income[1] in the specified quantile group of the combined self-employed distribution	Percentage with employment income[2] in the specified quantile group of the combined self-employed distribution
	£ pa	%	%	%	%
Top 1 per cent	17,496	0·7	0·0	0·2	0·0
Top 5 "	9,036	3·9	0·1	1·3	0·2
Top 10 "	6,244	8·2	0·2	2·9	1·5
Top 20 "	3,978	18·3	2·4	10·3	12·4
Top 50 "	2,053	40·1	44·3	54·4	82·7
Top 80 "	986	68·4	98·7	98·1	99·5
Total number	1,657,701	246,561	(1,364)	375,433	(8,013)

Table 11.10 (cont'd)   Comparison of the Self-employed and Employees within Trade Groups: Agriculture (1), Building and Contracting; Industry Basis; 1976-77[4]

Quantile	Quantile as percentage of the median for the combined self-employed distribution[1,5]	AGRICULTURE (1)		BUILDING AND CONTRACTING (2)	
		SELF-EMPLOYED	EMPLOYEES	SELF-EMPLOYED	EMPLOYEES
		Quantile[1] as percentage of the median[5]	Quantile[2] as percentage of the median[5]	Quantile[1] as percentage of the median[5]	Quantile[2] as percentage of the median[5]
	%	%	%	%	%
Top percentile : :	852	966	244	473	253
Highest decile : :	304	348	150	187	156
Upper quartile : :	167	192	123	138	125
Median : :	100	100	100	100	100
Lower quartile : :	57	44	84	71	82
Lowest decile : :	23	17	73	43	68
Mean £ pa : :	2,961	2,515	2,119	2,448	2,907

Sources: SPI (self-employed), NES (employees).

Notes: [1] Schedule D cases I and II excluding the incomes of wives.
[2] Derived from weekly earnings (Basis D).
[3] Though the income unit is shown as "tax unit" (because of the nature of the SPI database), the figures do in fact relate to individuals (main source).
[4] The SPI data for the self-employed relate to 1976–77 but because of time lags the comparison is with 1975 NES data for employees.
[5] Quantiles as percentages of their respective medians are shown rounded to the nearest percentage point.

187

Table 11.11 Comparison of the Self-employed and Employees within Trade Groups: Retail Distribution (3), Catering (4); Industry Basis; 1976-77[4]

Percentage of self-employed and employees who fall into given quantile groups of the self-employment income distribution[1] for all trade groups. Quantiles as percentages of the median for the self-employed and employees. Mean incomes for the self-employed and employees.

United Kingdom (self-employed)
Great Britain (employees)

Income unit: tax unit[3] (self-employed),
Full-time men and women (employees)

Quantile group	Self-employment income[1] range (lower limit)	RETAIL DISTRIBUTION (3)		CATERING (4)	
		SELF-EMPLOYED	EMPLOYEES	SELF-EMPLOYED	EMPLOYEES
		Percentage with self-employment income[1] in the specified quantile group of the combined self-employed distribution	Percentage with employment income[2] in the specified quantile group of the combined self-employed distribution	Percentage with self-employment income[1] in the specified quantile group of the combined self-employed distribution	Percentage with employment income[2] in the specified quantile group of the combined self-employed distribution
	£ pa	%	%	%	%
Top 1 per cent	17,496	0·4	0·0	0·1	0·1
Top 5 ,, ...	9,036	3·0	0·3	2·0	0·1
Top 10 ,, ...	6,244	7·7	0·8	7·6	0·2
Top 20 ,, ...	3,978	18·5	4·4	22·0	4·0
Top 50 ,, ...	2,053	48·1	36·1	54·7	34·4
Top 80 ,, ...	986	79·8	95·4	83·6	89·9
Total number	1,657,701	224,183	(6,296)	64,685	(909)

Table 11.11 (*cont'd*) Comparison of the Self-employed and Employees within Trade Groups: Retail Distribution (3), Catering (4); Industry Basis; 1976-77[4]

Quantile	Quantile as percentage of the median for the combined self-employed distribution[1,5]	RETAIL DISTRIBUTION (3)		CATERING (4)	
		SELF-EMPLOYED	EMPLOYEES	SELF-EMPLOYED	EMPLOYEES
		Quantile[1] as percentage of the median[5]	Quantile[2] as percentage of the median[5]	Quantile[1] as percentage of the median[5]	Quantile[2] as percentage of the median[5]
	%	%	%	%	%
Top percentile : : :	852	693	344	475	299
Highest decile : : :	304	279	185	252	176
Upper quartile : : :	167	169	138	164	131
Median : : :	100	100	100	100	100
Lower quartile : : :	57	57	78	56	72
Lowest decile : : :	23	26	66	28	56
Mean £ pa : : :	2,961	2,685	2,029	2,759	1,921

Sources: SPI (self-employed), NES (employees).

Notes: [1] Schedule D cases I and II excluding the incomes of wives.

[2] Derived from weekly earnings (Basis D).

[3] See footnote 3 to Table 11.10.

[4] See footnote 4 to Table 11.10.

[5] See footnote 5 to Table 11.10.

11.55   Points that deserve mention here are that in the NES analysis Barristers and Solicitors cannot be separated from each other or from Judges and Advocates. In the case of Accountancy, the SPI as opposed to the NES covers only qualified accountants. Distributions from the Road Transport 'trade group' were produced on both industry and occupation bases so that some comparisons of the merits of each would be possible.

11.56   The numbers of individuals in some of the NES distributions are rather small but adequate to produce satisfactory analysis, except in the case of Dentistry where only 20 individuals were identified. It was therefore decided to produce an aggregate distribution for Medicine and Dentistry in addition to that for Medicine alone.

Earnings of the self-employed and employees

11.57   The results for each of the thirteen comparisons described above appear in Tables 11.10 to 11.16. In each table the upper half is produced in a similar way to the analysis given in Table 11.2. Comparison of the percentage columns in this part of the table will show what proportions of employees have earnings at the various levels of self-employment income selected (which are those for the combined distribution), the self-employed in each group having already been allocated to these ranges. The lower part of each table gives a picture of the dispersion within each distribution, as does Table 11.6. We will briefly consider each 'trade group' selected and then give an overview of the results.

11.58   In the Agriculture (industry basis) trade group (Table 11.10) we see that very few employees reach the level of the top 20 per cent of the self-employed, either in absolute terms or relatively to the self-employed in the same trade group. Conversely, a slightly greater fraction of employees than self-employed reach the combined self-employed median and only very few employees are in the combined bottom quintile, while the self-employed in this category had a noticeably large proportion in this situation. In view of this, the amount of dispersion among earnings in this group is moderate, while for the corresponding group of self-employed it is extremely large. The Agriculture group was previously exemplified as being one where the nature of an employee's work was likely to be very different from that of a self-employed person under this heading. The mean earnings of employees in this group are some 16 per cent below the mean main source self-employment income.

11.59   Turning to Building and Contracting (industry basis, Table 11.10) it is noticeable that apart from the top 10 per cent combined level and above, employees tend to have greater incomes than their self-employed counterparts, and their mean earnings are also greater. The dispersion for this group, as in the case of the previous one, is rather typical of an earnings distribution.

11.60   The next two groups analysed on an industry basis may be taken together, as they exhibit certain similarities. In Retail Distribution and Catering (Table 11.11) employees do not do well in achieving earnings equivalent to the median self-employed income or above. Though the earnings distributions are dispersed well above the median, the mean incomes for employees in these groups are about 25 and 30 per cent below the corresponding self-employment incomes.

Table 11.12   Comparison of the Self-employed and Employees within Trade Groups: Motor Repairs (5); Industry Basis; 1976-77[4]

Percentage of self-employed and employees who fall into given quantile groups of the self-employment income distribution[1] for all trade groups. Quantiles as percentages of the median for the self-employed and employees. Mean incomes for the self-employed and employees.

United Kingdom (self-employed)
Great Britain (employees)

Income unit: tax unit[3] (self-employed),
Full-time men and women (employees)

Quantile group	Self-employment income[1] range (lower limit)	MOTOR REPAIRS (5)	
		Self-employed	Employees
		Percentage with self-employment income[1] in the specified quantile group of the combined self-employed distribution	Percentage with employment income[2] in the specified quantile group of the combined self-employed distribution
	£ pa	%	%
Top 1 per cent	17,496	0·4	0·0
Top 5 ,, ...	9,036	2·5	0·2
Top 10 ,, ...	6,244	7·3	0·8
Top 20 ,, ...	3,978	19·4	4·5
Top 50 ,, ...	2,053	53·2	52·1
Top 80 ,, ...	986	85·4	97·5
Total number	1,657,701	47,719	(2,066)

Quantile	Quantile as percentage of the median for the combined self-employed distribution[1,5]	MOTOR REPAIRS (5)	
		Self-employed	Employees
		Quantile[1] as percentage of the median[5]	Quantile[2] as percentage of the median[5]
	%	%	%
Top percentile	852	592	290
Highest decile	304	257	157
Upper quartile	167	161	123
Median	100	100	100
Lower quartile	57	62	77
Lowest decile	23	37	60
Mean £ pa	2,961	2,818	2,241

Sources: SPI (self-employed), NES (employees).
Notes: [1] Schedule D cases I and II excluding the incomes of wives.
   [2] Derived from weekly earnings (Basis D).
   [3] See footnote 3 to Table 11.10.
   [4] See footnote 4 to Table 11.10.
   [5] See footnote 5 to Table 11.10.

Table 11.13 Comparison of the Self-employed and Employees within Trade Groups: Barristers and Solicitors (7, 8), Accountancy (9); Occupation Basis; 1976–77[1]

Percentage of self-employed and employees who fall into given quantile groups of the self-employment income distribution[1] for all trade groups. Quantiles as percentages of the median for the self-employed and employees. Mean incomes for the self-employed and employees.

United Kingdom (self-employed)
Great Britain (employees)

Income unit: tax unit[2] (self-employed),
Full-time men and women (employees)

Quantile group	Self-employment income[1] range (lower limit)	BARRISTERS AND SOLICITORS (7, 8)		ACCOUNTANCY (9)	
		SELF-EMPLOYED — Percentage with self-employment income[1] in the specified quantile group of the combined self-employed distribution	EMPLOYEES — Percentage with employment income[2] in the specified quantile group of the combined self-employed distribution	SELF-EMPLOYED — Percentage with self-employment income[2] in the specified quantile group of the combined self-employed distribution	EMPLOYEES — Percentage with employment income[2] in the specified quantile group of the combined self-employed distribution
	£ pa	%	%	%	%
Top 1 per cent	17,496	12·4	0·0	8·5	0·1
Top 5 ,, ...	9,036	47·7	6·0	34·1	0·3
Top 10 ,, ...	6,244	67·5	13·3	50·6	6·2
Top 20 ,, ...	3,978	83·4	37·3	66·4	36·4
Top 50 ,, ...	2,053	91·6	73·3	84·8	88·4
Top 80 ,, ...	986	95·4	92·7	93·4	98·8
Total number	1,657,701	23,354	(150)	16,258	(773)

Table 11.13 (cont'd) Comparison of the Self-employed and Employees within Trade Groups: Barristers and Solicitors (7, 8), Accountancy (9); Occupation Basis; 1976-77[1]

Quantile	Quantile as percentage of the median for the combined self-employed distribution[1,5]	BARRISTERS AND SOLICITORS (7, 8)		ACCOUNTANCY (9)	
		SELF-EMPLOYED Quantile[1] as percentage of the median[5]	EMPLOYEES Quantile[2] as percentage of the median[5]	SELF-EMPLOYED Quantile[1] as percentage of the median[5]	EMPLOYEES Quantile[2] as percentage of the median[5]
	%	%	%	%	%
Top percentile :: ::	852	421	384	593	225
Highest decile ::	304	216	238	261	153
Upper quartile ::	167	152	153	174	127
Median :: ::	100	100	100	100	100
Lower quartile ::	57	61	64	48	77
Lowest decile ::	23	27	37	23	56
Mean £ pa :: :: ::	2,961	10,147	3,789	8,126	3,665

Sources: SPI (self-employed), NES (employees).
Notes: [1] Schedule D cases I and II excluding the incomes of wives.
[2] Derived from weekly earnings (Basis D).
[3] See footnote 3 to Table 11.10.
[4] See footnote 4 to Table 11.10.
[5] See footnote 5 to Table 11.10.

193

Table 11.14   Comparison of the Self-employed and Employees within Trade Groups: Architecture (10), Surveying (19); Occupation Basis; 1976–77[4]

Percentage of self-employed and employees who fall into given quantile groups of the self-employment income distribution[1] for all trade groups. Quantiles as percentages of the median for the self-employed and employees. Mean incomes for the self-employed and employees.

United Kingdom (self-employed),
Great Britain (employees)

Income unit: tax unit[3] (self-employed),
Full-time men and women (employees)

Quantile group	Self-employment income[1] range (lower limit)	ARCHITECTURE (10)		SURVEYING (19)	
		SELF-EMPLOYED	EMPLOYEES	SELF-EMPLOYED	EMPLOYEES
		Percentage with self-employment income[1] in the specified quantile group of the combined self-employed distribution	Percentage with employment income[2] in the specified quantile group of the combined self-employed distribution	Percentage with self-employment income[1] in the specified quantile group of the combined self-employed distribution	Percentage with employment income[2] in the specified quantile group of the combined self-employed distribution
	£ pa	%	%	%	%
Top 1 per cent	17,496	10·5	0·0	8·2	0·0
Top 5 "	9,036	31·4	0·5	27·4	0·0
Top 10 "	6,244	46·6	4·0	46·2	4·1
Top 20 "	3,978	63·2	35·5	60·9	33·0
Top 50 "	2,053	76·6	89·0	78·8	83·4
Top 80 "	986	87·9	98·7	87·7	98·4
Total number	1,657,701	7,907	(372)	5,147	(367)

194

Table 11.14 (*cont'd*) Comparison of the Self-employed and Employees within Trade Groups: Architecture (10), Surveying (19); Occupation Basis; 1976–77[4]

Quantile	Quantile as percentage of the median for the combined self-employed distribution[1,5]	ARCHITECTURE (10)		SURVEYING (19)	
		SELF-EMPLOYED Quantile[1] as percentage of the median[5]	EMPLOYEES Quantile[2] as percentage of the median[5]	SELF-EMPLOYED Quantile[1] as percentage of the median[5]	EMPLOYEES Quantile[2] as percentage of the median[5]
	%	%	%	%	%
Top percentile : : :	852	611	218	653	238
Highest decile : : :	304	311	156	278	152
Upper quartile : : :	167	185	129	169	126
Median : : :	100	100	100	100	100
Lower quartile : : :	57	38	78	43	78
Lowest decile : : :	23	13	55	11	47
Mean £ pa : : :	2,961	7,901	3,633	7,586	3,529

Sources: SPI (self-employed), NES (employees).
Notes: [1] Schedule D cases I and II excluding the incomes of wives.
[2] Derived from weekly earnings (Basis D).
[3] See footnote 3 to Table 11.10.
[4] See footnote 4 to Table 11.10.
[5] See footnote 5 to Table 11.10.

195

Table 11.15 Comparison of the Self-employed and Employees within Trade Groups: Medicine (12), Medicine and Dentistry (12, 13); Occupation Basis; 1976–77[4]

Percentage of self-employed and employees who fall into given quantile groups of the self-employment income distribution[1] for all trade groups. Quantiles as percentages of the median for the self-employed and employees. Mean incomes for the self-employed and employees.

United Kingdom (self-employed)
Great Britain (employees)

Income unit: tax unit[3] (self-employed),
Full-time men and women (employees)

Quantile group	Self-employment income range (lower limit)	MEDICINE (12)		MEDICINE AND DENTISTRY (12,13)	
		SELF-EMPLOYED	EMPLOYEES	SELF-EMPLOYED	EMPLOYEES
		Percentage with self-employment income[1] in the specified quantile group of the combined self-employed distribution	Percentage with employment income[2] in the specified quantile group of the combined self-employed distribution	Percentage with self-employment income[1] in the specified quantile group of the combined self-employed distribution	Percentage with employment income[2] in the specified quantile group of the combined self-employed distribution
	£ pa	%	%	%	%
Top 1 per cent : : :	17,496	1·0	0·0	2·3	0·0
Top 5 ,, : : :	9,036	31·2	7·0	32·7	6·5
Top 10 ,, : : :	6,244	70·2	30·5	67·4	28·9
Top 20 ,, : : :	3,978	85·6	59·3	84·3	60·1
Top 50 ,, : : :	2,053	92·2	96·7	93·1	96·6
Top 80 ,, : : :	986	96·0	99·2	96·2	99·2
Total number : :	1,657,701	22,639	(243)	35,350	(263)

Table 11.15 (*cont'd*) Comparison of the Self-employed and Employees within Trade Groups: Medicine (12); Medicine and Dentistry (12, 13); Occupation Basis; 1976–77[4]

Quantile	Quantile as percentage of the median for the combined self-employed distribution[1,5]	MEDICINE (12)		MEDICINE AND DENTISTRY (12, 13)	
		SELF-EMPLOYED Quantile[1] as percentage of the median[5]	EMPLOYEES Quantile[2] as percentage of the median[5]	SELF-EMPLOYED Quantile[1] as percentage of the median[5]	EMPLOYEES Quantile[2] as percentage of the median[5]
	%	%	%	%	%
Top percentile	852	216	246	257	240
Highest decile	304	144	198	159	193
Upper quartile	167	119	159	127	153
Median	100	100	100	100	100
Lower quartile	57	73	77	70	77
Lowest decile	23	35	67	37	66
Mean £ pa	2,961	7,715	5,239	7,852	5,207

Sources: SPI (self-employed), NES (employees).

Notes: [1] Schedule D cases I and II excluding the incomes of wives.
  [2] Derived from weekly earnings (Basis D).
  [3] See footnote 3 to Table 11.10.
  [4] See footnote 4 to Table 11.10.
  [5] See footnote 5 to Table 11.10.

Table 11.16 Comparison of the Self-employed and Employees within Trade Groups: Road Transport (16); Industry and Occupation Bases; 1976–77[4]

Percentage of self-employed and employees who fall into given quantile groups of the self-employment income distribution[1] for all trade groups. Quantiles as percentages of the median for the self-employed and employees. Mean incomes for the self-employed and employees.

United Kingdom (self-employed)
Great Britain (employees)

Income unit: tax unit[3] (self-employed),
Full-time men and women (employees)

Quantile group	Self-employment income range (lower limit)	ROAD TRANSPORT (16) INDUSTRY BASIS		ROAD TRANSPORT (16) OCCUPATION BASIS	
		SELF-EMPLOYED	EMPLOYEES	SELF-EMPLOYED	EMPLOYEES
		Percentage with self-employment income[1] in the specified quantile group of the combined self-employed distribution	Percentage with employment income[2] in the specified quantile group of the combined self-employed distribution	Percentage with self-employment income[1] in the specified quantile group of the combined self-employed distribution	Percentage with employment income[2] in the specified quantile group of the combined self-employed distribution
	£ pa	%	%	%	%
Top 1 per cent	17,496	0·2	0·0	0·2	0·0
Top 5 ,, ...	9,036	1·1	0·0	1·1	0·0
Top 10 ,, ...	6,244	4·3	0·6	4·3	0·2
Top 20 ,, ...	3,978	12·8	13·8	12·8	10·7
Top 50 ,, ...	2,053	43·6	87·4	43·6	86·1
Top 80 ,, ...	986	83·2	99·5	83·2	99·8
Total number	1,657,701	64,997	(2,821)	64,997	(4,111)

198

Table 11.16 (cont'd) Comparison of the Self-employed and Employees within Trade Groups: Road Transport (16); Industry and Occupation Bases; 1976-77[4]

| Quantile | Quantile as percentage of the median for the combined self-employed distribution[1,5] | ROAD TRANSPORT (16) INDUSTRY BASIS | | ROAD TRANSPORT (16) OCCUPATION BASIS | |
		SELF-EMPLOYED Quantile[1] as percentage of the median[5]	EMPLOYEES Quantile[2] as percentage of the median[5]	SELF-EMPLOYED Quantile[1] as percentage of the median[5]	EMPLOYEES Quantile[2] as percentage of the median[5]
	%	%	%	%	%
Top percentile ∴ ∴ ∴	852	488	189	488	178
Highest decile ∴ ∴ ∴	304	234	139	234	139
Upper quartile ∴ ∴ ∴	167	152	119	152	120
Median ∴ ∴ ∴	100	100	100	100	100
Lower quartile ∴ ∴ ∴	57	66	82	66	82
Lowest decile ∴ ∴ ∴	23	35	65	35	66
Mean £ pa ∴ ∴	2,961	2,330	3,050	2,330	2,947

Sources: SPI (self-employed), NES (employees).

Notes: [1] Schedule D cases I and II excluding the incomes of wives.
   [2] Derived from weekly earnings (Basis D).
   [3] See footnote 3 to Table 11.10.
   [4] See footnote 4 to Table 11.10.
   [5] See footnote 5 to Table 11.10.

11.61 The income characteristics of employees in the Motor Repairs group (industry basis, Table 11.12) resemble those of Agriculture more than they do the other three groups so far mentioned. They are, however, more likely to fall into the region of the distribution just above the combined self-employed median though their mean does not match up so well.

11.62 We next consider the professions, NES comparisons for which have been worked out on an occupation basis. Table 11.13 shows the results for Barristers and Solicitors aggregated[1] and incidentally, therefore, gives for this group material for the self-employed not shown in Tables 11.2 and 11.6. While dispersion of earnings for the employees in this group is not much different from that for the self-employed, the mean earnings figure is only 37 per cent of the mean income from self-employment, and the proportions falling into high ranges of income are in accordance with this.

11.63 In the case of employees in Accountancy (Table 11.13), Architecture (Table 11.14) and Surveying (Table 11.14) there are broad similarities in the results. They have only about half the proportion of employees in the top 20 per cent combined that the self-employed have, but they tend to be more concentrated in the region above the combined median and have notably less representation in the bottom 20 per cent. Their mean earnings in each case are about 45 per cent of the relevant mean for the self-employed.

11.64 As we have noted before there are several features of the income distribution for Medicine which are peculiar to that group. A comparison between the self-employed and employees in Medicine is afforded by Table 11.15. Here the proportions of employees in the top 20 per cent ranges are significantly higher than for the professional groups already discussed, though not as great as those for the self-employed. The situation regarding the top 1 per cent is rather different though, as mentioned in paragraph 11.19. The mean earnings for employees in this group are greater than those in any other of the NES analyses undertaken, whereas Table 11.6 shows that the self-employed Medicine distribution exhibits only the fifth highest mean among the self-employed. The inclusion of Dentistry with Medicine (Table 11.15) has little effect on the figures for employees, as the number of individuals in Dentistry shown by the NES is very small. It is useful, however, to have an aggregated distribution for the self-employed of these two groups. In this respect, inclusion of Dentistry with Medicine produces a distribution which is more balanced than that shown for Medicine alone in Table 11.2.

11.65 For employees in the Road Transport trade group we have two distributions of earnings, on industry and occupation bases, respectively (Table 11.16). The situation here is that this group of employees is in a similar position within their trade group to those in Building and Contracting (see Table 11.10 and paragraph 11.59). The differences in the results on the two different bases employed in analysing this group are reasonably small. They arise, of course,

---

[1] Only 150 employed Barristers and Solicitors are identified in the NES survey where the *overall* sampling fraction for full-time employees is about 1 in 133, while the SPI estimates 23,354 self-employed in these groups. This implies a rough estimate for the incidence of self-employment among Barristers and Solicitors (aggregated) of 54 per cent (see paragraph 11.21).

because of differing definitions of coverage (see Appendix M). These comparisons help to give an indication of what variations in the figures for employees between NES 'trade groups' should be considered significant.

11.66 The general points emerging from these results, with the exceptions noted in the foregoing paragraphs, are that employees on the whole have lower earnings than the amounts that the self-employed receive from their main source in similar broad areas of work defined by the trade groups. This is demonstrated by the mean income figures cited and the generally smaller concentrations into the higher income ranges. On the other hand, in every group studied (except Barristers and Solicitors combined) employees have a smaller proportion of their numbers falling below the bottom 20 per cent range of the combined distribution. These effects go hand in hand with the fact that the extreme dispersions prevalent in the self-employed distributions do not occur in the case of employees.

11.67 It should be stressed that while we have sought, as far as possible, to match up groups based on descriptions given in the surveys, in the final analysis the value of the comparisons is a matter for judgement based on knowledge of the industries or occupations in question.

Summary

11.68 Data supplied by the Inland Revenue have enabled comparisons to be made of the self-employment incomes of main source Schedule D tax units according to each of twenty-two trade groups identified. The major results of the analysis of these data appear in Tables 11.2 and 11.6 and are summarised in the form of a rank table in Table 11.9.

11.69 The greatest point of interest in the analysis of self-employment incomes by trade group has been the contrast between the professional groups and the remainder, though there are three groups which display intermediate characteristics, namely Engineering, Insurance, Stockbrokers and Jobbers and, to a lesser extent, Wholesale Distribution. This is consistent with the known or believed makeup of these groups.

11.70 Among the professional groups the Medicine trade group stands somewhat apart having a high average level of income and few low incomes, but no more than the average number of incomes in the top 1 per cent of the combined distribution (ie of the self-employment income distribution for all trade groups combined). For the other professional trade groups the results have tended to be more consistent between groups. Solicitors are shown to occupy a prominent position among the professional groups. The numbers of professionals are quite small but they account for large shares of high incomes and have high mean incomes, with very little representation in the lowest income ranges.

11.71 Four groups show up as faring badly compared with other trades in the classification of groups by reward. These are Road Transport, the Other Services group, Entertainments and Gambling, and Advertising and Business Services. Generalisations are difficult to make, however, because much depends upon which criteria are selected as the basis for such remarks. For example, judged by the proportion falling in the top one per cent of the combined distribution (a statistic for which rankings are given in Table 11.9), the Retail Distribution group falls below the last two of the four groups mentioned at the beginning of this paragraph.

11.72 The analysis of other components of income by trade group reveals considerable variation in relation to the wives' self-employment component and also as far as employment income is concerned. Data on all other components are limited, though a variation between groups is noted in the incidence of deductions. In particular, the proportionate amount of retirement annuity relief is substantially greater in the case of the one professional trade group, namely Surveying, for which figures are available, and the incidence of this component is considerably more frequent as compared with other groups analysed. Other income (that is, investment income) is a not unimportant component for most trade groups, but little more can be said about its differing impact between groups. For all the components mentioned, further analysis by level of main source income might be revealing. It would also be useful to be able to examine how employees' other components of income vary by trade.

11.73 Certain comparisons can be made, though with the greatest caution because of the different sources of data as well as the differing nature of the income, between the self-employment income of those self-employed in a trade group and employees in an associated occupation or industry. For a number of trade groups no such parallel group of employees can be found. The broad conclusions from such comparisons as can be made are that the corresponding employees have generally lower incomes, have less dispersion of incomes *and* are less likely to figure in the lowest income ranges (under £1,000 pa in 1976–77) than their self-employed opposite numbers. A major qualification of these results concerns the difficulty of identifying groups of employees whose jobs are comparable with the trade groups of the self-employed.

11.74 The professions differ widely in the opportunities offered for self-employment and salaried employment, respectively. Those self-employed in the professions are usually not allowed to form close companies as is common in other businesses. As we have seen in the previous Chapter, directors of close companies tend to have very high incomes not matched by the professional or other self-employed groups analysed in this Chapter, and in turn we now see that employees in general, within trade groups, do not have as much propensity to reach higher levels of income as do the self-employed. The group of those analysed in this Chapter to which this remark applies with least force is Building and Contracting, where the median and mean of employees are greater than in the corresponding self-employed group. In this particular group, labour-only subcontracting is an important element in the self-employed workforce and under-recording of incomes is likely to occur. In all groups, however, the effects of other components of income may be significant when assessing the overall situation.

CHAPTER 12

Assets, Income and Tax: Distinctive Features of Self-employment

Introduction

12.1   We examine in this chapter a number of aspects in which self-employment differs from employment, in order to throw light on the comparisons that were made in Chapters 10 and 11, and to ensure that the results are not open to mis-interpretation. We examine first, in the next three sections, the issues arising from the fact that the self-employed typically invest capital in their businesses, look to the appreciation of capital for a substantial part of their reward, and are subject to capital taxation. In the remaining sections we turn to the distinctive features of the income of the self-employed, the consequences of its assessment to tax under a separate schedule, the benefit that can be obtained from a wide variety of allowances and reliefs, and the opportunities for abuse to which this may give rise; and try to assess the comparability, in the light of these factors, of the income statistics for the self-employed and for employees that have been set alongside one another in the last two Chapters. The common starting point of the two parts of this Chapter is that self-employment income can be regarded as hybrid, being partly a return to the entrepreneur on his labour and partly a return on the capital invested, including a reward for risk. The reader is referred to the further discussion of this in Chapter 3 (paragraph 3.15–3.21).

Aggregate data on the business assets of the self-employed

12.2   The personal sector balance sheet for the United Kingdom can be broken down in order to identify the major elements of the net worth of unincorporated businesses, thereby producing a separate (if somewhat partial) balance sheet for the business assets of the self-employed. Such calculations were undertaken by Revell for 1961[1] and the Central Statistical Office (CSO) has been able to produce more recent estimates (for 1975 and 1976) on a broadly comparable basis.

12.3   These balance sheets are summarised in Table 12.1. It should be noted that some of the estimates for financial assets and liabilities are subject to a higher degree of error than the physical assets:

(a) Revell's estimate of 'cash' covered only bank deposits but the CSO were also able to make a very approximate estimate of the amount of cash held within businesses based on a study of holdings of cash by the Cash Distribution Study Group under the chairmanship of the Inter-Bank Research Organisation.

---

[1] Revell, Jack, *The wealth of the nation*, Cambridge University Press, 1967.

(b) Unincorporated businesses were assumed by Revell to have zero net trade credits. His estimates were based on estate duty figures, while the CSO estimates are incomplete, and do not provide data for unincorporated businesses. We cannot, therefore, improve on Revell's assumptions.

(c) His figure for hire purchase debt was an estimate based on an analysis of hire purchase debt outstanding (by type of asset) which is no longer available. There is some evidence to suggest that this form of finance may not be important (certainly not for farmers).

12.4   According to Table 12.1 the total net worth of unincorporated businesses amounted to £31 billion in 1976 and constituted a not insubstantial proportion of total personal sector wealth in that year (nearly 11 per cent). An important omission from the figures is the net worth of close companies, for which no separate estimates are available.

12.5   We have already pointed out that the average income of the self-employed is higher than that of employees. It is natural to ask what relation this difference might bear to the capital invested by the self-employed in their businesses, on which some return would be expected. The question is not easy to answer, because the sources of data on the value of capital employed, on total self-employment income, and on numbers of self-employed are all different and are not necessarily consistent. No pretence can be made, therefore, at an accurate calculation, as is evident from the fact that, when allowance is made for various uncertainties, we arrive at a range for the average return on capital of $2\frac{1}{2}$ to 8 per cent[1].

12.6   A result in such broad terms does not say much about the profitability of self-employment as compared with other uses of capital. In any case an average, taken over the whole self-employed population where the capital invested varies from zero up to large amounts, may not represent very well the general experience. Whatever the 'right' figure may be in the aggregate there would certainly be considerable variation around it in the experience of individuals

---

[1] For capital we take the figure of *£28 billion* which is the estimated value of physical assets of the self-employed sector in Table 12.1. To be consistent we should subtract some (probably small) quantity for the capital of the secondary source self-employed but we ignore this in view of the much larger uncertainties elsewhere in the calculation. Next we seek an estimate of total net income, from which to subtract a notional 'return on labour' leaving the 'return on capital' as the remainder. The gross income from self-employment in 1976 was estimated (National Income and Expenditure 1967–77, Table 4.3) at £10$\frac{1}{2}$ billion of which about £10 billion would be the income of main source self-employed. Net income allowing for capital depreciation and stock relief would be about £8 billion. There are grounds for thinking that this total may be an under-estimate to the extent of perhaps £$\frac{1}{2}$ billion on account of under-reporting (see paragraph 12.39 below), so we finally arrive at a figure of *£8$\frac{1}{2}$ billion* as a realistic estimate of net income. There is no way of distinguishing, within this total, between the return on labour and the average return on capital in self-employed income: the separation into the two parts has to be done arbitrarily. Assuming first that the 1·66 million main source self-employed have 'labour' income of £3,750 per annum (the average for full-time male employees in 1976), we reach a total labour income of about £6·2 billion. We could equally reasonably have assumed that many of the self-employed would regard their equivalents in employment as professionals or managers with much higher expectations of earnings: allowing for this, a return on labour of, say, 1$\frac{1}{4}$ times average earnings overall could well be justified. That would give a range of *£6·2–7·7 billion* for this item. Subtracting it from total net income gives £0·8–2·3 billion, and hence a range for the average return on capital of 2$\frac{1}{2}$–8 per cent.

Table 12.1 Balance Sheet Estimates for the Self-employed Sector (Business Assets only); 1961, 1975 and 1976

United Kingdom

	1961 (Revell)	1975 (CSO)	1976 (CSO)
	£ million	£ million	£ million
Physical assets			
Stocks & work in progress	2,203	5,386	6,244
Vehicles, plant & machinery	1,800	4,781	5,920
Developed land & buildings	1,220	6,036	6,818
Agricultural land[1]	2,069	9,601	9,226
Financial assets			
Deposits at banks	1,761	4,208	4,640
Total assets	9,053	30,012	32,848
Liabilities			
Bank borrowing	486	1,248	1,402
Hire purchase	84	N/A[3]	N/A[3]
Other identified borrowing	55	351	395
Total liabilities	625	1,599	1,797
Net wealth	8,428	28,413	31,051
Total net wealth of the household component of the personal sector[2]	69,890	265,369	288,314
Net worth of unincorporated businesses as percentage of total net wealth of the household component of the personal sector	12·1%	10·7%	10·8%

Sources: Revell (1967) and CSO.

Notes: [1] The figures cover all agricultural land and therefore overstate the value of such land held by the self-employed.

[2] Excluding pension fund assets.

[3] Data not available.

bearing in mind the high degree of risk in some forms of self-employment. Nevertheless, there is perhaps some value in drawing out this comparison, crude and inconclusive as it is, between earnings and capital in the self-employed sector as a whole.

Capital gains and losses: goodwill

12.7 Most forms of self-employment to some degree, and some to a very high degree, enjoy the potential benefit from the growth in the capital value of a business as it develops goodwill. Since this is, by its nature, a capital profit, it is not generally liable to income tax and will not be captured in statistics of income. Further, it may or may not be reflected in the balance sheet of a business and, if it is so reflected, it may appear as a change in either the book values of the assets or the valuation placed on goodwill itself, or in both. The capital profit resulting from such growth will not be subject to tax until it is realised, by sale or otherwise, when it may be chargeable to capital taxes. There is no reliable source of information on the distribution of goodwill.

205

12.8 Goodwill has been defined[1] as the excess of the going-concern realisable value of a business over the sum of the replacement or realisable values of the separable assets, less liabilities. Its value—however calculated—may bear little relation to the cost of the separable assets, individually or collectively. It may be acquired intact from the previous owner, or may arise in the course of building up a business from scratch. If through enterprise, foresight, efficiency and good fortune a business prospers, it will develop goodwill and that goodwill can be sold to a purchaser of the business. It is the building up of this value over the years with the ultimate prospect of a profitable sale at some future date that—for many people—will provide the motivating force to embark upon a business enterprise. This was recognised by the Royal Commission on the Taxation of Profits and Income when they said "Goodwill is part of the normal reward of a successful enterprise: indeed under present day conditions it is by far the most important part of that reward, the expectation of which is a crucial factor in the supply of risk capital and business ability to new ventures."[2]

12.9 For some forms of partnerships, especially in the professions, goodwill is often the main form of capital holding, and new partners effectively purchase part of this goodwill as their initial capital contribution. Close companies can have quite unrealistic net worth valuations in their accounts compared with their realisable market values and, for the very successful, the difference may represent a personal fortune to the owners if the company is sold.

12.10 The counterpart of the prospect of this reward is, of course, the possibility that goodwill may not be developed or, if developed, may be lost, leading to a sale at a loss, or even to bankruptcy. The latter can have most serious implications for the proprietors of unincorporated businesses because their personal assets are legally indistinguishable from their business assets and their personal wealth is at risk.

12.11 The fact that some businesses do make losses is recorded in the income statistics, and this is one reason for the more unequal income distribution of the self-employed compared with employees. However, just as the absence of capital appreciation tends to understate the total rewards to self-employment at the top of the income distribution, the absence of statistics of capital loss resulting from bankruptcy and business failure understates the significance of the losses at the lower end of the income distribution of the self-employed.

12.12 There is published information on bankruptcies, and data from the Department of Industry on the number of receiving orders applied to the self-employed, together with the average net values of the debts concerned, are shown in Table 12.2. This table also shows the bankruptcy rate among different trade groups of the self-employed (to derive these figures the number of tax assessments on individuals and partnerships made by the Inland Revenue was used as a proxy for the total number of enterprises in each group). This estimate is subject to a margin of error because some self-employed persons may have

---

[1] Lee G A, *Modern Financial Accounting*, Second Edition, Nelson, 1973.

[2] *Final Report, Royal Commission on the Taxation of Profits and Income*, (Cmnd 9474), HMSO, July 1955. While that report was written prior to the introduction of capital gains tax, their general point is still valid.

Table 12.2 Number of Bankruptcies (Receiving Notices) Among the Self-employed (Unincorporated Companies only) by Trade Group; 1975 to 1977

England and Wales

Trade group	Number of receiving orders administered			Ratio of receiving orders to number of self-employed businesses	Average net debt on bankruptcy
	1975	1976	1977	1975	1975
	No.	No.	No.	Ratio	£
Agriculture	167	135	72	1 : 1,492	19,248
Manufacturing	199	185	130	1 : 719	7,319
Construction	1,543	1,564	986	1 : 335	4,840
Road haulage	458	405	252	1 : 193	5,790
Wholesaling	122	137	106	1 : 581	8,294
Retailing	1,098	1,146	790	1 : 285	6,408
Financial and professional	306	317	213	1 : 1,086	42,719
Other services	814	840	566	1 : 460	6,672
Other industries	82	69	36	1 : 512	6,972
Total	4,789	4,798	3,151	—	—

Source: Department of Industry.

been subject to more than one assessment in any one year. These figures do nevertheless show that there were considerable differences in the risk of bankruptcies between trade groups, the risk being particularly low in agriculture and the professions, and highest in transport, retailing and construction. However, the highest net debts on bankruptcy occurred in the lowest 'risk' trades, namely agriculture and the professions.

Capital transfer tax

12.13   In our Third Report on the Standing Reference (Report No 5, Cmnd. 6999, published in November 1977) we noted that the introduction of capital transfer tax in place of estate duty was likely to affect the pattern of wealth transmission through inheritance in a number of ways. In our Fourth Report (Report No 7, Cmnd. 7595, published in July 1979) we examined trends in the total amounts of personal capital taxes collected over the period 1966–67 to 1977–78 (see paragraphs 4.32 to 4.37 of that Report). The impact of capital transfer tax on the estates of the self-employed is relevant to this Report because, in particular occupations, the self-employed may have substantial wealth in the form of business assets. In others, private assets will be used to underpin the business of the self-employed and may be used to guarantee business loans.

12.14   Capital transfer tax is a progressive tax charged on the cumulative total of all non-exempt lifetime transfers made after 26 March 1974 and of 'deemed' transfers on death after 12 March 1975 (ie for the purpose of capital transfer tax a person is deemed to transfer the whole of his estate when he dies). No tax is payable on the first £25,000 of transfers on death. Transfers between husbands and wives in life and on death are exempt from tax whereas previously, under estate duty, property left to a spouse valued up to £15,000 was exempt from tax.

207

12.15   In our Fourth Report (paragraph 4.32) we noted that the new exemptions in favour of transfers on death between husbands and wives were one of the causes of the recent decline in the annual yield of capital transfer tax. In such instances these new provisions may act as a postponement of liability to capital transfer tax rather than a total exemption. Under the previous arrangements, property covered by surviving spouse settlements would be liable to estate duty on the death of the first spouse and subject to a measure of relief on the death of the second. Under the new arrangements, liability is postponed until the death of the second spouse.

12.16   Before 27 October 1977, business relief took the form of a reduction in value of 30 per cent for transfers of shareholdings which gave the transferor control of a company immediately before the transfer, for transfers of interests in unincorporated businesses and for transfers of certain business assets. Under the terms of the Finance Act 1978, after 26 October 1977, that reduction in value was increased to 50 per cent for most categories of property qualifying for business relief and, in addition, relief was also given by way of a 20 per cent reduction in the value of gifts of shareholdings in unquoted companies. These increased reliefs were also applied to transfers of farming businesses etc on the same terms as other businesses, and were applied in addition to any 'agricultural relief' for other property.

12.17   It will be noted that the relief is the more effective in that it operates by way of percentage deductions made from the value transferred and not from the amount of tax that would otherwise be payable. Two examples are worked through in Appendix N to show the extent of the change on estates of various sizes between March 1974 (under estate duty) and March 1978 (under capital transfer tax and with the business reliefs in operation). Comparisons between estate duty and capital transfer tax are not easy. For example, gifts *inter vivos* more than 7 years before death were exempt from estate duty but charged to capital transfer tax and increase the tax payable on other assets on the occasion of the donor's death. There are also other differences. For example, as explained in paragraph 12.15, it should be remembered that under capital transfer tax there may be a subsequent liability to tax on death of the second spouse. The examples at Appendix N do, however, show that where business relief applies, the effective rates of capital transfer tax will often be much lower than in March 1974.

Tax assessment of the self-employed

12.18   We now enquire what differences there are between the income tax regime that applies to profits from a business (Schedule D) and the regime that applies to income from employment (Schedule E), and what effect these differences have on the incomes recorded in the SPI and in our sample survey of the incomes of close company proprietors. Our main aim in the following sections of this Chapter is to explore the various grounds for believing that the true economic income of the self-employed and of employees may not be fully reflected in a comparison of their income as recorded in the SPI.

12.19   There are differences in kind between the rules covering allowable deductions for expenses under Schedules D and E. Providing, however, that the expenses are "wholly and exclusively laid out or expended for the purpose of the trade, profession or vocation" as is required by the expenses rule, there is no reason why the deduction of Schedule D expenses from gross receipts—in arriving at total net income as recorded in the SPI—should produce a misleading picture of the true income of a self-employed person. We discuss later the opportunities for abuse (through understatement of income or overstatement of expenses) to which the system of allowances and deductions gives rise.

12.20   Despite the wording of the expenses rule, it is usual for certain types of expenditure incurred by the self-employed to be apportioned between business and private use, only the former being allowed for tax purposes. This is when a definite part of the expenditure can be said to satisfy the wording of the legislation, and examples would include expenditure on cars, telephones, and home accommodation used partly as workshop or office.

12.21   The self-employed frequently operate as family businesses and if, say, a spouse becomes a partner or director, then this brings with it the associated responsibilities; and, if he or she is really involved in the business, then no particular tax advantage will follow from the payment of a wage or other emolument. Moreover, the SPI will normally cover the total income of the tax unit concerned, just as it does for employee tax units where the spouse is also employed.

12.22   On the other hand, employees may receive fringe benefits, some of which have no taxable value and are not, therefore, counted in the SPI. Examples of these would be employers' contributions to pensions, paid sick leave, holiday entitlements, preferential loans for house purchase, subsidised meals, company cars provided for private use and concessionary prices for goods or services purchased from the employer. As 'employees', in the sense that they are taxed under Schedule E, close company proprietors can benefit from these items. The 1976 Finance Act introduced new rules relating to fringe benefits received by higher paid employees (above £8,500 per annum in 1979–80) and by company directors, and the result is that most benefits received by these groups now have a taxable value.

12.23   As we noted in paragraphs 9.23 to 9.26 above, the use of a company car for private purposes can often represent a benefit in monetary terms well in excess of the flat-rate 'benefit' that is added on to income for tax purposes. If so, the income recorded will be less than the income that would be necessary, other things being equal, to support the expense of a similar car that was privately owned. This provision is available to close company proprietors, as to any employee who has the use of a company car, so long as the business use is more than 10 per cent of the total. It therefore introduces distortions as between these two categories on the one hand, and on the other the self-employed assessed under Schedule D and the general run of employees who do not have company cars. Illustrative calculations in support of this point will be found in Chapter 9.

Capital allowances and stock relief

12.24   The SPI statistics of self-employment incomes are of income after deduction of Schedule D losses, capital allowances and stock relief and, to the extent that such deductions do not reflect the true economic position, the SPI statistics will understate or overstate true economic income from self-employment. Depreciation, as such, is not allowed as a tax deductible expense; instead capital allowances are available, as deductions from taxable income, for certain categories of investment, whether by unincorporated businesses or by companies. First year tax allowances of up to 100 per cent of cost are available for plant and machinery (except cars); and 25 per cent annual allowances are available on the remaining cost (or, for cars, on the whole cost); a 50 per cent initial allowance (on new buildings only) plus additional annual allowances of 4 per cent of cost are available for industrial buildings. No allowance is granted for some kinds of assets, including commercial buildings and rented houses. Some of the higher rates of first year tax allowances would normally represent a rate of depreciation in excess of the true economic rate, although the exact relationship would depend on the rate of inflation and on the pattern of investment over the years. It is evident that the recorded income figures are liable to fluctuate widely from year to year on this account.

12.25 The aggregate value of capital allowances granted to the self-employed in 1974 was £773 million (14·3 per cent of gross income from self-employment) whereas the corresponding National Accounts figure for depreciation of the assets of the self-employed at replacement cost was £615 million.

12.26 The turnover of stocks introduces a distortion of a different kind. In order to maintain the substance of a trading business, it is necessary to replace stocks as they are sold. In times of high inflation the replacement stocks may cost more than those recently sold. Not only does this distort the real value to the proprietor of his profits determined on an historic cost basis, but it can also lead to cash flow and liquidity problems, especially where stocks are replaced out of profits that are subject to tax. A special relief was introduced by the Finance Act 1975 for certain companies and this was later extended by the Finance No 2 Act 1975 to all businesses, including those run by individuals and partners. As they affect the self-employed, the current regulations allow, broadly, for increases in stock values (beyond an amount equal to 15 per cent of profits) to be deducted from such profits for tax purposes. This relief is allowed irrespective of whether the increase in value arises from an increase in unit cost or from an increase in volume (subject to anti-avoidance provisions relating to the contrived enhancement of stock levels) and is in terms of a deferral of a charge to tax on an equivalent amount of profits. When stocks fall over an accounting period, past relief is withdrawn up to the level of the fall in the value of stocks. However, the Government has now enacted proposals to write off, after accounting periods ending in 1978–79, any unrecovered past relief given for the first base period (broadly the accounting periods ended in 1973–74 and 1974–75) and to institute a rolling write-off relief after 6 years for subsequent periods. Once any past relief is written off under these rules, it will not be available for subsequent recovery charges (ie for 'withdrawal') on a fall in stock values.

12.27 The first reference period for the relief comprised the two years ended March 1975, so any relief claimed over that period did not enter into the SPI until 1975–76. Because the 1973–74 and 1974–75 SPI data are on a total income basis (after 'deductions') and because of the high rate of inflation in that period, the SPI data will therefore tend to overstate true economic self-employment income. The magnitude of this can be gauged by the National Accounts estimates of stock appreciation for self-employment income. These amounted to £809 million for 1974 and £849 million for 1975, or to about one-fifth of gross self-employment income as recorded by the SPI over that period.

12.28   Although the 1975–76 SPI data will contain adjustments reflecting stock relief, the amount actually claimed by the self-employed was only about £60 million, so it appears likely that the overstatement of income will continue. Appendix O describes the main features of the relief claimed in respect of the first reference period and examines possible reasons why the amount claimed by the self-employed appears to be so low.

Under-reporting of income

12.29   The extent of under-reporting cannot by its nature be estimated with any precision. We collect together below the few facts—fragmentary as they are —that can be drawn from published sources, and also report on evidence given to the Expenditure Committee recently by the Chairman of the Board of Inland Revenue on the extent of under-reporting by both the self-employed and employees.

12.30   We refer first to tax avoidance which has the effect of reducing the amount of income assessable to tax and about which it is also difficult to say anything quantitative. A tax avoidance scheme may be defined as any legal way of minimising taxes and includes the discovery and exploitation of loopholes in the law neither intended nor envisaged by Parliament. Since personal tax matters are private, we do not have access to information that would enable us to review the likely impact of such schemes. A recent report[1] by the Comptroller and Auditor General drew attention to one particular form of avoidance which may be cited by way of illustration. Examination of a number of cases suggested that many partnership changes were contrived to secure the maximum advantage from the commencement and cessation provisions. It is not possible to determine the precise extent of the avoidance that takes place in this way; it has been estimated at £5 million a year, but it may be considerably more. While such a sum would not seriously affect the overall accuracy of SPI income data, we have no means of knowing whether it is typical of the amount of tax lost by other types of schemes.

12.31   Turning to tax evasion, some under-reporting of income comes to light as a result of investigations by the Inland Revenue, and the Department's annual reports provide details of the amounts of detected under-assessment (see Table 12.3). However, these figures give no indication of the total extent of under-reporting because they contain no estimate of the amount of undetected under-assessment, and include only the more significant cases of evasion on which interest and penalties have been charged. The figures in Table 12.3 are almost wholly attributable to omitted trading income. They exclude under-assessments

---

[1] See paragraph 1576 of *Sixth Report from the Committee of Public Accounts, Session 1977–78.*

on which interest and penalties were not charged, and smaller cases of under-assessment of non-trading income (such as those concerning, say, interest which had been received or credited without deduction of tax and had not been shown on taxpayers' returns).

Table 12.3   Under-assessment to Tax[1]; 1964 to 1977

Year ended 31 March	Number of charges raised	Total charges raised	Penalties included in total charges
	000's	£ million	£ million
1964	12·2	15·6	4·7
1965	12·4	16·0	4·9
1966	11·6	14·2	4·6
1967	11·2	14·7	4·7
1968	10·5	13·6	4·3
1969	9·0	13·2	4·2
1970	8·5	11·3	3·7
1971	9·0	11·8	4·0
1972	11·1	13·3	4·3
1973	11·8	15·4	5·3
1974	11·8	16·1	5·5
1975	11·7	17·3	5·9
1976	12·7	23·2	8·2
1977	14·1	27·1	9·1

Source: Inland Revenue.
Note: [1] The table does not include the smaller cases of under-assessment to tax.

12.32   The under-reporting of trading income is difficult to detect because the income is usually the outcome of a profit and loss account which summarises many—sometimes thousands—of different transactions including, particularly, sales and purchases. The profit figure can be reduced by omitting receipts or increasing the figure for payments. Reference has been made above to the wide range of expenses that are normally allowed to the self-employed, the scope for apportionment of accommodation, car and telephone between business and private use, and the practice of employing a spouse or other members of the family in the business. All these provisions are susceptible of manipulation in the interests of reducing the taxable profit. An employee has much less opportunity for under-reporting his income because this would normally require the collusion of the person operating the PAYE system and because the provisions concerning allowable expenses are more restrictive.

12.33   On the other hand, the self-employed are required to make returns to the Inland Revenue and, if their sales are above the Value Added Tax (VAT) limit, to the Customs and Excise also. Both these bodies seek to detect under-reporting and, although unincorporated businesses are not legally required to keep separate accounts, the practice of the Inland Revenue is to require some form of accounts to be submitted with tax returns for all but the smallest businesses. Inspectors of Taxes have recently become more selective in taking up cases for investigation and more flexible in the way they quantify understated income, with the result that the yield from their investigations has increased. The Inland Revenue estimate that total charges raised from their investigations are currently amounting to about £55 million a year, including about £10 million from settlements which do not include interest or penalties.

12.34 In recent years the extent of under-reporting in certain industries has received much publicity. Legislation was enacted in 1971 and 1975 to counter under-reporting of earnings by sub-contractors in the construction industry, ie by the so-called 'lump'. These special provisions required that, unless a sub-contractor was the holder of a certificate issued by an inspector of taxes, any contractor making a payment to him for construction work should deduct a proportion (30 per cent before September 1975 and 35 per cent thereafter) from that payment and pay it over to a collector of taxes. The qualifications for obtaining a certificate were tightened up by the 1975 Act.

12.35 More recently, early in 1979 extensive publicity was given to the Inland Revenue's special drive against under-reporting by printing workers employed by newspaper publishers in Fleet Street. For neither of these are there reliable quantitative estimates.

12.36 Indeed, by its very nature, under-reporting is difficult to quantify. There are no authoritative surveys on the subject, whether covering its extent in particular industries, occupations or regions, or its extent in the whole economy. There is much anecdotal evidence but little beyond that.

12.37 When, on 26 March this year, Sir William Pile, Chairman of the Board of Inland Revenue, gave evidence to the Expenditure Committee of the House of Commons on the possible extent of the under-reporting of income in the whole economy, he told the Committee it was not implausible that, overall, unreported income could amount to as much as $7\frac{1}{2}$ per cent of GDP, ie to roughly £10 billion annually[1].

12.38 Sir William stressed that this figure of $7\frac{1}{2}$ per cent was no more than a judgement by himself and other senior tax officials of what was plausible; if it was right, it implied that, on average, one income earner in eight was not declaring £1,000 of his income each year. He added that he believed that the problem had been growing over the past ten years.

12.39 No breakdown is available of the figure of $7\frac{1}{2}$ per cent of GDP. Some part must, however, be due to undeclared receipts of interest payments, leaving a figure of less than $7\frac{1}{2}$ per cent for income unreported by both employees and the self-employed. Not all of this would represent taxable income (some earnings from part-time work would, for example, fall below the tax threshold). It does not seem possible to draw any immediate conclusions from these estimates as to their implications for the distribution of income of main source self-employment or for that of the incomes of employees.

12.40 We report the above as the only recent estimate from an authoritative source on the subject and are in no position to test it. Direct verification is in any case impossible. However, the compilation of the National Accounts throws some light on the matter indirectly. When the initial estimates of national income and expenditure are compared, the expenditure estimate usually

---

[1] *Minutes of Evidence, Expenditure Committee (General Sub-committee) Session 1978–79*, Administration of Inland Revenue 312–i (Monday 26 March 1979), HMSO.

exceeds the corresponding income estimate. An adjustment is therefore incorpo-rated in the income estimates to allow for unrecorded income from employment and self-employment, which is currently around $2\frac{1}{2}$ per cent of GDP. This is not necessarily the full extent of unreported income since certain transactions may escape the formal sources of both income and expenditure statistics.

12.41 Evidently, there is a wide range within which the truth may lie and no amount of research is likely to get the right answer. However, we would support the continuing effort, both in Inland Revenue and within the Government Statistical Service generally, to find ways of approaching somewhat closer to an estimate of the extent of unrecorded income and its effect on the distribution of total income.

Retained profits of close companies

12.42 Although our special sample survey of the incomes of close company proprietors covered that part of close companies' profits that was distributed by way of remuneration and dividends, similar data are not available on that part of close companies profits which is retained within the businesses. To maintain a consistent definition of income as between the two forms of self-employment (ie between Schedule D self-employment income and close com-pany proprietors' income taxed under Schedule E), retained profits should be regarded as part of the total remuneration of close company proprietor tax units, the total being divided between the proprietors in some suitable way.

12.43 For the self-employed taxed under Schedule D, any profits retained within their businesses are treated as personal income. In other words, all income is treated as though it had been distributed to the persons concerned. The decision to retain taxed profits within a business may, of course, be virtually dictated by the exigencies of cash flow etc. None the less, the omission of retained profits from the income distributions included in this study is likely to result in a significant understatement of the economic welfare of close company proprietors.

12.44 Because the retained profits of close companies attract corporation tax but are not normally subject to personal income tax at higher rates, there are provisions which, in certain circumstances, impose a charge to income tax on undistributed income of the amount of the difference between the higher rates and the basic rate. These provisions set a standard which is broadly equivalent to investment income plus 50 per cent of the property or trading income of a company (both net of tax). If distributions fall below this standard, then income tax may be levied on the difference as if it had been paid out as a dividend. Trading companies with total profits below a certain level are exempt from these arrangements. In addition, if trading companies can satisfy the Inland Revenue that they cannot distribute their income without prejudice to the current or future requirements of the company's business, then that income will not be subject to income tax. The threshold below which the trading income of a trading company is exempt from income tax was substantially increased by the Finance Act 1978 to £25,000 (net of corporation tax). Accordingly, the great majority of close companies will not now be affected by these provisions, but close investment companies continue to be subject to them.

214

The 'preceding year' method of tax assessment

12.45 The self-employed person taxed under Schedule D is on a different footing from the employee taxed under Schedule E, in that what the latter receives from his employer broadly constitutes taxable income, whereas the trader's receipts are simply one side of the account, and the amount of his income or profit cannot be known until both sides of the account—receipts and expenditures—can be calculated. Mainly for this reason, tax has been assessed for many years on what is known as the 'preceding year' basis.

12.46 The preceding tax year basis takes, as a measure of taxable profits for a tax year, the profits earned in the accounting year ending in the preceding year. Its advantage is that it should give sufficient time for the profits to be computed and agreed with the Inland Revenue before they come to be used as a basis for tax assessment. It is not, however, a simple system, mainly because of the special rules for when a business begins or ends.

12.47 When a business is started, there are no preceding year's profits to refer back to, so special rules are required. The effect of these rules is that while some of the profits at the commencement of a business are used more than once for the computation of tax, other profits at its cessation are not used at all[1]. These provisions, though clearly needed to deal with a particular problem, themselves create their own difficulties. They lead to a mismatching of profits earned and profits taxed, so that—over the life of a business—only by coincidence will the total profits taxed equal the total profits earned; they frequently involve time-consuming reworking of settled assessments; and they have, as noted above, provided scope for tax avoidance.

12.48 Generally, the preceding year basis will work to the advantage of the self-employed person, as profits in the early years of a business are usually modest, but in some cases assessed profits may be the greater figure. It is not known to what extent this distorts the SPI income data which are based on assessed profits, but it is unlikely to be great.

12.49 Although the Schedule D rules ensure that a self-employed person will pay tax for each year that he is in business, the income used as a basis for tax will actually have been earned between one and two years before the date when payment becomes due. This means that incomes currently being assessed are not in general representative of incomes currently being earned. It also means that if the money value of *current* profits is greater (because of rising profits or inflation or a combination of the two), then the employee with the same current earnings will pay tax currently on that greater amount. This will bring a continuing advantage to the self-employed, by comparison with an employee on a similar income, for as long as, and to the extent that, the money value of his profits increases.

12.50 Conversely, when profits fall and high tax bills from previously successful years have to be met, the 'preceding year' method can lead to cash flow difficulties:

---

[1] The Inland Revenue have estimated that the annual turnover of Schedule D cases, ie the proportion of the total numbers of self-employed taxed under Schedule D that are represented by the numbers of Schedule D commencements and cessations, is around 10 per cent for both commencements and cessations.

indeed the inability to pay tax bills in such circumstances is known to be a common reason for bankruptcy, especially since self-employment earnings are liable to fluctuation from year to year.

12.51 The Inland Revenue has recently announced that it is undertaking a broad-based review of the way in which Schedule D tax is assessed and collected, including the possibility of moving from a preceding year basis of assessment to a current year basis.

National Insurance and occupational pensions

12.52 Though not strictly a taxation matter, we should mention for completeness the differential treatment of the self-employed under National Insurance. Under the new State pension scheme they pay a separate class of contributions and are entitled to only a proportion of the full range of benefits available to employees. Unlike employees, the self-employed are not eligible for unemployment benefit, industrial injuries benefits, or for the earnings-related addition to invalidity and retirement pensions. However, like employees, they are eligible to receive basic sickness, invalidity, widow's and maternity benefits, death grant and basic retirement pensions (see Table P.1 in Appendix P). Their contributions have been fixed on lines similar to, and at a lower level than the contributions in respect of employees who are 'contracted-out' of the pension scheme. The details are set out in Appendix P. From this it appears that, in broad terms, the self-employed contribute at the rate of about 5 per cent of their reckonable earnings under the new State scheme, compared with about 8 per cent in recent years (1976–77 and 1977–78) under the previous scheme (including an element for the National Health Service in both cases). The range of benefits for which they are eligible has not changed. The new contribution rates represent, therefore, a substantial reduction on the rates payable in preceding years. However, as the contributions of the 'contracted-out' rise over the years, so will those of the self-employed (see paragraph P.2 of Appendix P).

12.53 It has sometimes been argued that the rates previously payable discriminated against the self-employed. This is now perhaps of no more than academic interest, and in any case as a matter of public debate on which we have taken no evidence it is not one for us to judge: but Appendix P includes some estimates from DHSS which we think will be of interest. They show how the national insurance contributions in 1976–77 and 1977–78 can be apportioned notionally to the various benefits according to the cost of each benefit to the National Insurance Fund. From this it would be possible to see, for any group whose eligibility for benefits is limited or whose take-up of benefits differs from the average by an ascertainable amount, what difference is implied for the average cost per individual in that group. But we have not attempted the calculation for 1978–79, for the reasons mentioned in the Appendix (see paragraph P.7 of Appendix P).

12.54 Not being eligible for the new State earnings-related pension scheme, the self-employed have to make their own provision for any additions to their flat-rate State retirement pensions. A common method is to take out a retirement annuity policy with premiums which attract full tax relief on that part equal to a maximum of 15 per cent of annual earnings (up to a premium limit of £3,000).

Under such policies a lump sum can be taken at the time a pension starts. This is tax free and can amount to up to one-quarter of the total value of the pension.

12.55 The 15 per cent limit is comparable with rates of contribution to other types of pension schemes. A recent Government Actuary's report estimated that, on average, the combined employee/employer contribution to company occupational pension schemes was about $17\frac{1}{2}$ per cent[1].

12.56 Working proprietors of close trading companies can make provision for their pensions by allocating part of their business profits to a company pension scheme, and such contributions are fully deductible against corporation tax. The regulations relating to the amount of contribution payable are the same as for employees who are members of company pension schemes.

Summary

12.57 In 1976, the total net worth of unincorporated businesses, at £31 billion, amounted to nearly 11 per cent of total personal sector wealth (Table 12.1). These figures exclude the net worth of close companies, for which separate estimates are not available.

12.58 Although recognising that the income of a self-employed person is hybrid, being partly a return to the entrepreneur on his labour and partly a return on the capital involved (including a reward for risk), it is not possible to distinguish between the two components in practice. Because of uncertainties in the aggregate statistics of income and wealth, even if we arbitrarily assign a value to the return on labour, we can only infer that the average return on capital lies within a wide range ($2\frac{1}{2}$–8 per cent).

12.59 Data are not available on the aggregate value of goodwill, nor on the average rate of growth, though these are clearly a most important part of the potential reward both for unincorporated businesses and for close companies. Some information is available on bankruptcies and Table 12.2 shows that, in 1975, there were considerable differences in the risk of bankruptcies between different trade groups. The risk was high in road transport and retailing, and low in agriculture and the professions where the greatest sums are at stake.

12.60 A comparison of the effective rates of tax on business assets left to a son in 1974 and 1978, respectively, illustrates the consequences of the changes made when capital transfer tax was introduced and of the subsequent provisions for business relief under the Finance Act 1978. The effective rate of tax on that part of an estate which comprised business assets is seen to be much lower than it was in 1974: but this is an incomplete comparison so far as any transfer to a surviving spouse is concerned because of changes in the liability to tax on the death of the second spouse.

12.61 Our review of the application of income tax through Schedules D and E suggests that statistics of self-employment incomes are likely to be incomplete in coverage and so fall short of 'true economic incomes' to a greater extent than

---

[1] *Fifth Government Actuary's report into the Occupational Pension Scheme*, HMSO, 1978.

statistics of employment incomes. Incomes of employees will be understated to the extent of any fringe benefits that do not have a taxable value and, in some cases, of unreported earnings from second jobs etc. The understatement of self-employment incomes reflects the combined effects of a number of factors: notably the operation of the system of capital allowances, the omission of the retained profits of close companies and the under-reporting of income. Under the last head we include the effects of certain tax avoidance schemes, as well as tax evasion, and refer to the recent statement by the Chairman of the Board of Inland Revenue about the possible overall extent of unreported income, a problem which has been growing over the past ten years. This implied that unreported income might amount to around $7\frac{1}{2}$ per cent of GDP. On the other hand, the relatively small amount of stock relief claimed (by comparison with the amount of stock appreciation due to increases in unit costs) may cause self-employment incomes to be overstated. It seems clear, however, that in aggregate the under-recording will far outweigh the over-recording.

12.62   The 'preceding year' method of tax assessment of Schedule D incomes is described. This gives rise to the need (explained in Chapter 4) to introduce a 'lag' of one year when comparing distributions of self-employment and employment incomes, if these comparisons are to be on a proper statistical footing. It is further shown in this Chapter that the method will generally work to the advantage of the self-employed person, in that the self-employment income brought to assessment will actually have been earned between one and two years before the date when payment becomes due. Under the PAYE system, an employee pays tax on his current year's earnings. If incomes are rising then an employee will pay more tax than a self-employed person whose *current* income is the same.

12.63   We summarise the system of National Insurance contributions and benefits as it applies to the self-employed. We note that the current contributions of the self-employed, which are related to the contributions levied on employees who have 'contracted-out' of the earnings-related pension scheme, represent a significant reduction upon the contribution they made prior to 1978–79 for the same range of benefits. These contributions, will not, for many years, reflect the full value of the benefits received. However, as the contributions of 'contracted-out' employees rise over the years, so will those of the self-employed.

12.64   Because the self-employed are not eligible for earnings-related retirement pensions, we also consider the tax provisions on premiums for retirement pensions. The tax-allowable retirement annuity premiums of the self-employed may not exceed 15 per cent of annual earnings (subject to a premium limit of £3,000 per annum). This is not out of line with the Government Actuary's recent estimate that, on average, the combined employee/employer contribution to company pension schemes was about $17\frac{1}{2}$ per cent of annual earnings.

CHAPTER 13

Self-employment Incomes
in Eleven Countries

13.1   This study of the available data on the income distributions of the self-employed in a number of developed countries was carried out for us by Dr T Stark, who is a member of the Department of Economics at the New University of Ulster, Coleraine. In addition, Dr Stark's examination looks briefly at the importance of self-employment in the economies of those countries, as measured either by the share of self-employment income in total personal income or by the proportion of the self-employed in the total labour force.

The importance of self-employment

13.2   International comparisons of the structure of aggregate personal income are possible using data from the UN Yearbooks of National Accounts Statistics (SNA). However, all estimates from this source are net of depreciation and stock appreciation, and the Yearbooks do not identify self-employment income as such but, instead, use the concept of entrepreneurial income. In addition, the definition of entrepreneurial income was changed from 1970 onwards. Before then the definition had been very similar to our own National Accounts definition of self-employment income (ie the net proceeds from unincorporated enterprises). Since 1970 that concept has been expanded to include the economic rent of buildings and structures (other than owner-occupied dwellings), and the pure economic (imputed) rent from owner-occupied dwellings. For some countries, information is only available on the basis of the pre-1970 definition.

13.3   Table 13.1 presents these data in terms of percentage shares of entrepreneurial income in total household income. For those countries listed in the top half of the Table, imputed rent from owner-occupied dwellings has been deducted from total income, so that the difference remaining between the two halves of the Table represents rent on buildings and structures. Figures on both bases are available for the USA and these show that the change in basis does not make a large difference to the percentage share of entrepreneurial income.

13.4   The overall impression which emerges from Table 13.1 is that, in all the countries shown, there had been a general decline in the share of entrepreneurial income within total household income. The rate of decline has been uneven, however, and in the early 1970s several countries (Australia, Canada, the United Kingdom, the United States and Ireland) experienced an increase in the entrepreneurial share, albeit temporary in nearly all cases. The decline in the

219

Table 13.1 Entrepreneurial Income in Selected Countries; 1960 to 1975

Ratios of entrepreneurial income to the total income of households and private (non-financial) bodies, eleven selected countries

Country	Years				
	1960	1965	1970	1973	1975
	%	%	%	%	%
(A) PRESENT SNA DEFINITION OF SELF-EMPLOYMENT[1]					
Australia	18·7	15·9	11·9	14·7	10·2
Canada[2]	12·2	11·5	8·6	9·3	8·4
Sweden	16·6	13·1	9·4	7·8	7·2
United Kingdom[2]	8·5	9·7	7·4	8·6	6·9
United States	11·2	10·1	7·6	8·1	6·6
(B) FORMER SNA DEFINITION OF SELF-EMPLOYMENT[1]					
United States	10·9	10·3 (1963)	7·7	—	—
Belgium[3]	23·4	21·6	17·9	—	12·7
France[3]	25·1	21·3	18·5	—	—
Germany[3]	26·4	23·6	21·5	—	17·7
Ireland	26·9	23·4	18·7	20·8	—
Italy	—	28·1 (1963)	24·4	20·4	—
Japan	29·1	24·3	21·6	—	—

Source: UN Yearbooks of National Accounts Statistics (various).

Notes: [1] For SNA definitions see text.
   [2] Includes rent on land.
   [3] Includes 'withdrawals from the entrepreneurial income of quasi-corporate enterprises'.

entrepreneurial share was continuous in Sweden, Belgium and Germany so that, by 1975, the spread in the percentage shares between countries was much less than in 1960. Nevertheless, considerable differences existed between countries at the end of the period covered.

13.5 The relative importance of self-employment in particular countries can also be expressed in terms of the percentage of those in civilian employment who are self-employed. Table Q.1 in Appendix Q, drawn from OECD statistics, provides these percentages for eleven countries for selected years between 1960 and 1975. To illustrate the main points, we extract and give in Table 13.2, a comparison between France, West Germany and the United Kingdom, showing separate figures for the agricultural sector whose behaviour, as we shall see, is of particular significance.

13.6 In the United Kingdom self-employment as a proportion of all civil employment was slightly higher in 1975 than in 1960; but in both France and Germany it was very much lower, and reference to Appendix Q shows that the same was true of countries as different in other respects as the United States and Japan. Among the eleven countries examined, the rise in the proportion of civil employment in the UK that was self-employed was unique. The explanation of the contrast is two-fold: in the other countries the proportion self-employed in industries and services other than agriculture fell, whereas in the UK it rose; and the fall in the proportion of the labour force employed in agriculture (where in

Table 13.2 Employment and Self-employment in Agriculture and Other Industries; 1960 and 1975

	France		West Germany		United Kingdom	
	1960	1975	1960	1975	1960	1975
	%	%	%	%	%	%
1. Distribution of civil employment:						
Agriculture, hunting, forestry, fishing..	22·4	11·3	14·0	7·4	4·1	2·7
Industries and services other than agriculture etc ..	77·6	88·7	86·0	92·6	95·9	97·3
Total civil employment	100·0	100·0	100·0	100·0	100·0	100·0
2. Self-employed and family workers as proportion of all civil employment:						
Agriculture, hunting, forestry, fishing..	77·6	79·4	85·3	86·7	39·5	40·0
Industries and services other than agriculture etc ..	16·9	11·3	12·7	9·5	5·9	6·8
All civil employment	30·5	19·0	22·8	15·9	7·3	7·7

Sources and Notes: See Table Q.1, Appendix Q.

all countries the self-employed are a much higher proportion of the labour force than in the rest of the economy) was much greater.

13.7 The rise in self-employment as a proportion of civil employment in industries and services other than agriculture in the UK (which we showed in Chapter 2, paragraph 2.52, to have been primarily the consequence of the growth of self-employment in the construction industry) was unique. Elsewhere, self-employment outside agriculture was falling relative to total employment, but at a slower rate than the overall self-employment ratio. As Table 13.2 shows, in Germany it had reached a level in 1975 not very much higher than in the UK.

13.8 Still more important, however, as a cause of the fall in the proportion of self-employed in all countries was the reduction in the proportion of total employment in agriculture. The figures for France and Germany in Table 13.2 show this clearly: in 15 years the proportions virtually halved (and Appendix Q shows that similar changes took place in other countries). In the UK, in contrast, agriculture by 1960 employed so small a proportion of the labour force that further reductions could have had only a small effect on the national total of the self-employed. Reductions in employment in agriculture of the magnitude that took place in France, Germany and Japan, for instance, in the 1960s and 1970s took place in Britain in the nineteenth century, though more slowly.

Income distributions compared

13.9 The same large number of data sources have been used here as were used for Chapter 6 of our Fifth Report on the Standing Reference and for our Background paper No 4 to that Report. In nearly all the sources used, the

221

concept of self-employment income was broadly comparable (representing gross receipts from a trade or business or shares in a partnership, less operating costs).

13.10 There was a wide variety in the definition of income recipients. The four main types encountered in the data sources were individuals, consumer units, households and tax units.[1] The distributions presented here are for income units who were either classified as self-employed or whose main source of income was self-employment. Most of the distributions are pre-tax, but the only available data for Germany are on a post-tax basis. As well as the use of the Gini coefficient to summarise the shape of the income distributions, we also use, in the following tables on international comparisons, two further summary statistics: the location scale ratio and the distribution scale ratio. The former is the ratio of the mean income of the self-employed group under analysis to that of all incomes in the distribution, and the latter is the ratio of the respective Gini coefficients.

13.11 There are four countries (including the UK) which have data on the income of self-employed individuals and these are shown in Table 13.3. Distributions in this Table are based on individuals who either had self-employment as their principal income source or who had been occupationally classified as self-employed (as in the UK Census Follow-up Survey). For Canada, distributions on both definitions are available and the change alters the pattern of income shares considerably, especially in the top half of the distribution. It is not clear why this is so.

13.12 The Table shows that for the UK, the USA, and Canada there is a common pattern of higher mean incomes for the self-employed compared with all individuals, and for the income distribution of the self-employed to be more unequal (characteristics summarised by a location scale ratio or a distribution scale ratio greater than one). The USA and Canadian distributions of the income of the self-employed were more unequal than the UK's.

13.13 The Australian distribution is quite distinct, in that it has a low Gini coefficient and a distribution scale ratio of less than one. The mean and median incomes of the self-employed were, however, considerably higher than for other individuals.

13.14 Income distributions for five countries derived on the basis of consumer units or households[1] are shown in Table 13.4. In all the pre-tax distributions, the level of inequality of the self-employed group was greater than for the equivalent distributions for all households. The mean incomes of the self-employed were also higher, though in Canada and Ireland the difference was only marginal (median incomes for the self-employed in these two countries were broadly the same as for all households).

13.15 This Table also shows post-tax distributions for Canada and Germany. For Canada, the tax system has little effect on the summary statistics describing

---

[1] The consumer unit is broadly either a family or persons in a household related by blood or marriage, or unrelated individuals living 'singly' together or with a family. Households are a larger grouping of persons but with common housekeeping and this is likely to bias the comparisons to less inequality in the household distributions.

222

Table 13.3 Distribution of Self-employment Income of Individuals; 1971–72 to 1974

Distribution of the total income of individuals with self-employment income, four selected countries

Country	Year	Source	Top 1%	Top 5%	Top 20%	21–40%	41–60%	61–80%	81–100%	Gini coefficient	Location scale ratio[1]	Distribution scale ratio[2]
			%	%	%	%	%	%	%	%	Ratio	Ratio
Individuals with principal source self-employed income												
Australia..	1973–74	ABS	4·6	16·8	44·7	23·0	16·1	11·1	5·1	39·1	1·59(1·50)	0·868
Canada ..	1973	CFS	12·7	28·5	57·2	21·6	13·0	6·8	1·4	59·3	1·39(1·15)	1·270
Canada ..	1974	CFS	15·7	31·8	58·5	20·6	12·8	7·1	1·0	63·1	1·64(1·31)	1·337
Individuals classified as self-employed												
Canada :	1973	CFS	17·7	33·9	59·5	18·8	11·8	7·3	2·6	55·8	1·52(1·33)	1·195
Canada :	1974	CFS	23·4	40·2	64·0	16·7	10·5	6·4	2·4	60·3	1·60(1·38)	1·277
USA .. :	1973	CPS	25·2	42·4	66·3	16·3	10·2	5·7	1·4	63·3	1·29(1·18)	1·251
UK .. :	1971–72	CIF	17·8	32·9	59·7	18·1	12·3	8·2	1·7	—	—	—

Sources: ABS — Australian Bureau of Statistics, *Income Distribution 1973–74*, Table 17.
CFS — Statistics Canada, *Income Distributions by Size in Canada*, 1974, Tables 54, 64 and 65.
CPS — Bureau of Census, US Department of Commerce, Current Population Reports, *Consumer Income, Money Income in 1973 of Families and Persons in the United States*, Series P-60, No 97, January 1975.
CIF — Follow-up Income Survey to the 1971 Census of Population.

Notes: [1] This is the ratio of the mean income of the self-employed group under analysis to that of all incomes in the distribution. The ratio of median incomes is shown in parentheses. (See paragraph 13.10).

[2] This is the ratio of the Gini coefficient for the self-employed group under analysis to that of all incomes in the distribution. (See paragraph 13.10).

223

Table 13.4 Distribution of Self-employment Income of Consumer Units and Households; 1970 to 1975

Distribution of the total income of consumer units and households with heads with self-employment income, five selected countries.

Country	Year	Source	Unit	Top 1%	Top 5%	Top 20%	21-40%	41-60%	61-80%	81-100%	Gini coefficient	Location scale ratio	Distribution scale ratio
				%	%	%	%	%	%	%	%	Ratio	Ratio
(A) BEFORE TAX DISTRIBUTIONS													
By heads with principal source self-employment income													
Canada	1973	CFS	Consumer unit	9·7	24·0	52·1	21·6	14·1	9·3	2·9	48·7	1·20	1·25
Canada	1974	CFS	Consumer unit	12·0	26·9	53·8	21·4	13·4	8·5	2·9	58·8	1·41	1·51
By heads classified as self-employed													
USA	1973	CPS	Consumer unit	10·9	25·4	52·6	20·8	14·1	9·0	3·5	48·3	1·60	1·16
UK	1974	FES	Household	9·4	22·5	47·7	20·7	14·9	10·9	5·8	40·8	1·35	1·17
UK	1975	FES	Household	7·9	20·4	45·9	21·4	15·3	11·3	6·1	38·9	—	1·12
Ireland	1973	HBI	Household	7·6	20·1	46·3	23·8	14·6	10·0	5·3	45·0	1·05	1·14
(B) AFTER TAX DISTRIBUTIONS													
Canada	1973	CPS	Consumer unit	12·3	26·5	52·0	20·4	13·7	9·4	4·5	47·1	1·16	1·20
Germany	1970	DIW	Household	—	—	41·7	21·8	16·3	12·3	7·9	32·8	2·07	0·80
Germany	1975	DIW	Household	—	—	42·4	20·7	16·2	12·5	8·2	32·2	2·18	0·80

Sources: CFS — Statistics Canada, *Income Distribution by Size in Canada, 1973*, Tables 44 and 45; and 1974, Tables 31 and 32.
CPS — Bureau of Census, US Department of Commerce, Current Population Reports, *Consumer Income, Money Income in 1973 of Families and Persons in the United States*, series P-60, No 97, January 1975, Table 41.
FES — Family Expenditure Survey 1974 and 1975.
HBI — Central Statistics Office, *Household Budget Survey 1973*, Vol 1, Summary results, Dublin, 1976.
DIW — (1) Gerhard Göseke and Klaus-Dietrich Bedau, ' *Verteilung und Schichtung der Einkommen der privaten Haushalte in der Bundesrepublik Deutschland 1950 bis 1975*', D.I.W. Beitrage zur Strukturforschung, Heft 31, 1974, Duncker and Humblot Berlin; and (2) ' *Das Einkommen soziaer Gruppen in der Bundesrepublik Deutschland in Jahre 1973*', Wochenbericht 35/74, August 1974.

the distribution, compared with the pre-tax distributions. The distribution for Germany[1], however, is very untypical of the other distributions, as it shows very high incomes for the self-employed, compared with other households, but a less unequal income distribution.

13.16   The final set of comparisons is for distributions based on tax units and these are shown in Table 13.5 for the USA, the UK and Sweden (the UK statistics are taken from the SPI). The USA and Swedish distributions had higher Gini coefficients than the UK distribution, although the share of income accruing to the top quintile of the UK and Swedish distributions was the same, at around 50 per cent of the total income. The Swedish distribution was characterised by the very small percentage going to the bottom quintile (0·1 per cent), although the size of this share may be a result of definitional peculiarities.

Table 13.5   Distribution of Self-employment Income of Tax Units; 1972 to 1975-76

Distribution of total income of tax units classified as self-employed, three selected countries

Quantile group	USA (TM) 1972 (1)	UK (SPI) 1973-74 (2)	UK (SPI) 1975-76 (3)	Sweden(OTS) 1974 (4)
	%	%	%	%
Top 1 per cent	10·4	9·3	8·9	9·2
Top 5 ,, ...	26·4	24·7	23·7	22·8
Top 20 ,, ...	54·4	51·0	50·4	50·1
21–40 ,, ...	20·7	19·7	20·3	23·8
41–60 ,, ...	13·4	13·9	14·1	16·0
61–80 ,, ...	8·3	10·0	10·1	10·0
81–100 ,, ...	3·2	5·4	5·1	0·1
Gini coefficient	—	44·7	44·2	50·5
Location scale ratio	n.a. (1.18)	1·20	n.a.	1·21(1·24)
Distribution scale ratio	1·09	1·18	n.a.	1·37

Sources: Internal Revenue Service, US Department of the Treasury, 'Individual Income Tax Returns', *1972 Statistics of Income*, Publication 1979, Table 14; Statistiska Central-byran, Inkomst och Förmogenhets-fördelningen Ar 1974, *Statistiska Meddelanden*, Series N, 1976:4, Stockholm, Table 7; and *Survey of Personal Incomes*.

Notes: Col. 1—tax units liable to self-employment tax. Cols. 2 to 4—tax units with main source self-employment income (trade and business in Sweden, Schedule D classes I and II in UK).

Summary

13.17   The observations in the above brief survey of the international income structure of the self-employed are too few to draw any firm conclusions. However, it is possible to make some tentative concluding remarks about the pattern of self-employment income in the UK relative to other countries.

13.18   The most striking feature of the international comparisons is the extent of the difference in the importance of the self-employed in the various countries.

---

[1] The German distribution is classified by occupational status and excludes the retained profits of the self-employed. It is not known how important this latter effect is likely to be.

Although this may be due in part to differences of definition (for example the inclusion or exclusion of family workers, or the exclusion of family companies), it is clear that in the UK self-employment is considerably less important than in most other countries. The main reason for this is that the agricultural sector— where self-employment is relatively high as a proportion of total employment in all countries—is so much smaller in the UK than elsewhere. This is also the main reason why the trend of self-employment has been different in the UK; in most other countries the rapid contraction of agriculture has been the main reason for the fall in self-employment in total, but in the UK, with so small an agricultural sector, the further contraction did not offset the effect of the growth of self-employment in the construction industry—an increase which had no parallel elsewhere.

13.19   Higher average income and a more unequal distribution (characteristics which are shown in the UK's SPI data for the self-employed) are also evident in the income distribution of the self-employed in nearly all the other countries for which data are available. The exceptions are Australia and Germany, where the incomes of the self-employed are less unequal (as shown by the distribution scale ratio) than for other income recipients.

PART IV

CHAPTER 14

The Main Findings

Introduction

14.1   In this report we investigate the structure of earnings, both of employees and of the self-employed. Earnings from employment are numerically the more important—in the 1970s about 70 per cent of aggregate personal incomes were obtained from working for an employer and 10 per cent from self-employment, the rest being other types of income eg investment income and rent. Employees were much more numerous than the self-employed—there were nearly 22 million employees in employment in 1971 as against just over 1·8 million self-employed. Nevertheless, there are distinctive features of the distribution of incomes from self-employment that make such incomes of special importance for the distribution of personal incomes as a whole. We therefore give particular attention to the distribution of incomes from self-employment, and to the incomes of directors of close companies, which are usually classified as employment incomes but are in many ways like those of the self-employed.

14.2   We investigate the extent to which the structure of earnings as a whole is influenced by differences in earnings within occupations and within industries, as opposed to differences between occupations and between industries; and the way in which these factors have contributed to the changes over time in the distribution of earnings.

The structure of employment and self-employment

14.3   As an introduction to our work on the effect of occupation and industry on the structure of earnings from employment, and on self-employment incomes, we review the change over time in the age, sex and occupational structure of the labour force, the connection between the occupational and industrial structure of employment, and the changes in the industrial structure of employment since the 1930s.

14.4   Because there have been a number of major changes in the ways in which occupations have been classified in the Census and other statistical sources, it is possible to show long term changes only for very broad groups. But certain trends are unmistakable, and are summarised in Table 14.1. Over the past half century there has been a growth of employment in non-manual occupations, both for men and women. Within the non-manual occupations, numbers in professional and managerial work have grown faster than numbers in clerical work; and within the manual occupations there has been a growth of employment in skilled occupations relative to semi-skilled and unskilled (Chapter 2, paragraphs 2.19 to 2.23 and Table 2.7).

14.5 Turning to the composition of employment in terms of industries, the most strongly marked trend has been the rapid rise in employment in services, both absolutely and proportionately. Between 1961 and 1971 nearly all the growth in employment in services was due to the increase in the number of women workers, most of them working part-time. The growth in service employment has been to a substantial degree associated with the expansion of employment in publicly financed services—in particular the National Health Service, and education; but by no means exclusively. Up to the early 1960s, employment in manufacturing increased, except in the textiles and clothing industry where a falling trend of employment goes back to the inter-war years; but since the early 1960s manufacturing employment has declined even in absolute terms. Employment in agriculture and in mining has declined throughout the last half century (Chapter 2, paragraphs 2.28 to 2.32, and Tables 2.9 and 2.10).

Table 14.1   Distribution of Employees by Occupational Class; 1921 to 1978

Great Britain

Occupational class		1921	1931	1951	1961	1971	1978[1]
		%	%	%	%	%	%
Professional and managers	men	7·6	8·1	12·8	17·8	24·1	31·9
	women	9·2	8·4	11·5	15·7	18·6	26·2
Clerks	men	6·1	6·2	6·9	7·4	6·7	5·3
	women	10·8	11·1	21·3	31·1	34·2	30·5
Total non-manual occupations	men	13·7	14·3	19·7	25·2	30·8	37·2
	women	20·0	19·5	32·8	46·8	52·8	56·7
Skilled manuals	men	36·7	34·3	35·3	41·0	38·5	40·0
	women	20·9	19·8	14·0	14·7	12·4	14·5
Semi and unskilled manuals	men	49·6	51·4	45·0	33·8	30·7	22·8
	women	59·1	60·7	53·2	38·5	34·8	28·8
Total manual occupations	men	86·3	85·7	80·3	74·8	69·2	62·8
	women	80·0	80·5	67·2	53·2	47·2	43·3
Overall total	men	100·0	100·0	100·0	100·0	100·0	100·0
	women	100·0	100·0	100·0	100·0	100·0	100·0

Source: Table 2.7, Chapter 2.

Note: [1] The 1978 estimates are projections of the 1971 figures, based on New Earnings Survey data. They should therefore be treated with some caution (see footnotes to Table 2.7, Chapter 2).

14.6 Self-employment is heavily concentrated in a fairly small proportion of occupations and industries—in particular farming, the construction industry, retailing, a heterogeneous group of services ranging from garages to cafés, and the professions. In 1971 some 50 per cent of self-employed men were concentrated in the three Census occupation 'Orders': sales workers; farmers, foresters and fishermen; and construction workers. These roughly correspond to the three industry 'Orders': distribution; agriculture, forestry and fishing; and construction. With one major exception—the rise in self-employment in the construction industry from the mid-1960s onwards—the trend of self-employment as a proportion of total civil employment has been downwards. This is due partly to structural changes like the falling number of small farms and small shops, and partly to a relative shift towards salaried employment even in growing occupations like the main professions. A closer look at employment in two of the professions (architects and solicitors) shows, however, that the factors influencing the choice between self-employment and salaried employment differ considerably between different professions (Chapter 2, paragraphs 2.33 to 2.52 and Tables 2.11 to 2.19).

Factors associated with differences in earnings

14.7   There are many reasons why variations in earnings can arise, both between different occupations and within any occupational category. We have identified three strands to the theory of the structure of earnings: (i) 'labour market' theories, which treat the structure of wages and salaries as being determined by market processes, ie prices are regarded as being set for labour services in a way which is not intrinsically different from the setting of prices in other markets; (ii) 'human capital' theories, which regard the acquisition of knowledge and skills as an investment on which a return can be earned; and (iii) 'institutional' theories, which regard the influence of customary relativities, collective agreements, and Government regulation as so pervasive that they transform the nature of the labour market. These strands are not mutually exclusive. However, their relative importance is a matter of disagreement, with implications for the structure of earnings (Chapter 3, paragraphs 3.5 to 3.14).

14.8   Earnings from self-employment can be regarded as comprising earnings from labour services, returns on capital employed, and the profit or loss from the bearing of business risk. Institutional factors may reduce the degree of competition in certain professions, which is reflected in customary or agreed scales of charges rather than market-determined rates. This may explain in part why, as shown in Chapter 11, variations in incomes in some professions are lower, and average incomes higher, than in other professions or trades. In those trades and professions where there are both employed and self-employed workers the choice between employment and self-employment depends mainly on people's desire to control their own work and on their attitude to risk. For the employee, it is his employment that is at risk: for the self-employed, it may be everything he has. The distinctive influences on the distribution of earnings from self-employment lead to the expectation that the dispersion of earnings from self-employment will be greater than the dispersion of employees' earnings (Chapter 3, paragraphs 3.15 to 3.21).

14.9   Arising from these considerations, we set out in Chapter 3 (paragraph 3.25) the questions that we have explored in this Report. These are:

1 To what extent is the distribution of earnings related to differences in occupation and to differences in industry?

2 How have the earnings of different occupational groups changed over time?

3 What has been the relationship between changes in the occupational and industrial structure and the distribution of earnings?

4 What is the relationship between the age of employees and their earnings in different occupations, and how stable are the relative earnings of individuals through time?

5 How have non-cash benefits grown in relation to earnings?

229

6 What is the relationship between institutional factors and the structure of earnings?

7 On what basis is it possible to make legitimate comparisons between incomes of the self-employed and incomes of employees?

8 How does the structure of incomes from self-employment differ from the structure of incomes from employment?

The following sections summarise our findings.

Differences in occupation: differences in industry (Question 1)

14.10 Part II of the report analyses earnings from employment, with special regard to the first five of these questions. Statistics derived from the New Earnings Survey (NES) show that in 1978 the earnings of all categories of employees were widely dispersed but that the degree of dispersion was greater for non-manual than manual employees, and somewhat greater for men than for women. Using variance as the measure of dispersion, we enquire to what extent earnings depend on occupation or, putting it another way, how much of the dispersion of earnings can be explained by differences between occupations, using for this purpose the classification into 441 occupations of the NES. We find that this 'occupation effect' is rather more important for women than for men, and much more important for non-manual employees than for manual employees. The greater dispersion in non-manual employees' earnings, therefore, can be attributed in part to greater differences in earnings between occupations: on average, however, occupation explains much less than half of the overall variance for men and about a half for women (Chapter 5, paragraphs 5.4 to 5.10). Preliminary results from a study by Professor Saunders and Mr David Marsden at the European Research Centre, University of Sussex, of industrial earnings show that occupation is a more important factor in France and Italy than in Britain (paragraph 5.17). The results are published as a background paper to this report[1].

14.11 Some occupations are specific to particular industries (eg coal miners to 'mining and quarrying') but others (for example, managers and cleaners) are found in virtually all industries. An employee's occupation, therefore, does not usually indicate that he works in a particular industry. Consequently, there is no simple relationship between industrial and occupational grouping of different jobs. When we enquire whether there is an 'industry' effect equivalent to the 'occupation' effect, we find that it is much less significant for all groups. But the combined 'occupation-and-industry' effect has considerable explanatory power for women, accounting for seventy per cent of the total variance (Chapter 5, paragraphs 5.11 to 5.13).

Occupations over time (Questions 2 and 3)

14.12 To study changes over time we have to turn to a broad classification of the population into eight occupational classes—higher and lower professionals, managers, foremen, clerks and three grades of manual workers (skilled, semi-skilled and unskilled). A number of strands have to be distinguished:

---

[1] Background paper No 8, *A six country comparison of the distribution of industrial earnings in the 1970s'* C T Saunders and D Marsden.

(a) Work done by Dr Routh and not hitherto published shows the movements of average earnings in the various classes over the last 65 years. If we compare these (for men) with movements in average earnings of all male employees, the most notable feature is the fall in the relative position of higher professionals from $3\frac{1}{2}$ times the average in 1913–1914 to $1\frac{3}{4}$ times the average in 1978. In contrast, the position of unskilled manuals has remained fairly stable: their earnings have fluctuated around 70 per cent of average earnings. A general contraction from 1971 to 1978 in the spread between occupational classes can be detected from the NES.

(b) We have already mentioned (paragraph 14.4) that there has been a tendency for people to move towards jobs in higher paid occupational classes. Between 1971 and 1978 changes in occupational structure accounted for one-third of the growth in men's earnings adjusted for the increase in prices and less than one-fifth of the growth in women's earnings.

(c) The effect of this movement between occupations has been to increase slightly the inequality of the distribution of men's earnings. Had the occupational structure remained as it was in 1971 the highest percentile, highest decile and upper quartile would all be closer to the median than they actually were in 1978. A similar result was found for the distribution of women's earnings. Data for earlier years are not so reliable but they tend to suggest that from 1961 to 1971 the effect of the change in occupational structure was, again, to increase the dispersion of earnings.

Despite the change in occupational structure and the rapid increase in average earnings in money terms, the overall distribution has remained remarkably stable. This suggests that any effects of structural change have been offset by other changes (Chapter 6, paragraphs 6.12 to 6.26).

14.13 A study of more than 50 individual occupations showed considerable dispersion of earnings in virtually every case: in contrast, the differences in median earnings from one occupation to another were relatively small and there was a lot of overlapping even between occupations at very different positions (ranked in order of medians) (Chapter 7, paragraphs 7.3 to 7.5).

14.14 Over the period 1973 to 1978, the gap between men's and women's earnings narrowed, but women were still much worse off than men in 1978. In other European countries studied by Saunders and Marsden this difference was found to be not so great. In fact, differences between men's and women's earnings in Britain were still greater in 1978 than had been those in the other countries in 1972 (the only year for which comparable figures were available for all the countries) (Chapter 7, paragraphs 7.8 to 7.13).

Earnings by age and fluctuations over time (Question 4)

14.15 Data from the NES show earnings by age range for occupational groups. As Figure 14.1 shows, the earnings profiles typically have a steep increase in average earnings in the first years of working life followed by a plateau and then a decline in the last years. Non-manual workers take longer to reach their maximum earnings than manual workers, but their maximum is higher. Women's earnings rise more slowly and to a lower plateau than men's. Age affects earnings

231

Figure 14.1   Average Gross Weekly Earnings by Age Group for Four Groups of Employees; 1978

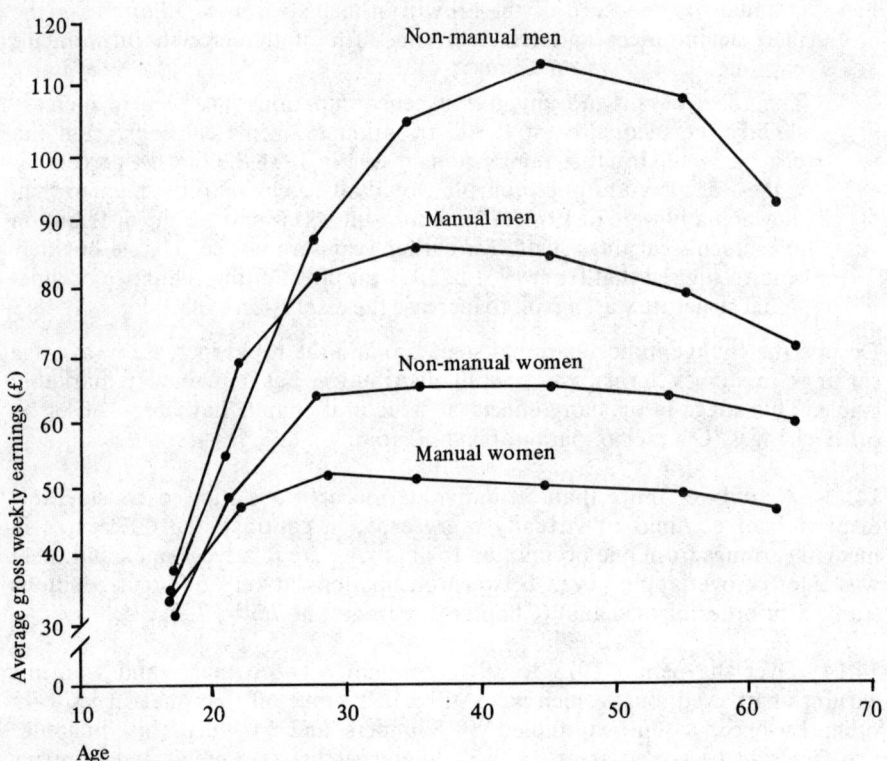

Source: New Earnings Survey 1978.

to a greater extent in higher paid occupations. These profiles are based on average earnings in different age groups at one particular time. It is important to note that the probable earnings progression of individuals through their lifetimes cannot be inferred from such profiles except by making a number of hypothetical assumptions (Chapter 8, paragraphs 8.4 to 8.7).

14.16   It is possible to look directly at the changes in earnings of individuals over time using the NES matched sample data, which cover the period from 1971 to 1978. There is a continuous run from 1975 to 1978 but owing to a change in the composition of the sample it is possible to trace only a small part of the sample back to 1974 and earlier years. The four-year matched sample showed that employees in given quantiles in 1978 were spread across other quantiles in earlier years but that the greatest number remained in the original quantile group. The nearer the year to 1978 the less were they dispersed around the quantile group. There was not much difference in the degree of movement between quantile groups by manual and non-manual men at the bottom of the distribution but the latter were considerably more stable at the top of the distribution. Non-manual women had moved less than manual women at both top and bottom of the distribution. We also examined the eight-year matched sample (1971 to 1978). Many people in the sample in 1978 could not be traced in the earlier year, possibly leading to bias, and so the results should be treated with caution. However, the general trends in the data are similar to those observed from the four-year matched sample (Chapter 8, paragraphs 8.10 to 8.13).

Non-cash benefits (Question 5)

14.17   It is clear that cash earnings alone are an imperfect measure of employees' remuneration. Employee benefits form a large part of many employees' total earnings, and the non-cash element has been growing quite fast over the last five years (paragraph 9.21). The data on this subject are somewhat impressionistic, but there is little doubt that if account were taken of employee benefits, working conditions and other aspects of employment, the dispersion of the earnings distribution would be increased. The effect within the top one per cent of employees must be particularly marked (Chapter 9).

Institutional factors (Question 6)

14.18   It is not possible to isolate and measure the effect on earnings of institutional factors, such as incomes policies, collective bargaining, legislation etc. Repeated rounds of incomes policy have had as one of their aims an improvement in the position of the lower paid relative to the higher paid. However, it has not been possible to establish a direct correlation between the timing of such changes, as can be observed in the distribution and the periods covered by particular incomes policies. The Equal Pay Act of 1970 has been associated with the rapid improvement in the pay of women relative to men which has taken place. It was put to us in the context of our Report on Lower Incomes that lack of collective bargaining was an important factor explaining the low earnings of groups of workers, and we reported then (Report No 6, paragraph 6.14) that statistical studies presented to us were consistent with this view. We are unable to go beyond this on the evidence presented in this report.

Comparability of incomes of employees and the self-employed (Question 7)

14.19   Part III of the report is devoted to a study of the income of the self-employed, a heterogeneous group drawn from very different walks of life (see paragraph 14.6 above) who have one thing in common: they are working on their own account. The main source of data is the Survey of Personal Incomes (SPI) based on returns of taxable income, but comparing the incomes of the self-employed and employees from this source is far from straightforward for a number of reasons. In the first place, self-employment income has to be regarded as hybrid, being partly a return to the entrepreneur on his labour and partly a return on the capital he has invested, including a reward for risk. (The amount of capital of course will vary enormously.) The system of capital allowances applicable to the self-employed can give rise to somewhat artificial fluctuations from year to year in taxable income. Then, for the generality of the self-employed who are taxed under Schedule D, taxable income is business profit, that is the gross income of the business less allowable deductions such as business expenses, capital allowances and stock relief. Employees do not have scope for similar deductions but on the other hand they do generally receive fringe benefits from their employer which are not necessarily included in taxable income. Being self-employed gives wider opportunities for the under-reporting of income or the overstating of expenses than receiving pay from an employer under PAYE. Undeclared income is a major source of uncertainty in all our work on the distribution of income. We quote the rather different results of two attempts to estimate the proportion of Gross Domestic Product that is undeclared income from employment and self-employment: one of something under $7\frac{1}{2}$ per cent based on an estimate by senior tax officials and one of $2\frac{1}{2}$ per cent used by the Central Statistical Office to reconcile figures in the National Accounts. We give our support to the continuing effort, both by the Inland Revenue and within the Government Statistical Service generally, to approach nearer to an estimate of the extent of this phenomenon and its effect on the distribution of total income (Chapter 10, paragraphs 10.2 to 10.9, and Chapter 12, paragraphs 12.18 to 12.41).

14.20   Close company proprietors—that is, directors of close companies whose main source of income is the company—form a category that has to be examined separately. They are taxed under Schedule E along with employees and are so classified in the SPI, but for our purposes we classify them with the self-employed whom they resemble in that they control the enterprises in which they work. We therefore carried out a special survey with the Inland Revenue to provide information on the total incomes in 1974–75 of an anonymous sample of close company proprietors, and were thus enabled for that year to establish distributions of income for the self-employed (including close company proprietors) and for employees (Chapter 4, paragraphs 4.12 to. 4.15 and Chapter 10, paragraph 10.6). A particular feature that makes comparisons of incomes with this group difficult is that profits retained within the business and not distributed in salaries or dividends do not appear as income. For the self-employed taxed under Schedule D all profits, whether withdrawn or not, are treated as having been 'distributed' (Chapter 12, paragraphs 12.42 to 12.44).

14.21   Thus many distortions are present in the figures provided by the SPI which make it difficult to draw a true comparison between the incomes of

234

employees and of the self-employed derived from that source, and again between the self-employed taxed under Schedule D and close company proprietors taxed under Schedule E. Though the distortions are not all in the same direction it seems clear that in aggregate the incomes of the self-employed will tend to be understated relative to those of employees, in terms of comparable purchasing power. This conclusion is supported by comparing the proportions of households in each group who own washing machines, cars etc at similar levels of apparent income; and also supported, especially strongly in the case of close company proprietors, by analysis of the levels of tax deductions including deductions for retirement annuities (Chapter 12, paragraph 12.61 and Chapter 10, paragraphs 10.30 to 10.39).

14.22 Another point of difficulty is that under Schedule D the self-employed are taxed on a 'preceding year' basis. This not only works generally to the advantage of the self-employed person but also makes it necessary to introduce a 'time lag' when comparing distributions of self-employment and employment incomes. Wherever possible in the body of the report we have lagged self-employment incomes by one year (Chapter 4, paragraphs 4.18 to 4.21 and Chapter 12 paragraphs 12.45 to 12.51).

Income of the self-employed (Question 8)

14.23 The distribution of income of the self-employed, however defined, is more unequal than that of employees. If close company proprietors are transferred to the self-employed distribution the inequality is increased. This can be shown by comparison of Gini coefficients, and also by examining the upper quantiles of the combined distribution. Though less than 9 per cent of the tax units in the combined distribution are self-employed, they constitute over one-quarter of the top decile group and nearly three-quarters of the top one per cent group. Their share of total net income is correspondingly high. Below the top decile the self-employed form a roughly constant proportion of each decile group. The major difference between the two groups, therefore, is the relatively large number of self-employed with high incomes. If we look at the separate distributions of each group the differences are striking: for example the average incomes of the top 10 per cent of each distribution were:

	£
1974–75 Close company proprietors (Sch. E)	21,068
1975–76 Main source Sch. D self-employed	12,290[1]
1974–75 Main source Sch. E employees	5,482

Any such comparisons have to be made bearing in mind the cautions about comparability that have been set out in the previous section (Chapter 10, paragraphs 10.10 to 10.22).

14.24 The self-employed received significant amounts of income from sources other than self-employment and, generally, the higher the total income the larger was this component. For employees, dividends and other investment income were significant only for the top 10 per cent. Many employees are also

---

[1] The top 10 per cent of the self-employed distribution is dominated by the professional groups, as is shown in the next section.

235

recorded as having small subsidiary incomes from self-employment, but this is an area where a lot of income is believed to be under-recorded or not recorded at all (Chapter 10, paragraphs 10.25 to 10.29).

14.25   The pattern of higher average earnings and more unequal distribution that we have observed for the self-employed in the UK was repeated in nearly all the other countries included in the survey of the income structure of the self-employed which was carried out for us by Dr T Stark of the New University of Ulster. There are considerably fewer self-employed in the UK than in most of the other countries. The long-run decline in the numbers of the self-employed elsewhere contrasts with the relative stability of the numbers in the UK in recent years. Part of the decline in other countries is due to the rapid contraction of the numbers employed in agriculture (where self-employment is prevalent): in the UK the numbers in agriculture have been very low for many years, the contraction having taken place earlier (Chapter 13).

Occupational analysis of the self-employed (Questions 3 and 8)

14.26   The self-employment incomes of main source Schedule D tax units are classified in Chapter 11 into 22 'trade groups', some of which correspond approximately to occupations and some to industries recognised in the NES. The findings of our analysis consist of a great number of figures and comparisons which are difficult to summarise but which bring out well the heterogeneous nature of self-employment. Some of the main features can be picked out from the summary presentations in Tables 11.8 and 11.9.

14.27   The most striking feature is the contrast between on the one hand the professional groups, with their small numbers and relatively very large share of the high incomes, high mean incomes and low incidence in the bottom income range, and on the other hand the remainder which lack most or all of these characteristics. But three groups emerge with intermediate or 'mixed' characteristics—Engineering, Stockbrokers etc and, less distinctly, Wholesale Distribution. These have, on the whole, high dispersions and a considerable presence among both the very high and the very low incomes. And among the professions Medicine stands somewhat apart, having a high average level of income and few low incomes but no more than the average number of very high incomes (above the top percentile of the overall distribution of self-employment income) (Chapter 11, paragraphs 11.1 to 11.31 and 11.39 to 11.42).

14.28   The comparisons above are of income from self-employment alone. The other components of income, especially wives' self-employment income, vary considerably between trade groups but are generally not unimportant (Chapter 11, paragraphs 11.32 to 11.38).

14.29   Certain comparisons can be made, though with the greatest caution because of the different sources of data as well as the differing nature of the income, between the self-employment income of those self-employed in a trade group and employees in an associated occupation or industry. For a number of trade groups no such parallel group of employees can be found. The broad conclusions from such comparisons as can be made are that the corresponding employees:

a have less dispersion of incomes,

b have generally lower incomes and yet,

c are less likely to figure in the lowest income ranges (say, less than £1,000 per annum in 1976–77)

than their self-employed opposite numbers (Chapter 11, paragraphs 11.47 to 11.67).

14.30 It should be noted that those self-employed in the professions cannot form close companies, as is common in other businesses. As we have already seen, close company proprietors tend to have very high incomes—even higher than the professional, let alone the other self-employed groups discussed here: and we now see that employees in their turn do not have the same propensity to reach higher levels of income as do the self-employed (Chapter 11, paragraph 11.74).

Improvements in data

14.31 The Royal Commission has been in a good position to assess the strengths and weaknesses of official statistics in the field of income and wealth. The recommendations we have made from time to time in earlier reports have normally been adopted and we are grateful to Government departments for the alacrity with which most of our suggestions have been followed up. As a result the statistical coverage has, we believe, steadily improved over the past five years. One general problem to which we have referred earlier in this chapter (paragraph 14.19) is the need to estimate the degree to which both employment and self-employment income are under-recorded by the Survey of Personal Incomes.

14.32 The work of compiling the present report has taken us deeper into employment matters than we have been before, and the difficulties we have encountered lead us to make two specific recommendations. The first concerns occupational structure and applies both to the employed and self-employed workforce. Our studies of occupational variations in earnings make it clear that the spread of earnings and the way it changes over time cannot be understood without a clear picture of changes in occupational structure. The prime source of information on trends in the spread of occupations is the Census of Population, conducted once every 10 years. The official household surveys are on too small a scale (of the order of 0·1 per cent) to be reliable in the required detail: the New Earnings Survey, though on a larger scale (one per cent), is not designed to provide information on numbers in occupations and does not cover the self-employed. Moreover each source uses a different occupational classification so that there is difficulty in combining data from more than one source. We draw attention in particular to the considerable room for improvement in the available annual statistics on the self-employed, which, being based on the Census, are likely at any given time to be rather out of date and do not provide adequate information on occupational and industrial distribution. We therefore find a strong case for a relatively large scale household survey, more frequent than the Census though not in full Census detail. The EEC Labour Force Survey (LFS), a biennial household survey which the UK has taken part in since 1973, could be a suitable vehicle for the collection of the required data, with appropriate development (Chapter 2, paragraphs 2.27, 2.35 and 2.36).

14.33 The second recommendation concerns the New Earnings Survey. The advent of this Survey and its development over the last 10 years have provided an inexhaustible supply of material for informed comment by journalists and other commentators, for use in collective bargaining by employees and trade unions, and for studies in universities and in Government departments. The field is one of perennial interest, and despite the large number of tables published (regularly and with commendable speed) there is still a considerable need among a variety of users for further analyses of the data. The Department of Employment rightly gives higher priority to maintaining this timetable than to producing tabulations to meet special requirements of individual users. However, we consider that such a valuable source should be exploited as fully as possible. The Department should give serious consideration to the possibility of making the data available, on a basis which protects confidentiality, to users to carry out their own analyses. If this should not prove possible, then the Department might consider developing the facility to respond readily and flexibly to requests for analyses from *bona fide* users of their data (Chapter 4, paragraphs 4.7 and 4.8).

A final word

14.34 This report was nearing completion when it was announced in Parliament that the work of the Royal Commission was to come to an end. It is therefore our final report on the standing reference. As a final word in our final report, we wish to stress the importance we attach to the continuing maintenance and development of the valuable body of statistics on the distribution of income and wealth now available in this country.

14.35 Various developments since 1974, associated with the Commission's investigations, have greatly enhanced the usefulness of the official statistics on the distribution of income and wealth by adjusting them in various ways and extending their coverage. This has resulted in the establishment, exemplified particularly in the standing reference reports, of a single integrated system of statistics on the distribution of income and wealth; there now exists in this country a substantial and comprehensive body of knowledge on this important subject. The Commission's reviews of the distribution of income and wealth in other countries have established that the standard of statistical information achieved in this country in this field is higher than in most other western countries. The development of these statistics has required considerable effort both on the part of the Commission and on that of the Government Departments concerned. The generally favourable reactions in this country and the extent of the interest shown in other countries show that the investment in time and resources has been well worthwhile, and it is considered important that the benefits achieved to date should not be lost. Priority should be given, therefore, to the maintenance and continuing development of the various data sources within a single statistical system and the publication on a regular basis of papers and articles on the shape of and trends in the distribution of income and wealth.

14.36 Our detailed recommendations to this end have been conveyed to the Government Departments concerned. We have also urged upon them the continuing need, if this body of statistics is to be developed, for investigations from time to time into specific aspects of the distribution of income and wealth. To our heirs and successors, both inside and outside Government, we earnestly commend these continuing tasks.

ALL OF WHICH WE HUMBLY SUBMIT FOR YOUR MAJESTY'S
GRACIOUS CONSIDERATION

DIAMOND (CHAIRMAN)
ANTHONY B ATKINSON
NEVILLE BUTTERWORTH
ANTHONY CHRISTOPHER
JOHN GREVE
DAVID LEA
DERYK VANDER WEYER

17 July 1979

The Census of Population and Department of Employment Estimates of the Labour Force[1]

A.1 The Census of Population estimate of the labour force in 1971 is that of the "economically active" population, ie all those over the statutory school leaving age who are either in employment or out of employment (but actively seeking work). Persons in employment include all those (apart from students) who worked for pay and profit at any time during the week before the Census (April 1971), including work on own account, part-time work, casual or temporary work and unpaid work in a family business. Students were excluded from the labour force, even if they had a job in the week before the Census. However, people temporarily away from work during that week, because of holidays, sickness or injury, industrial dispute or temporary lay-off were counted as "in employment" if their job was waiting for them on their return. The category "in employment" therefore covers all those who have a job in the contractual sense, irrespective of whether they were actually at work in the week before the Census, and all others who did work for pay and profit in that week.

A.2 Persons out of employment throughout the week before the Census comprise those who were out of work but prevented by temporary sickness or injury from seeking work, and those who were either seeking work or waiting to take up a job already obtained. The category "out of employment" is therefore much wider than that of the registered unemployed, since many of those seeking work, in particular women and pensioners, will not be registered as unemployed.

A.3 Since the Census of Population enumerates the population in this country on Census night it includes, in the category "in employment", only those members of the armed forces in this country at that time. Since a sizeable part of HM Forces is stationed abroad, particularly in Germany, the omission of the overseas contingents is a significant source of difference between Census of Population estimates of the labour force and those of the Department of Employment, which includes all HM Forces (home and overseas) in its estimates of the working population.

A.4 The Department of Employment (DE) describes the labour force as the "working population". This comprises employees in employment, employers and the self-employed, HM Forces and the registered unemployed. Estimates of

---

[1] For a more detailed discussion see N K Buxton and D I Mackay, *British Employment Statistics*, Oxford, Blackwell, 1977.

employees in employment were based on counts of National Insurance cards up to June 1971 and on annual Censuses of Employment from that date onwards. The Department of Employment has, however, constructed a continuous series of mid-year estimates of employees in employment for the period since 1959 which adjusts for the change in the source of basic data in 1971. The card count used to include full-time students who were in employment at any time during the year, and casual and seasonal workers, even if they were not working at the time of the count. These are now excluded, and so the definition of employees in employment is now rather closer to that of the Census of Population.

A.5   However, the Census of Employment excludes some categories, which are included in the Census of Population: eg

  a   working proprietors; partners; the self-employed; directors not under a contract of service; wives working for husbands; husbands working for wives;

  b   persons working in their own homes, eg taking in sewing;

  c   private domestic staff working in private households (239,000 in the 1971 Census of Population).

A.6   Because of the exclusion of employers and the self-employed from the Census of Employment, estimates of this category based on Census of Population data, updated (to 1974) by the DHSS sample of Class 2 National Insurance cards (and to 1975 by EEC Labour Force Survey data) have to be added on to the DE estimates of employees in employment, in order to arrive at estimates of civil employment. The lack of direct estimates of the self-employed after 1975 is proving to be quite a handicap in trying to estimate the current size of the working population. Of the other categories excluded from the Census of Employment but included in the Census of Population, domestic servants are probably the largest in size.

A.7   The Census of Employment is carried out in June, while the Census of Population relates to April. Thus part-year or casual workers will not be included to the same extent in the two Censuses and this will cause the estimates of employed workers to diverge. Another major difference between the Census of Employment and the Census of Population is that the Census of Employment counts jobs rather than people, ie a person holding two jobs with different employers will be counted twice. (The old card count system and the Census of Population would only count the person once.) This element of 'double-jobbing' is one reason why the Census of Employment's employees in employment estimates may exceed those of the Census of Population.

A.8   The DE estimates of employees in employment in Great Britain for June 1971 are 21,648,000 (13,424,000 men and 8,224,000 women). The April 1971 Census of Population estimates of employees in employment are 21,890,000 (13,560,000 men and 8,330,000 women)—based on the 10 per cent sample. The Census of Population estimates are, on balance, higher, because they include part of HM Forces, domestic servants, and unpaid family workers. The element of 'double-jobbing' in the DE estimates is not sufficient to counter balance the

Census of Population's wider coverage. (DE estimates based on the card count were usually higher than Census of Population estimates, mainly because of the inclusion of full-time students and other casual workers who held insurance cards but were not at work at the time of the Census.)

A.9 The DE estimate of the working population in 1971 was 24,545,000 compared with the Census of Population figure of 25,103,000 for the economically active population. The main reason for the greater difference between the Census total of the 'economically active' population and the Department of Employment's estimate of the working population, than between the estimates from the same sources of employees in employment, is that the working population includes (in addition to employees in employment, the self-employed, and HM Forces) only the registered unemployed, whereas the economically active population includes all who describe themselves as out of employment (including those who would have been looking for work but for temporary sickness). The working population includes all the armed forces, including those stationed abroad, whereas the 'economically active' population includes HM Forces stationed in this country and foreign and Commonwealth armed forces stationed here at the Census date—though the latter are fewer in number than HM Forces stationed outside Great Britain, so that the armed forces component of the economically active population is smaller than that of the working population.

A.10 The coverage of the Census of Population's estimates of the labour force has varied somewhat over time. Before 1961 the "occupied" population consisted of those who said that they were in work. In 1921 it included some people, in particular the long-term sick, who had been employed previously but in fact were unlikely to return to work. The 1931 and 1951 Censuses excluded the long-term sick and those who worked but were not essentially part of the work-force, such as students. The 1961 and subsequent Censuses also excluded these categories, concentrating on the "economically active" population. This comprises all persons actually in work in the week before the Census and those currently available for work. For purposes of comparison over time, the 1921 estimates of the labour force, therefore, probably cover a slightly larger section of the population than those for 1931 and 1951; the effect of the change in concept from occupied to economically active population in 1961 probably makes very little difference in total (since any fall in the numbers included as actually in work could well be counter balanced by a rise in the estimated numbers currently available for work, as opposed to 'unemployed' in previous Censuses).

The Industrial Structure of Civil Employment

B.1 The Department of Employment's continuous series of employees in employment[1] provides consistent figures since 1959; and from 1961 onwards estimates are available of self-employment on the same definitions[2] and the two can be added to provide a consistent run of figures from 1961 to 1975 for the whole civilian labour force excluding the unemployed. This continuous series does not, however, span the change from the 1948 Standard Industrial Classification (SIC) to the 1958 SIC. An approximate comparison is made between 1951 and 1961 by using estimates classified according to the 1948 SIC from 1951 to 1959, and according to the 1958 SIC from 1959 to 1961; the link was made from the 1959 estimates which were made according to both SICs[3]. Comparisons cannot be taken back before 1951 on the basis of employment data collected by the Departmental predecessors of the Department of Employment; so use is made of the work of Buxton and Mackay[4] in which they estimated a re-classification of the industry data from the 1931 and 1951 Censuses according to the 1978 SIC. The amount of estimation involved in re-classifying the 1931 Census figures was considerable, so the changes between 1931 and 1951 are broad indications of what happened rather than precise measures. In the interest of brevity the original twenty-seven 'Orders' of the Standard Industrial Classification are condensed to nine groups:

A   Order I

B   Order II

C   Orders VI to XII

D   Orders XIII, XIV, XV

E   Orders III, IV, V, XVI, XVII, XVIII, XIX

F   Order XX

G   Orders XXI, XXII

H   Order XXIII

I   Orders XXIV to XXVII

---

[1] *Department of Employment Gazette*, March 1975, and subsequent updating.
[2] *Department of Employment Gazette*, December 1976 and June 1977.
[3] *Annual Abstract of Statistics*, 1963, Table 132.
[4] N K Buxton and D I Mackay, *British Employment Statistics*, Blackwell, Oxford, 1977.

1951–61

B.2   Between 1951 and 1961 the changes in employment are those estimated by the Ministry of Labour from exchanges of National Insurance cards. Owing to the change in SIC, the calculation was made in two parts: from 1951 to 1959 on the basis of the 1948 SIC; and from 1959 (the year for which the figures are available on both bases) to 1961. The composition of the nine groups (using the nomenclature of the 1958 SIC) was:

A   Order I

B   Order II

C   Orders V, VI, VII, VIII, IX

D   Orders X, XI, XII

E   Orders III, IV, XIII, XIV, XV, XVI

F   Order XVII

G   Orders XVIII, XIX

H   Order XX

I   Orders XXI, XXII, XXIII, XXIV

The source from which the figures were taken was the *Annual Abstract of Statistics*, 1960, Table 133; 1963, Table 132.

1961–75

B.3   The figures are the sum of the Department of Employment's continuous series of employees in employment, and of self-employment. *Department of Employment Gazette*, March 1975, July 1976, December 1976, and June 1977.

Survey of the Incomes of Close Company Directors

C.1   In broad terms, a close company is one which is controlled by five or fewer individuals and their respective families. There are currently some 400,000 active close companies registered at the Company Registration Office, ranging from the very small, run typically by a man and his wife, to large family companies employing thousands of people. In this latter category come companies like Laker Airways, Littlewoods and Sainsburys. Directors of close companies have considerable flexibility (within limits set by the profitability of the company) in determining the amount of income they can take out of the company and the manner in which they take it (as earnings, non-cash benefits or dividends). The ownership of the company frequently represents a considerable investment and the directors generally have very wide discretion in deciding how to manage the company. In these respects, close company directors are more analogous to the self-employed than to employees with whom they are grouped for income tax purposes.

C.2   As a consequence of their treatment for tax purposes, they are also treated as employees in the SPI but are not separately identified. We considered it important to have separate data on the incomes of this group which could be used to compare them with both employees and the self-employed, and to adjust the SPI data to subtract their incomes from the employment income distribution and to combine them with the self-employed. The Inland Revenue agreed to carry out a special survey of the tax records of close company directors. The confidentiality of these records was protected by ensuring that, in the analyses, individual cases could not be identified.

C.3   The survey covered approximately 1,000 cases. The aim was to obtain information which would be comparable with that available in the SPI for 1974–75, but which would also shed light on aspects of the incomes of close company directors which appeared to be of particular interest. Accordingly, the survey sought separate information on income from close companies in the form of Schedule E income, investment income and benefits; on tax paid in respect of an apportionment under the close companies legislation; and, on other items of income, including income of spouse, deductions and income tax which were considered necessary for a comparison with the SPI data on the incomes of the self-employed and employees.

C.4   A random sample of 1,300 close companies was drawn from the records held at Companies House, and the Inland Revenue searched their records for the tax returns of one director from each of these companies. Usable information was available for 1,000 directors (most of the remaining 300 companies proved, on closer inspection, to be either non-close or inactive).

C.5 The information covered total tax unit income but individual items as indicated in paragraph C.3 above were identified. For 800 of the total of 1,000 close company directors, income from close companies represented their main source (defined here as the largest single source). This sample was too small to permit detailed breakdowns by categories of close company directors but it was sufficiently large to give a satisfactory measure of the overall distribution of their income, subject, of course, to the usual deficiencies associated with Inland Revenue data (see Appendix C, Report No 5).

C.6 We estimated from the available evidence on the numbers of close companies, the average number of directors per company in our survey and the average number of directorships held by each director, that there were in the whole UK population some 309,000 tax units whose main source of income was from close company directorships. The available SPI tabulations have all been grossed up to the total population of tax units (excluding those whose incomes are not recorded by the Revenue). In order to disaggregate the income distribution of close company directors from the SPI main source Schedule E distribution, it was necessary to gross up the close company sample to the estimated population total of 308,980. The tables presented in this report are based on the survey results grossed up to this total.

Time Lags in Recording Self-employment Incomes

D.1 This Appendix presents the detailed information which we were able to collect concerning time lags in the SPI and FES data on self-employment incomes.

D.2 Table D.1 presents the results of a sampling exercise carried out by the Inland Revenue to estimate the extent of the time lag in the SPI data on self-employment income. The income data presented in the SPI relates to the fiscal year of assessment which, for Schedule E income, will be the current year and, for Schedule D income, will be income earned in an accounting period ending sometime in the previous fiscal year. For each calendar month, the figures in Table D.1 show the numbers of individuals and partnerships whose accounting year ends in that month.

D.3 The figures for April are broken down between those businesses ending their accounting year before 5 April (the end of the fiscal year) and those ending after 5 April. This distinction is crucial to the time lag effect as the minimum

Table D.1   Schedule D Accounting Periods

Accounting period ending in month shown	Numbers of cases				
	Individuals	Partnerships	Status not reported	Total	
	No.	No.	No.	No.	%
January	30,520	12,640	30,800	73,960	4·45
February	27,080	10,240	27,600	64,920	3·90
March	118,680	48,600	98,960	266,240	16·01
April 1–5	213,760	28,200	176,320	418,280	25·16
April 6–30	53,240	17,800	29,680	100,720	6·06
May	44,920	15,240	28,440	88,600	5·33
June	45,000	15,880	28,880	89,760	5·40
July	40,480	11,760	26,360	78,600	4·73
August	40,040	12,480	24,000	76,520	4·60
September	54,280	19,200	34,680	108,160	6·51
October	44,840	15,000	33,200	93,040	5·60
November	29,360	10,360	23,440	63,160	3·80
December	64,760	26,600	49,280	140,640	8·46
Total	806,960 (48·5%)	244,000 (14·7%)	611,640 (36·8%)	1,662,600 —	— 100

Source: Inland Revenue.

time lag possible (one year) occurs when the accounting period ends on 5 April, while the maximum possible (one year and 364 days) occurs when it ends on 6 April.

D.4   The average time lag was calculated by weighting the number of businesses ending their accounting years in each month by the appropriate time lag for that month. The figure derived thereby was 15 months.

D.5   The Central Statistical Office has similarly investigated time lags in the FES data on self-employment incomes. In this case, however, account needed to be taken of the fact that interviews are carried out throughout the year.

D.6   The FES exercise covered two separate quarterly periods. Taken together, the results of the two sets of data indicated an average time lag of 9 months. However, because the earnings of employees recorded in the Survey are their earnings for the prior week, the lag for self-employment incomes needs to be extended to the mid-points of the accounting periods for self-employment incomes. The total time lag thus becomes 9 months plus 6 months, ie 15 months.

The Calculation of Occupation and Industry Effects

E.1　This Appendix describes the methods used in deriving the results shown in Chapter 5. The analyses were based on tabulations showing, for each occupation and industry order identified in the NES, the dispersion of gross weekly earnings in 1978 of full-time employees over 18 whose pay for the survey pay period was unaffected by absence. There were separate tabulations for manual and non-manual men and manual and non-manual women. The Department of Employment provided additional NES tabulations which were used in deriving the combined effect of occupation and industry.

E.2　The analyses were based on the assumption that the variance in the earnings distribution could be broken down into two components; the occupation effect and the non-occupation effect in the case of the occupational analyses. This assumption implies that occupation effects and other effects contribute to the overall variance in the earnings distribution in a purely additive way such that the overall variance is equal to the sum of the component of variance due to occupation effect and that due to non-occupation effects.

E.3　The variances were not calculated directly. We relied instead on an approximate relationship between the variance and the interdecile range (IDR) such that the variance $= \left\{ \dfrac{\text{IDR}}{1 \cdot 3} \right\}^2$

This is a rather rough approximation based on the assumption that the distribution is normal in shape. However, the analysis does not rely on a precise estimate of the variance but rather on a satisfactory allocation of the proportion of the variance due to the occupation effect. We show later that this allocation process was fairly robust in the face of a different approach to deriving the occupation effect (by estimating the non-occupation effect) and of a different assumption about the shape of the distribution (log-normal). In addition, it proved possible to measure the industry effect using conventional analysis of variance and the results obtained were of the same order as those obtained by relying on inter-decile range based estimates.

E.4　The methodology can be illustrated by reference to Table E.1 which shows the various quantile points of the NES distributions for all men and women expressed as a percentage of their respective medians. These are compared with similar statistics calculated on the basis that there were no differences in earnings between individuals in the same occupation (column 3 of Table E.1). Then using the relationship between the interdecile range and the variance the proportion of the overall variance accounted for by the between occupation effect is:

$$\left\{\frac{IDRB}{1\cdot3}\right\}^2 \bigg/ \left\{\frac{IDR\ overall}{1\cdot3}\right\}^2$$

where IDRB is the IDR of the 'between occupations' distribution which for men is equal to $\left\{\dfrac{57\cdot0}{94\cdot2}\right\}^2 = 0\cdot37$

leaving a residual of 0·63 to be explained by differences arising within occupations.

E.5 As a check on this residual estimate, an estimate of the dispersion which would emerge if all differences in levels of earnings between occupations were removed was derived and is shown in column 2 of Table E.1. This was done by weighting (according to the number of employees in each occupation) for each occupation, earnings as a percentage of the median at various quantile points, and summing across occupations for each quantile group. For example, suppose we are given the following dispersions of five theoretical occupations:

Occupation	No. in sample	As percentage of the median				
		Lowest decile	Lower quartile	Median	Upper quartile	Highest decile
		%	%	%	%	%
a	100	60	80	100	120	140
b	200	65	80	100	125	150
c	150	65	85	100	120	150
d	100	70	90	100	130	160
e	250	70	85	100	125	150
Total	800					

Then, for instance, the lowest decile of the 'within occupation' distribution would be calculated thus:

Occupation	No. in sample	Lowest decile	No. in sample x Lowest decile
		%	%
a	100	60	6,000
b	200	65	13,000
c	150	65	9,750
d	100	70	7,000
e	250	70	17,500
Total	800		53,250

The lowest decile as a percentage of the median $= \dfrac{53,250}{800} = 67$ per cent.

Estimates of the lowest decile and the other quantile points specified in Table E.1 were calculated in a similar way. The resulting interdecile range for men was

251

76·3 which suggests that the proportion of the variance due to within occupation effects is $\left\{\dfrac{76\cdot3}{94\cdot2}\right\}^{2} = 0\cdot66$. This is reasonably close to the proportion found in paragraph E.4 above.

Table E.1   Dispersion of Earnings 'Between Occupations' for Full-time Men and Women; 1978

Quantile points as percentages of the median, quantile points as percentages of the median on the basis that there is no variation in average earnings between occupations, and quantile points as percentages of the median on the basis that there is no earnings variation within occupations; 1978

Great Britain

Quantile group	NES distribution	'Within occupation' distribution	'Between occupations' distribution
	Percentage of median %	Percentage of median %	Percentage of median %
	All full-time men, pay unaffected by absence		
Lowest decile	64·6	70·5	79·6
Lower quartile	79·5	83·1	87·7
Median	100·0	100·0	100·0
Upper quartile	125·6	121·4	115·6
Highest decile	158·8	146·8	136·6
Highest percentile	270·4	210·6	180·0
Median £ pw	80·4	—	83·0
Mean £ pw	87·2	—	87·0
Gini coefficient %	20·9	19·1	12·3
	All full-time women, pay unaffected by absence		
Lowest decile	69·1	74·0	85·0
Lower quartile	82·2	85·3	96·0
Median	100·0	100·0	100·0
Upper quartile	125·3	117·3	111·3
Highest decile	161·4	136·9	152·2[1]
Highest percentile	242·0	169·5	183·3
Median £ pw	51·8	—	51·8
Mean £ pw	56·4	—	56·3
Gini coefficient %	19·3	15·8	12·4

Source: NES 1978.

Note: [1] This figure is the result of smoothing between quantiles adjacent to the highest decile. Two occupations which form a large proportion of the sample (secondary and primary teachers) have average earnings around the highest decile, thus making it difficult to locate this point by more precise means.

E.6   For other groups the correspondence achieved between the two approaches was of the same order. Tables E.2 to E.7 show the results of the quantile point calculations carried out in order to assess separately the occupation effect for manual and non-manual groups (Tables E.2 and E.3), the industry effects for all men and all women (Table E.4) and for manual and non-manual men and women (Tables E.5 and E.6) and the combined effect of occupation and industry (Table E.7).

E.7   The results of the cases in which two approaches (ie estimating separately the "between" and the "within" effect) were pursued, are summarised below:

	Percentage of variance explained by occupation effect	Percentage of variance explained by within occupation effect
	%	%
All men	37	66
All women	53	46

	Percentage explained by industry effect	Percentage explained by within industry effect
	%	%
All men	5	92
All women	18	74

The extent to which the "within" and "between" effects do not sum to 100 provides an indication of the scope for estimation error in the results.

E.8   The basic assumption underlying all these calculations was that the earnings distributions were approximately normal. It might, however, be better to assume that earnings are lognormally distributed, since the distributions are highly skewed. Below, we compare estimates of the overall variance attributable to differences obtained using both distributions; between occupation, between industry and between occupation and industry combined.

	Percentages of overall variance attributable to *occupational* earnings differences	
	Normal	Lognormal
	%	%
Manual men	15	17
Non-manual men	42	48
All men	37 (66)	36 (66)
Manual women	13	13
Non-manual women	49	41
All women	53 (46)	47 (53)

	Percentages of overall variance attributable to *industrial* earnings differences	
	Normal	Lognormal
	%	%
Manual men	10	12
Non-manual men	4	5
All men	5 (92)	6 (90)
Manual women	9	10
Non-manual women	12	18
All women	18 (74)	23 (77)

The figures in brackets represent our estimates, from the 'within occupation' and "within industry" distributions, of the percentages of overall variance attributable to differences in earnings within occupations and industries for all men and all women using both normal and lognormal distributions.

	Percentage of overall variance attributable to *occupational and industrial* earnings differences	
	Normal	Lognormal
	%	%
All men	45	45
All women	70	65

E.9   As the results above show, normal and lognormal distributions give approximately the same estimates for the 'between' and 'within' components of variance. So, in the interests of simplicity the normal estimates were used in our analyses. In Chapter 5 the results are shown rounded to the nearest 5 per cent, which is the appropriate degree of accuracy.

E.10   As a final check on the robustness of the estimates, an analysis of variance was carried out on the NES distributions of earnings of full-time manual and non-manual men and manual and non-manual women by industry orders. The results are shown in Table E.8. The large F-ratios obtained (column d) indicate that industry had a significant effect in all four cases. The proportion of the variance attributable to between industry effects which is given by the ratio of the "between industries" sum of squares (column a) to the overall sum of squares is shown below for each group and for comparison, the estimates derived by the interdecile range method are also shown. The results are similar.

	Proportion of variance due to industry effect	
	By analysis of variance	By interdecile range method
	%	%
Manual men	10	10
Non-manual men	3	4
Manual women	12	9
Non-manual women	14	12

Table E.2 Dispersion of Earnings 'Between Occupations' for Manual and Non-manual Men; 1978

Quantile points as percentages of the median and quantile points as percentages of the median on the basis that there is no earnings variation within occupations; 1978.

Great Britain

Quantile group	NES distribution	'Between occupations' distribution
	Percentage of median %	Percentage of median %
	Manual men, pay unaffected by absence	
Lowest decile	67·6	82·5
Lower quartile	81·5	89·0
Median	100·0	100·0
Upper quartile	121·8	106·6
Highest decile	147·2	113·5
Highest percentile	213·5	132·0
Median £ pw	75·4	80·0
Mean £ pw	79·2	79·0
Gini coefficient %	17·5	7·5
	Non-manual men, pay unaffected by absence	
Lowest decile	60·2	67·9
Lower quartile	77·2	82·2
Median	100·0	100·0
Upper quartile	128·9	115·7
Highest decile	165·0	136·1
Highest percentile	286·1	161·5
Median £ pw	90·1	97·3
Mean £ pw	98·7	98·4
Gini coefficient %	23·1	13·9

Source: NES 1978.

255

Table E.3 Dispersion of Earnings 'Between Occupations' for Manual and Non-manual Women; 1978

Quantile points as percentages of the median and quantile points as percentages of the median on the basis that there is no earnings variation within occupations; 1978

Great Britain

Quantile group	NES distribution	'Between occupations' distribution
	Percentage of median %	Percentage of median %
	Manual women, pay unaffected by absence	
Lowest decile	70·8	88·3
Lower quartile	83·2	94·1
Median	100·0	100·0
Upper quartile	119·6	107·5
Highest decile	140·9	113·4
Highest percentile	196·3	139·5
Median £ pw	47·6	48·8
Mean £ pw	49·3	49·3
Gini coefficient %	15·8	6·3
	Non-manual women, pay unaffected by absence	
Lowest decile	68·8	90·3
Lower quartile	81·9	95·9
Median	100·0	100·0
Upper quartile	127·4	118·9
Highest decile	164·7	157·4[1]
Highest percentile	241·4	191·5.
Median £ pw	53·9	52·7
Mean £ pw	59·1	59·0
Gini coefficient %	19·7	13·3

Source: NES 1978.

Note: [1] This figure is the result of smoothing between quantiles adjacent to the highest decile. Two occupations which form a large proportion of the sample (secondary and primary teachers) have average earnings around the highest decile, thus making it difficult to locate this point by more precise means.

Table E.4 Dispersion of Earnings 'Between Industries' for Full-time Men and Women; 1978

Quantile points as percentages of the median, quantile points as percentages of the median on the basis that there is no variation in average earnings between 27 industry orders, and quantile points as percentages of the median on the basis that there is no earnings variation within orders; 1978

Great Britain

Quantile group	NES distribution	'Within industry' distribution	'Between industries' distribution
	Percentage of median %	Percentage of median %	Percentage of median %
	All full-time men, pay unaffected by absence		
Lowest decile	64·6	66·9	87·2
Lower quartile	79·5	80·5	94·2
Median	100·0	100·0	100·0
Upper quartile	125·6	125·2	104·7
Highest decile	158·8	157·2	109·2
Median £ pw	80·4	—	86·9
Mean £ pw	87·2	—	87·0
Gini coefficient %	20·9	22·8	5·3
	All full-time women, pay unaffected by absence		
Lowest decile	69·1	71·6	78·3
Lower quartile	82·2	83·4	87·3
Median	100·0	100·0	100·0
Upper quartile	125·3	124·6	116·4
Highest decile	161·4	151·0	117·9
Median £ pw	51·8	—	55·9
Mean £ pw	56·4	—	56·2
Gini coefficient %	19·3	19·9	8·6

Source: NES 1978.

257

Table E.5   Dispersion of Earnings 'Between Industries' for Manual and Non-manual Men; 1978

Quantile points as percentages of the median and quantile points as percentages of the median on the basis that there is no earnings variation within industries; 1978

Great Britain

Quantile group	NES distribution	'Between industries' distribution
	Percentage of median %	Percentage of median %
	Manual men, pay unaffected by absence	
Lowest decile	67·6	82·4
Lower quartile	81·5	89·9
Median	100·0	100·0
Upper quartile	121·8	102·7
Highest decile	147·2	107·5
Median £ pw	75·4	82·8
Mean £ pw	79·2	80·8
Gini coefficient %	17·5	5·9
	Non-manual men, pay unaffected by absence	
Lowest decile	60·2	85·2
Lower quartile	77·2	96·4
Median .. .. ∴·	100·0	100·0
Upper quartile	128·9	101·5
Highest decile	165·0	106·1
Median £ pw	90·1	102·1
Mean £ pw	98·7	100·7
Gini coefficient %	23·1	4·0

Source: NES 1978.

Table E.6 Dispersion of Earnings 'Between Industries' for Manual and Non-manual Women; 1978

Quantile points as percentages of the median and quantile points as percentages of the median on the basis that there is no earnings variation within industries; 1978

Great Britain

Quantile group	NES distribution	'Between industries' distribution
	Percentage of median %	Percentage of median %
	Manual women, pay unaffected by absence	
Lowest decile	70·8	89·9
Lower quartile	83·2	91·9
Median	100·0	100·0
Upper quartile	119·6	109·3
Highest decile	140·9	111·3
Median £ pw	47·6	48·4
Mean £ pw	49·3	49·5
Gini coefficient %	15·8	5·6
	Non-manual women, pay unaffected by absence	
Lowest decile	68·8	74·7
Lower quartile	81·9	92·5
Median	100·0	100·0
Upper quartile	127·4	103·5
Highest decile	164·7	107·7
Median £ pw	53·9	59·6
Mean £ pw	59·1	59·3
Gini coefficient %	19·7	8·2

Source: NES 1978.

Table E.7 Dispersion of Earnings 'Between Occupation within Industries'; 1978

Quantile points as percentages of the median and quantile points as percentages of the median on the basis that there is no earnings variation within occupations within industry orders; 1978

Great Britain

Quantile group	Men, pay unaffected by absence		Women, pay unaffected by absence	
	NES distribution	'Between occupations and industries' distribution	NES distribution	'Between occupations and industries' distribution
	Percentage of median %	Percentage of median %	Percentage of median %	Percentage of median %
Lowest decile	64·6	75·8	69·1	79·0
Lower quartile	79·5	86·9	82·2	90·7
Median	100·0	100·0	100·0	100·0
Upper quartile	125·6	116·2	125·3	112·9
Highest decile	158·8	138·8	161·4	156·3[1]
Highest percentile ..	270·4	197·5	242·0	190·2
Median £ pw	80·4	83·2	51·8	53·0
Mean £ pw	87·2	87·1	56·4	56·7
Gini coefficient % ..	20·9	13·6	19·3	13·6

Source: NES 1978.

Note: [1] This figure is the result of smoothing between quantiles adjacent to the highest decile. Two occupations which form a large proportion of the sample (secondary and primary teachers) have average earnings around the highest decile, thus making it difficult to locate this point by more precise means.

Table E.8   Analysis of Variance of NES Distributions of Earnings by Industry Orders; 1978

Great Britain

	Sum of squares	Degrees of freedom	Mean square	F-ratio
Full-time manual men 1978				
Between industries	3,656,244	25	146,250	222·3
Within industry	32,175,883	48,901	658	
Total	35,832,127	48,926		
Full-time non-manual men 1978				
Between industries	2,010,512	25	80,420	41·1
Within industry	68,901,104	35,192	1,958	
Total	70,911,616	35,217		
Full-time manual women 1978				
Between industries	267,513	18	14,862	75·1
Within industry	2,028,135	10,234	198	
Total	2,295,648	10,252		
Full-time non-manual women 1978				
Between industries	1,910,564	21	90,979	203·1
Within industry	11,995,904	26,755	448	
Total	13,906,468	26,776		

Source: NES 1978.

NES Occupational Classification Systems and Occupational Classes

F.1 It was mentioned in paragraph 6.6 that in order to carry out an analysis of changes in occupational structure over time, it was necessary to reclassify the NES data as individual occupations into Routh's occupational classes.

F.2 This appendix describes the two occupational class systems used in the NES, the first used for the 1970, 1971 and 1972 Surveys, the second used from 1973 onwards and indicates to which of Routh's seven occupational classes each NES occupation was allocated.

NES system 1970–72

F.3 The survey form included a list of 189 occupations. The employer was asked to classify the employee to the occupation that most nearly described the employee's job; the employer also recorded the employee's job title and a brief description of the main duties. Apprentices and other trainees or learners were classified to the occupations for which they were being trained. The listed occupations were arranged under 16 broad headings which are described as main groups:

1 Managers
2 Supervisors and foremen
3 Engineers, scientists and technologists
4 Technicians
5 Academic and teaching staff
6 Medical, dental, nursing and welfare staff
7 Other professional and technical staff
8 Office and communications staff
9 Sales staff
10 Security staff
11 Catering, domestic and other service staff
12 Farming, forestry and horticultural occupations
13 Transport occupations
14 Building, engineering etc occupations
15 Textile, clothing and footwear occupations
16 Other occupations

The individual occupations are listed below and the occupational class to which each one has been allocated is entered alongside each occupation title. For main groups 14, 15 and 16 an analysis by skill level, corresponding to Routh's Groups 5, 6 and 7 is given in the survey.

262

Grouped List of Occupations Used in the Survey; 1971

GROUP 1. MANAGERS

2B   Company chairman; director
2B   General manager; divisional manager (with other managers under their control)
2B   Company secretary
2B   Works manager/superintendent, production manager
2B   Marketing, advertising, sales manager
2B   Personnel or training manager
2B   Transport manager
2B   Office manager (including departmental office manager)
2B   Site or yard manager
2B   Retail shop manager or departmental manager
2B   Hotel, catering, club or entertainments manager
2B   Other managerial staff

GROUP 2. SUPERVISORS and FOREMEN

4   Office supervisor
4   Sales supervisor, section head, first assistant
4   Catering supervisor
4   Transport inspector
4   Senior or higher level foreman (eg works foreman)
4   Other foreman or supervisor

GROUP 3. ENGINEERS, SCIENTISTS, TECHNOLOGISTS (performing work normally requiring university degree or equivalent)

1A   Engineer—civil, structural or municipal
1A   Engineer—electrical, electronic
1A   Engineer—mechanical
1A   Engineer—planning and production
1A   Engineer—other
1A   Natural scientist (biologist, chemist, physicist etc)
1A   Social or other scientist
1A   Technologist

GROUP 4. TECHNICIANS

1B   Draughtsman
1B   Systems analyst, computer programmer
1B   Technician—laboratory, scientific, medical, dental
1B   Technician—design, costing, production
1B   Other technician

GROUP 5. ACADEMIC AND TEACHING STAFF

1B   University academic staff (professors, readers, lecturers and others)
1B   Teachers in establishments for further education
1B   School teachers, secondary, primary, nursery, special schools
1B   Other teachers and instructors

GROUP 6. MEDICAL, DENTAL, NURSING AND WELFARE STAFF

1A   Medical or dental practitioner
1B   Medical auxiliary (radiographer, physiotherapist etc)
1B   Nursing matron, sister
1B   Staff nurse, enrolled nurse, registered nurse, midwife
1B   Nursing assistant
1B   Welfare worker (including probation officer, childrens' officer, hospital almoner)
5   Ambulance man, hospital or ward orderly
1B   Other medical, dental, nursing and welfare staff

GROUP 7. OTHER PROFESSIONAL AND TECHNICAL STAFF

1A   Accountant (professional)
1A   Architect, planner
1A   Surveyor
1A   Solicitor
1A   Author, editor, journalist
1B   Artist, musician, photographer, entertainer, sportsman

1B	Purchasing officer, buyer
1B	Aircrew officer, ships officer, pilot
1B	Other professional and technical staff

GROUP 8. OFFICE AND COMMUNICATIONS STAFF

3	Clerk—senior level
3	Clerk—intermediate level
3	Clerk—routine or junior level
3	Secretary, shorthand typist
3	Copy/audio typist
3	Receptionist
3	Telephonist
3	Office machine operator (including punch and telex)
6	Postman, mail sorter, messenger
3	Other office and communications staff not listed elsewhere

GROUP 9. SALES STAFF

2B	Sales representative, traveller, agent, technical salesman
6	Cashier—retail shop
6	Shop salesman, sales assistant, shop assistant
6	Roundsman—retail sales, van salesman
6	Petrol pump attendant
6	Other sales staff not listed elsewhere

GROUP 10. SECURITY STAFF

2B	Police officer (inspector and above)
5	Police sergeant or constable
5	Fire officer
5	Fireman
5	Prison officer
7	Guard, watchman
6	Caretaker, office keeper
6	Other security staff

GROUP 11. CATERING, DOMESTIC and OTHER SERVICE STAFF

6	Chef/cook
5	Steward, stewardess, hostess—aircraft, railways, ships
6	Waiter, waitress
7	Kitchen/counter hand, schoolmeals helper
6	Barman, barmaid
6	Other catering staff
5	Hairdresser, barber
6	Car park attendant, lift attendant
7	Cleaner, charwoman
6	Housekeeper, house warden
6	Maid, valet etc, domestic gardener
6	Other domestic and service staff

GROUP 12. FARMING, FORESTRY and HORTICULTURAL OCCUPATIONS

6	Stockman
6	Agricultural machinery driver/operator
6	General farm worker
6	Groundsman, gardener—non-domestic
6	Horticultural worker
6	Other farming, forestry or horticultural occupations

GROUP 13. TRANSPORT OCCUPATIONS

5	Railway engine driver, motorman, secondman
5	Railway signalman
5	Railway guard
6	Railway porter, ticket collector, railman
5	Railway lengthman
6	Bus conductor
6	Bus or coach driver
6	Taxi driver, other private hire driver
6	Lorry or van driver (vehicles up to 5 tons)

6	Lorry or van driver (vehicles 5 to 10 tons)
6	Lorry or van driver (vehicles 10 to 15 tons)
6	Lorry or van driver (vehicles over 15 tons)
5	Deck or engine-room hand, seaman, boatman, fisherman
5	Docker, stevedore
6	Other transport occupations not listed elsewhere

NES System 1973–78

F.4   The List of Key Occupations has over 400 entries arranged within 18 main groups, namely:

I	Managerial (general management)
II	Professional and related supporting management and administration
III	Professional and related in education, welfare and health
IV	Literary, artistic and sports
V	Professional and related in science, engineering, technology and similar fields
VI	Managerial (excluding general management)
VII	Clerical and related
VIII	Selling
IX	Security and protection service
X	Catering, cleaning, hairdressing and other personal service
XI	Farming, fishing and related
XII	Materials processing (excluding metal)
XIII	Making and repairing (excluding metal and electrical)
XIV	Processing, making, repairing and related (metal and electrical)
XV	Painting, repetitive assembling, product inspecting, packaging and related
XVI	Construction, mining and related not identified elsewhere
XVII	Transport operating, materials moving and storing and related
XVIII	Miscellaneous

Within each main group, a number of particular occupations or groups of associated occupations are distinguished; for example, in group II, systems analysts and computer programmers are not listed separately but are grouped together, but accountants are listed separately. Except for groups I, VII and VIII, each main group includes some occupations in addition to those so distinguished; these are treated as a residual category which is described in the list as, for example, "all other professional and related occupations supporting management and administration" in group II.

F.5   The individual occupations are listed below and the occupational class to which each one has been allocated is entered alongside each occupation title.

Grouped List of Occupations used in the Survey

GROUP I—MANAGERIAL (GENERAL MANAGEMENT) '

2B	Top managers—national government and other non-trading organisations
2B	General, central, divisional managers—trading organisations

GROUP II—PROFESSIONAL AND RELATED SUPPORTING MANAGEMENT AND ADMINISTRATION

1A	Judges, barristers, advocates and solicitors
2B	Company secretaries
2B	Town clerks and clerks to local authorities
1B	Secretaries of trade associations, trade unions, professional bodies and charities
1A	Accountants
2B	Estimators, valuers and assessors
2B	Finance, investment, insurance and tax specialists
2B	Personnel and industrial relations officers and managers
1A	Organisation and methods, work study and operational research officers
1B	Systems analysts and computer programmers
2B	Marketing and sales managers and executives
2B	Advertising and public relations managers and executives
2B	Purchasing officers and buyers
2B	Property and estate managers
1B	Librarians and other information officers
2B	Public health inspectors
2B	Other statutory and similar inspectors
2B	General administrators—national government
2B	General administrators—local government
2B	All other professional and related supporting management and administration
1A	Economists, statisticians and actuaries

GROUP III—PROFESSIONAL AND RELATED IN EDUCATION, WELFARE AND HEALTH

1B	University academic staff
1B	Teachers in establishments for further and higher education
1B	Secondary teachers
1B	Primary teachers
1B	Pre-primary teachers
1B	Special education teachers
1B	Vocational/industrial trainers
2B	Directors of education, education officers, school inspectors
1A	Social and behavioural scientists
1B	Welfare workers—social, medical, industrial, educational and moral
1A	Clergy, ministers of religion
1A	Medical practitioners
1A	Dental practitioners
2B	Nurse administrators and nurse executives
1B	State registered and state enrolled nurses and state-certified midwives
1B	Nursing auxiliaries and assistants
1B	Pharmacists
1B	Medical radiographers
1B	Ophthalmic and dispensing opticians
1B	Remedial therapists
1B	Chiropodists
1B	Medical technicians and dental auxiliaries
1B	Veterinarians
1B	All other professional and related in education, welfare and health

GROUP IV—LITERARY, ARTISTIC AND SPORTS

1A	Journalists
1B	Artists, commercial artists
1B	Industrial designers
1B	Actors, musicians, entertainers, stage managers
1B	Photographers and cameramen
1B	Sound and vision equipment operators
1B	Window dressers
1B	Professional sportsmen, sports officials
1A	All other literary, artistic and sports, including authors and writers

GROUP V—PROFESSIONAL AND RELATED IN SCIENCE, ENGINEERING, TECHNOLOGY AND SIMILAR FIELDS

1A	Biological scientists and biochemists
1A	Chemical scientists
1A	Physical and geological scientists and mathematicians

266

1A	Civil, structural and municipal engineers
1A	Mechanical engineers
1A	Electrical engineers
1A	Electronic engineers
1A	Electrical/electronic engineers
1A	Production engineers
1A	Planning and quality control engineers
1A	Mining, quarrying and drilling engineers
1A	Aeronautical engineers
1A	Chemical engineers
1A	Heating and ventilating engineers
1A	General and other engineers
1A	Metallurgists
1A	All other technologists
1B	Architectural draughtsmen
1B	Engineering and other draughtsmen
1B	Laboratory technicians—scientific and medical
1B	Engineering technicians and technician engineers
1A	Architects and town planners
1B	Town planning assistants, architectural and building technicians
1A	Quantity surveyors
1A	Building, land and mining surveyors
1B	Aircraft, flight deck officers
1B	Air traffic planners and controllers
1B	Ships' masters, deck officers and pilots
1B	Ships' engineer officers
1B	Ships' radio officers
1B	All other professional and related in science, engineering and other technologies and similar fields

GROUP VI—MANAGERIAL (EXCLUDING GENERAL MANAGEMENT)

2B	Production managers, works managers, works foremen
2B	Engineering maintenance managers
2B	Site and other managers, agents, clerks of works, general foremen (building and civil engineering)
2B	Managers—underground mining and public utilities
2B	Transport managers—air, sea, rail, road, harbour
2B	Managers—warehousing and materials handling
2B	Office managers—national government
2B	Office managers—local government
2B	Other office managers
2B	Managers—wholesale distribution
2B	Managers—department stores, variety chain stores, supermarket and departmental managers
2B	Branch managers of shops other than above
2B	Managers of independent shops (employees)
2B	Hotel and residential club managers
2B	Publicans (employees)
2B	Catering and non-residential club managers
2B	Entertainment and sports managers
2B	Farm managers
2B	Police officers (inspectors and above)
2B	Fire service officers
2B	Prison officers (chief officers and above)
2B	All other managers

GROUP VII—CLERICAL AND RELATED

4	Supervisors of clerks
3	Costing and accounting clerks
3	Cash handling clerks
3	Finance, investment and insurance clerks
3	Production and materials controlling clerks
3	Shipping and travel arranging clerks
3	Record keeping and library clerks
3	General clerks and clerks not identified elsewhere
6	Retail shop cashiers
6	Retail shop check-out and cash and wrap operators
3	Receptionists

4	Supervisors of typists
3	Personal secretaries, shorthand writers and shorthand typists
3	Other typists
4	Supervisors of office machine operators
3	Accounting and calculating machine operators
3	Key punch operators
3	Automatic data processing equipment operators
3	Office machine operators not identified elsewhere
4	Supervisors of telephonists, radio and telegraph operators
3	Telephonists
3	Radio and telegraph operators
4	Supervisors of postmen, mail sorters and messengers
6	Postmen, mail sorters, and messengers

GROUP VIII—SELLING

4	Sales supervisors
6	Salesmen, sales assistants, shop assistants, and shelf fillers
6	Petrol pump/forecourt attendants
6	Roundsmen and van salesmen
2B	Technical sales representatives
2B	Sales representatives (wholesale goods)
2B	Other sales representatives and agents

GROUP IX—SECURITY AND PROTECTIVE SERVICE

4	Supervisors (police sergeants, fire fighting and related): principal prison officers
5	Policemen (below sergeant)
5	Firemen
5	Prison officers below principal officer
5	Security officers and detectives
6	Security guards, patrolmen
6	Traffic wardens
6	All other in security and protective service

GROUP X—CATERING, CLEANING, HAIRDRESSING AND OTHER PERSONAL SERVICE

4	Catering supervisors
6	Chefs, cooks
6	Waiters, waitresses
6	Barmen, barmaids
6	Counter hands/assistants
7	Kitchen porters/hands
4	Supervisors—housekeeping and related
4	Supervisors/foremen—caretaking, cleaning and related
6	Domestic housekeepers
6	Home and domestic helpers, maids
6	School helpers and school supervisory assistants
5	Travel stewards and attendants
5	Ambulancemen
6	Hospital/ward orderlies
7	Hospital porters
7	Hotel porters
7	Caretakers
7	Road sweepers (manual)
7	Other cleaners
6	Railmen, stationmen
6	Lift and car park attendants
6	Garment pressers
4	Hairdressing supervisors
5	Hairdressers
6	All other in catering, cleaning, hairdressing and other personal service

GROUP XI—FARMING, FISHING AND RELATED

4	Foremen
6	General farm workers
6	Dairy cowmen
6	Pig and poultrymen
6	Other stockmen

6	Horticultural workers
6	Domestic gardeners (private gardens)
6	Non-domestic gardeners and groundsmen
6	Agricultural machinery drivers/operators
6	Forestry workers
4	Supervisors/mates (fishing)
4	Fishermen
4	All other in farming, fishing and related

GROUP XII—MATERIALS PROCESSING (EXCLUDING METAL)
(Hides, textiles, chemicals, food, drink, tobacco, wood, paper and board, rubber and plastics)

4	Foremen—tannery production workers
6	Tannery production workers
4	Foremen—textile processing
5	Preparatory fibre processors
6	Spinners, doublers/twisters
6	Winders, reelers
5	Warp preparers
5	Weavers
5	Knitters
5	Bleachers, dyers and finishers
5	Burlers, menders, darners
4	Foremen—chemical processing
6	Chemical, gas and petroleum process plant operators
6	Bread bakers (hand)
5	Flour confectioners
5	Butchers and meat cutters
4	Foremen—paper and board making
5	Beatermen, refinermen—paper and board making
5	Machinemen, dryermen, calendarmen, reelermen—paper and boardmaking
4	Foremen—processing—glass, ceramics, rubber and plastics etc
5	Glass and ceramic furnacemen and kilnmen
5	Kiln setters
5	Masticating millmen—rubber and plastics
5	Rubber mixers and compounders
5	Calendar and extruding machine operators—rubber and plastics
5	Man-made fibre makers
4	Foremen—food and drink processing
6	Sewage plant attendants
6	All other in materials processing (other than metal)

GROUP XIII—MAKING AND REPAIRING (EXCLUDING METAL AND ELECTRICAL)
(Glass, ceramics, printing, paper products, clothing, footwear, woodworking, rubber and plastics)

4	Foremen—glass working
5	Glass formers and shapers
5	Glass finishers and decorators
4	Foremen—clay and stone working
5	Casters and other pottery makers
5	Cutters, shapers and polishers—stone
4	Foremen—printing
4	Foremen—paper products making
4	Foremen—bookbinding
5	Compositors
5	Electrotypers, stereotypers
5	Other printing plate and cylinder preparers
6	Printing machine minders (letterpress)
6	Printing machine minders (lithography)
6	Printing machine minders (photogravure)
6	Printing machine assistants (letterpress, lithography, and photogravure)
5	Screen and block printers
5	Bookbinders and finishers
6	Cutting and slitting machine operators (paper and paper products making)
4	Foremen—textile materials working
5	Bespoke tailors and tailoresses
5	Dressmakers

5	Clothing cutters and markers (measure)
5	Other clothing cutters and markers
5	Coach trimmers
5	Upholsterers, mattress makers
5	Milliners
5	Furriers
5	Hand sewers and embroiderers
5	Linkers
5	Sewing machinists (textile materials)
4	Foremen—leather and leather substitute working
5	Boot and shoe makers (bespoke) and repairers
5	Leather and leather substitute cutters
5	Footwear lasters
5	Leather and leather substitute sewers
6	Footwear finishers
4	Foremen—woodworking
5	Carpenters and joiners (construction sites and maintenance)
5	Carpenters and joiners (ship and stage)
5	Carpenters and joiners (other)
5	Cabinet makers
6	Case and box makers
5	Wood sawyers and veneer cutters
6	Woodworking machinists (setters and setter-operators)
6	Other woodworking machinists (operators and minders)
5	Patternmakers (moulds)
7	Labourers and mates to woodworking craftsmen
4	Foremen—rubber and plastics working
5	Tyre builders
6	Moulding machine operators/attendants (rubber and plastics)
6	Dental mechanics
6	All other in making and repairing (excluding metal and electrical)

GROUP XIV—PROCESSING, MAKING, REPAIRING AND RELATED (METAL AND ELECTRICAL)
(Iron, steel, and other metals, engineering [including installation and maintenance] vehicles and shipbuilding)

4	Foremen—metal making and treating
5	Blast furnacemen
5	Furnacemen (steel smelting)
5	Other furnacemen—metal
5	Rollermen (steel)
5	Moulders and moulder/coremakers
5	Machine moulders, shell moulders and machine coremakers
5	Die casters
5	Metal drawers
5	Smiths, forgemen
5	Electroplaters
5	Annealers, hardeners, temperers (metal)
4	Foremen—engineering machining
5	Press and machine tool setters
5	Roll turners, roll grinders
5	Other centre lathe turners
5	Machine tool setter—operators
6	Machine tool operators (not setting up)
6	Press and stamping machine operators
6	Automatic machine attendants/minders
5	Metal polishers
5	Fettlers/dressers
4	Foremen—production fitting (metal)
5	Toolmakers, tool fitters, markers-out
5	Precision instrument makers
5	Metal working production fitters (fine limits)
5	Metal working production fitter-machinists (fine limits)
5	Other metal working production fitters—(not to fine limits)
4	Foremen—installation and maintenance—machines and instruments
5	Machinery erectors and installers
5	Maintenance fitters—non-electrical plant and industrial machinery
5	Knitting machine mechanics (industrial)

5	Motor vehicle mechanics (skilled)
6	Other motor vehicle mechanics (oilers, greasers)
5	Maintenance and service fitters—aircraft engines
5	Watch and clock repairers
5	Instrument mechanics
5	Office machine mechanics
4	Foremen—production fitting and wiring (electrical/electronic)
5	Production fitters—electrical/electronic
5	Production electricians
4	Foremen—installation and maintenance (electrical/electronic)
5	Electricians—installation and maintenance (plant and machinery)
5	Electricians—installation and maintenance (premises, ships)
5	Telephone fitters
5	Radio, television and other electronic maintenance fitters and mechanics
5	Cable jointers and linesmen
4	Foremen/supervisors—metal working—pipes, sheets, structures
5	Plumbers, pipe fitters
5	Heating and ventilating engineering fitters
5	Gas fitters
5	Sheet metal workers
5	Platers and metal shipwrights
5	Caulker burners, riviters and drillers (constructional metal)
5	General steel workers—shipbuilding and repair
5	Steel erectors
5	Scaffolders, stagers
5	Steel benders, bar benders and fixers
5	Welders—skilled
6	Other welders
4	Foremen—other processing, making and repairing (metal and electrical)
5	Goldsmiths, silversmiths and precious stone workers
5	Engravers and etchers (printing)
5	Coach and vehicle body builders/makers
5	Aircraft finishers
5	Maintenance and installation fitters—mechanical and electrical
5	Setter operators of woodworking and metal working machines
5	{ All other skilled in processing, making and repairing (metal and electrical) { All other non-skilled in processing, making and repairing (metal and electrical)

GROUP XV—PAINTING, REPETITIVE ASSEMBLING, PRODUCT INSPECTING, PACKAGING AND RELATED

4	Foremen—painting and similar coating
5	Painters and decorators
5	Pottery decorators
5	Coach painters
5	Other spray painters
5	French polishers
4	Foremen—product assembling (repetitive)
4	Foremen—product inspection
6	Repetitive assemblers (metal and electrical goods)
4	Inspectors and testers (skilled)—metal and electrical goods
4	Viewers—metal and electrical engineering
4	Foremen—packaging
6	Packers, bottlers, canners, fillers
6	All other in painting, repetitive assembling, product inspecting, packaging and related

GROUP XVI—CONSTRUCTION, MINING AND RELATED NOT IDENTIFIED ELSEWHERE

4	Foremen—building and civil engineering not identified elsewhere
5	Bricklayers
5	Fixer/walling masons
5	Plasterers
5	Floor and wall tilers, terrazzo workers
5	Roofers and slaters
5	Glaziers
5	Railway trackmen and platelayers
6	Asphalt and bitumen road surfacers
7	Other roadmen
6	Concrete erectors/assemblers

6	Concrete levellers/screeders
6	General builders
6	Sewermen (maintenance)
5	Mains and service layers and pipe jointers (drainage, gas, oil, water)
4	Waste inspectors (water supply)
7	Craftsmen's mates and other builders' labourers not identified elsewhere
7	Civil engineering labourers
4	Foremen/deputies—coalmining (including shot-firers and gate-end supervisors)
5	Face-trained coalmining workers
5	Tunnellers
6	All other in construction, mining, quarrying, well-drilling and related not identified elsewhere

GROUP XVII—TRANSPORT OPERATING, MATERIALS MOVING AND STORING AND RELATED

4	Foremen—ships, lighters and other vessels
4	Foremen—rail transport operating
4	Foremen—road transport operating
5	Deck and engine room hands (sea-going)
5	Bargemen, lightermen, boatmen, tugmen
5	Locomotive drivers, motormen
5	Secondmen (railways)
5	Railway guards
5	Railway signalmen and shunters
4	Bus inspectors
6	Bus and coach drivers
6	Heavy goods drivers (over 3 tons unladen weight)
6	Other goods drivers
6	Other motor drivers
6	Bus conductors
7	Drivers' mates
4	Foremen—civil engineering plant operating
6	Mechanical plant drivers/operators—earth moving and civil engineering
4	Foremen—materials handling equipment operating
6	Crane drivers/operators
6	Fork lift and other mechanical truck drivers/operators
4	Foremen—materials moving and storing
5	Storekeepers, warehousemen
5	Stevedores and dockers
6	Furniture removers
7	Warehouse, market and other goods porters
7	Refuse collectors/dustmen
7	All other in transport operating, materials moving and storing and related, not identified elsewhere

GROUP XVIII—MISCELLANEOUS

4	Foremen—miscellaneous
6	Electricity power plant operators and switchboard attendants
6	Turncocks (water supply)
7	General labourers—engineering and shipbuilding
7	Other general labourers
7	All other in miscellaneous occupations, not identified elsewhere

Allocation of Occupations Identified in the Census to the Broader Occupational Groups Adopted by Routh; 1961 and 1971

G.1   It was mentioned in paragraph 6.7 that in order to carry out an analysis of changes in occupational structure over time, it was necessary to reclassify Census data on individual occupations into the broader occupational groups of Routh.

Classification of Occupations—1961 Census
Numbers of employees (England and Wales, and Scotland).
Census tables 1, 5, 6.

Group 1A   Higher professional
Occupational classes: 280, 281, 288–293, 296–299.   Columns b, c, d, e, l, m, n, o. *Plus* officers in the armed forces.
Minus corresponding numbers in Tables 5 and 6.

Group 1B   Lower professional
Occupational classes: 282–287, 294, 295, 310–314, 190, 192, 265.   Columns b, c, d, e, l, m, n, o.
Minus corresponding numbers in Tables 5 and 6.

Group 2B   Managers and administrators
Occupational classes: Columns b, c, l, m of all except those in category XXV and classes 190, 192, 220, 221, 265.
Plus columns d, e, n, o of classes 001, 153, 230, 231, 236–239, 253, 255, 270–278, 222, 223.
Minus corresponding numbers in Tables 5 and 6.

Group 3   Clerical
Occupational classes: 220, 221.   Columns b, c, d, e, l, m, n, o.
Minus corresponding numbers in Tables 5 and 6.

Group 4   Foremen, supervisors and inspectors
Occupational classes: Columns d, n of all classes except those in categories XXI, XXIV, XXV and 001, 153, 190, 192, 230, 231, 236–239, 253, 255, 265.
Plus classes 077, 198.   Columns e, o.

Group 5 Skilled manual

Occupational classes: 010, 011, 013, 014, 030–033, 040–043, 050–054, 056, 060–064, 066–070, 072–076, 080–085, 090–093, 102–107, 110, 111, 113, 120–122, 130–135, 140, 142, 150–152, 161, 171, 172, 174, 193, 194, 199, 200, 210, 250, 251, 263. Columns e, o.
Plus share of inadequately described.

Group 6 Semi-skilled manual

Occupational classes: 000, 002–005, 012, 015, 020, 021, 034, 044, 045, 055, 065, 071, 078, 100, 101, 108, 112, 123, 124, 141, 143, 154, 160, 180, 191, 195–197, 201–203, 205, 206, 209, 211, 232–235, 252, 254, 256–261, 264, 266, 267. Columns e, o.
Plus other ranks of the armed forces.
Plus share of inadequately described.

Group 7 Unskilled manual

Occupational classes: 170, 173, 181–188, 204, 207, 208, 262.
Plus share of inadequately described.

Classification of Occupations—1971 Census

Total numbers of employees: Table 4 of 1971 Census, Economic Activity, Part II.

Group 1A Higher professional

Occupational classes: 181, 182, 195–206, 209, 212–214, 217, columns f, p in all cases.
Plus officers in armed forces.

Group 1B Lower professional

Occupational classes: 183–189, 191–194, 207, 208, 211, 215, 216, 218–220, 115, 117, 169, columns f, p in all cases.

Group 2B Managers and administrators

Occupational classes: Columns c and m of all occupations except those in Category XXV and classes 115, 117, 169, 147.
Plus columns d, e, n, o of classes 096, 138, 142, 148–150, 157, 190, 210, 173–180.
Plus columns e, o of classes 002, 143, 154, 156, 159, 171.
Plus column m of classes 190, 210.

Group 3 Clerical

Occupational classes: 139, 140, 141, columns d, e, n, o.

Group 4 Foremen, supervisors and inspectors

Occupational classes: all except 096, 115, 117, 147–150, 157, 169 and those in categories XXI, XXIV, XXV columns d and n.
Plus classes 031, 053, 123, columns e, o.

274

Group 5 Skilled manual

Columns e, o of the following occupations:
007, 009, 013–016, 018–021, 024–028, 030, 032–038, 040–046, 048–052, 055–063, 067–072A, 074, 075, 077, 078–080, 083–089, 091, 093–095, 100–101, 103–105, 118, 119, 124, 125, 126, 136, 151, 152, 167.

Group 6 Semi-skilled manual

Columns e, o of the following occupations:
001, 003–006, 008, 010, 011, 012, 017, 022, 023, 029, 039, 047, 054, 064–066, 073, 076, 081, 082, 090, 092, 097–099, 106, 116, 120–122, 127–129, 131, 132, 135, 137, 144–146, 153, 155, 158, 160–165, 168, 170, 172.
Plus other ranks of the armed forces.

Group 7 Unskilled manual

Columns e, o of the following occupations:
102, 107–114, 130, 133, 134, 166.

Trends in the Earnings of Selected Occupations

Average gross weekly earnings, median and quantile points as a percentage of the median 1973 to 1978 of 55 selected occupations for men, and 35 selected occupations for women

Table H.1   Trends in Earnings of Selected Occupations; 1973 to 1978

Average gross weekly earnings, medians and quantile points as a percentage of the median; 1973 to 1978

Men

Quantiles as % of median

Year	Number in sample	Mean £ pw	Median £ pw	Lowest decile %	Lower quartile %	Upper quartile %	Highest decile %
Medical practitioners							
1973	238	82·9	60·0	71·5	84·2	172·8	216·0
1974	202	88·9	71·0	66·8	77·7	170·2	208·9
1975	206	106·7	92·0	64·5	72·6	159·7	187·3
1976	229	139·3	123·3	60·8	74·8	147·8	184·8
1977	234	153·2	145·0	63·9	79·5	130·5	157·0
1978	230	163·3	154·2	63·8	80·5	132·2	153·9
University academic staff							
1973	248	82·5	73·4	55·8	76·7	130·2	156·8
1974	276	83·3	82·2	60·1	78·4	116·8	141·1
1975	241	97·5	97·3	60·2	73·1	119·6	145·7
1976	241	121·6	120·4	61·5	78·5	120·9	139·4
1977	239	125·7	125·6	60·1	79·0	119·5	139·4
1978	238	136·0	135·7	64·1	79·1	119·7	139·2
Teachers in establishments for further education							
1973	530	59·2	56·5	72·4	85·8	116·0	135·3
1974	431	64·2	63·3	70·0	83·8	115·8	133·5
1975	566	87·1	85·5	74·5	85·3	112·7	138·6
1976	607	107·1	105·6	75·5	86·6	113·5	133·2
1977	598	113·5	111·9	77·7	84·8	112·3	132·5
1978	624	121·8	118·8	76·9	85·0	112·8	134·6

Table H.1 (*continued*)

Quantiles as % of median

Year	Number in sample	Mean £ pw	Median £ pw	Lowest decile %	Lower quartile %	Upper quartile %	Highest decile %
Police inspectors and above, fire service officers							
1973	—	—	—	—	—	—	—
1974	107	73·7	68·8	77·6	87·0	123·4	142·0
1975	168	94·6	85·8	75·7	87·4	127·6	155·8
1976	167	113·7	103·7	71·5	81·9	137·0	159·9
1977	168	116·0	105·9	81·6	87·5	126·5	151·4
1978	164	133·0	121·6	83·0	90·1	125·0	153·4
Engineers—electrical, electronic							
1973	704	55·0	51·4	72·1	85·1	120·4	144·7
1974	616	60·8	58·5	68·9	84·1	118·1	142·8
1975	613	81·7	79·6	71·1	83·7	117·9	137·4
1976	702	97·4	95·0	69·8	82·0	117·8	137·7
1977	713	104·4	101·9	70·2	82·5	119·2	136·7
1978	733	117·1	112·3	68·9	84·1	121·6	142·9
Secondary teachers							
1973	889	47·5	47·0	63·6	76·8	119·1	138·7
1974	791	52·8	53·1	64·8	77·8	117·2	133·2
1975	1,064	73·5	71·2	68·6	84·2	120·2	138·4
1976	1,303	90·3	88·1	69·0	83·1	119·9	134·3
1977	1,303	94·1	92·2	70·0	83·1	117·7	131·7
1978	1,318	102·7	101·0	71·0	81·9	117·4	131·3
Production and works managers, works foremen							
1973	1,402	55·0	49·7	70·4	82·7	124·9	155·4
1974	1,243	59·5	55·7	69·9	82·7	121·6	151·7
1975	1,137	72·5	67·6	68·9	82·2	123·2	159·8
1976	721	89·6	83·7	68·9	83·5	123·8	153·7
1977	868	98·1	92·0	71·1	83·8	122·4	153·5
1978	850	110·2	104·4	70·4	82·9	120·4	147·3
Primary teachers							
1973	366	44·4	45·3	63·9	76·6	115·6	130·4
1974	300	50·8	50·6	66·4	80·4	119·1	135·8
1975	413	70·8	70·8	67·8	81·4	116·2	134·3
1976	475	87·3	86·3	69·4	82·4	117·9	135·1
1977	469	91·9	91·9	69·1	82·6	115·5	131·0
1978	494	99·8	99·5	68·3	82·9	115·7	131·6
Accountants							
1973	791	53·5	48·7	53·4	75·9	133·5	168·5
1974	747	58·3	55·1	47·5	75·4	128·3	168·7
1975	729	71·7	69·0	56·7	77·5	125·7	153·4
1976	884	84·7	80·6	51·3	75·0	129·5	159·9
1977	879	93·4	88·3	56·6	77·6	130·6	157·3
1978	914	106·5	102·1	54·2	77·2	126·5	156·6

Quantiles as % of median

Year	Number in sample	Mean £ pw	Median £ pw	Lowest decile %	Lower quartile %	Upper quartile %	Highest decile %
Foremen, electricians, installation and maintenance							
1973	408	49·6	47·9	77·3	87·1	114·7	132·7
1974	402	52·7	51·1	75·5	89·5	113·8	132·3
1975	163	69·3	64·6	74·8	86·2	126·1	147·9
1976	174	84·2	80·3	70·6	81·1	119·6	145·9
1977	612	89·9	86·5	83·6	91·6	112·2	130·8
1978	176	98·0	88·4	76·1	89·1	124·4	159·9
Face-trained coalminers							
1973	687	41·7	38·2	89·0	93·9	119·2	139·4
1974	653	51·2	47·6	89·4	95·8	114·1	135·9
1975	675	74·2	69·2	85·0	93·1	117·3	139·7
1976	691	80·5	74·8	84·1	91·7	119·5	142·8
1977	626	84·6	78·6	86·3	91·5	120·9	140·4
1978	545	109·1	103·4	77·4	85·5	118·8	141·8
Electricians—installation and maintenance—plant etc							
1973	800	43·2	41·8	67·6	82·0	120·3	142·4
1974	869	49·5	47·0	69·9	82·4	123·2	148·2
1975	803	62·4	59·7	68·7	82·8	122·7	145·5
1976	957	72·5	69·6	68·4	83·6	121·9	144·2
1977	885	79·3	76·3	68·6	83·8	122·0	145·8
1978	891	91·8	88·2	68·4	81·2	122·7	145·8
Supervisors of clerks							
1973	1,164	41·6	40·6	69·9	82·4	114·1	135·2
1974	1,109	49·7	49·3	71·4	81·8	114·3	132·0
1975	1,215	59·7	58·2	72·4	84·0	114·9	136·4
1976	966	72·6	72·4	71·6	83·3	113·1	126·0
1977	1,073	76·7	76·5	74·4	84·7	113·1	123·9
1978	1,024	84·8	84·6	73·5	85·0	111·2	125·7
Policemen							
1973	795	43·6	42·4	68·2	83·5	118·2	142·9
1974	619	46·8	44·7	69·8	85·0	121·7	150·0
1975	707	62·1	60·0	73·3	85·5	117·6	138·7
1976	759	76·0	73·2	71·5	84·9	116·6	143·6
1977	808	78·3	74·9	73·8	83·5	117·9	145·9
1978	812	88·4	86·1	74·9	84·9	117·4	134·5
Bus and coach drivers							
1973	724	40·0	39·4	73·1	84·1	115·9	131·4
1974	645	46·7	46·0	72·4	84·8	117·1	133·5
1975	643	63·7	63·5	71·3	83·8	117·3	131·1
1976	672	71·6	71·1	71·3	84·0	115·1	132·7
1977	680	77·3	76·4	71·5	84·9	116·5	132·7
1978	625	87·3	85·8	71·4	83·7	118·2	135·7

Table H.1 (*continued*)

Year	Number in sample	Mean £ pw	Median £ pw	Lowest decile %	Lower quartile %	Upper quartile %	Highest decile %
Welders—skilled							
1973	423	43·2	40·5	70·8	84·2	122·3	144·7
1974	463	47·6	46·6	68·8	83·9	116·3	135·6
1975	525	61·6	59·2	70·8	83·3	119·6	143·4
1976	643	72·1	68·0	73·0	84·7	120·0	142·5
1977	651	78·9	73·8	72·4	85·0	120·4	144·8
1978	635	87·3	82·0	72·3	86·4	121·2	146·6
Inspectors and testers (metal and electrical)							
1973	741	40·5	39·1	76·5	86·6	116·3	135·7
1974	748	44·7	43·7	75·0	87·9	116·2	130·3
1975	683	58·2	56·4	75·6	86·4	117·7	135·7
1976	704	68·8	65·7	77·9	87·7	119·5	135·1
1977	734	74·6	72·0	77·2	87·4	117·1	133·7
1978	639	85·2	81·8	77·7	87·7	115·8	137·5
Welfare workers							
1973	237	41·6	37·4	68·2	83·1	132·1	157·9
1974	217	44·1	40·0	62·4	81·1	130·5	156·5
1975	303	55·7	51·3	69·5	81·0	129·2	156·5
1976	388	70·2	64·1	68·2	81·7	130·8	157·5
1977	391	78·6	72·1	69·1	82·4	128·3	153·5
1978	423	83·6	79·9	69·9	82·2	120·2	143·8
Sales supervisors							
1973	304	41·9	38·0	68·4	79·2	123·2	162·4
1974	291	45·8	42·7	67·2	77·7	123·4	149·8
1975	203	57·7	54·1	67·7	78·9	123·5	147·6
1976	191	65·1	63·2	65·0	78·6	120·0	143·8
1977	237	72·0	69·9	63·3	76·4	123·5	143·4
1978	223	75·5	70·3	71·2	82·5	126·5	151·9
Machine tool operators (not setting up)							
1973	695	39·7	38·4	72·4	83·7	120·0	138·5
1974	693	45·4	44·3	73·1	84·6	117·2	135·5
1975	679	55·2	53·7	73·8	85·1	116·8	134·6
1976	786	64·3	62·3	75·2	86·3	116·7	136·8
1977	725	71·1	69·8	73·7	84·6	114·4	133·2
1978	782	81·2	78·9	72·8	85·2	116·4	137·8
Bus conductors							
1973	196	37·1	36·1	76·3	87·2	115·8	132·1
1974	152	40·2	38·9	74·2	87·4	118·3	136·2
1975	156	59·9	60·2	71·3	84·6	115·9	124·4
1976	158	68·0	65·3	72·2	85·9	120·5	141·1
1977	142	74·3	71·0	76·2	86·6	119·5	140·7
1978	119	82·7	78·8	78·7	88·1	121·0	136·7

Table H.1 (*continued*)

Year	Number in sample	Mean £ pw	Median £ pw	Lowest decile %	Lower quartile %	Upper quartile %	Highest decile %
Firemen							
1973	217	39·9	39·5	79·2	87·3	107·7	122·8
1974	230	48·0	47·2	78·4	87·0	109·9	125·1
1975	280	60·9	59·1	79·5	89·5	112·3	125·0
1976	264	65·4	65·0	82·3	90·7	107·9	116·8
1977	303	70·6	69·6	83·8	89·4	107·8	116·4
1978	285	79·6	78·1	81·8	90·5	113·0	123·0
Press and stamping machine operators							
1973	247	39·8	38·8	69·6	79·9	120·4	141·1
1974	255	46·1	44·4	73·5	86·3	119·1	137·7
1975	172	52·1	50·6	73·2	84·1	117·9	135·1
1976	185	64·7	63·6	71·6	84·0	115·2	136·0
1977	195	70·9	69·6	73·6	85·6	114·5	136·1
1978	198	82·4	80·8	70·9	82·6	116·6	137·4
Telephonists							
1973	146	35·0	30·1	76·9	87·5	124·0	162·9
1974	131	43·5	37·4	73·9	86·9	122·5	185·4
1975	158	55·6	49·8	77·4	88·9	122·5	152·2
1976	151	62·0	59·3	79·7	90·4	112·1	134·9
1977	133	73·9	69·4	73·9	84·3	116·1	149·1
1978	119	73·1	68·1	74·9	86·6	121·9	147·2
Laboratory technicians							
1973	536	37·1	35·0	59·7	78·2	124·4	157·4
1974	518	39·8	37·8	66·0	80·2	124·8	152·6
1975	469	55·1	52·6	64·7	79·5	121·0	153·3
1976	593	66·0	61·6	68·7	82·5	121·9	154·1
1977	580	72·2	67·4	71·2	82·7	122·7	155·0
1978	572	79·2	73·7	68·1	81·7	125·8	154·0
Railway guards							
1973	123	35·8	34·8	72·1	86·0	115·4	134·5
1974	124	38·7	38·1	73·8	87·9	115·5	131·9
1975	113	56·3	54·3	74·4	85·5	118·5	134·7
1976	115	66·1	64·2	76·5	85·6	118·1	134·0
1977	105	69·8	68·2	79·1	86·9	112·4	127·3
1978	98	77·5	74·6	75·4	86·3	116·9	129·4
Supervisors/foremen—caretaking, cleaning, etc							
1973	104	37·0	35·0	72·2	83·5	123·8	143·8
1974	94	42·0	41·8	67·8	77·2	116·0	133·3
1975	89	57·0	54·8	68·4	79·5	118·4	146·4
1976	84	69·6	68·0	65·2	80·9	115·4	148·5
1977	114	73·3	71·0	67·9	82·7	118·8	138·9
1978	110	82·7	80·5	62·7	81·0	117·6	147·0

Year	Number in sample	Mean £ pw	Median £ pw	Lowest decile %	Lower quartile %	Upper quartile %	Highest decile %
Repetitive assemblers (metal and electrical)							
1973	539	37·9	36·9	70·2	83·5	119·9	136·6
1974	541	43·1	41·7	73·5	85·3	119·4	135·0
1975	508	52·4	50·0	74·0	88·2	119·6	140·3
1976	518	61·5	60·5	72·2	84·9	114·8	132·3
1977	626	68·1	66·2	74·1	84·9	117·2	135·7
1978	604	76·8	74·7	71·5	84·9	117·5	139·3
Plumbers, pipe fitters							
1973	530	38·4	37·1	72·2	82·6	118·7	139·2
1974	461	44·9	42·3	72·7	83·5	122·8	143·9
1975	534	57·1	52·4	74·5	84·2	127·6	159·9
1976	553	65·5	60·2	76·0	85·7	127·1	155·8
1977	529	70·8	64·5	76·7	85·0	128·2	160·7
1978	557	81·9	74·4	73·4	84·3	122·9	155·9
Bricklayers							
1973	530	40·6	38·2	73·2	83·7	120·0	146·4
1974	489	45·8	42·3	76·2	85·9	122·9	150·7
1975	414	56·1	51·8	76·6	87·2	122·0	152·9
1976	504	62·9	57·8	75·7	87·0	124·5	151·2
1977	449	69·5	64·7	81·2	87·9	118·9	141·9
1978	433	77·0	71·8	76·4	85·2	123·5	152·8
Finance, insurance, etc clerks							
1973	373	37·2	35·5	60·2	79·7	122·2	147·8
1974	413	42·2	40·6	60·2	77·7	122·1	150·8
1975	394	50·3	50·0	61·2	75·8	119·9	141·1
1976	366	61·1	58·2	67·6	78·9	123·2	145·6
1977	391	63·2	62·5	63·2	79·8	119·3	139·1
1978	412	75·6	71·6	62·4	79·6	126·5	150·9
Motor vehicle mechanics—skilled							
1973	1,118	34·3	33·1	59·4	79·8	124·6	150·0
1974	1,015	39·4	38·7	62·6	80·5	119·6	141·7
1975	912	49·9	48·6	63·9	80·6	121·9	144·1
1976	1,134	57·7	56·0	63·9	80·9	120·7	144·9
1977	990	64·5	62·3	65·6	81·6	120·2	145·5
1978	1,077	73·0	70·7	65·0	80·4	121·1	147·1
Refuse collectors, dustmen							
1973	275	31·4	30·3	76·5	87·8	117·8	133·0
1974	222	35·7	34·5	75·4	89·9	116·0	131·5
1975	271	49·4	47·7	81·1	90·0	115·5	132·8
1976	273	57·6	56·1	84·3	91·2	113·6	127·8
1977	272	64·5	62·9	81·1	88·1	112·3	128·4
1978	283	70·2	67·5	82·7	90·0	114·9	129·5

Table H.1 (*continued*)

Year	Number in sample	Mean £ pw	Median £ pw	Lowest decile %	Lower quartile %	Upper quartile %	Highest decile %
Cash handling clerks							
1973	664	33·9	32·7	64·8	82·7	118·9	143·5
1974	673	38·2	36·7	66·4	81·2	120·8	146·2
1975	559	51·5	48·4	63·4	79·9	126·3	157·0
1976	528	58·3	56·8	67·9	81·3	119·8	141·6
1977	515	63·7	60·7	69·9	83·7	122·8	144·5
1978	590	68·6	65·9	69·3	83·8	120·9	145·2
Packers, bottlers, canners, fillers							
1973	647	34·7	33·0	67·9	82·2	123·8	149·6
1974	628	39·1	37·4	66·7	80·8	123·9	149·5
1975	546	48·6	47·0	69·4	81·6	118·0	140·7
1976	546	58·1	56·8	67·5	82·7	119·9	142·4
1977	592	64·7	61·8	68·0	82·0	122·7	149·9
1978	607	74·8	72·4	68·0	81·0	120·0	141·0
Shipping and travel clerks							
1973	235	35·6	32·6	64·8	80·6	132·0	162·7
1974	244	40·4	37·4	70·0	82·4	123·6	149·5
1975	211	51·4	46·6	66·6	81·1	123·4	167·6
1976	218	57·7	54·8	65·6	81·8	123·9	155·4
1977	219	63·1	59·6	61·2	83·9	124·0	157·9
1978	238	69·8	67·1	64·9	83·6	122·3	145·4
Production & materials controlling staff							
1973	917	33·3	31·8	69·8	84·1	120·1	144·3
1974	950	38·4	36·9	72·4	83·7	119·5	142·2
1975	986	47·1	45·4	72·4	85·6	118·5	139·2
1976	971	56·8	54·5	74·1	85·7	117·4	137·3
1977	1,026	61·6	59·1	75·3	86·6	116·6	136·5
1978	1,027	69·3	67·1	73·5	85·4	118·4	137·9
Footwear workers							
1973	—	—	—	—	—	—	—
1974	146	42·2	41·8	62·9	73·7	125·6	143·0
1975	114	45·1	42·5	70·7	84·3	126·8	152·0
1976	123	54·9	53·0	66·7	81·7	121·5	139·5
1977	129	60·8	57·3	66·3	82·6	124·7	150·9
1978	134	68·5	65·3	69·1	84·5	120·7	150·6
Costing & accounting clerks							
1973	1,043	31·4	30·5	62·5	80·5	120·4	146·8
1974	989	35·7	34·3	66·3	82·9	122·2	146·8
1975	997	45·8	44·6	67·6	83·1	118·6	143·7
1976	1,122	54·4	52·8	71·5	83·4	117·5	138·9
1977	1,167	59·6	58·0	71·1	83·4	116·5	136·8
1978	1,115	66·1	63·6	71·2	83·2	118·3	140·3

Table H.1 (*continued*)

Year	Number in sample	Mean £ pw	Median £ pw	Lowest decile %	Lower quartile %	Upper quartile %	Highest decile %
General clerks & clerks not included elsewhere							
1973	2,198	29·2	28·1	63·1	80·7	119·7	146·2
1974	2,107	35·0	34·0	69·3	83·3	115·6	139·5
1975	1,982	43·6	41·2	70·2	85·0	119·0	144·9
1976	2,027	54·4	52·7	68·0	82·5	118·1	140·7
1977	1,906	59·0	57·5	70·2	82·5	116·2	138·9
1978	1,650	64·9	62·4	70·2	83·3	117·8	142·9
Records & library clerks							
1973	373	32·6	30·9	70·8	84·7	120·2	148·6
1974	320	35·6	33·5	70·2	82·2	122·0	144·3
1975	252	48·5	45·9	73·3	83·9	121·3	145·8
1976	292	54·7	52·4	71·4	86·3	120·2	141·9
1977	274	60·7	58·3	72·6	86·3	118·0	141·2
1978	310	69·7	67·3	68·8	81·8	118·2	145·3
Registered & enrolled nurses & midwives							
1973	199	26·2	24·2	67·5	78·7	133·6	154·8
1974	160	31·6	30·9	64·8	78·4	117·9	143·3
1975	148	50·2	49·0	63·8	76·0	123·3	153·9
1976	188	56·8	53·6	75·0	82·6	120·7	144·0
1977	177	60·5	56·9	74·8	83·3	123·7	148·2
1978	189	63·1	58·4	74·6	80·2	125·5	160·0
Storekeepers etc							
1973	2,148	31·5	30·1	70·2	82·5	122·2	145·3
1974	2,002	35·9	34·4	71·2	82·8	121·8	144·3
1975	1,911	45·5	43·5	71·7	82·8	121·1	144·5
1976	2,054	53·7	51·8	70·4	82·7	119·9	144·0
1977	1,932	59·3	56·6	71·9	84·1	120·2	145·5
1978	1,953	68·1	64·6	70·5	82·0	121·0	148·7
Chefs/cooks							
1973	290	30·9	29·6	62·5	78·1	124·3	153·2
1974	251	36·9	35·7	60·7	78·0	124·7	150·2
1975	243	47·7	45·9	58·4	78·7	125·4	152·1
1976	253	52·1	50·9	59·6	77·2	122·6	150·5
1977	267	56·9	54·6	56·7	75·0	126·3	157·7
1978	276	64·7	60·2	56·2	71·4	128·3	167·7
Other motor vehicle mechanics							
1973	149	35.9	34·3	63·9	79·5	126·4	153·2
1974	167	39·8	39·9	54·8	74·5	121·4	144·3
1975	163	44·6	40·8	61·4	82·2	135·1	165·4
1976	79	54·9	53·8	61·1	71·3	122·1	152·5
1977	84	59·6	52·0	76·5	86·5	142·3	166·5
1978	114	66·2	64·8	68·3	76·8	120·7	144·9

Table H.1 (*continued*)

Year	Number in sample	Mean £ pw	Median £ pw	Lowest decile %	Lower quartile %	Upper quartile %	Highest decile %
Postmen, mail sorters & messengers							
1973	—	—	—	—	—	—	—
1974	1,269	41·3	36·9	73·7	80·1	134·9	171·1
1975	1,347	53·8	48·5	73·6	82·0	129·4	165·7
1976	1,370	66·8	61·0	79·0	87·3	126·5	157·5
1977	1,354	69·4	64·3	78·8	86·8	122·1	150·7
1978	1,305	74·0	67·7	76·8	83·4	129·7	157·3
Tailors, cutters, dressmakers etc							
1973	—	—	—	—	—	—	—
1974	110	36·0	35·2	65·4	81·0	122·0	139·3
1975	91	42·2	42·1	63·6	82·1	118·9	134·0
1976	105	49·6	48·4	70·8	87·7	114·9	131·3
1977	111	55·6	55·3	68·2	82·9	116·9	130·2
1978	91	62·6	59·8	68·2	84·8	125·7	144·1
Salesmen, shop assistants & shelf fillers							
1973	1,090	30·7	26·8	60·7	78·1	131·9	173·5
1974	994	34·1	30·5	65·1	80·4	127·5	164·0
1975	747	41·1	37·9	64·6	81·4	124·7	160·7
1976	822	45·9	41·5	68·4	83·0	126·0	156·6
1977	822	50·6	45·7	68·4	81·3	123·3	162·9
1978	799	61·2	52·3	67·4	78·6	128·5	174·6
General farm workers							
1973	326	25·2	23·6	82·3	89·0	120·1	140·6
1974	268	32·4	29·4	73·9	85·6	135·1	160·2
1975	390	36·6	34·0	82·5	88·8	121·5	147·1
1976	439	46·0	43·1	83·4	89·6	120·1	138·8
1977	466	50·9	46·9	83·6	90·2	121·5	145·8
1978	444	56·0	52·8	81·1	86·9	123·2	139·4
Waiters							
1973	149	26·0	23·7	47·3	69·9	140·5	174·6
1974	114	31·5	32·1	47·9	65·8	123·4	148·8
1975	98	38·4	38·0	50·4	74·0	130·3	147·9
1976	95	48·1	43·5	49·4	69·8	142·0	185·1
1977	96	44·8	41·0	56·6	66·7	139·0	180·7
1978	80	48·0	45·0	56·3	72·2	140·0	163·9
Mechanical engineers							
1973	—	—	—	—	—	—	—
1974	289	59·8	58·1	67·5	80·6	116·3	141·9
1975	241	79·3	78·2	66·6	81·3	121·1	137·5
1976	281	95·8	96·1	64·6	81·3	117·0	138·7
1977	310	101·9	101·7	67·0	85·4	114·2	130·9
1978	354	113·3	110·8	69·8	83·2	117·6	135·9

Table H.1 (*continued*) **Trends in Earnings of Selected Occupations; 1973–1978**
Average gross weekly earnings, medians and quantile points as a percentage of the median; 1973 to 1978

Women

Quantiles as % of median

Year	Number in sample	Mean £ pw	Median £ pw	Lowest decile %	Lower quartile %	Upper quartile %	Highest decile %
Teachers in establishments for further education							
1973	105	49·9	48·7	67·4	82·7	121·2	140·5
1974	104	54·9	53·5	66·7	81·6	119·6	147·3
1975	142	77·2	75·0	66·9	84·1	120·2	143·1
1976	160	96·5	91·8	76·6	85·8	118·7	141·6
1977	175	99·1	94·8	75·5	87·6	119·4	136·7
1978	169	102·3	99·1	74·9	87·1	117·5	133·4
Nurse administrators and executives							
1973	423	36·1	36·0	76·4	85·9	110·6	127·0
1974	361	37·8	38·0	72·7	83·6	110·8	128·7
1975	359	63·6	65·5	58·5	84·5	112·4	125·0
1976	489	72·8	76·1	61·3	85·3	107·8	117·5
1977	525	78·2	80·8	74·1	87·6	107·3	114·6
1978	479	80·5	82·0	77·3	89·6	107·3	115·2
Secondary teachers							
1973	693	39·9	37·2	68·9	82·2	127·8	153·1
1974	652	45·3	43·3	70·6	82·3	122·3	144·8
1975	807	63·9	62·0	67·8	82·1	119·4	139·5
1976	972	78·8	76·8	72·0	81·5	116·6	140·1
1977	1,008	82·3	79·8	72·4	82·9	117·8	137·2
1978	1,013	90·1	88·1	71·9	82·8	118·3	135·2
Primary teachers							
1973	1,098	36·1	33·8	75·4	82·4	127·7	144·2
1974	953	41·1	39·4	73·1	83·9	122·8	140·9
1975	1,267	57·7	55·0	73·4	83·9	123·8	139·8
1976	1,643	73·9	72·0	74·3	84·2	118·7	134·0
1977	1,615	78·2	76·2	75·4	85·1	118·9	131·8
1978	1,584	86·0	84·4	75·2	86·6	116·1	129·3
Supervisors of clerks							
1973	580	30·3	28·6	70·5	84·1	122·9	150·7
1974	558	37·5	35·9	67·7	81·0	124·3	149·3
1975	658	46·3	44·3	73·2	85·9	121·1	142·6
1976	625	57·4	55·7	69·1	82·5	122·2	141·1
1977	770	62·1	60·4	69·7	83·4	122·8	138·4
1978	775	69·3	66·9	73·6	84·8	119·8	138·2

Table H.1 (continued)

Quantiles as % of median

Year	Number in sample	Mean £ pw	Median £ pw	Lowest decile %	Lower quartile %	Upper quartile %	Highest decile %
Welfare workers							
1973	381	29·6	29·1	59·2	75·9	122·2	144·2
1974	351	31·7	31·8	60·3	75·1	116·3	139·5
1975	437	45·5	43·4	66·2	80·6	122·2	151·9
1976	503	54·7	51·8	62·2	79·0	121·9	152·9
1977	554	60·6	58·0	64·4	80·4	123·1	148·3
1978	615	64·3	62·6	66·5	79·8	119·9	146·0
Machine tool operators (not setting up)							
1973	183	22·5	22·3	71·3	83·7	114·1	132·1
1974	114	25·7	24·9	77·5	89·9	115·6	131·5
1975	130	35·0	35·5	70·4	84·3	111·6	121·1
1976	120	46·1	45·6	71·6	87·0	112·7	131·6
1977	133	52·6	53·7	71·0	84·0	108·7	126·7
1978	127	56·5	54·8	73·4	83·9	119·2	135·4
Laboratory technicians							
1973	191	26·4	24·4	67·6	81·2	124·7	151·4
1974	203	29·2	27·0	69·3	82·4	123·1	154·9
1975	187	41·1	39·6	68·2	83·3	119·6	138·4
1976	248	50·0	47·4	71·1	85·6	119·7	144·8
1977	228	56·7	53·5	76·6	87·7	117·0	145·5
1978	237	63·6	59·5	78·8	88·7	117·1	144·5
Secretaries, shorthand typists							
1973	2,740	24·6	23·8	68·9	83·0	119·4	139·8
1974	2,480	29·0	28·1	71·4	83·5	119·2	138·2
1975	2,482	36·8	36·1	70·4	83·3	117·5	136·5
1976	2,481	45·2	44·0	69·7	83·4	118·3	137·1
1977	2,574	51·1	49·9	72·6	85·7	116·8	134·9
1978	2,505	57·6	55·6	74·6	85·1	116·9	137·1
Registered & enrolled nurses & midwives							
1973	1,421	22·7	21·2	66·8	80·4	127·5	158·5
1974	964	26·0	24·5	68·4	82·1	124·9	154·8
1975	1,144	42·8	39·4	72·9	81·3	126·3	160·5
1976	1,493	49·7	46·4	80·1	86·3	120·9	155·2
1977	1,577	52·4	49·7	80·7	86·3	116·5	144·2
1978	1,641	54·0	51·2	78·6	84·7	118·0	149·0
Inspectors & testers							
1973	132	22·3	21·3	78·2	86·3	119·5	136·4
1974	148	26·9	24·9	83·4	92·1	119·1	141·5
1975	87	35·6	35·3	74·3	88·0	109·4	133·9
1976	105	46·0	45·7·	74·2	90·5	112·0	123·6
1977	109	49·8	49·5	80·7	89·8	110·0	122·3
1978	112	56·6	56·6	76·7	87·6	109·1	127·8

286

Table H.1 (continued)

Quantiles as % of median

Year	Number in sample	Mean £ pw	Median £ pw	Lowest decile %	Lower quartile %	Upper quartile %	Highest decile %
Telephonists							
1973	729	21·4	21·4	68·9	82·9	113·1	126·5
1974	629	25·0	25·0	71·1	81·3	112·4	128·6
1975	601	34·6	34·7	69·6	81·0	114·0	131·9
1976	632	41·2	41·8	67·6	79·8	115·7	128·2
1977	588	47·1	47·0	70·0	82·0	115·1	129·5
1978	582	49·7	48·8	73·5	84·9	114·3	129·3
Records & library clerks							
1973	630	21·4	20·1	73·7	83·9	121·8	146·4
1974	522	25·0	23·7	74·5	85·1	120·8	142·2
1975	459	34·8	33·7	72·4	84·7	115·4	138·2
1976	660	42·8	41·4	72·8	87·2	117·2	136·7
1977	552	47·9	46·8	74·4	86·2	116·5	135·6
1978	616	52·8	51·3	73·3	87·0	117·0	134·8
General clerks & clerks not included elsewhere							
1973	4,025	21·9	21·2	70·0	83·6	121·1	138·6
1974	3,911	26·9	26·6	69·1	81·5	118·8	136·7
1975	4,199	34·7	34·0	73·0	86·1	117·8	132·8
1976	4,285	43·1	42·6	69·7	83·9	117·0	133·6
1977	4,271	47·7	46·6	73·6	86·8	116·9	133·0
1978	3,991	51·9	50·7	73·5	86·4	116·9	132·6
Nursing auxiliaries & assistants							
1973	563	19·3	18·6	77·2	88·3	115·7	132·3
1974	646	21·1	20·3	74·0	86·8	116·3	137·1
1975	414	35·4	34·2	79·6	90·4	114·6	129·4
1976	444	43·5	43·1	79·6	90·2	109·6	124·3
1977	427	47·4	46·5	83·6	90·7	111·8	126·2
1978	454	47·9	46·7	83·1	91·9	110·4	123·6
Repetitive assemblers (metal and electrical)							
1973	677	21·2	20·8	74·4	86·1	114·1	130·7
1974	682	25·2	24·6	75·8	86·5	115·4	133·3
1975	539	33·9	33·0	76·0	87·3	115·7	132·1
1976	615	42·8	42·6	75·2	87·3	112·7	127·2
1977	676	46·8	46·0	75·9	89·5	112·8	126·7
1978	673	54·1	52·8	76·9	88·5	113·4	129·7
Shipping and travel clerks							
1973	120	23·9	21·6	68·5	83·2	128·0	164·3
1974	112	27·5	26·5	65·4	80·5	121·0	147·2
1975	114	36·9	33·9	66·4	85·4	124·4	165·6
1976	161	44·3	42·8	68·4	81·3	120·5	143·7
1977	156	47·6	45·5	67·3	83·5	123·5	147·8
1978	179	54·2	51·4	67·6	84·4	122·7	146·4

Table H.1 (*continued*)

Year	Number in sample	Mean £ pw	Median £ pw	Lowest decile %	Lower quartile %	Upper quartile %	Highest decile %
Cash handling clerks							
1973	744	22·2	21·0	70·8	81·8	123·5	149·0
1974	861	25·9	24·8	70·2	83·3	119·8	147·1
1975	758	33·8	32·5	70·3	80·9	119·5	143·2
1976	738	41·4	40·2	70·4	82·3	119·7	141·6
1977	788	46·7	45·2	75·2	85·1	119·3	137·2
1978	860	52·9	51·0	73·8	84·2	120·8	139·2
Finance, insurance etc clerks							
1973	298	24·9	23·2	67·5	80·7	124·7	153·5
1974	271	27·7	26·3	70·6	85·4	120·3	146·7
1975	282	37·1	34·9	69·3	81·9	120·8	153·5
1976	373	43·3	42·2	72·0	83·2	116·9	138·0
1977	341	47·4	45·2	74·1	84·3	123·3	142·3
1978	369	53·5	51·4	68·7	82·7	123·1	143·3
Costing and accounting clerks							
1973	1,304	21·2	19·9	72·7	85·9	123·4	148·1
1974	1,227	24·9	23·4	74·9	85·9	123·0	147·6
1975	1,463	32·9	31·5	75·1	86·4	118·0	139·8
1976	1,814	40·4	38·9	73·2	84·3	120·1	139·6
1977	2,075	45·9	44·9	74·0	85·0	117·3	133·6
1978	2,098	51·2	49·8	74·1	85·0	117·9	133·2
Press and stamping machine operators							
1973	140	19·8	19·5	72·7	85·9	114·7	129·0
1974	131	23·9	23·3	71·4	84·1	115·1	127·8
1975	99	31·4	30·5	73·1	84·6	117·7	138·9
1976	106	40·7	41·0	66·3	82·2	116·5	125·7
1977	106	45·3	44·3	69·2	85·7	117·1	136·5
1978	124	52·8	52·0	68·1	84·1	117·3	133·9
Packers, bottlers, canners, fillers							
1973	878	20·0	19·4	72·8	84·0	116·9	137·3
1974	930	22·9	22·2	73·7	86·6	117·6	137·2
1975	785	31·4	30·8	70·9	84·2	117·0	136·1
1976	791	39·2	38·6	69·3	83·8	117·9	134·2
1977	812	44·2	43·8	71·9	84·1	114·1	130·1
1978	853	49·4	48·5	73·8	85·5	115·0	131·0
Other typists							
1973	1,277	20·4	19·8	73·3	86·2	117·0	135·4
1974	1,275	23·9	23·5	73·0	85·2	116·0	133·9
1975	989	31·9	31·7	73·0	84·1	114·0	128·7
1976	1,137	39·8	39·1	71·1	83·6	117·9	133·5
1977	1,225	43·8	43·6	73·5	86·2	113·8	126·5
1978	1,242	50·1	49·4	76·4	87·7	114·0	128·7

Quantiles as % of median

Year	Number in sample	Mean £ pw	Median £ pw	Lowest decile %	Lower quartile %	Upper quartile %	Highest decile %
Sales supervisors							
1973	187	21·4	20·0	76·5	85·6	121·2	150·8
1974	185	24·9	23·3	78·7	89·3	119·6	145·0
1975	176	33·6	32·5	72·9	83·7	119·0	139·7
1976	159	40·4	38·5	74·9	86·4	117·7	137·9
1977	188	46·4	43·2	80·5	91·3	118·8	142·3
1978	202	51·1	47·3	79·4	90·6	118·5	151·6
Home and domestic helpers, maids							
1973	561	18·0	17·7	63·4	83·1	116·7	141·4
1974	418	22·6	21·9	64·4	82·8	122·0	143·6
1975	544	32·5	32·0	64·1	84·0	120·0	136·3
1976	728	39·9	40·0	68·1	83·9	115·0	130·9
1977	686	43·0	42·8	71·9	85·7	114·1	131·4
1978	601	47·8	46·6	71·1	85·6	114·5	130·0
Production and materials controlling clerks							
1973	482	21·1	19·8	75·6	85·7	119·9	148·2
1974	472	24·1	22·8	79·9	87·6	117·7	143·9
1975	449	31·6	30·5	75·6	86·2	118·6	138·4
1976	513	39·2	38·0	74·6	85·5	117·6	136·6
1977	607	43·6	42·3	75·3	87·7	115·4	136·8
1978	741	50·8	49·1	76·5	86·7	117·3	136·0
Storekeepers etc							
1973	195	19·7	18·9	73·8	84·4	120·7	135·6
1974	164	23·3	22·7	75·1	85·3	116·7	133·6
1975	182	31·8	30·8	70·8	85·6	118·6	139·5
1976	202	38·8	37·6	70·3	85·7	117·0	140·1
1977	199	43·1	41·9	76·3	85·9	117·7	133·9
1978	189	50·0	47·1	74·9	85·0	120·9	144·4
Footwear workers							
1973	—	—	—	—	—	—	—
1974	163	26·8	25·4	71·3	83·8	125·2	147·0
1975	91	32·8	30·6	70·8	85·2	119·5	165·1
1976	102	40·5	37·6	70·6	82·0	121·7	161·0
1977	135	43·0	40·6	71·2	84·2	122·5	152·2
1978	129	47·8	46·4	72·5	81·0	117·6	141·4
Other cleaners							
1973	648	17·1	16·6	67·3	84·0	118·0	142·0
1974	593	21·7	21·4	67·9	81·5	117·0	137·2
1975	419	31·7	30·7	67·4	83·8	120·6	139·5
1976	442	37·2	36·5	62·7	83·8	121·7	139·3
1977	428	40·7	40·2	68·3	83·1	119·4	134·2
1978	410	46·6	44·7	70·7	85·5	120·6	143·3

Table H.1 (*continued*)

Year	Number in sample	Mean £ pw	Median £ pw	Lowest decile %	Lower quartile %	Upper quartile %	Highest decile %
Chefs/cooks							
1973	468	19·3	18·4	75·9	86·3	116·2	142·5
1974	404	23·2	22·0	75·0	85·4	123·0	145·0
1975	429	32·4	30·5	78·0	88·3	119·2	142·7
1976	446	38·1	36·6	76·1	87·2	117·6	139·8
1977	450	42·0	39·4	79·6	88·0	119·1	144·2
1978	454	46·4	43·7	80·2	87·5	117·6	141·2
Sewing machinists, textiles							
1973	735	19·1	18·3	70·1	84·0	119·7	141·8
1974	723	22·8	22·2	69·6	83·3	116·9	141·8
1975	644	29·1	28·1	72·4	84·1	119·4	140·9
1976	675	34·9	33·5	72·6	84·5	120·6	140·0
1977	696	39·3	38·3	73·0	83·8	116·7	134·8
1978	721	45·2	43·0	75·7	85·5	119·9	142·8
Counter hands							
1973	550	17·6	16·4	72·1	84·8	123·3	150·7
1974	396	20·6	19·6	69·4	82·0	123·9	150·5
1975	389	29·2	27·7	71·0	80·8	123·4	146·2
1976	455	35·0	32·6	74·1	86·6	123·4	148·0
1977	453	39·8	37·6	71·1	84·7	122·0	144·7
1978	450	44·3	41·1	74·9	85·9	123·9	145·7
Receptionists							
1973	297	18·4	17·2	70·6	83·8	122·6	148·7
1974	301	21·1	20·2	72·0	84·4	120·4	141·8
1975	342	27·8	26·2	75·3	86·0	121·1	147·3
1976	332	33·3	31·1	75·5	87·8	123·0	147·9
1977	373	37·5	35·9	72·5	85·7	118·4	143·9
1978	354	41·5	40·7	72·3	83·7	116·0	133·5
Salesmen, shop assistants and shelf fillers							
1973	1,964	16·1	15·3	75·8	87·9	115·4	137·5
1974	1,803	18·8	18·1	77·4	88·2	113·5	137·3
1975	1,636	25·3	24·5	74·4	87·1	114·0	132·6
1976	1,801	29·8	29·1	77·0	88·0	113·5	128·8
1977	1,786	34·7	34·0	77·6	89·4	110·2	125·7
1978	1,803	38·4	37·3	78·4	89·2	110·9	130·8
Waiters							
1973	171	16·3	14·6	67·8	81·5	132·7	162·2
1974	171	19·7	17·7	70·3	84·8	128·3	168·6
1975	116	26·8	25·2	63·2	78·3	126·9	162·0
1976	108	33·8	30·8	65·5	74·8	129·0	171·1
1977	118	36·3	32·6	71·9	83·3	127·6	163·1
1978	117	39·2	35·6	70·0	87·1	125·2	159·5

Age-earnings Relationships for
Full-time Males and Females; 1978

Figure I.1   Median, and highest and lowest deciles of gross weekly earnings by age group for men in certain occupations; 1978.

Figure I.2   Median, and highest and lowest deciles of gross weekly earnings by age group for women in certain occupations; 1978.

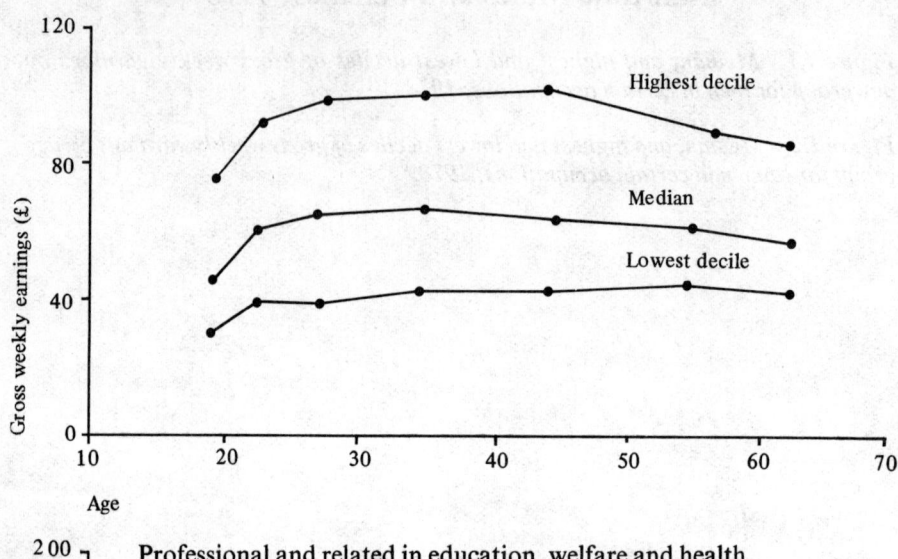

Figure I.1 Median, and Highest and Lowest Deciles of Gross Weekly Earnings by Age Group for Men in Certain Occupations; 1978

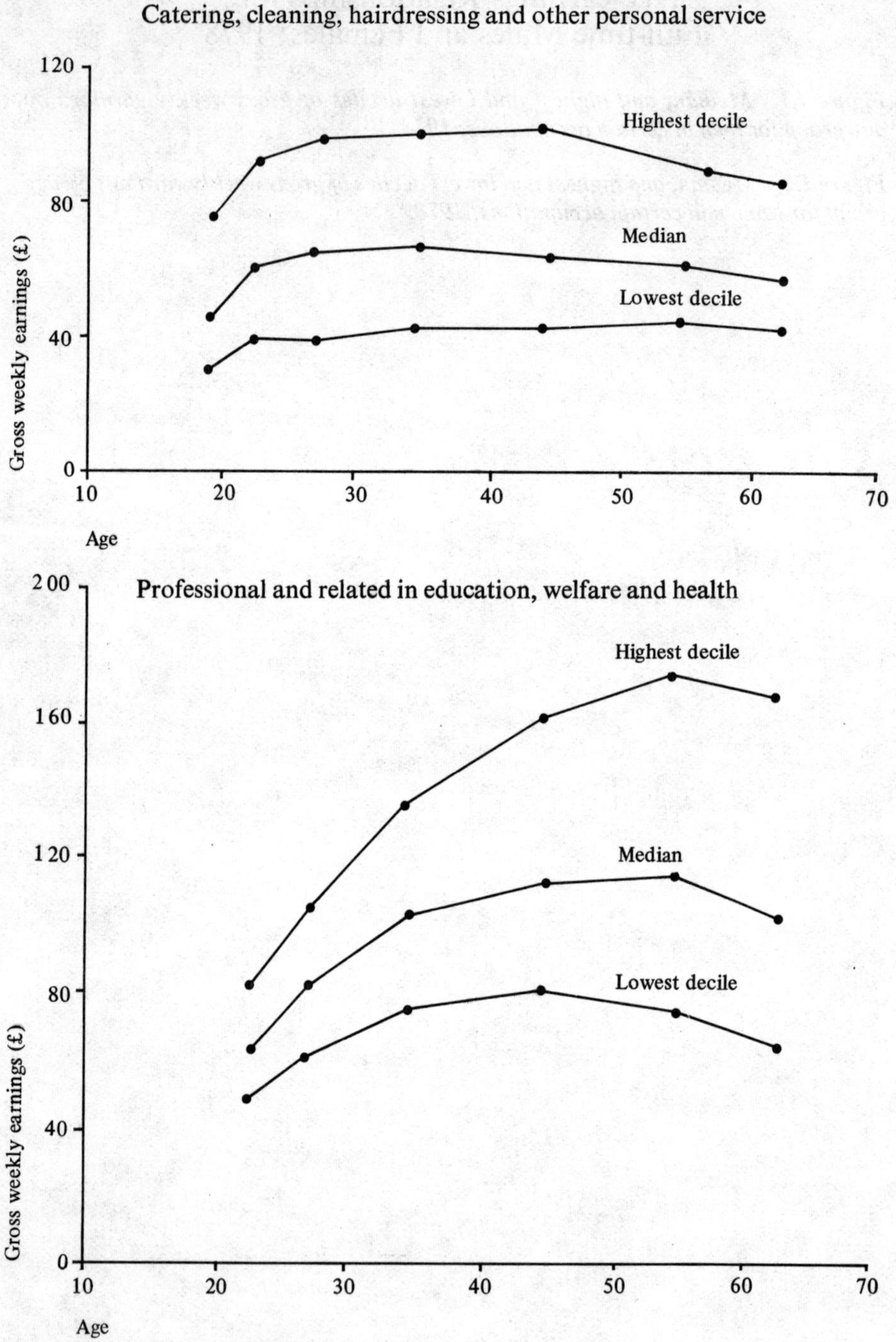

Catering, cleaning, hairdressing and other personal service

Professional and related in education, welfare and health

Source: New Earnings Survey 1978.

292

Figure I.1 (*continued*)   **Median, and Highest and Lowest Deciles of Gross Weekly Earnings by Age Group for Men in Certain Occupations; 1978**

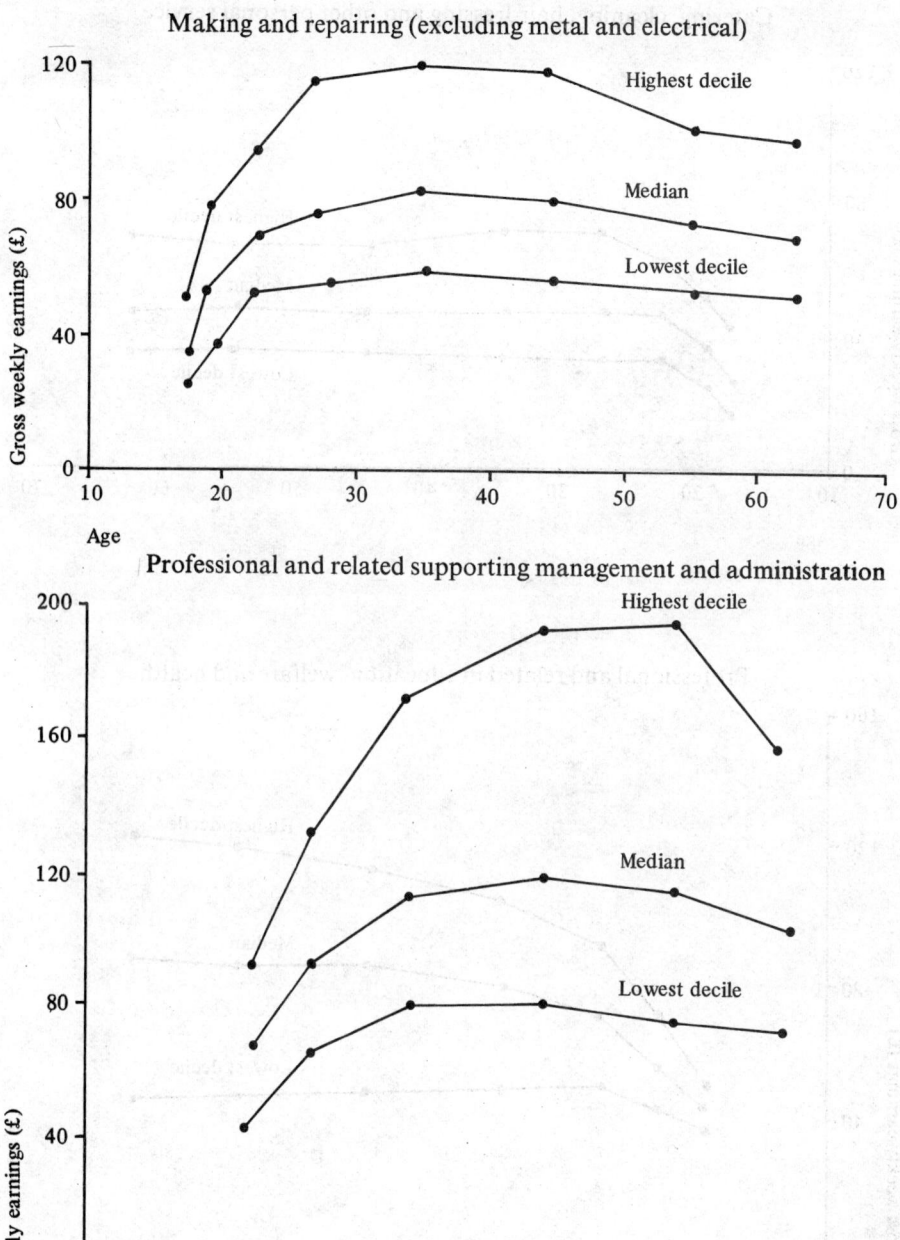

Making and repairing (excluding metal and electrical)

Professional and related supporting management and administration

Source: New Earnings Survey 1978.

Figure I.2 Median, and Highest and Lowest Deciles of Gross Weekly Earnings by Age Group for Women in Certain Occupations; 1978

Catering, cleaning, hairdressing and other personal service

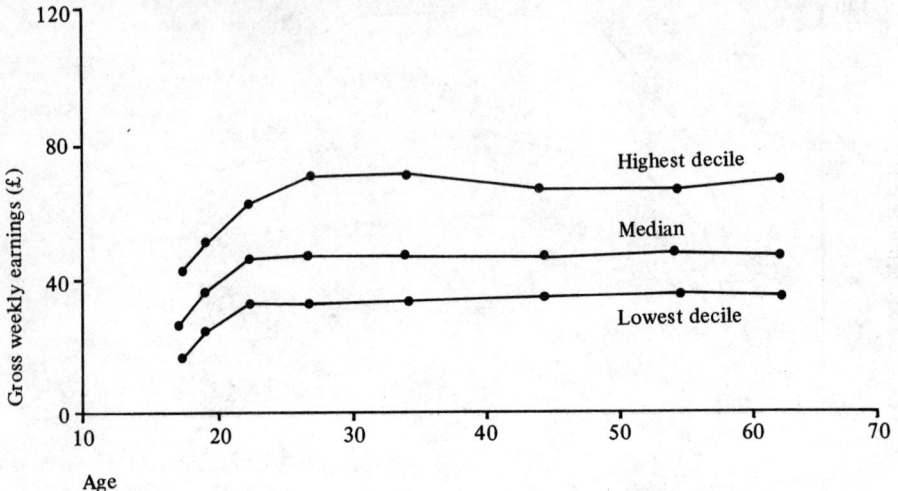

Professional and related in education, welfare and health

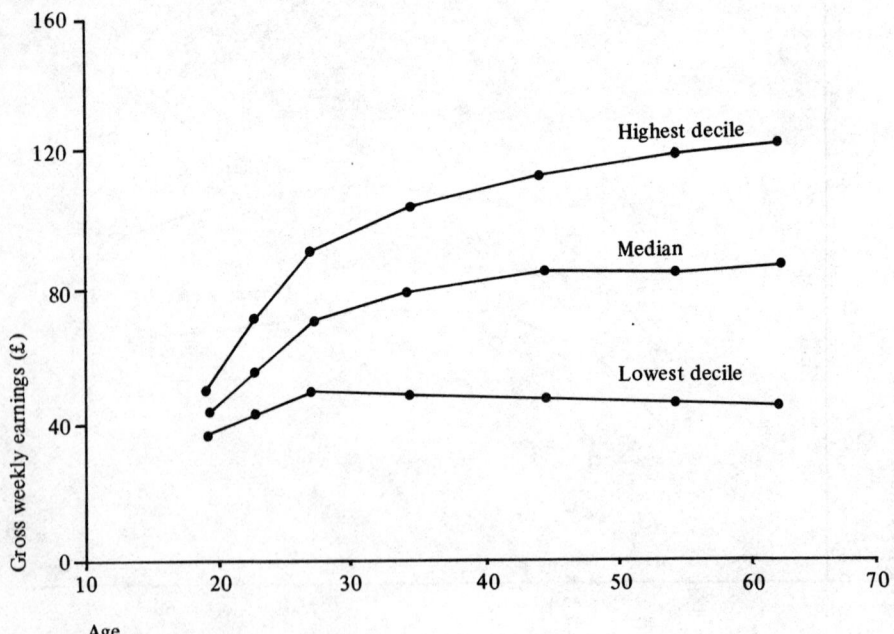

Source: New Earnings Survey 1978.

Making and repairing (excluding metal and electrical)

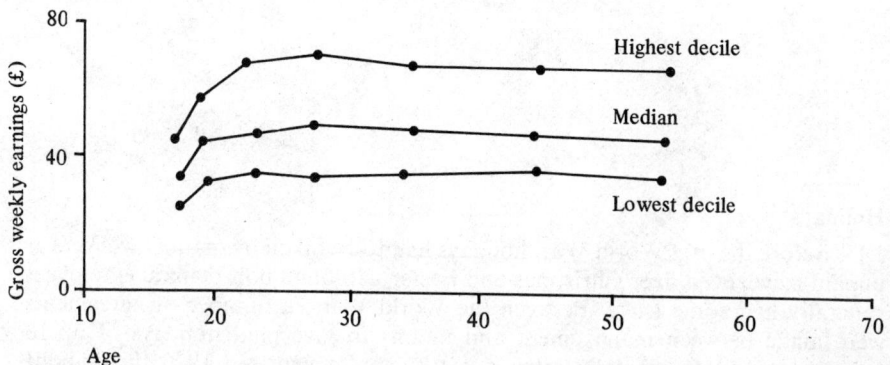

Professional and related supporting management and administration

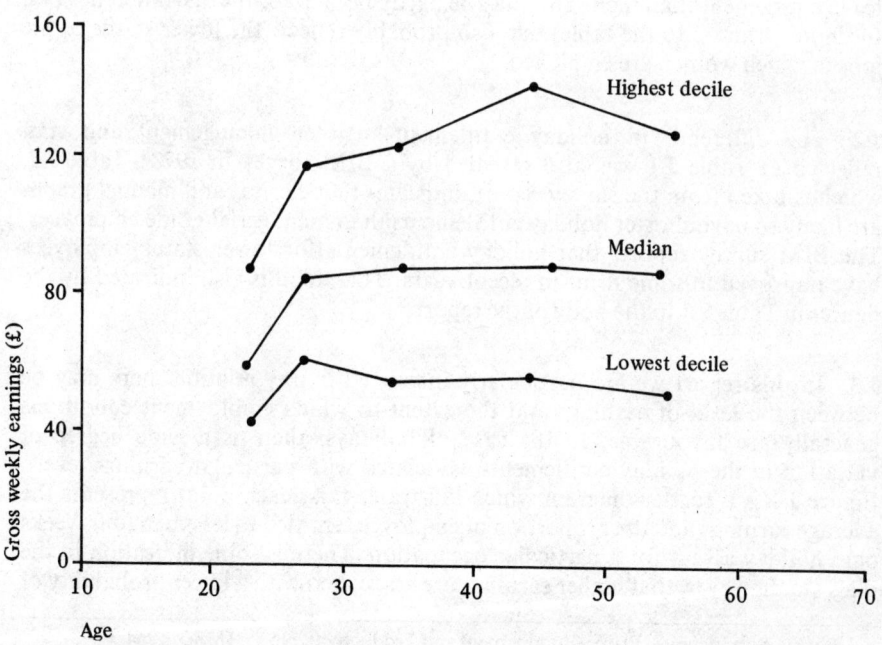

Source: New Earnings Survey 1978.

295

Holidays and Hours in Different Occupations

Holidays

J.1 Before the first World War, holidays had to be taken by manual workers as unpaid leave, even over Christmas and Easter, although non-manual employees generally had some leave. Between the World Wars, a number of agreements were made between management and unions to give paid holidays of up to twelve days a year, usually after a year's employment. In 1929 the Labour Government introduced five days statutory holiday plus eight days paid holiday a year for its employees. By 1964 96 per cent of manual workers were entitled to two weeks' basic paid holiday, with 15 per cent getting additional days for long service[1]. Table J.1 shows that by 1974 a third week's paid holiday had become almost standard, while a quarter of male manual employees and three-fifths of male non-manual employees were entitled to four weeks or more paid holiday a year. The table also shows that for almost every occupation, women had a lower leave entitlement than men. This may be partly because of the age difference (see footnotes 1 and 2 to the table) but also probably reflects the lower status of the jobs in which women are employed.

J.2 The difference in holiday entitlement between management and staff reflected in Table J.1 was also revealed by a BIM survey in 1978[2]. Table J.2, which is taken from the survey report, indicates that clerical and manual grades are likely to have shorter holiday entitlements than managerial grade employees. The BIM survey reports that holiday entitlements for lower status employees have improved in some firms in recent years. This trend is also indicated by the figures in Table 9.1 in the body of the report.

J.3 In this report we are particularly interested in any relation there may be between the level of earnings and the extent to which employment conditions generally are favourable. In the case of holidays, there is a wide degree of variation in the holiday entitlements associated with particular earnings levels. Figure J.1 is a scatter diagram which illustrates this: each point represents the average earnings and the proportion of employees entitled to less than four weeks paid holiday a year for a particular occupation. There is some indication in the diagram, however, that higher earnings are associated with a lower probability of

---

[1] Statistics on Incomes, Prices, Employment and Productivity No 8, HMSO, 1964.
[2] H Murlis, Employee benefits: a survey of practice in 400 companies, *Management Survey Report No 37*.

Table J.1 Length of Annual Holiday Entitlements by Occupational Group; 1974

Great Britain   Percentages

Occupation Group		3 Weeks+		4 Weeks+	
		Men[1]	Women[2]	Men	Women
I	Management (general management)	94·6	n.a.	63·4	n.a.
II	Professional and related supporting management and administration ..	98·3	98·2	67·1	51·2
III	Professional and related in education, welfare and health	97·5	97·5	88·8	84·8
IV	Literary, artistic and sports	97·1	93·1	67·2	43·7
V	Professional and related in science, engineering, technology and similar fields	98·5	96·2	72·0	44·0
VI	Managerial (excluding general management)	95·5	90·7	51·0	27·4
VII	Clerical and related	97·6	94·1	53·3	32·3
VIII	Selling	91·9	84·8	26·0	10·8
IX	Security and protective services ..	97·4	95·1	48·2	16·7
X	Catering, cleaning, hairdressing and other personal service	89·5	89·8	12·9	11·5
XI	Farming, fishing and related ..	88·5	80·4	6·8	3·9
XII	Materials processing (excluding metals)	92·9	90·6	27·0	10·9
XIII	Making and repairing (excluding metal and electrical)	94·3	91·5	29·6	15·3
XIV	Processing, making and repairing and related (metal and electrical) ..	96·1	92·7	23·3	9·5
XV	Painting, repetitive assembling and related	95·6	91·4	21·1	12·1
XVI	Construction, mining and related not identified elsewhere	93·9	n.a.	27·9	n.a.
XVII	Transport operating, materials moving and storing and related	93·1	92·6	20·2	15·0
XVIII	Miscellaneous	93·4	93·4	22·1	10·3
All manual employees		94·3	90·9	23·3	12·2
All non-manual employees		97·0	94·0	60·4	42·1

Source: NES 1974.

Notes: [1] Full-time men over 21.
[2] Full-time women over 18.

less than four weeks' holiday and this is borne out by the result of a simple linear regression. There is a significant relationship (characterised by the straight line entered on the graph) between level of earnings and the proportions in each occupation with holiday entitlement of less than 4 weeks. This relationship explains only about 30 per cent of the total variation in the proportions.

J.4 Britain has eight statutory public holidays and any further holiday entitlements (apart from those laid down in Wages Council Orders) are the results of collective agreements or individual arrangements between employer and employee. Basic holiday entitlements are not laid down by law. The ILO Convention of June 1978 stated that all employees should receive paid holidays of not less than three working weeks after one year's service, however, and in the EEC at least three weeks is the standard holiday entitlement for employees in

Table J.2   Basic Annual Holiday Entitlements by Employee Category[1]; 1977

Percentages of companies

Working days	All employees with same entitlement (N=208)	Employees having varying entitlement					
		Directors (N=190)	Senior managers (N=192)	Middle managers (N=192)	Junior managers (N=192)	Clerical (N=192)	Manual (N=184)
Less than 15 ..	—	—	—	—	—	1	1
15	12	1	1	5	13	26	29
16–19	7	—	3	7	16	30	34
20	66	34	41	49	43	35	31
21–24	9	19	26	27	26	8	5
25 or more ..	7	45	29	13	3	1	—
	100	100	100	100	100	100	100

Source: BIM.

Notes: [1] Excluding Public Holidays.
   N=number of companies.

manual jobs. In France there is a statutory entitlement of four weeks. Figure 9.1 in Chapter 9 shows that the United Kingdom has shorter holidays generally than any other EEC country apart from Ireland; it is likely that the UK will catch up in the next few years, under the influence of EEC practice.

J.5   Annual holidays are also likely to increase in coming years because of the general pressure from trade unions for the improvement of employee benefits and because of the employment problem. The BIM surveys on employee benefits found that a number of companies intended to extend holidays or to give equal allowances to all employees once counter-inflation legislation was relaxed[1].

---

[1] Employee Benefits Today, *BIM Management Survey Report No* 19, 1974; Employee Benefits, *BIM Management Survey Report No 37, 1978.*

Figure J.1   Average Gross Weekly Earnings and Annual Holiday Entitlement by Occupational Group; 1974

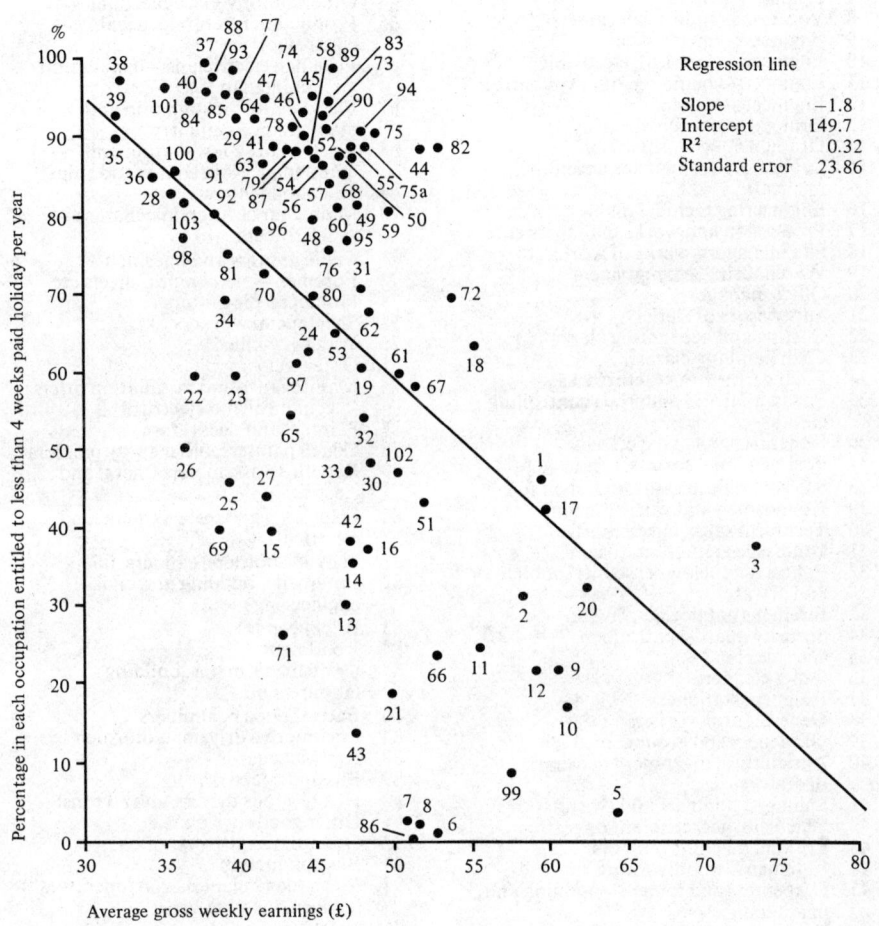

Source: New Earnings Survey 1974.

LIST OF OCCUPATIONS IN FIGURE J.1 (1974)

1 Accountants
2 Systems analysts, computer programmers
3 Marketing and sales managers executives
4 Civil servants (administration and executive) nie
5 Teachers in establishments for further education
6 Secondary teachers
7 Primary teachers
8 Vocational/Industrial trainers
9 Engineers—mechanical
10 Engineer—electrical, electronic
11 Engineers—planning, quality control
12 Engineers—others
13 Draughtsmen—engineering
14 Draughtsmen—other
15 Laboratory technicians (scientific, medical)
16 Engineering technicians etc
17 Production and works managers etc
18 Site managers, clerks of works etc
19 Warehousing, etc managers
20 Office managers
21 Supervisors of clerks
22 Costing and accounting clerks
23 Cash handling clerks
24 Finance, insurance, etc clerks
25 Production and materials controlling clerks
26 General clerks and clerks nie
27 Postmen, mail sorters, messengers
28 Salesmen, shop assistants, shelf fillers
29 Roundsmen and van salesmen
30 Technical sales representatives
31 Other sales representatives and agents
32 Policemen (below sergeant) (public and private)
33 Firemen (public and private)
34 Security guards, patrolmen
35 Caretakers
36 Other cleaners
37 Railmen, stationery
38 General farm workers
39 Gardeners and groundsmen
40 Agricultural machinery drivers/operators
41 Spinners, doublers and twisters
42 Chemical, gas, etc plant operators
43 Printing machine minders
44 Foremen—woodworking
45 Carpenters and joiners—building and maintenance
46 Carpenters and joiners—others
47 Woodworking machinists and sawyers
48 Moulding machine operators (rubber, plastics)
49 Furnacemen
50 Moulders, coremakers, diecasters
51 Foremen—engineering machinery
52 Press and machine tool setters
53 Roll turners, roll grinders
54 Other centre lathe turners
55 Machine tool setter-operators
56 Machine tool operators

57 Press stamping machine operators
58 Automatic machine attendants/minders
59 Toolmakers, tool fitters etc
60 Metal working production fitters (fine limits)
61 Foremen—installation and maintenance of machines etc
62 Maintenance fitters (non electrical)
63 Motor vehicle mechanics (skilled)
64 Other motor vehicle mechanics
65 Production fitters (electrical/electronic)
66 Foremen electricians—installation and maintenance
67 Electricians—installation and maintenance—plant, etc
68 Electricians—installation and maintenance—premises and ships
69 Telephone fitters
70 Maintenance fitters/mechanics—radio, TV etc
71 Cable jointers and linesmen
72 Foremen—metal pipes, sheets etc
73 Plumbers, pipe fitters
74 Sheet metal workers
75 Welders (skilled)
75a Other welders
76 Maintenance and installation fitters (mechanical and electrical)
77 Painters and decorators
78 Coach painters, other spray painters
79 Repetitive assemblers (metal and electrical)
80 Inspectors and testers (metal and electrical)
81 Packers, bottlers, canners, fillers
82 Foremen—building and civil engineering nie
83 Bricklayers
84 Roadmen
85 Craftsmen's mates, building labourers nie
86 Face-trained coalminers
87 Locomotive drivers, motormen
88 Railway guards
89 Bus and coach drivers
90 Heavy goods drivers (over 3 tons)
91 Other goods drivers
92 Other motor drivers
93 Bus conductors
94 Mechanical plant drivers/operators (civil engineering)
95 Crane drivers/operators
96 Fork lift, etc drivers/operators
97 Foremen—materials moving and storing
98 Storekeepers etc
99 Stevedores and dockers
100 Goods porters—warehouse, market etc
101 Refuse collectors, dustmen
102 Electricity power plant operators, switchboard attendants
103 General labourers (including engineering, shipbuilding)

The timing of leave

J.6 Industrial Relations Review and Report (IR-RR) carried out a survey, reported in December 1977, of holiday entitlements among 205 organisations employing over half a million people. 60 per cent of the organisations said their manual workers could not normally take more than 10 days together. 47 per cent of organisations had the same restriction on non-manual employees. 30 per cent place no restriction on non-manual employees and 23 per cent placed no restriction on manual employees.

Hours

J.7 The relationship between earnings and hours was explored by Layard *et al* in a recent Background Paper commissioned by the Royal Commission (see paragraph 9.7 of the main text). We used the 1977 New Earnings Survey to investigate the relationships further by plotting, for a large sample of occupations, average earnings against basic hours and against average hours worked. Figure J.2 is a scatter diagram showing the basic hours/basic earnings relation for different occupations. The observations in the bottom right-hand corner are largely for non-manual occupations but although it is fairly clear that non-manual employees have a shorter working week and relatively high earnings, these data, are not representative of all non-manual employees. There are many non-manual occupations for which "hours worked" is not a meaningful concept, and for which hours and hourly earnings are not recorded in the New Earnings Survey. Many people in professional jobs work outside office hours to maintain their professional competence, for example, while university academic staff spend time on preparation and research as well as actual teaching, those in management are likely to adapt their hours of work to the needs of the moment. For employees in most manual and many non-manual jobs, hours of work are generally laid down in their contract of employment. In 1977 basic weekly hours for most occupations were in the range $39\frac{1}{2}$–$40\frac{1}{2}$, regardless of wage levels. There is no clear association between hourly earnings and the length of the basic working week[1].

J.8 The relation between total hours worked per week (including overtime) and the basic hourly earnings is also unclear, as illustrated by Figure J.3. Overtime was worked in most manual occupations, somewhat more in those with low basic earnings than in those with high basic earnings. Those who are recorded in the 1977 NES as working an average of forty-eight or more hours a week are heavy goods drivers, security guards, bus and coach drivers, bus conductors, mechanical plant drivers, firemen, agricultural machinery drivers, stockmen, other motor vehicle drivers, and roundsmen. Their basic hourly earnings (before overtime) range from 113 pence per hour to 153 pence per hour. Those who worked an average of forty-three hours per week or less were nearly all non-manual employees whose employer specified the number of hours they worked, plus coalminers, telephone fitters, policemen, television maintenance fitters, gardeners and butchers. The range of earnings in this case was from 120 pence

---

[1] J Marquand found that, of the thirty-two industries below the lower quartile of average weekly earnings, only seven had above average weekly hours. "In general, workers with very low hourly rates of pay cannot be shown . . . to be working particularly long hours." "Which are the lower paid workers?" *British Journal of Industrial Relations*, 1967. This was still true in 1977, as shown by the data for broad occupational groups in Table 9.5.

Figure J.2   Normal Weekly Hours and Hourly Earnings by Occupational Group, Males; 1977

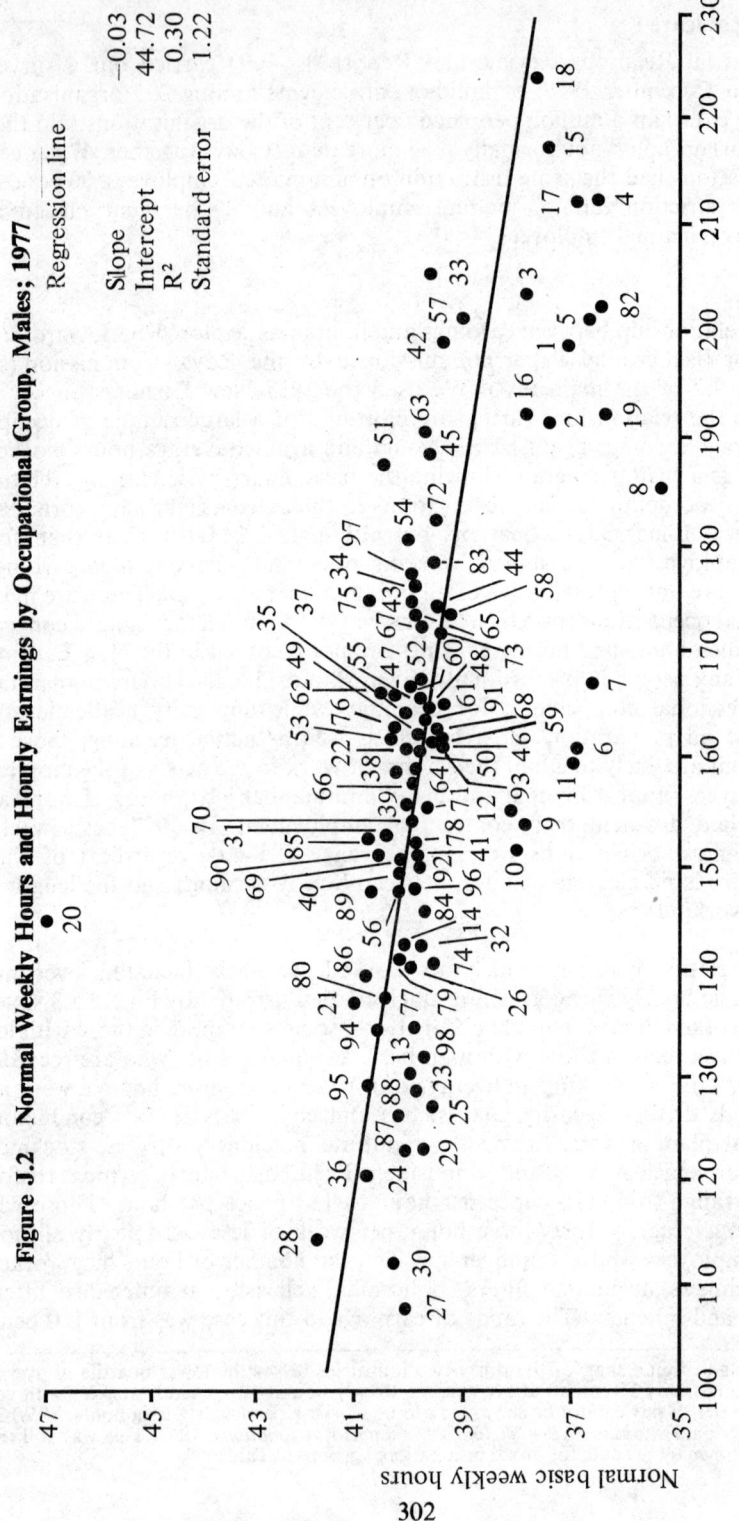

Regression line	
Slope	−0.03
Intercept	44.72
R^2	0.30
Standard error	1.22

Hourly earnings, excluding overtime pay and hours (pence)

Source: New Earnings Survey 1977.

302

Figure J.3 Average Hours Worked and Hourly Earnings by Occupational Group, Males; 1977

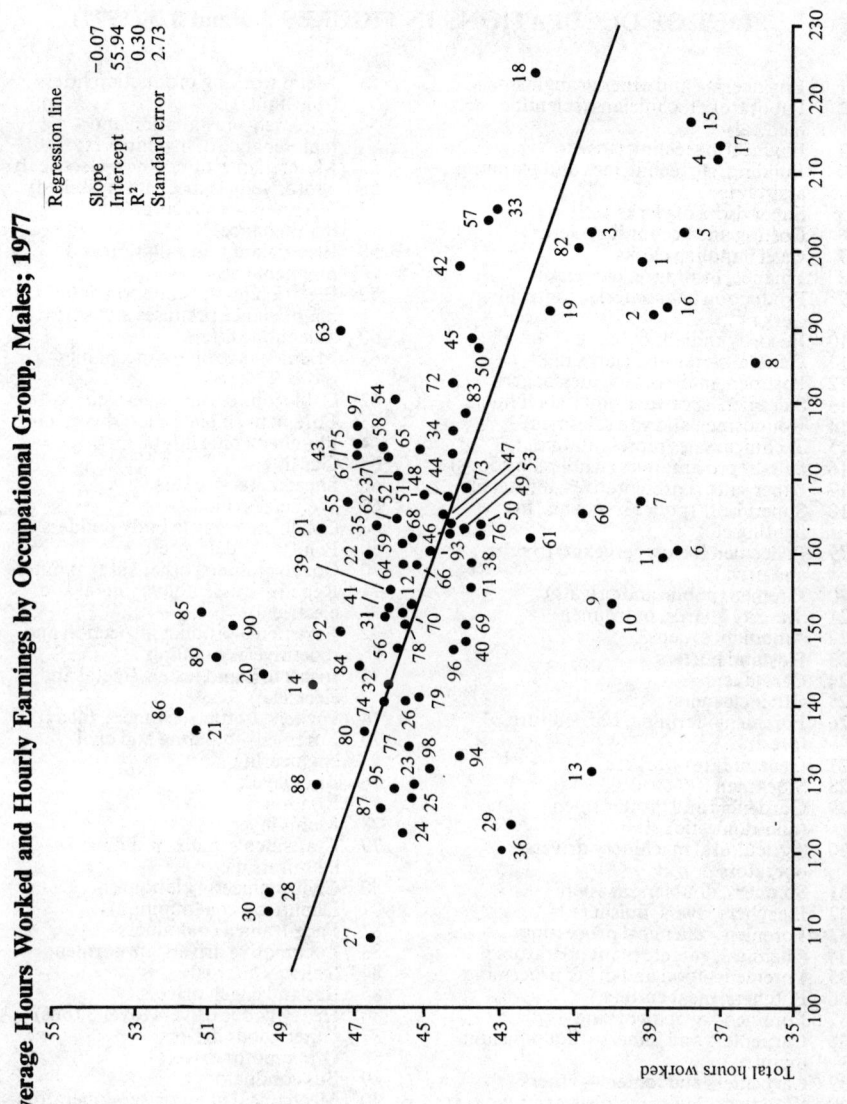

Regression line	
Slope	−0.07
Intercept	55.94
R²	0.30
Standard error	2.73

Total hours worked

Hourly earnings excluding overtime pay and hours (pence)

Source: New Earnings Survey 1977.

LIST OF OCCUPATIONS IN FIGURES J.2 and J.3 (1977)

1 Engineering and other draughtsmen
2 Laboratory technicians (scientific, medical)
3 Engineering technicians etc
4 Building, etc technicians and planning assistants
5 Supervisors of clerks
6 Costing and accounting clerks
7 Cash handling clerks
8 Finance, insurance, etc clerks
9 Production and material controlling clerks
10 Records and library clerks
11 General clerks and clerks nie
12 Postmen, mail sorters, messengers
13 Salesmen, shop assistants, shelf fillers
14 Roundsmen and van salesmen
15 Technical sales representatives
16 Sales representatives (wholesale goods)
17 Other sales representatives and agents
18 Supervisors (police sergeants, fire fighting etc)
19 Policemen (below sergeant) (public and private)
20 Firemen (public and private)
21 Security guards, patrolmen
22 Ambulance men
23 Hospital porters
24 Caretakers
25 Other cleaners
26 Foremen—farming, horticulture, forestry
27 General farm workers
28 Stockmen
29 Gardeners and groundsmen (non-domestic)
30 Agricultural machinery drivers/operators
31 Spinners, doublers, twisters
32 Bleachers, dyers, finishers
33 Foremen—chemical processing
34 Chemical, gas, etc plant operators
35 Foremen—food and drink processing
36 Butchers, meat cutters
37 Foremen—woodworking
38 Carpenters and joiners—building and maintenance
39 Carpenters and joiners—others
40 Woodworking machinists and sawyers
41 Moulding machine operators
42 Foremen—metal making and treating
43 Furnacemen
44 Moulders, coremakers, diecasters
45 Foremen—engineering, machinery
46 Press and machine tool setters
47 Other centre lathe turners
48 Machine tool setter—operators
49 Machine tool operators (not setting up)
50 Press and stamping machine operators
51 Foremen—production fitting (metal)
52 Toolmakers, tool fitters, etc
53 Metal working production fitters (fine limits)
54 Foremen—installation and maintenance of machines etc
55 Maintenance fitters (non-electrical)
56 Motor vehicle mechanics (skilled)
57 Foremen—installation and maintenance
58 Electricians—installation and maintenance—plant, etc
59 Electricians—installation and maintenance premises and ships
60 Telephone fitters
61 Maintenance fitters/mechanics—radio, TV etc
62 Cable jointers and linesmen
63 Foremen—metal pipes, sheets, etc
64 Plumbers, pipe fitters
65 Gas fitters
66 Sheet metal workers
67 Welders (skilled)
68 Coach and vehicle body builders
69 Painters and decorators
70 Coach painters, other spray painters
71 Repetitive assemblers (metal and electrical)
72 Foremen—product inspection and repetitive assembling
73 Inspectors and testers (metal and electrical)
74 Packers, bottlers, canners, fillers
75 Foremen—building and civil engineering nie
76 Bricklayers
77 Roadmen
78 Mains layers
79 Craftsmen's mates, building labourers nie
80 Civil engineering labourers
81 Deputies—coal mining
82 Face-trained coalminers
83 Locomotive drivers, motormen
84 Railway guards
85 Bus and coach drivers
86 Heavy goods drivers (over 3 tons)
87 Other goods drivers
88 Other motor drivers
89 Bus conductors
90 Mechanical plant drivers/operators (civil engineering)
91 Crane drivers/operators
92 Fork lift, etc drivers/operators
93 Foremen—materials moving and storing
94 Storekeepers
95 Goods porters—warehouse, market etc
96 Refuse collectors, dustmen
97 Electricity power plant operators, switchboard attendants
98 General labourers (including engineering, shipbuilding)

per hour to 224 pence per hour. Most employees (61 per cent of those in the individual occupations listed in the NES) worked an average of between forty-three and forty-eight hours per week. It is likely that the relation between industry and hours worked is more important than that between occupation and hours worked.

J.9   Most of the variation in hours was caused by the difference between manual and non-manual jobs. Most of this difference was caused by overtime working as can be seen from Table J.3. The difference in average basic hours was only two and a half hours per week, but the inclusion of overtime work increased this to seven hours per week. The relation between long hours (including overtime) and low basic rates of pay is weak; and adding overtime pay to basic pay has the effect of widening the dispersion of earnings slightly[1].

J.10   To test the relationship between hourly earnings and basic and average hours worked simple linear regressions were fitted. The regression lines are shown in Figures J.2 and J.3 and have a slight downward slope.

J.11   Employees in manual jobs work about the same number of hours as their counterparts in the EEC. Table J.4 gives the average weekly hours of work for manual employees in the different EEC countries[2]. Table J.5 shows the average hours worked by male employees in eleven different industries in the EEC.

---

[1] For NES 1977 data, we analysed the earnings of manual employees only, as overtime is not a meaningful concept in many non-manual jobs. The inclusion of overtime pay in weekly earnings reduced the ratio of the lowest decile to the median from 74 per cent to 70 per cent, and increased the ratio of the highest decile to the median from 137 per cent to 144 per cent.

[2] The figures include hours worked by employees who were absent for part of the week; this is why they look lower than the gross weekly hours in Figure 9.4.

Table J.3 Hours and Earnings of Full-time Men by Occupational Group; 1977

Great Britain

Occupational Category	Average weekly hours		Average gross hourly earnings	
	normal basic	overtime	excluding overtime	including overtime
			pence	pence
I Managerial (general management)	n.a.	n.a.	n.a.	n.a.
II Professional and related supporting management and administration	n.a.	n.a.	n.a.	n.a.
III Professional and related in education, welfare and health ..	n.a.	n.a.	n.a.	n.a.
IV Literary, artistic and sports ..	n.a.	n.a.	n.a.	n.a.
V Professional and related in science, engineering, technology and similar fields	n.a.	n.a.	n.a.	n.a.
VI Managerial (excluding general management)	n.a.	n.a.	n.a.	n.a.
VII Clerical and related..	37·3	2·8	167·1	167·8
VIII Selling	38·6	1·5	175·7	174·6
IX Security and protective service ..	39·7	6·1	171·5	172·1
X Catering, cleaning, hairdressing and other personal service	40·0	5·7	128·2	130·1
XI Farming, fishing and related ..	40·3	5·2	118·3	120·1
XII Materials processing (excluding metals)	40·1	5·8	153·8	155·2
XIII Making and repairing (excluding metal and electrical)	39·9	4·3	159·0	161·1
XIV Processing, making, repairing and related (metal and electrical) ..	39·8	5·4	166·4	169·4
XV Painting, repetitive assembling, product inspecting, packaging and related	39·7	4·6	156·6	158·7
XVI Construction, mining and related not identified elsewhere	39·7	5·2	158·5	159·6
XVII Transport operating, materials moving and storing and related ..	40·1	7·6	145·6	148·3
XVIII Miscellaneous	39·8	5·6	143·4	145·9
All non-manual occupations	37·3	1·4	227·9	227·2
All manual occupations	39·9	5·8	154·3	156·5
All occupations	38·9	4·1	181·5	181·1

Source: NES 1977, Table 86.

306

Unit: hours (and decimals)

Table J.4 Average Weekly Hours of Work per Manual Worker in the EEC; 1967 to 1977

	1967	1972		1973		1974		1975		1976		1977
	X¹	IV²	X	IV	X	IV	X	IV	X	IV	X	IV
Manufacturing industries												
W. Germany	42·8	43·0	43·0	43·0	42·8	42·0	41·6	40·4	40·6	41·4	42·2	41·8
France	45·7	44·1	44·1	43·7	43·5	43·1	42·8	41·7	41·5	41·7	41·6	41·3
Italy	44·7	42·0	42·0	41·7	41·9	41·7	41·7	41·4	41·5	41·5	41·7	—
Netherlands	45·2	43·2	43·3	43·2	43·2	42·5	41·8	40·6	40·7	40·9	41·3	40·9
Belgium	43·7	41·4	41·4	40·7	40·8	40·6	39·5	36·4	36·3	37·8	38·2	36·9
Luxembourg	43·9	42·3	42·4	42·1	42·3	43·0	42·4	40·1	40·8	39·5	40·6	40·3
United Kingdom	—	—	42·3	—	42·7	—	42·1	—	41·1	—	41·7	—
Building and civil engineering												
W. Germany	44·1	44·0	44·2	42·9	43·6	42·5	42·4	41·3	42·5	42·0	42·9	41·8
France	50·2	48·2	48·5	48·0	48·0	47·4	47·4	46·0	45·8	45·3	44·4	43·6
Italy	44·0	40·7	41·1	40·7	41·1	41·0	41·4	40·8	41·4	40·6	41·3	—
Netherlands	46·2	43·7	43·4	43·4	43·1	42·5	42·4	41·2	41·2	41·1	41·0	40·9
Belgium	44·7	44·0	43·2	41·8	41·9	42·2	39·2	38·0	40·2	39·2	39·4	38·2
Luxembourg	52·2	50·7	50·7	51·4	51·4	51·1	48·4	42·7	41·6	41·1	41·5	41·2
United Kingdom	—	—	46·6	—	46·8	—	46·4	—	44·8	—	44·0	—
All industries												
W. Germany	43·0	43·1	43·2	43·0	42·9	42·1	41·7	40·6	40·9	41·4	42·3	41·8
France	46·7	44·9	45·0	44·6	44·4	44·0	43·8	42·6	42·4	42·5	42·2	41·8
Italy	44·6	41·9	41·9	41·6	41·8	41·7	41·7	41·3	41·5	41·5	41·6	40·9
Netherlands	45·4	43·4	43·9	43·3	43·2	42·5	41·9	40·8	40·8	41·0	41·2	40·9
Belgium	43·8	41·8	41·7	40·9	41·0	40·9	39·5	36·8	37·1	38·2	38·5	37·3
Luxembourg	45·8	43·8	43·0	43·7	43·4	44·6	42·9	40·6	40·9	39·8	40·3	40·4
United Kingdom	—	—	43·0	—	43·4	—	42·9	—	41·8	—	42·2	—

Source: Eurostat, I–1978, Table 16.

Notes: ¹ Old series.
       ² New series.

307

Table J.5 Average Hours Worked per Week by Male Employees in EEC Countries by Industry; 1975

Industry sector	Average number of hours worked per week by Male employees in									
	West Germany	France	Italy	Nether-lands	Belgium	Luxem-bourg	United Kingdom	Ireland	Denmark	All EEC
1 Agriculture, forestry, fishing	46·5	48·0	43·0	46·5	47·8	45·3	49·5	49·6	45·7	45·9
2 Energy and water	41·0	40·5	41·5	39·3	40·3	40·4	41·9	40·5	40·7	41·2
3 Extraction and processing non-energy producing minerals and derived products chemical industry	41·1	41·4	40·5	39·7	40·9	40·2	43·1	43·9	40·7	41·6
4 Metal manufacture; mechanical electrical and instrument engineering	40·6	40·7	40·1	38·8	40·1	40·4	42·4	41·5	40·3	40·9
5 Other manufacturing industries	41·7	42·5	41·0	39·5	40·6	40·5	42·8	42·1	40·7	41·7
6 Building and civil engineering	41·6	43·9	41·9	39·6	40·7	41·4	44·6	42·4	39·7	42·6
7 Distributive trade, hotels, restaurants and cafes, repairs	43·4	45·3	43·6	42·3	42·5	42·3	44·1	43·1	41·8	43·9
8 Transport and communications	42·6	42·9	42·1	42·3	41·2	41·5	45·4	41·8	42·4	43·1
9 Financing, insurance etc	42·6	41·5	40·5	40·0	41·2	39·8	41·4	40·5	40·6	41·5
10 Public administration	41·3	42·8	41·0	39·8	41·3	40·1	42·5	42·6	41·5	41·7
11 Other services	43·4	39·7	38·5	39·1	36·7	39·8	40·8	41·5	40·0	40·3
12 All	41·8	42·6	41·1	40·2	40·6	40·7	43·1	42·6	41·0	42·0

Source: Eurostat, 1975 Labour Force Survey, Table IV/3.

Identified Trade Groups in the SPI

		Number of tax units in group; 1976/77
1	AGRICULTURE (including market gardening, fruit, flower and seed growing)	246,561
2	BUILDING AND CONTRACTING (construction of buildings, bridges, roads, etc and other civil engineering; jobbing building; carpenters, plumbers, gasfitters, decorators; electric wiring and contracting)	375,433
3	RETAIL DISTRIBUTION (including retail distribution of food and drink; excluding dealing in fuel, agricultural and industrial materials and machinery; excluding miscellaneous services)	224,183
4	CATERING (excluding hotels, motels, holiday camps, other residential establishments, sports and gaming clubs; including residential clubs, night clubs, public houses, restaurants, cafes, catering contractors)	64,685
5	MOTOR REPAIRS (wholesale and retail distribution of cars, motor cycles and cycles, garage and filling stations, motor and motor cycle repairs)	47,719
6	OTHER SERVICES (laundries, laundrettes, dry cleaners and dyers, boot and shoe repairing, hairdressing and manicure; welfare and community services not elsewhere specified; trade unions, trade associations; others assessed under cases I and II; hotels, motels, holiday camps, other residential establishments excluding clubs; letting of furnished and service flats, rooms, houses, offices and halls)	114,895
7	BARRISTERS	3,612
8	SOLICITORS	19,742
9	ACCOUNTANCY (qualified accountants, chartered or incorporated)	16,258

			Number of tax units in group; 1976/77

10 ARCHITECTURE .. .. — 7,907

11 ENGINEERING (civil, consulting, inspecting and mining engineers in private practice) .. .. — 5,976

12 MEDICINE .. .. — 22,639

13 DENTISTRY .. .. — 12,711

14 MANUFACTURING INDUSTRY (fuel, oils, greases; chemicals, drugs, pharmaceuticals; iron, steel, metals; instruments; shipbuilding, motor vehicles, cycles, aircraft, rolling stock; other mechanical and machinery, electrical and electronic; spinning and weaving, wool, textiles, leather, fur, clothing, footwear; food, drink, tobacco; timber, furniture, paper, printing, publishing; bricks, pottery, glass, cement, other building materials; musical instruments; linoleum, floor-covering, rubber; miscellaneous stationery; plastics not elsewhere specified; toys, games, sports requisites, baby carriages; brushes, brooms, mops; bone and ivory workings; and other miscellaneous) .. .. — 100,607

15 WHOLESALE DISTRIBUTION (including wholesale distribution of food and drink and petroleum products; excluding dealing in fuel, agricultural and industrial materials and machinery; excluding miscellaneous services) .. .. — 24,922

16 ROAD TRANSPORT (including road haulage, contracting for general hire or reward; tramway and omnibus services; taxis, car hire services, and coach tours) .. — 64,997

17 ENTERTAINMENTS AND GAMBLING (sport and recreation; betting and gambling; theatres and broadcasting; musicians, actors, entertainers; cinemas; film production) .. .. — 39,045

18 OTHER MEDICAL SERVICES .. .. — 8,354

19 SURVEYING.. .. .. — 5,147

20 ADVERTISING AND BUSINESS SERVICES (including market research) .. .. — 4,669

21 INSURANCE, STOCKBROKERS AND JOBBERS (including share brokers) .. .. — 9,815

22 ALL OTHER TRADE GROUPS (forestry and fishing; coal mines, other mining and quarrying; gas, electricity, water, railways, shipping; other transport, communications and storage; dealing in fuel, agricultural and industrial materials and machinery; brokers and agents not being property, theatre or financial agents; charitable, domestic and foreign government services; veterinary surgery; research and development services; literature and art, musical composition; accountants not in group 9; religion, education; other professional and scientific services; national and local government wages and salaries; pensions; property owning and management, house and estate agents, rent collecting agents; banking and finance except as in group 21)   237,824

TOTAL SELF-EMPLOYED (ALL TRADE GROUPS)   ..   1,657,701

Additional Summary Tables of Other Components of Income by Trade Group

Table L.1   Comparison of Incomes by Trade Groups: Losses and Capital Allowances[1]; 1976-77

Amounts of losses and capital allowances (excluding and including wife) as percentage of main source self-employment income (excluding wife) gross of losses and capital allowances; 1976–77

United Kingdom   Income unit: tax unit[2]

Trade group	Losses and Capital Allowances as percentage of main source self-employment income (excluding wife) gross of losses and capital allowances	
	Excluding wife	Including wife
	%	%
14 Manufacturing Industry	11·1	11·8
15 Wholesaling Distribution	10·1	10·4
16 Road Transport	20·3	21·4
17 Entertainment and Gambling	6·2	6·7
18 Other Medical Services	5·8	6·6
19 Surveying	3·3	3·3
20 Advertising and Business Services	4·6	4·9
21 Insurance, Stockbrokers and Jobbers	4·2	4·4
22 All Other Trade Groups	9·1	9·8

Source: SPI.

Notes: [1] Including stock relief.

        [2] Though the income unit is shown as "Tax Unit" (because of the nature of the SPI database), the figures do in fact relate to individuals (main source), except where otherwise stated.

312

Table L.2 Comparison of Incomes by Trade Groups: Retirement Annuity Relief and Other Deductions[1]; 1976-77

Numbers of tax units with retirement annuity relief and other deductions as percentages of total numbers of self-employed tax units and amounts of retirement annuity relief and other deductions as percentages of total self-employment incomes (excluding wives); 1976-77

United Kingdom   Income unit: tax unit[2]

Trade group	Retirement Annuity Relief		Other Deductions	
	Number of tax units as % of total number of self-employed tax units	Amount as % of total self-employment incomes (excluding wives)	Number of tax units as % of total number of self-employed tax units	Amount as % of total self-employment incomes (excluding wives)
	%	%	%	%
14 Manufacturing Industry ..	16·4	2·2	50·9	6·8
15 Wholesale Distribution ..	19·4	3·4	49·9	6·7
16 Road Transport	9·8	1·0	50·6	7·2
17 Entertainment and Gambling	7·1	1·4	38·0	8·4
18 Other Medical Services ..	18·9	1·9	38·9	7·2
19 Surveying	47·5	5·6	72·0	8·7
20 Advertising and Business Services	13·2	2·3	37·9	8·9
21 Insurance, Stockbrokers and Jobbers	21·3	3·9	59·7	11·8
22 All Other Trade Groups ..	15·8	2·6	46·3	8·5

Source: SPI.

Notes: [1] Building society interest allowable, other interest paid, small maintenance payments etc, Schedule E expenses, charges and family allowance deduction.
[2] See footnote 2 to Table L.1.

Table L.3 Comparison of Incomes by Trade Groups: Other Income[1]; 1976-77

Other income as a percentage of total self-employment income (excluding wives); 1976-77

United Kingdom   Income unit: tax unit[2]

Trade group	Other Income as % of total self-employment income (excluding wives)
	%
14 Manufacturing Industry	8·4
15 Wholesale Distribution..	13·2
16 Road Transport..	4·9
17 Entertainment and Gambling	12·8
18 Other Medical Services..	17·9
19 Surveying	15·4
20 Advertising and Business Services	29·5
21 Insurance, Stockbrokers and Jobbers	22·9
22 All Other Trade Groups	19·0

Source: SPI.

Notes: [1] Schedule D cases III to VI, Schedule A rents, Building Society interest, dividends from UK companies and any other income taxed before receipt.
[2] See footnote 2 to Table L.1.

Definitions of NES "Trade Groups"

		Number of employees in group; 1975

INDUSTRY BASIS

1 *AGRICULTURE* (farming and stock-rearing, agricultural contracting, market gardening, fruit, flower and seed growing)   1,364

2 *BUILDING AND CONTRACTING* (erection and repair of buildings, construction and repair of roads and bridges, erection of steel and reinforced concrete structures, other civil engineering including sewers, gas, water and electricity, erecting overhead lines, supports and aerial masts; extraction of coal from opencast workings etc; including building and civil engineering establishments of government, local authorities and New Town bodies, and on-site industrialised building; demolition work; asphalting, electrical wiring, flooring, glazing, installing heating and ventilating apparatus, painting, plastering, plumbing, roofing, including hire of contractors' plant and scaffolding)   8,013

3 *RETAIL DISTRIBUTION* (retail distribution of grocery, provisions and other food; confectionery, tobacco and newspapers, clothing and footwear, household goods, other non-food goods; including general stores).. ..   6,296

4 *CATERING* (restaurants, cafes, snack bars, public houses, clubs and catering contractors)   909

5 *MOTOR REPAIRS* (motor repairers, distributors, garages and filling stations)   2,066

16 *ROAD TRANSPORT* (omnibus and tramway service, taxis and private hire cars, road haulage contracting for general hire or reward, other road haulage)   2,821

		Number of employees in group; 1975

OCCUPATION BASIS

7 + 8   *BARRISTERS AND SOLICITORS* (judges, barristers, advocates and solicitors)   150

9   *ACCOUNTANCY* (accountants)   773

10   *ARCHITECTURE* (architects and town planners, town planning assistants, architectural and building technicians)   372

12   *MEDICINE* (medical practitioners)   243

13   *DENTISTRY* (dental practitioners)   20

16   *ROAD TRANSPORT* (road transport operating foremen, bus inspectors, bus and coach drivers, heavy goods drivers over 3 tons unladen weight, other goods drivers, goods drivers category unspecified, other motor drivers, bus conductors, drivers' mates, furniture removers)   4,111

19   *SURVEYING* (quantity surveyors, building, land and mining surveyors)   367

Effective Rates of Capital Transfer Tax on Bequests of Business Assets

N.1   In circumstances where half an estate is left to the surviving spouse and the other half, consisting of business assets, is left to a son, Table N.1 below shows the effective rates of tax for estates of various sizes in March 1974 and March 1978, respectively, ie before the introduction of capital transfer tax and after the introduction of the changes made by the Finance Act 1978. For the purpose of calculation, it has been assumed that asset values have risen in line with the Retail Prices Index. It will be seen that in the particular circumstances to which Table N.1 relates, the fall in the effective rate of tax due to the combined impact of both surviving spouse and business relief has indeed been very considerable.

N.2   Some idea of the impact of business relief alone can be obtained from Table N.2 below. This shows the same situation as in Table N.1 except that the estates do not contain any business assets. It will be seen that the effect of business relief is to reduce the effective rate of tax, in March 1978, on an estate of, say, £374,000, from 19·0 per cent (where the estate does not contain any business assets) to 5·6 per cent (where half the estate comprises business assets).

N.3   If it is assumed that an estate valued at £374,000 in March 1978 would have been valued at £200,000 in March 1974 at prices then current, the comparable effective rates of tax in March 1974 would have been 45 per cent where the estate did not contain any business assets and 37·7 per cent where half the estate comprised business assets and two-thirds of these qualified for estate duty business relief.

N.4   This comparison gives an incomplete picture however. The change in the rules for taxing transfers on death between husbands and wives makes a dramatic difference in the impact of tax on the death of the first spouse. But the new rules can be regarded as a postponement of liability rather than a total exemption. Under the previous arrangements, property covered by surviving spouse settlements would be liable to estate duty on the death of the first spouse and exempt on the death of the second. Under the new arrangements, liability is postponed until the death of the second spouse.

Table N.1 Effective Rates of Tax Applying where Half an Estate Passes to a Surviving Spouse and the Other Half, Consisting of Business Property, Passes to a Son; March 1974 and March 1978

Value of estates in March 1974	Effective rate of tax in March 1974[1]	Assumed value of estate in March 1978	Effective rate of tax in March 1978
£	%	£	%
15,000	—	28,000	—
20,000	—	37,400	—
30,000	—	56,100	—
40,000	5·2	74,800	—
50,000	9·4	93,500	—
60,000	13·0	112,200	0·27
80,000	19·1	149,600	1·1
100,000	23·9	186,900	2·1
150,000	32·4	280,500	4·0
200,000	37·7	374,000	5·6
500,000	50·6	934,500	10·6
1,000,000	57·1	1,869,500	12·8
2,000,000	60·4	3,739,000	14·5

Source: Written answers, House of Commons Hansard 9 June 1978, columns 288–90.

Note: [1] It has been assumed that two-thirds of the business property would have qualified for the estate duty business relief.

Table N.2 Effective Rates of Tax Applying where Half an Estate Passes to a Surviving Spouse; March 1974 and March 1978

Value of estates in March 1974	Effective rate of tax in March 1974	Assumed value of estate in March 1978	Effective rate of tax in March 1978
£	%	£	%
15,000	—	28,000	—
20,000	—	37,400	—
30,000	—	56,100	0·5
40,000	6·9	74,800	2·3
50,000	12·0	93,500	4·2
60,000	16·3	112,200	5·9
80,000	23·4	149,600	8·8
100,000	29·0	186,900	11·1
150,000	38·8	280,500	15·6
200,000	45·0	374,000	19·0
500,000	59·9	934,500	25·6
1,000,000	67·4	1,869,500	28·9
2,000,000	71·2	3,739,000	31·9

Source: as Table N.1.

Claims for Stock Relief

O.1   Tables O.1 and O.2 give details of the stock relief claimed in respect of the first reference period, ie 1973-74 and 1974-75. Table O.1 shows that the amount of relief claimed in 1974-75 for that two year period amounted to under £58 million. The self-employment income of the businesses which claimed that relief amounted to only £108 million for the two years 1973-74 and 1974-75. This amount of £108 million can be compared with total self-employment income of the main source self-employed as recorded in the 1974-75 and 1975-76 SPI of £8,309 million. Stock relief therefore represented only 0·7 per cent of total self-employment income in the first reference period.

O.2   Table O.1 analyses total relief claimed by range of income. It will be seen that, for those businesses which claimed stock appreciation relief, the relief was an important deduction against taxable profit equalling, on average, 53 per cent of profit before relief, with higher proportionate deductions in the lower income ranges.

Table O.1   Stock Relief Claimed by the Self-employed by Range of Profit; 1973–74 and 1974–75[1]

Lower limit of range of profit for the two year period	Number of cases (businesses)	Total relief claimed	Relief as percentage of profits in each range	Percentage of total relief	Average relief per case
£	No.	£ million	%	%	£ 000's
Negative	170	1·87	—	3·2	10·9
Nil	758	1·06	(113)	1·8	1·4
2,000	822	1·55	75	2·7	1·9
3,000	780	1·46	53	2·6	1·9
4,000	1,360	3·55	53	6·2	2·6
6,000	945	3·62	55	6·3	3·8
8,000	743	3·65	55	6·3	4·9
10,000	1,155	7·72	55	13·3	6·7
15,000	720	6·23	51	10·8	8·7
20,000	1,150	15·36	45	26·6	13·4
50,000	247	11·73	50	20·3	47·5
Total	8,850	57·80	53	100·0	—

Source: Derived from Inland Revenue data.

Note: [1] Amounts of profit and relief relate to the full 2 year base period April 1973 to March 1975.

O.3   Table O.2 shows the importance of stock relief to particular trade groups. It will be seen that agriculture claimed 31·0 per cent of the total amount of relief claimed, and that the retail trade claimed 25·9 per cent and manufacturing 15·8 per cent. Not surprisingly, stock relief was relatively small in construction (6·2 per cent) despite the large numbers of self-employed workers in that industry (many of whom are labour-only subcontractors).

Table O.2   Stock Relief Claimed by the Self-employed by Trade Group;
1973 to 1975

Trade group	Number of cases (businesses) —excluding losses	Average profit before relief	Total relief claimed	Relief as percentage of profit	Percentage of total relief
	No.	£ 000's	£ million	%	%
Agriculture.. ..	2,873	14·1	17·34	42·6	31·0
Manufacturing ..	758	16·7	8·85	70·0	15·8
Construction ..	432	12·1	3·48	67·0	6·2
Wholesale	223	15·0	2·30	69·0	4·1
Retail	3,092	8·0	14·46	58·0	25·9
Services (STC 78) ..	627	10·8	4·13	60·9	7·4
Professional ..	276	40·7	3·08	27·4	5·5
Rest..	381	11·9	2·24	49·4	4·0
Total	8,662	—	55·88	—	100·0

Source: Derived from Inland Revenue data.

O.4   There appear to be two principal reasons why the self-employed have not made use of the new relief against stock appreciation to the extent suggested by the allowance for stock appreciation given in the National Accounts. Firstly, the provision that only relief above 15 per cent of profit is deductible, means that the self-employed received rather harsh treatment. This is because the relevant profit figure is calculated before deduction of proprietors' drawings or salary whereas, for close companies, directors' fees will already have been deducted. To overcome this problem, the Government has reduced the profit restriction for unincorporated businesses from 15 per cent to 10 per cent for accounting periods ending in and after 1979–80.

O.5   Secondly, the tax relief is deferred, implying that if, in future years, the value of stocks held fall, that liability will again arise. This may have had a disincentive effect on small businesses which are more likely to experience good and bad years in terms of profitability. However, the Government has now enacted proposals for writing-off some of the deferred tax liabilities resulting from stock appreciation. They involve writing-off relief given for the first two years of the scheme at the end of the accounting period ending in 1978–79 and thereafter having a rolling write-off limiting the build-up of deferred relief to a maximum period of six years.

The Self-employed and National Insurance

P.1 The self-employed are treated separately under the National Insurance Scheme. They pay a separate class of contributions (Class 2 and Class 4) and are entitled to only a proportion of the full range of benefits available to employees. Unlike employees, the self-employed are not eligible for unemployment benefit, industrial injuries benefits, earnings-related supplements to sickness, widow's

Table P.1   Apportionment of National Insurance Contributions; 1976–77 and 1977–78

Type of benefit	Cost of benefit to the National Insurance Fund		Apportionment of Class 1 contributions (with allowance for administration costs)	
	1976–77	1977–78	1976–77	1977–78
	£ million	£ million	%	%
Unemployment benefit*	559	629	0·99	0·95
Sickness benefit (flat-rate)	406	475	0·71	0·70
Sickness benefit (earnings-related supplement)*	112	138	0·20	0·20
Widow's benefit (flat-rate)	425	456	0·69	0·64
Widow's benefit (earnings-related supplement)*	11	12	0·02	0·02
Retirement pensions (flat-rate)	5,583	6,511	9·03	9·03
Graduated retirement benefit*	68	81	0·11	0·11
Invalidity benefit	563	701	0·95	1·01
Maternity benefits (flat-rate)	65	73	0·11	0·11
Maternity benefits (earnings-related supplement)*	16	19	0·03	0·03
Death grant	15	15	0·03	0·03
Industrial injury benefits*	242	275	0·43	0·42
Total	8,066	9,385	13·30	13·25
NI benefits to which self-employed are entitled	7,057	8,231	11·52	11·52
National Health Service	—	—	1·00	1·00

Source: DHSS and Government Actuary's Department.

Notes: 1 Benefits marked * are those to which the self-employed are not entitled.

2 Sickness benefit expenditure includes payments in lieu of benefit foregone made to employers under Section 136 of the Social Security Act 1975.

3 Widow's benefit includes guardian's allowance and child's special allowance.

4 Columns do not always add up to totals due to rounding.

and maternity benefits, or for graduated retirement benefit or earnings-related pensions. However, like employees, they are eligible to receive flat-rate sickness, widow's and maternity benefits, death grant and flat-rate retirement pensions (see Table P.1 for details as to which benefits the self-employed were not entitled in 1976–77 and 1977–78).

P.2   Following the introduction of the new State earnings-related pension scheme in 1978–79, the contributions of the self-employed have been derived on lines similar to those of employees who 'contract-out' of the earnings-related pension scheme[1]. The current (1978–79) low initial rates for those 'contracted-out' arise from the fact that a deduction representing the full value of the part of the new earnings-related benefits that are foregone is made from a 'pay as you go' contribution which will not, for many years, reflect the full value of benefits. As the contributions of the 'contracted-out' rise over the years, so will those of the self-employed.

P.3   Accordingly, the starting point is the total contribution rate for employees who are not 'contracted-out' and deductions are made on account of the benefit rights which the self-employed do not acquire[2]. Table P.2 shows that the total

Table P.2   National Insurance Contributions for 'Contracted-out' Employees and for the Self-employed; 1978–79

Class of contributions	Level of earnings/profits or gains							
	£950	£1,000	£2,000	£3,000	£4,000	£5,000	£6,000	£6,250
EMPLOYEES: Class 1	£	£	£	£	£	£	£	£
employees (6·5%/4%)	60·75	62·75	102·75	142·75	182·75	222·75	262·75	272·35
employers (10%/5·5%)	93·20	95·95	150·95	205·95	260·95	315·95	370·95	384·15
Total (16·5%/9·5%)	153·95	158·70	253·70	348·70	443·70	538·70	633·70	656·50
SELF-EMPLOYED: Class 2 & 4 Class 2								
(flat-rate) (£1.90)	98·80	98·80	98·80	98·80	98·80	98·80	98·80	98·80
Class 4 (5%)	—	—	—	50·00	100·00	150·00	200·00	212·50
Total	98·80	98·80	98·80	148·80	198·80	248·80	298·80	311·30

Source: DHSS.

Notes: For 1978–79, contracted-out employees' Class 1 contributions amounted to 6·5 per cent of earnings up to and including £17·50 a week plus a contribution of 4 per cent on earnings between £17·50 and £120 a week. Their employers' contributions (excluding the National Insurance surcharge) amounted to 10 per cent and 5·5 per cent over the same earnings range. The Class 2 flat-rate contributions of the self-employed amounted to £1·90 a week and the Class 4 contributions to 5 per cent of annual profits or gains between £2,000 and £6,250 (Class 4 contributions are generally assessed and collected by the Inland Revenue along with Schedule D income tax).

[1] Employees who are members of occupational pension schemes providing an acceptable level of benefits can be 'contracted-out' of the earnings-related pension benefits of the State scheme and pay reduced contributions.

[2] For a full explanation, see the Report by the Government Actuary on the draft of the Social Security (Contributions, Re-rating) (No 2) Order 1977 (Cmnd 7036).

contributions for 'contracted-out' employees (ie the combined employees' *and* employers' contributions) are considerably higher than the total contributions of the self-employed. The main reason for this is that the contracted-out employees will receive part of the new earnings-related benefits as well as those, mainly short-term, benefits for which the self-employed are not eligible. Although questions of taxation are irrelevant to the position of the National Insurance Fund, it should be noted that employers' contributions on behalf of their employees are allowed as deductions from taxable income. The contributions of employees and of the self-employed are not tax deductible.

P.4 In broad terms the self-employed now contribute to the scheme at the rate (including a National Health Service contribution) of about 5 per cent of their reckonable earnings. Under the earlier arrangements which applied from 1975–76 to 1977–78 their contributions (including an element for the National Health Service) were equivalent to about 8 per cent of reckonable earnings. The range of benefits for which the self-employed are eligible did not change between 1975–76 and 1978–79. It is clear, therefore, that the new contribution rates payable by the self-employed for 1978–79 represent a substantial reduction on those payable in preceding years.

P.5 Data are available which compare National Insurance contributions and benefits for 1976–77 and 1977–78. The Department of Health and Social Security (DHSS) has provided us with the data in Table P.1 which, for 1976–77 and 1977–78, notionally apportions between various benefits, employees' Class 1 contributions to the National Insurance Fund. By deleting from the calculation those benefits for which the self-employed were ineligible in 1976–77 and 1977–78, the Department has indicated the size of the contribution which would have been required for employees if they qualified only for the benefits available to the self-employed. That figure was 11·52 per cent of reckonable earnings for both 1976–77 and 1977–78, to which may be added the 1 per cent contribution which is allocated to the National Health Service (NHS).

P.6 Because of the principle of 'pooling of risks', no attempt is made by the DHSS to take into account the relative extent that individual groups (such as the self-employed) claim particular benefits. It has been estimated, however, that if allowance were to be made for the lower level of claims to sickness and invalidity benefit by the self-employed, this would reduce the figure of 11·52 per cent to about 11 per cent. Any tendency for the self-employed to defer receipt of their retirement pension for longer than the average person would, on average, be adequately compensated for by the extra pension earned during deferment.

P.7 Precise information as to the cost of benefits in 1978–79 is not yet available but, in any event, it is no longer possible to apportion contributions in exactly the same way as before because employees' contributions are at two rates according to whether or not they are 'contracted-out'.

P.8 As we have already noted, the self-employed paid Class 2 and Class 4 contributions for 1976–77 and 1977–78 which, including the element for the NHS were, in general, equivalent to 8 per cent of reckonable earnings. Employees' contributions for equivalent benefits were then equivalent to about

12·5 per cent of reckonable earnings (or about 12·0 per cent if allowance is made for the lower level of claims to sickness and invalidity benefits by the self-employed).

The Extent of Self-employment in Eleven Countries

Q.1 Table Q.1 shows for eleven countries, for selected years between 1960 and 1973: (a) the division (in percentage terms) of total civil employment between the agricultural and non-agricultural sectors; (b) self-employment (including unpaid family workers) as a percentage of total civil employment; (c) self-employment as a percentage of total employment in agriculture; and (d) self-employment as a proportion of total non-agriculture employment. Of these (a) is shown in the first row for each country—in Australia in 1965, for example, 9·9 per cent of total civilian employment was in agriculture and 90·1 per cent in the rest of the economy; (b), (c) and (d) are shown in the second row—taking Australia in 1965 again as an example, the self-employed and family workers were 16·3 per cent of total civilian employment, 64·0 per cent of employment in agriculture and 11·1 per cent of employment in the rest of the economy.

Q.2 The figures are derived from OECD published statistics and are on a broadly comparable basis. However, some countries do not follow the OECD definitions closely, and so international comparisons should be made with caution. The coverage of those in civil employment (ie employees, plus self-employed), and of the two broad sectors (agriculture, and other industries and services) shown in the Table is not the same in all countries (eg forestry and fishing is not included in the agricultural sector in all the countries covered, in particular the United States).

Q.3 The major problem of comparability with the figures in Table Q.1 relates to family workers. The definition of self-employed status covers, broadly, persons principally working on their own account, whether alone or as employers, and this conforms with the UK Census of Population definition. Family workers, however, are defined as persons regularly assisting an enterprise even if remuneration is not clearly defined[1]. Figures for family workers are not available for the UK but are included in the percentages shown for all other countries. The importance of family workers in some countries is indicated by the last column in Table Q.1 which gives their share of total civil employment in 1975.

---

[1] Those working less than one-third of the normal working week are excluded.

Table Q.1 Self-employed and Family Workers as Proportion of those in Civil Employment by Sector for Selected Countries; 1960 to 1975

Country	Status of employment	All industries and services					Agriculture, hunting, forestry, fishing					Industries and services other than agriculture					Family workers as % of civil employment
		1960	1965	1970	1973	1975	1960	1965	1970	1973	1975	1960	1965	1970	1973	1975	1975
Australia[1]	Total civil employment	—	100·0	100·0	100·0	100·0	—	9·9	8·3	7·2	6·7	—	90·1	91·7	92·8	93·3	0·3
	Self employed and family workers	—	16·3	14·5	13·9	14·3	—	64·0	62·8	63·4	66·2	—	11·1	10·2	10·1	10·5	
Belgium[2]	Total civil employment	100·0	100·0	100·0	100·0	100·0	8·7	6·4	4·7	3·8	3·6	91·3	93·6	95·3	96·2	96·4	3·7
	Self employed & F.W.	26·2	22·2	18·9	17·1	16·8	92·6	88·3	92·5	91·7	91·2	19·9	17·5	15·2	14·2	14·0	
Canada[3]	Total civil employment	100·0	100·0	100·0	100·0	100·0	13·3	10·1	6·5	5·4	6·1	86·7	89·9	93·5	94·6	93·9	1·4
	Self employed & F.W.	18·8	16·1	11·6	9·9	9·8	75·0	74·1	71·9		63·9	10·2	9·5	8·3	6·3	6·3	
France	Total civil employment	100·0	100·0	100·0	100·0	100·0	22·4	17·7	14·3	12·2	11·3	77·6	82·3	85·7	87·8	88·7	—
	Self employed & F.W.	30·5	25·9	22·2	19·9	19·0	77·6	79·0	78·9	79·2	79·4	16·9	14·5	12·7	11·6	11·3	
West Germany[4]	Total civil employment	100·0	100·0	100·0	100·0	100·0	14·0	10·9	8·6	7·5	7·4	86·0	89·1	91·4	92·5	92·6	5·7
	Self employed & F.W.	22·8	19·4	16·9	15·8	15·9	85·3	87·2	87·0	86·8	86·7	12·7	11·1	10·3	10·1	9·5	
Ireland[5]	Total civil employment	(100·0)	100·0	100·0	100·0	100·0	(36·3)	32·0	27·1	24·9	24·3	(63·7)	68·0	72·9	75·1	75·7	—
	Self employed & F.W.	(38·6)	34·6	31·4	29·5	29·2	(84·7)	85·9	86·9	87·3	88·1	(12·3)	10·4	10·8	10·3	10·3	
Italy	Total civil employment	100·0	100·0	100·0	100·0	100·0	32·8	26·0	19·5	17·4	15·8	67·2	74·0	80·5	82·6	84·2	6·2
	Self employed & F.W.	41·6	36·3	31·7	28·7	27·6	73·6	69·2	66·8	62·2	61·9	25·9	24·7	23·2	21·7	21·2	
Japan[6]	Total civil employment	100·0	100·0	100·0	100·0	100·0	30·2	23·5	17·4	13·4	12·8	69·8	76·5	82·6	86·4	87·2	12·0
	Self employed & F.W.	46·6	39·2	35·0	31·1	30·0	92·6	92·2	94·8	93·3	93·0	28·1	22·9	22·4	21·5	20·9	
Sweden	Total civil employment	—	100·0	100·0	100·0	100·0	—	11·3	8·1	7·1	6·4	—	88·7	91·9	92·9	93·6	1·4
	Self employed & F.W.	—	14·2	10·9	9·2	8·5	—		64·0	62·7	64·8	—		6·2	5·1	4·7	
United Kingdom[7]	Total civil employment	100·0	100·0	100·0	100·0	100·0	4·1	3·8	3·2	2·9	2·7	95·9	96·2	96·8	97·1	97·3	—
	Self employed	7·3	6·9	7·8	7·9	7·7	39·5	36·5	40·3	39·3	40·0	5·9	5·7	6·7	7·0	6·8	
United States[8]	Total civil employment	100·0	100·0	100·0	100·0	100·0	8·3	6·1	4·4	4·1	4·0	91·7	93·9	95·6	95·9	96·0	1·0
	Self employed & F.W.	16·1	13·6	10·2	9·7	9·7	67·7	68·2	66·7	63·7	62·2	11·4	10·0	7·6	7·4	7·5	

Sources: OECD *Labour Force Statistics*, 1960–1971, and 1965–1976; Paris 1973 and 1978.

Notes:
1 Major revision of data and industrial classification for Australia in 1972. Figures not strictly comparable 1960–1975.
2 New data series for Belgium in 1970. Figures not strictly comparable 1960–1975.
3 Revised data series for Canada from 1970.
4 Sector breakdown revised for Germany from 1972.
5 Figures in brackets for Ireland refer to 1961. No separate figure for family workers given for 1975, but in 1965 they constituted 8·9 per cent of total civil employment.
6 From 1973 major data change to include Okinawa prefecture. Figures not strictly comparable 1960–1975 for Japan.
7 UK figures not strictly comparable with those given in Chapter 2, because on UK not GB basis, and adjustments for standardisation on OECD classification.
8 US data covers agriculture only.
— Indicates no data available.

Index

327